LANDSCAPES OF PROTEST IN THE SCOTTISH HIGHLANDS AFTER 1914

Studies in Historical Geography

Series Editor: Professor Robert Mayhew, University of Bristol, UK

Historical geography has consistently been at the cutting edge of scholarship and research in human geography for the last fifty years. The first generation of its practitioners, led by Clifford Darby, Carl Sauer and Vidal de la Blache presented diligent archival studies of patterns of agriculture, industry and the region through time and space.

Drawing on this work, but transcending it in terms of theoretical scope and substantive concerns, historical geography has long since developed into a highly interdisciplinary field seeking to fuse the study of space and time. In doing so, it provides new perspectives and insights into fundamental issues across both the humanities and social sciences.

Having radically altered and expanded its conception of the theoretical underpinnings, data sources and styles of writing through which it can practice its craft over the past twenty years, historical geography is now a pluralistic, vibrant and interdisciplinary field of scholarship. In particular, two important trends can be discerned. Firstly, there has been a major 'cultural turn' in historical geography which has led to a concern with representation as driving historical-geographical consciousness, leading scholars to a concern with text, interpretation and discourse rather than the more materialist concerns of their predecessors. Secondly, there has been a development of interdisciplinary scholarship, leading to fruitful dialogues with historians of science, art historians and literary scholars in particular which has revitalised the history of geographical thought as a realm of inquiry in historical geography.

Studies in Historical Geography aims to provide a forum for the publication of scholarly work which encapsulates and furthers these developments. Aiming to attract an interdisciplinary and international authorship and audience, Studies in Historical Geography will publish theoretical, historiographical and substantive contributions meshing time, space and society.

Landscapes of Protest in the Scottish Highlands after 1914

The Later Highland Land Wars

IAIN J.M. ROBERTSON
University of Gloucestershire, UK

Routledge
Taylor & Francis Group
LONDON AND NEW YORK

First published 2013 by Ashgate Publishing

Published 2016 by Routledge
2 Park Square, Milton Park, Abingdon, Oxfordshire OX14 4RN
711 Third Avenue, New York, NY 10017, USA

First issued in paperback 2016

Routledge is an imprint of the Taylor & Francis Group, an informa business

British Library Cataloguing in Publication Data
A catalogue record for this book is available from the British Library

The Library of Congress Cataloging in Publication Data
A catalog record for this book is available from the Library of Congress

ISBN 13: 978-1-138-27980-3 (pbk)
ISBN 13: 978-1-4724-1137-2 (hbk)

Contents

List of Figures and Tables

Figures

Tables

For James McPherson Robertson
(1918–1996)

Acknowledgements

Not unlike the actions of the cottars and crofters who are its subjects, it has taken some time to bring this work to fruition. The temptation is to push this analogy even further and to suggest that the trajectory to final publication matches that of the Land Wars as a whole: initial furious activity of only partial success followed by a period of comparative inactivity, which in turn is replaced by a resumption of peak levels stimulated by external influences. Whether this analogy holds or not, there can be no doubt that the journey to final fruition has been marked by many deviations and false turns, but also, and more significantly, the accumulation of many debts of thanks.

The most immediate of these is to the School of Humanities at the University of Gloucestershire whose generous support in the form of research leave ensured the completion of this work. I'd also like to thank my History colleagues for so uncomplainingly taking up those responsibilities I was fortunate enough to be able to cast off. I must also acknowledge the input of all the students who took my third year module on rural social protest over the years, notwithstanding the certain knowledge that they would hear yet more from E.P. Thompson. Special thanks here to the early modern cartographer and the imperialist, whose constant intelligent critique has ensured a stimulating teaching experience.

In the longer term this book has benefitted hugely from the diligent and unstinting assistance of staff at the National Archives of Scotland and National Library of Scotland, at the Bodleian in Oxford and the over-worked inter-library loan staff at the University of Gloucestershire. I thank you all. The catalyst, however, who enabled the archival research to go in new and exciting areas, was Leah Leneman. I owe her a great debt for alerting me to the existence of the Department of Agriculture for Scotland files and it is a great shame that Leah is not here to see the outcome of her intervention. I must also thank all the staff with whom I came into contact at the then Department (and now the Rural Payments and Inspections Directorate), but particularly Mr John Davidson who did so much to smooth my initial access to these files. Thanks also to the Department library staff who put up with a stranger in their midst for so long asking daft questions of long-settled estates and the files attaching to them. Any errors or omissions that have resulted from the many hours of effort spent working through these uncatalogued files are entirely my own.

A number of people have played important roles in the production of this work and I acknowledge their roles with thanks. Firstly to Robert Mayhew, the Historical Geography series editor at the University of Bristol and also to my editors at Ashgate: Valerie Rose and Pam Bertram. I must also thank Kathryn

Sharp for her brilliant initial cartographic efforts and Caroline Macintosh for her tireless endeavours in updating them. I owe much to Phil Toms, both for help with the graphs, but also for the many cups of coffee and constant refusal to talk about anything that might resemble historical geography. It has kept me sane.

There are many people encountered along the way, without whom this work would have been significantly the weaker. I'd like to acknowledge the help given in the initial stages by Donald Archie MacDonald then at the School of Scottish Studies in Edinburgh and also the unfailing support and encouragement offered throughout by both Willie Gillies and Donald Meek. Central to the oral history aspects of the work, however, was the inspirational John MacInnes, now retired from the School of Scottish Studies. My sincere thanks to John for guiding me through my first interviews, for sharing his deep love and knowledge of the people and places of the Outer Hebrides and for his encouragement and assistance with the project from the outset. The month spent with John on his croft in Cheesebay had a deep impact on my intellectual development. My thanks, but can I have my tapes back please?

On the islands I am grateful to Finlay MacLeod of Lewis for the interest he has shown and for sharing knowledge, and thanks go to John Murdo Morrison for allowing me access to material on the Harris disturbances he has in his possession. I would also like to acknowledge the unstinting assistance and encouragement offered by Angus 'Ease' Macleod, also from Lewis, which has had a profound influence on the shape of the work. It is wonderful to see Angus's life work included in the Angus Macleod archive at Ravenspoint (Lewis), even if it is a little odd to see one's own letters collected there.

My understanding of these events and their context and the way I have written them have been massively shaped by the many conversations, commentaries and feedback I have garnered along the way. The huge efforts of both Roy Jones and Martin Randall in reading multiple versions of various chapters have been much appreciated. I'd also like to thank James Hunter, Annie Tindley, Iain Black, Neil Wynn and Craig Fees for their equally helpful inputs on various drafts. The input of the "new guard" in protest studies at various seminars must also be acknowledged: Peter Jones, Briony Mcdonagh, Katrina Navickas, Steve Poole, Rose Wallis, but perhaps above all, for his constant encouragement to actually write something, Carl Griffin. I'd also like to thank Andrew Charlesworth for just being Andrew Charlesworth. But my deepest intellectual debt and gratitude goes to Charles Withers. His has been a shaping influence on this work and I owe him much.

All of these debts, however, pale in comparison with that I owe to my wife Andrea. She has lived with this project and my many absences to the far north west of Scotland for a considerable period of time and has done so with patience and much understanding. She has been wonderfully supportive and this could not have been done without her. It is conventional in hymns of praise such as this to say that one's children have provided a welcome reminder of the demands of the world outside the academy. But as both Elizabeth and Katherine are now too old for that sort of comment I will simply confine myself to dedicating this book to them and to Andrea.

Introduction

For someone of his strongly romantic nature [my father's] achievement of a place of his own in South Harris represented something akin to the emotion of the Jew returning to Israel; he was one of those people whose fairly immediate ancestors had been uprooted from the South during the evictions of the previous century ... for me the new village wove a spiritual and physical magic as I grew up with it. It was carved out from what had been the granary of the Clan MacLeod in the old days of that Clanship. The Atlantic thundered or shimmied according to its mood in mile upon mile of shell-white beach which, in turn, was selvedged to rolling green meadowland ... That was "below the road" on the setting sun side. Above the road were the crofts themselves, each consisting of thirteen or fourteen acres of arable land stretching up to an infinity of heather moorland which was too rough and sour for cultivation but ideal for summer pasture.

... Up on the moor the Black shepherd and his friends were getting restive ... Over the weeks they had quietly procured some sacks of grain, and one fine spring morning, they went out and parcelled out some of the landlord's best fields among themselves and began to plough and sow. ... Previously they had merely staked out claims to land ... but now they were planting [and] the landlord couldn't stand by and nod approval ... there was nothing he could do except drum up a regiment of some reluctant farm hands, to drive off the "raiders" who were, in all probability, their own kith and kin. Up on the hillside the women-folk saw their men being "attacked" by the landlord and his henchmen and they decided to take a hand. They formed a loose-knit human chain stretching from the pee-tubs to the landlords, and pail after pail of malodourous urine passed down the line to be generously thrown over the landlord ... soaking wet and with smarting eyes he was forced to retreat ... cheered on by the school-children whom even Miss Dalbeith could not control.[1]

Land disturbances at Scaristaveg, which began in 1926 and lasted for at least three years, was just one of the over 500 separate incidents of protest which took place in the Scottish Highlands after 1914. These took a hitherto un-recognised variety of forms, ranging from the simple and individual written (but rarely anonymous) threat to take action through to complex and mass acts of land seizure and beyond. Together, this was the final, successful and sadly much neglected, act of the Highland Land Wars which began in 1914 and lasted until at least 1939, albeit

1 Finlay, J. Macdonald, *Crowdie and Cream* (London, 1983), pp. 9–10 and 24–5.

with significantly decreasing intensity. Occurring in a greater diversity of places and far more frequently than has been previously recognised these events had a significant impact on the Highland landscape, particularly in the Outer Hebrides, on the nature of land-holding in the region and on the tri-partite relationship between landlords, tenantry and agencies of government which developed over the course of the first two decades of the twentieth century. At the same time, written into Highland land agitation were tensions and conflict within the tenantry which also demand greater attention than they have been given hitherto and which played a shaping role in protests' performances.

In examining the historical geography of rural social protest in Highland Scotland between 1914 and 1939 this book seeks to address and help to fill in some of these gaps. Three principal aims are here identified: to establish the geography of events of protest; to detail the chronology of protest; and to advance our understanding of the nature of protest, in the Highlands and more generally. First and foremost therefore the intention here is to detail and discuss at depth the nature, implications and underpinnings of an important set of protest events. The principle focus is thus on acts of rural resistance, something not attempted in Highland historiography for some considerable period. Alongside this a wider context is embraced in order to say a little (sadly not enough) about the role of the factor and Board of Agriculture sub-commissioner in Highland land disturbances, and thereby aims to make a contribution to a deeper understanding of twentieth century crofting society, and to embrace a view of protest from above alongside that from below.

With this focus on rural resistance comes the associated responsibility of addressing and integrating a much wider literature. This is the protest paradigm first established, largely in an English context, in the 1960s as part and as first pillar of the history from below movement. One of the major weaknesses of this paradigm has been this English focus and the fact that it has embraced only a geographically narrow range of events. Until comparatively recently the attentions of protest historians of the modern period has overwhelmingly been on southern England, and most often on the late eighteenth and early nineteenth centuries. Moreover, when historians and historical geographers have turned to a consideration of Highland protest, they have taken the protest paradigm with them and applied it to Highland events. Here, taking inspiration from the most recent work in protest studies, but also from some of the most recent thinking in human geography and the study of landscapes, social anthropology and social and cultural history, the intention is to concentrate on formulating explanation and interpretation from within. To look to the crofting landscape (partly captured in the opening passage from Finlay Macleod's elegiac *Crowdie and Cream*) as base, means and motive to disturbance and interpretation.

The protest literature is now considerable, with discussion either taking the form of a broad chronology or following significant themes and debates. Here both approaches are taken in order to facilitate comparison and allow local specificity to be considered as part of wider processes affecting the transformation of rural

Highland society and culture. Regardless of the basic approach the principal concern of students of social protest has often been the same: to identify incidents, to explain in terms of cause and motivation, and to relate such events to socio-economic change. Much of the template and paradigm for protest studies was set by Edward Thompson who, in common with Eric Hobsbawm and George Rudé, asserted that crowd actions were crucial to understanding the interaction between capitalism and those who worked the land.[2] From this view protest came to be understood as a central part of attempts to re-assert pre-capitalist social formations with subsequent studies taking Thompson's key thesis of moral economy in particular and applying it to studies of social protest chronologically and spatially disparate from that with which he was concerned. Indeed, our understanding of protest events has, in part, been based upon notions first applied to one protest type (the food riot) and explicated in a narrow range of work. It is this paradigm that has only comparatively recently been fully overturned.

Notwithstanding the fact that this was a somewhat limiting wellspring a number of fascinating and rewarding streams of engagement flowed. One such was the shift away from national and regional studies towards a focus on the local, whilst another was the important debate and differentiation around overt and covert protest. This debate was important much more for the fact that it demonstrated that the study of popular protest was reaching a mature stage and much less for the somewhat unhelpful categories it established. Into the category of overt protest was placed all those visible and collective manifestations, such as riot and land invasion, whilst the covert form was seen to be those events more often understood as rural crime and having the characteristics of anonymity, individuality and disguise. Such differentiation proved unsustainable, however, and much more weight has subsequently been given to the work of James C. Scott and to his notion of 'everyday forms of peasant resistance'.[3] Taking a diverse range of form, from foot dragging, dissimulation and false compliance through to poaching, these commonplace and everyday performances have been seen to be more enduring and significant expressions of discontent and resistance than the more spectacular but much less frequent overt acts.

It is a matter of considerable regret that, in common with the vast majority of other engagements with highland protest, this book almost wholly ignores acts of everyday resistance. In part this is a problem of the archive (and indeed popular memory – an important part of the evidential base here drawn on) but it is also an issue born of the belief that the greater need is the detailing of these hugely important overt acts at the level they deserve. Unlike many other

2 Edward P. Thompson, 'The moral economy of the English crowd in the Eighteenth Century', *Past and Present*, No. 50 (1971): 76–136; George, Rudé, *Ideology and Popular Protest* (London: Lawrence & Wishart, 1980); Eric J. Hobsbawm, and George Rudé, *Captain Swing* (London: Readers Union, 1970); Malcolm Thomis, *The Luddites: Machine-breaking in Regency England* (Newton Abbot, 1970).

3 Scott, James C. *Weapons of the Weak* (Yale, 1987).

protest performances – an example would be the Captain Swing riots in southern England in the 1830s where any consequent increase in wages and the parish dole were somewhat short-lived – events of the Highland Land Wars had positive impacts which endured. With the Crofters' Holdings (Scotland) Act of 1886, the Land Settlement Act of 1919 and with the establishment after 1918 of a number of crofting townships, a real and enduring impact on Highland society, culture and landscape had been effected. And it had been effected largely as a result of proactive protest performances; especially those of the Land Wars after 1914.

In turning to a detailed discussion of Highland protest, then, it will be argued that established and well-worked paradigms are incapable of satisfactorily encompassing the range and motivation of conflict that emerges from the monocular perspective here adopted. This move away from (but not a wholly abandoning of) the prioritising of class consciousness and class conflict as an analytical device is accompanied by an engagement with another important trend in the evolution of protest studies: a shift towards the local. Moreover, the differing spatial perspectives adopted here – from the regional, through the intra-regional to the local – matches that of the differing conceptual paths which can underlie the study of individual event and are based in part on the realisation of the complexities of the protest "moment" otherwise glossed over in a broader focus. But a turn to the local is also undertaken in order to more convincingly engage with an important evidential base – that of popular memory of land disturbances – and to adopt a frame and lens through which to explore new theories. This taking up of a new perspective is based upon the belief that in the study of landscapes of social protest the old shibboleth of space as passive setting and symbolic register needs substantial qualification at the very least. In what follows the argument will be made that a turn towards a focus on the crofting landscape (re-conceptualised as "taskscape") involves also a need to pay close attention to nature/culture interactions, to vernacular ecological beliefs and to the dynamic and formative role of landscape in people's lifespaces.

This work is also based on the belief that the Land Wars did not occur in a vacuum, that individual protestors had specific motivations based on their experiences and desires, and that disturbance had consequences. A further key hope as to what might emerge from this contribution to the recent upsurge of interest in acts of rural resistance, is both a definition of the essence of a Land Wars incident (if that is actually possible) and a demonstration of the ways in which these essentially localised protests were underlain by motives which had significantly wider resonances and connections and which ultimately drew the local into what we might understand as a meta-movement. It is suggested, therefore, that whilst the later Land Wars were clearly more than the sum of their parts, what we are witnessing in the Highlands falls short of constituting a protest movement, the key characteristics of which are that events in one place and at one time influence later events elsewhere and that the whole has some form of connection to even-wider political aims. In the post-1914 Highlands this latter connection seems tenuous at best; the same can be said of the evidence for the diffusion of and linkages between these events. In addition, there is limited direct evidence of protestors citing either the general success of land raiding or specific events as their motivation to action. More persuasive is the view which sees the influence of individual event as something akin to a pebble being thrown into a pond – a neat echo of the way in which decisions get made within a crofting township – in which the ripples have a clear but insubstantial influence on other protest performances. In this "meta-movement" the end to which all were working was access to land, and the means by which protestors chose to achieve this were shared across both time and space. Nevertheless, the more important connections and contexts were perhaps to earlier events in the same place with the nature of the demand for land – a belief in rights to small and specific pieces of land based on custom and inheritance – such that this did not coalesce into a wider movement for the transfer of land-holding. Rather, these were movements and moments of the locality; of local social relations and local cultures of resistance. When taken as a whole the post-1914 Land Wars were largely individual attempts to reaffirm and reinforce traditional cultural practices in the locality that were shared and evident (to a greater or lesser extent) across the whole of the Highlands, but which had at their heart the local landscape and the social relations which shaped and flowed from it.

The Highlands

Visually, as it faced the post-1914 protestors, the Scottish Highland landscape and lifespace, or at least the north and west Highland landscape (see Figure 1.2), was deeply dichotomous being divided between a vast empty wilderness organised principally for sport and sheep and a small-scale peopled landscape organised principally for crofting. Inevitably it was far more complex than that, not least because the two landscapes existed in symbiosis on many different levels, because the same people performed tasks in both landscapes and because the sporting landscape was once peopled and was emptied by what has become known as the Highland Clearances.

In engaging with these aspects of the Highland landscape, the concern is less with synthetic description of particular places but rather to link theoretical debate with empirical analysis in order, through (ultimately) something approaching thick description (see Chapters 6 and 7), better to understand the complex relationships among the specificities of place and with and between social and economic structures. At the same time concentration on particular places must be rooted in an engagement with processes generative of and generated within wider contexts in order to strike a balance between generalising tendencies and an unhelpful over-emphasis on uniqueness. Within this context, however, the principal emphasis is on process as it relates to the reciprocal, interactive and mutually constitutive relationship between the conduct of social life and place, space and landscape. The Highlands of Scotland are therefore here viewed principally in a cultural context, with wider political and economic processes seen to be rooted in particular Highland patterns of social organisation.

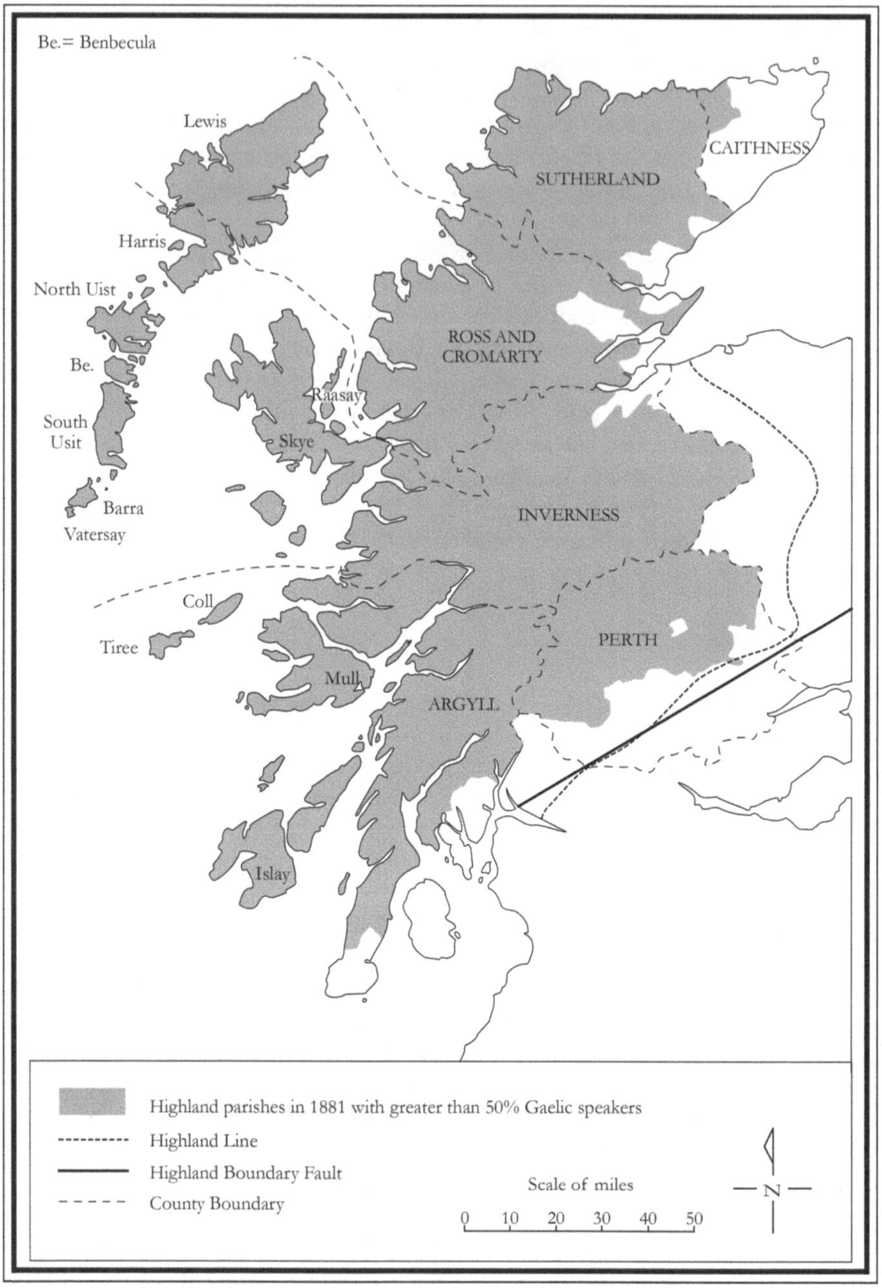

Figure I.1 The Highlands defined

Source: Withers, 1982.

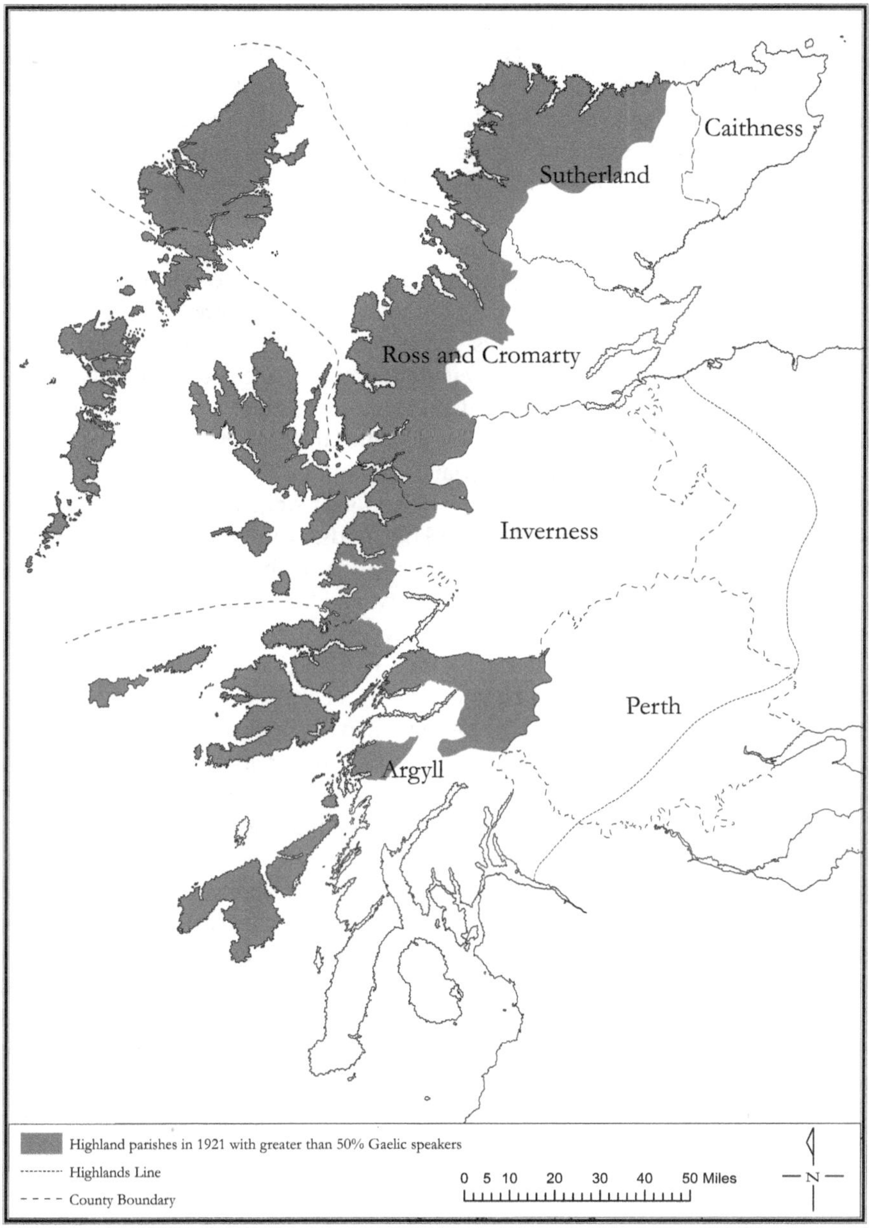

Figure I.2 Areas of predominant Gaelic speaking in 1921

Source: Withers, 1984.

This is not to suggest, however, that the reading and understanding of the Highland landscape arrived at here is solely that of an inert cultural construct. Undoubtedly the symbolic reading and register is both important and had significant impacts on the Highland way of life. But to adopt this view alone is a denial of the lifespaces that were made out of, from and by what we should properly call the crofting landscape. This denies also the often antagonistic associations of human and non-human out of which protest performances emerged and which shaped the tasks performed in this important 'scape. In short, we need to understand Highland disturbances and the taskscapes which shaped them as (the performing of) an embodied and mutually constitutive "more-than-representational" space.[4]

As made clear in Figure I.1, this space can be defined both physically and socially, with the physical boundary being either that of the (geological) Highland Boundary Fault or Highland Line. Of more direct interest to the present work, however, is the agrarian boundary which separates the crofting counties of Argyll, Inverness, Ross and Cromarty, Sutherland, Caithness, Orkney, and Shetland (as defined by the 1886 Crofters' Holdings (Scotland) Act), together with parts of northern Perthshire, from the rest of the Highlands. A further refinement of this, largely driven by an evidential divide, sees much of the effort in what follows concentrated on Inverness, Ross and Cromarty, and Sutherland.

To refine this a little further, and as hinted at above, the divide between the north and west and the remainder of the Highlands is social, economic and cultural. The north and west can be understood as constituting the *Gaidhealtachd* (see below) with the economy still largely shaped by crofting, fishing and the sporting estate. There can be no doubt that this intra-regional variation was of great significance in the chronology and geography of protest although within this the geography of language decline is of less importance than might be first imagined. In the past the Highlands could be equated with the area within which the Gaelic language was predominantly spoken or the clan the predominant social system. And whilst there are a number of issues associated with this (not everyone in the *Gaidhealtachd* spoke Gaelic only or to everyone in every social situation) perhaps the most significant for present purposes is that by the time the Land Wars can be said to have begun, in the 1880s, these two can no longer be said to have been cotemporaneous. The Gaelic speech community was already in the midst of an inexorable retreat to the western islands and seaboard, a trend only reinforced by 1921 (see Figure I.2). This separation of land and language raises the question as to whether we should be referring either to the Gael or the (perhaps much neglected) Highlander when we address issues of this period, even if we eschew the linguistic definition of the *Gaidhealtachd* in favour of that of "the land of the Gael". And yet, in the context addressed here the importance of this question is somewhat diminished as there is virtually no attempt to recognise a direct causal link between the geography of language decline and that of protest.

4 Hayden Lorimer, 'Cultural geography: the busyness of being "more-than-representational"', *Progress in Human Geography*, Vol. 29, No. 1 (2005): 83–94.

In addition, the "community" through which Highland land agitation is viewed is not a linguistic one but one based on agrarian and tenurial practices. Crofters, cottars and squatters could be either or both Highlanders and Gaels. In a further refinement of descriptive terminology the preference here is for "crofting tenantry" above that of community given the problematic nature of that term.

An additional and perhaps more vital context in which Highland land agitation must be viewed is that of population change. The actual figures are by now well established and will not detain us here but a reasonably detailed summary is called for, as the geography of population decline is closely related to the geography of protest. Whilst Highland society was periodically affected by famine crises there can be no doubt that a period of significant region-wide growth is evident from 1750 to about 1840. Population peaked in 1840 and then went into increasingly severe decline. This, however, is to hide significant variation with that of the western isles perhaps the most important in relation to the geography of protest. If we look at the region as a whole it is apparent that decline set in a decade later here than in other parts of the Highlands but even this level of analysis hides significant local variation. The population of the islands of Barra, Lewis and Harris continued to grow, not peaking on the last two until 1921. And when we descend to parish level we can see still further difference. The parish of Lochs on Lewis, for instance – the location for one of the case studies undertaken in Chapter 6 – started to decline in 1891.[5] Regardless of any actual decline, however, the vast bulk of the population of the north and west Highlands continued to be constituted by the crofting tenantry. Crofting was and is a way of life and agrarian practice which emerged in the first decades of the nineteenth century as a local response to the imposition of capitalism. This has been understood as a transitional form of 'petty commodity production' emerging from the 'articulation between the capitalist and pre-capitalist modes' of production with crofters possessing a status halfway between that 'of an independent peasantry and that of a totally dispossessed proletariat'.[6] Something of the nature of the croft emerges from *Crowdie and Cream* with its small acreage of arable accompanied by a share of the common grazing. Essentially and due to the poor quality of the soil and climate when combined with the size of the individual holding, crofting evolved as a part-time and subsistence occupation with cash income coming from cattle-rearing, fishing, forestry or kelping (or a combination thereof) within the region or seasonal migration to industrial towns outwith the region.

The crofting tenantry were sub-divided into two further groups, both of whom are a vital part of the story of the later Highland Land Wars as they formed the predominantly landless labouring groups largely untouched by the provisions of the 1886 Act. Cottars were occupiers of houses built on holdings of officially

5 Charles, W.J. Withers, *Gaelic Scotland* (London, 1988), pp. 179–81.

6 Geddes, Michael, 'Uneven Development and the Scottish Highlands,' Working Paper 17, *Urban Regional Studies Group* (University of Sussex, 1979), pp. 16–27; Withers, *Gaelic Scotland*, p. 222.

recognised crofting tenants to whom they were usually close relatives (often younger brothers or grandsons). Generally, cottars cultivated a part of the croft on which they lived and sometimes paid a share of the rent, though not always. Squatters, on the other hand paid no rent and usually had a house only, with a garden, reclaimed from the township common grazing. This they had usually built with the agreement of the township crofters but without the consent of the landowner. The fact of the lack of provision for cottars and squatters in the 1886 Act has long been recognised as a prime cause of the longevity of the Land Wars but one of the key arguments of this book is that these vital differences within the tenantry have been underplayed in the extant literature and that, in fact, growing division and conflict from within was perhaps of near equal significance in terms of motive to protest, as was conflict from without.

The regional and singular focus adopted here permits these insights as it is possible to essay a level of detail most often confined to single case studies. This has also permitted the development of an intra-regional (essayed in Chapter 4) focus to explore the thesis that the geography of protest may well be better understood at this level than at that of the region. The sub-divisions chosen are determined less by any administrative boundaries than by the belief that the islands would show a different pattern to the mainland and that the Outer Hebrides would be different again. Ultimately, in Chapter 6 we turn to an exploration of a number of case studies with the objective of offering a deep reading of the character of Highland protest as underpinned by the popular memory attaching to these particular places. Whilst there is much to be gained from this varying focus it does raise questions about the capacity to generalise upon Highland protest. If we are to see Highland disturbance as essentially local events there is then the problem of extrapolating from such localisms more general principles that may characterise protest as a regional issue. If individual complexity is to be allowed for, this may mean protest being seen as a record only of isolated "events" without wider significance. The hope is that in addressing all areal scales the systematic analysis thereby permitted, and attempted mainly in Chapter 7, will allow the local and sub-regional studies to be drawn back into the context of an outburst of protest which was felt from the islands of the far west and Shetland, through to rural Perthshire and beyond.

A Word about Words and Sources

Five principal source types have been utilised here: manuscript material stored at the National Archives of Scotland (hereafter N. A. S.); Department of Agriculture for Scotland records retained by the then Board of Agriculture for Scotland and now held by the Scottish Government, Rural Payments & Inspections Directorate (hereafter R. P. I. D.); local and national newspapers; published Parliamentary Papers; popular memory associated with a number of incidents and places. In what follows it will quickly become obvious that the weight of evidence is drawn from the manuscript material held in the main two archives and that there is a near total absence of any estate records. The reason for this is partly the sheer volume of material held in these archives but also for its quality. Much of what is captured contains both the private official response to the pressures generated by the agitation for land and the actual voice of the crofting tenantry, although it must be conceded that in writing in English many may not have been expressing themselves in their first language. In addition, with the material retained by the Board of Agriculture there is no archival indexing available. In order to ensure full coverage every file has been consulted; a total in excess of 5000. At the National Archives a further 286 estate files have been abstracted plus 53 Crofters' Commission files. The most compelling parts of this rich archive were the Board of Agriculture estate papers, located in both archives. These are files opened when a Highland estate was being considered by the Board of Agriculture for a scheme of land settlement. Files where the estate was purchased remain at the R. P. I. D. and have rarely been utilised. Similarly, whilst the AF83 papers at the N. A. S. have been previously used, they have not been drawn on in the way or in the depth that they are here. Such use has permitted more events and more detail of the nature of land disturbances to emerge. Taken together, it was felt that such was the richness and depth of the material and such was the importance of the need to draw attention to it, that this somewhat restricted approach was justified. What this archival and other material permits is the giving voice to the depth of moral and cultural feeling for land after 1914.

A similar depth of feeling is contained within Gaelic poetry and, as it does for earlier events, that relating to land disturbances after 1914 would have provided a useful counterpoint to the record as maintained in the formal archive. Unfortunately there is virtually no contemporary poetry addressing these later incidents. For Donald Meek this absence is the product of earlier population decline as there were insufficient people fully to maintain the poetic tradition.[7] This notwithstanding the power of the oral tradition attaching to places, events and beliefs is well attested to and has been drawn on here. Altogether 36 people were interviewed using both recorder and notepad methods with correspondence being entered into with ten additional informants. The information gathered is presented here mainly in abstract, accompanied by direct quotation with longer extracts kept to a minimum for economy and clarity. Similarly, repetition not for emphasis and hesitations are excluded. All interviewees waived anonymity and virtually all either took part in the incidents they were recalling or were kin of those who did.

In this way oral testimony has been utilised both to support and extend our knowledge of the protest performance as revealed in written records. This has also led to interpretation of events not alone dependant on and different from that confined to written sources. This is because written evidence may record only particular "moments" of an incident whereas oral testimony will be shown here to provide a more complete record of motivation. Indeed the Scaristaveg land seizure noted above, and as recorded by Finlay Macdonald, is a good example of what

7 Dr Donald Meek, personal correspondence, 11 November 1992.

might arise out of the use of popular memory. It is virtually certain that the author of *Crowdie and Cream* would have been one of the school children he identifies as witnesses of the soaking of the estate owner. His therefore is a direct memory of the events albeit one shaped by time and potential romanticisation of the past. There is an extensive archive for events at Scaristaveg and it includes reports on the incident by both the police and the Board of Agriculture's sub-commissioner for the area, but both these accounts vary from that recounted in *Crowdie and Cream*. At first glance this takes us to the heart of issues that have often been attached to the use of popular memory: questions of reliability and validity and the elaboration and distortion of memory. There remains, too, for this and all other events, the possibility that recollections may have been "borrowed", either consciously or unconsciously, from elsewhere, perhaps from the oral tradition pertaining to another location or via unwitting "transcription" from newspaper articles. The established response to such questioning is that the distortion of the past by memory demonstrates the process of negotiation between the individual and the social structure. In addition the nature of what is recalled of these events offers the possibility of more firmly placing them in the context of the community from which they arose and in which they are remembered. But at Scaristaveg a closer look at the archive reveals issues which may well raise direct questions over the comparative validity and reliability of the written record. It transpires that neither police officer nor sub-commissioner was a direct witness to the soaking and that their information was reported to them – a not uncommon form of recording these protests. The source of this information has not survived but if it were someone who had a vested interest in downplaying the affective force of such protest performances then the whole issue of reliability is perhaps inverted.

For institutions of government and absentee landowners protest often began in this way – as a second-hand report. In addition, the beginning of an act of seizure usually rested upon formal declaration of that act by those performing that act. Problematically, it will be demonstrated that for some protest events utilisation of land began well before any formal declaration and that there were other protest types embedded in the term "raid", a fact which further complicates the chronology of protest. A clear and unequivocal timing for the onset of cessation of a land protest is made all the more difficult once it is recognised that periods of explicit disturbance are often interspersed by periods of everyday forms of resistance. Such essentially passive events rarely appear in written records and thus, rather than the events themselves, it is the limitations of the records that often delimit an incident of protest.

Finally, in order for a full understanding to emerge it is vital that we appreciate that instances of opposition are not necessarily discrete typological events. What emerges most forcefully here, and apparent in the semantics of opposition, are the differing perceptions between Government and locality as to the nature of the event. Government, landlords and their agents saw such events as "raids"; to those who took part they were "seizures". The former attaches to these incidents a vocabulary of illegality unrecognised by the crofting tenantry which also carries connotations of wider political motivations and activities. This was something frequently claimed by landowners, their agents and agencies of government, but never by protestors. Here both "raid" and "seizure" are used depending on the language of the source utilised.

A recent contribution to Highland historiography has raised similar concerns over the use of the term "clearance", suggesting that if we apply only its precise meaning it was at best 'on a small and local scale'.[8] In many respects the intensity, depth and extent of Highlanders' ultimate reaction to this process suggests otherwise. It is also important to recognise that eviction/clearance/migration was as much a mental as it was material process, if not more so. People need other people to blame and to put a "face" on otherwise impersonal processes. As such clearance needs to be understood as less a synonym for wider socio-economic and cultural processes of change and more as a metonym for those self-same processes. Clearance is used here precisely because those who undertook acts of protest saw it that way. As such it probably says as much about popular memory as it does about the reality and actuality of the term, but, as with all popular memory and motives to protest, it is what is believed that is the important issue. It is possible that de-population is the less emotive term and more accurate reflection of what happened. Nevertheless clearance is retained here as indicator of the affective force both of the original processes which set de-population in train and of actions in protest.

It is for this latter reason also that the epithet "Highland Land Wars" is retained and preferred to "Crofters War" in order to better reflect the diversity of conflict and participants which come together in these disturbances. Even though these events were no conventional "war" violence can be affected and felt without recourse to physicality. Similarly, it needs noting that on occasion the actions of cottars and crofters in the period under consideration is referred to as "resistance". This is not to imply that they were attempting to resist ongoing processes of change, this was clearly not the case and neither is it to align with the somewhat problematic field of resistance studies.[9] What cottars and crofters were resisting against was, as they saw it, their ongoing dispossession and alienation from land and landscape.

The landscape in which this resistance and reassertion was taking place was a fluid one, of which place names are an obvious, symbolic and important and contentious example. Names vary; all the more so when linguistic hegemony is involved. Virtually all the source material here drawn upon (including the oral) uses often inaccurate Anglicisations of Gaelic originals. These names are highly variable and fluid and in a number of cases this caused significant miscommunication. The decision has been taken here to reproduce names as found in the archive, albeit with some attempt at standardisation. On occasion, however, some variation remains.

8 Michael Fry, *Wild Scots* (Edinburgh, 2005), p. 190.

9 Mitch Rose, 'The seductions of resistance; power, politics, and a performative style of systems', *Environment and Planning D: Society and Space*, Vol. 20 (2002): 383–400.

Structure

In the writing of this book two, if not three, audiences have always been envisaged: those interested in the Highlands; those interested in social protest more generally. The structure is in part a response to this. It is recognised that this dual approach may lead to accusations of a lack of overall coherence to the work but it is hoped that the structure adopted will minimise this potential impact. It is left to the reader to decide if this has worked, but the approach taken here is to split the work into a number of parts which in many respects mirror the areal foci the work adopts. Thus Part III turns to the local and oral and to place/space and landscape more specifically. Here the individual event is utilised as springboard from which to launch, in Chapter 7, a discussion of new ways of seeing Highland protest – as underpinned by vernacular environmental beliefs, by a dynamic and formative sense of place/space and by work tasks performed in an imaginative taskscape. This need to take a fresh look at Highland protest is clearly demonstrated in the chapters in Part II. This is where the rich depth of the archival material is most comprehensively essayed and put to use to detail the chronology (Chapter 3) and geography (Chapter 4) of the land agitation. Chapter 3 further discusses the various different forms protest took in this period and shows that in failing to recognise this diversity to type extant literature has also failed to fully come to terms with the geography of protest. These two chapters need therefore to be viewed as a whole and to be understood as leading directly to the following detailed discussion of explanation and interpretation of post-1914 events. Chapter 5 consequently acts very much as a bridge between the last two parts of the book.

Part I, to which we now turn, sets the scene for the protest performances which follow. The concern here is with broader context, firstly of processes of change in the Highlands and the earlier reaction to such hegemonic impositions. This established, Chapter 2 charts the various streams and eddies of the protest literature, placing past historians' understanding of the Land Wars into this important broader context. What emerges is that whilst protest studies in general has moved on from the foundational paradigm the same cannot be said for our understanding of the Land Wars. There is therefore an opportunity for a fresh look at these events and one which looks at them in all their rich detail. It is precisely this which this book aims to do.

PART I
The Background

Chapter 1

Agrarian Change and Rural Social Protest in Highland Scotland c.1700–1914

> *Whatever grounds are from their nature and situation peculiarly fitted for sheep pasture must be so arranged that the present occupiers may be removed to allotments which are for that purpose to be laid out for them.*[1]

> *Nothing can be more moving to the sensitive observer of Hebridean life than these lazy beds of the Bays district of Harris. Some are no bigger than a dining table, and possibly the same height from the rock, carefully built up with turves carried there in creels by the women and girls.*[2]

> *On behalf of the applicants from this township for ard-an-runnair on Balranald estate, I beg once more to remind the Board that they have ignored our letter of 20th February 1918 and letter of February last. In these letters we have stated our earnest desire clearly, and our claim to the land in question ... A number of the applicants [are] now full vexed that they refrained from ploughing the ground last year after manuring it.*[3]

This chapter seeks to identify the nature and geography of the demographic, socio-economic and cultural-ideological processes which lay behind changes in agrarian practices and land-holding and to which rural social protest in Highland Scotland was a reaction. Much of what follows will be a re-visiting of well-worn ground. No apologies are offered for this as, as discussed in the Introduction, this volume is firmly based on the anticipation of two significantly different readerships, one of which will almost certainly be unfamiliar, to a greater of lesser extent, with the discussion essayed here. Indeed, one of the enduring problems with discussions of Highland protest is that full understanding requires engagement with two distinct sets of literature and this has seldom been attempted or fully articulated. This and the following chapter thus attempts to carry off this difficult balancing act in the full and frank knowledge of the consequences of falling off. Thus, setting off in

1 Lord Seaforth 27 July 1819 quoted in James Hunter, *The Making of the Crofting Community* (Edinburgh, 1976), p. 43.

2 Frank Fraser Darling, *West Highland Survey: An Essay in Human Ecology* (Oxford, 1955), p. 44.

3 National Archives of Scotland, Crofting Files, AF67/252, Alexander Macdonald and others to Board of Agriculture, 29 May 1919.

trepidation of producing what MacAskill has called 'trite history',[4] the aim is not to engage in a detailed historiographical digression from the main focus of this book but to provide a frame, when viewed in conjunction with the following chapter, for the boundaries of our understanding of the events of protest which flowed from the momentous changes captured in this chapter. Frames need not be substantial and that offered here, whilst not insubstantial, does have something of the sketch about it in the belief that this meets the contextualising objective. In addition it is important to recognise that the reaction from the land working population was not necessarily synchronous with the socio-economic and cultural-ideological changes it opposed. Certainly the more successful protests of the 1920s occurred some time after these changes were complete, a delay that was the product of the slow emergence of crofting class consciousness and self-confidence. It thus becomes ever more important to set these events within their wider context – both the historical narrative and the historiography.

Pre-Crofting Highland Agriculture and Society

In early Highland society, and certainly prior to the seventeenth century, the clan (earlier *tuath*) shaped all socio-economic and cultural activity. Here was 'a set of men bearing the same surname and believing themselves to be related ... and descended from the same common stock ... [all] ... owing allegiance to the Supreme Chief of the clan[5]. Drawing on both tribal and feudal traditions, Highland society was multi-graded and held together by bonds of kinship and mutual obligation. The role of land and the holding of land in this was central. It was both stabilising and structuring agent and was used to verify and materialise patriarchal obligations. Land was about more than straightforward patronage, however, even though the military and social functions were significantly more important than any desire for agricultural efficiency. It was, in short, the material manifestation of cultural formulations and the holding of land was one of the most significant customary rights which appear to have pertained throughout the clan. Hereditary occupation of land perhaps related more closely to the tribal traditions this society inherited and was underpinned by and reflected in the contended notion of *duthchas*: 'an almost untranslatable Gaelic term which encapsulated a pervasive belief that clansfolk were entitled to a permanent stake in the territories pertaining to their clan'. This may have been a survival from a more substantive kin-based hereditary tenure similar to that recognisable in the Irish and Welsh law codes, or it may be related to the more feudal notion of individuals having a 'right and kindness'

4 John MacAskill, '"The most arbitrary, scandalous act of tyranny": The Crown, Private Proprietors and the Ownership of the Scottish Foreshore in the Nineteenth Century', *The Scottish Historical Review*, Volume 85, Number 2: No. 220 (2006): 279.

5 Duncan Forbes quoted in James Hunter, *The Making of the Crofting Community* (Edinburgh, 1976), p. 7.

of occupation. Indeed, there is substantial evidence from the Lowlands for the existence there of the practise of 'kindly tenure' embodying a sense of hereditary and customary right of occupation. Whether in Highland society this actually ever extended down to the level of the land-working tenantry must, however, be open to question. Richards suggests that the feudal nature of the relationship, land being held 'by a vassal of a superior', meant that landownership remained concentrated in one individual. Whilst for Fry, even if clansmen believed in a hereditary right of occupation 'this could not have amounted to a right to a specific plot because no such guarantees' could be made in an unstable society where the possession of land (and the population which resided upon it) was equated with power. Less polemically Withers asserts that as the differences between the feudal and tribal influences on clanship were of degree rather than type, Highland society was able to draw its practices from either system.[6]

The status of the clan chief depended on his military prowess and on the number of armed men he could command. This had a direct influence on the agricultural system. Subsistence demanded a labour-intensive agriculture but at the same time land was allocated by the chief and permitted to pass down through society for martial purposes, in order to bind a large population to a particular place. The role of land allocation in this system was therefore primarily 'to ensure the continued existence of the clan as a socially and military effective organisation'.[7]

Below the chief and usually related to him was the tacksman. He, too, usually fulfilled an economic and military function. Even if cash rents were rare, generally tacksmen leased large portions of an estate from their clan chief and then sub-let a large proportion. The tacksman was, therefore, the controller of land and rents, acted as farm "manager" – often for more than one holding – and was thus the 'functionary and collateral relation between highest and lowest kin'. It would seem that even if they only controlled a single settlement the tacksman's role was an administrative one and he rarely worked the land. This function was undertaken by their subtenants and by the cottars, mailers or servants 'who, as the subtenants of subtenants, constituted the lower orders of the clan'.

It is important to appreciate that any agrarian system is always in motion; never fixed and stable. This notwithstanding, for those at the bottom of early Highland society land was the means of subsistence with cattle trading providing cash income. Cattle swallowed up to one-third of total output from the land with a further third being held back for seed. The organisational and productive form

6 Eric Richards, *A History of the Highland Clearances*, Vol. 1 (London, 1982), pp. 54–60; Robert Dodgshon, 'West Highland and Hebridean Landscapes', *Journal of Historical Geography*, Vol. 19, No. 4 (1993): 383–98; Margaret Sanderson, *Scottish Rural Society in the 16th Century* (Edinburgh, 1982), 58–63; A. Collier, *The Crofting Problem* (Cambridge, 1959), p. 39; James Hunter, *Last of the Free* (Edinburgh, 1999); Allan, MacIness, *Clanship, Commerce and the House of Stuart, 1603–1788* (Edinburgh, 1996); Michael Fry, *Wild Scots* (Edinburgh, 2005); Withers, *Gaelic Scotland*, pp. 76–7.

7 Hunter, *The Making*, p. 9.

of these tenurial arrangements was the joint farm, in which land was cultivated in strips divided into infield and outfield, with common grazing beyond, run, perhaps, on 'egalitarian' lines with periodic reallocation of holdings and the tenantry jointly responsible for total rent. A further key component was transhumance, with sites (shielings) at some distance from the permanent settlement. Viewed as a unified whole, this system, sustained over time by custom, gave the land working population the means to subsist and a form of guarantee of an economic balance in their lives.[8] For cottars and servants balance came only from labouring on the land of others and even if other tenants had access to more land it was only sufficient to maintain a way of life only rarely raised above subsistence level and perhaps more frequently threatened by real dearth. It is thus clear that in this early system agricultural efficiency was decidedly subsidiary to the military needs of the clan. It was this, moreover, which created the mutuality of interest which served to bind the social organisation together. Social organisation and military and economic functions were based on and underpinned the land holding and land working system which was only maintained via the 'patriarchal will and the mutual coincidence of interests between landlord and tenant'.[9]

Whilst readily accepting that there were crucial inter-regional processes at work, it was this system that, from the seventeenth century onwards, was increasingly being drawn into the larger transformations of European agriculture. For Richards what this amounts to is the fact that change went 'beyond the influence of local agency'; the product of a recurrent theme in agrarian history: of repeated shifts in the use of land caused by 'land hunger, technological change and market forces'. The elements of structural change in the Highlands, the shift 'from small scale to large scale production and from low to high productivity' were those associated with the modernisation of economy and society and were a regional variant of a European pattern. Thus agricultural reorganisation and population growth are near-universally evident and in combination 'altered the relationship of people to the land'.[10]

Alternatively, James Hunter places greater emphasis on regional factors whilst continuing to see change as the product of modernisation. He believes that this began with increasing commerce between the Highlands and the rest of Britain, but more important was the increasing participation of Highland chieftains in society outwith the Highlands. During the eighteenth century the chiefs' twin roles of 'southern socialite' and 'tribal patriarch ... came into irreconcilable conflict' as the former demanded greater amounts of cash than the latter could provide. Critically, MacInnes traces the origins of this conflict to the early seventeenth

8 Gray, *Highland Economy*.

9 Hunter, *The Making*, p. 9; Malcolm Gray, *The Highland Economy 1750–1850* (London, 1957), p. 21.

10 Richards, *Highland Clearances, Vol. 1*, pp. 7–32.

century, but regardless of the time scale, from this growing landlord indebtedness the commercialisation of agriculture followed.[11]

On the ground this process of commercialisation needs to be understood as the material manifestation of a vast range of other less tangible processes: demographic; cultural; social. The drivers for change were therefore to be found both within the land-working tenantry and wider Highland society and outwith the Highlands in the form of the creation of a retrograde image of the Highlander and Highland society and culture. To Withers this is key and he points to the evolution of a complex and contradictory dialectic which in turn generated an important ideological context and justification for change. From the later 1600s the Highlands and Highlanders came to be perceived as 'inferior'. This led to attempts to remove the cultural forms upon which rested the region's supposed material and intellectual backwardness. Improvement (of self, society and (agri)culture) was thus both mental and material and drew on notions of civilisation as cultural progress: a conjunction of individual self-interest and communal good evident in the idea of culture as a process of societal development from less to more advanced and the claim of improvers to national prosperity and civil authority. Central to this was the adoption of the English language, the introduction of English schools and religious unification.[12]

Within the region increases in rental levels and the introduction of more formal leasing arrangements, in particular the move to direct letting by the landlord, can be said to be the first manifestation of change and led directly to the decline in importance of the tacksman with this group by the mid-eighteenth century turning from being members of 'a warrior caste' into 'middle managers' of the clan. This was accompanied by profound landscape change in the form of the systematic enclosure and engrossing of land as landowners sought to improve their estates. Part of the motivation for this was population pressure. Indeed, according to Flinn, by the mid-eighteenth century population levels began 'to press against the limits of the capacity of their usable resources of land' and for Fry virtually everything else flowed from this fact. Aided by the widespread take-up of inoculation which significantly reduced infant mortality, population growth was particularly rapid between 1755 and 1851 and was most marked in the north and west mainland and the islands. Nevertheless it impossible to deny that this period was primarily one of pursuit of profit and order, part of a policy aimed at the stabilisation and assimilation of the Highlands into the national space economy.[13]

The response of the labouring population to the increased rental demands consequent upon improvement took two forms. Firstly, attempts were made to

11 Hunter, *The Making*, pp. 6–11.

12 Withers, *Gaelic Scotland*, pp. 402–6; Michael. Hechter, *Internal Colonialism: The Celtic Fringe in British National Development, 1596–1966* (London, 1975), p. 343.

13 Michael Flinn, *Scottish Population History* (Cambridge: Cambridge University Press, 1977), pp. 30–31; Withers, *Gaelic Scotland*, p. 192 and 207–16; Eric Richards, *A History of the Highland Clearances, Vol. 2* (London, 1985); Michael Fry, *Wild Scots* (Edinburgh: John Murray, 2005), p. 154.

increase subsistence from land in order to free cash to pay for rent. Secondly, attempts were made to increase cash income from non-agricultural sources, such as linen production, distilling and fishing. Nevertheless, all three industries remained localised and made only minor contributions to cash income. Kelping was, however, different. Introduced into the Western Isles after 1750 this process involved burning seaweed (kelp) with the resultant ash used in the production of glass, soap and iodine. During the Napoleonic wars the industry rapidly expanded yet control of production remained in the hands of the landlords. Combined with the large labouring population and the seasonality of the industry, this meant that wage levels remained at a level below that which would have been sufficient for people to exist on. The consequence of this was that people continued to look to the land as means of subsistence. The landlord therefore recovered much of his wage bill in rental. Reliance on kelping was further increased by landlords re-locating their tenantry to the coast and sub-dividing the newly-created plots. The structure upon which crofting as agrarian form and landscape was to be based was now in place. Its main legacy was a tenantry, even in a normal year, unable to pay the rent, and, in an abnormal year, reliant on charity.[14]

Similar effects are evident with the expansion of large-scale sheep farming. From about 1760 large areas of the Highlands were being converted to single tenanted sheep run. At first confined to the south and east, sheep farming arrived late in the north and west but was everywhere accelerated by economic depression after 1815 and the harvest failure of 1816–17. For the landlord sheep farming offered the possibility of a regular and enhanced rental and with the end to reliance on peasant production the end of the concomitant reliance on a large population. The result was the depopulation of much of the inland parts of Highland estates with population re-settled on the coasts or wastes or emigrated. Whilst there remains much to be understood around the processes heretofore categorised as clearance, there can be no doubt the introduction of large-scale sheep farming was 'a singularly critical agency in the transformation of Highland agriculture' with the soil increasingly part and parcel of capital. This caution around the use of "clearance" stems in part from the fact that whilst landlords were content to move their tenantry around their estate at will, they also at times strove to set up model villages to encourage the adoption of a new way of life. Fry has also suggested that if any actual clearance took place it did so before the heaviest depopulation of the Highlands took place and that clan chiefs turned to improvement in the hope that they could maintain the old system alongside the new, thereby maintaining a substantial population on the land.[15]

14 James Caird, 'The making of the Scottish rural landscape', *Scottish Geographical Magazine*, Vol. 80, No. 2 (1964): 72–80; Malcolm Gray, 'The kelp industry in the Highlands and Islands', *Economic History Review*, Vol. 4, No. 2 (1952): 189–209.

15 Withers, *Gaelic Scotland*, pp. 224 and 228–9; Richards, *Highland Clearances Vol. 1*, pp. 1612, 169 and 249; Adam Collier, *The Crofting Problem* (Cambridge: Cambridge, 1953), pp. 44–5; Fry, *Wild Scots*, p. 172.

Whether we accept this somewhat over-extended revisionist position must be questionable at best, but what is beyond question is that the final piece in the jigsaw of transformation was the potato. It is likely that what was to become this ambivalent life-preserving and life-threatening dietary staple was first introduced into the Highlands in the late seventeenth century. At first unpopular, by a century later it had come to provide (in the Hebrides at least) up to four-fifths of the diet of the land-working population and, with the structure of kelping, fishing and agriculture, had become a crop of complete dependence. The advantages of the potato exactly matched the requirements of the socio-economic system as it evolved across the century after 1750 and proved to be the 'harbinger and agent of social and economic retrogression'.[16]

Regardless of whether we view this either in isolation or as 'part of the wider set of economic constraints which bound the region' the outcome is the same: Highland society and economy was transformed under the impetus of the ideology and institutions of agricultural improvement and demographic change. Nevertheless, it is perhaps better to understand this as a reciprocal relationship with all manifestations of change feeding off each other. For the Highland landlord, drawn into southern society and adopting the viewpoint of the market economy, the main purpose of landownership came to be the production of an enhanced cash income. Throughout the region tenant populations were increasingly confined to small plots on the coastal margins, reliant on potato mono-culture and part-time industrial by-employment. At the same time population growth 'was probably the greatest single determinant of change' creating pressure on resources, land, food supply, employment and prices.[17] It is nevertheless critical to acknowledge and appreciate that these socio-economic and cultural-ideological changes did not occur evenly across the Highlands, did not have the same effects, and did not operate on identical pre-improvement structures across the region. It is critical to pay attention to the geography of change, therefore.

The Geography of Change

In the first instance it is important to note that there was considerable variation in the agricultural practices of the Hebridean islands, the main determinants of which were environmental and traditional. Variation was also apparent across physical and intra-regional boundaries: the early introduction of commercialisation to the south and east of the region, for instance, being caused by an already existing strong commercial approach by certain proprietors. And whilst there are historical

16 Flinn, *Scottish Population History*, pp. 331 and 423–6; Withers, *Gaelic Scotland*, pp. 202–3; Redcliffe Salman, *The History and Social Influence of the Potato* (Cambridge, 1949), pp. 363–73.

17 Richards, *Highland Clearances Vol. 1*, p. 280; Eric Richards, 'Agricultural Change, Modernization and the Clearances', in Donald Ormand (ed.), *The Ross and Cromarty Book* (Golspie: 1984), p. 166.

factors which operated against divergence, Shaw, for instance,[18] arguing that the traditions of shared cultivation and communal pasture were important forces for uniformity, it is equally, if not more important to pay attention to the intra-regional geography of these crucial changes and (as will be shown in later chapters), perhaps mirroring and a product of the opposition to them.

Explanation of these intra-regional and chronological variations rests, in part, upon the particular balance between people and resources in the places concerned and in part also upon the policies of landlords, but perhaps more importantly, upon the differential impact of migration. Both Richards and Withers further persuasively argue that the consequences of structural change were often determined at the local and microhistorical scale. For the latter the geography of transformation may be best understood 'as the appearance of 'islands' of outside capital ... or authority and English – speaking ... within a shrinking Highland "sea"'. Withers further shows that the principal Highland industries had particular local geographies, as did the implementation and form of agricultural improvement. Differences between coastal margins and upland straths in soil type, differential population pressure, access to markets and returns from industry often 'determined ... enduring localisms of landscape and social experience'.[19]

Structural change only exacerbated and reflected such variation. Whilst the principal geographical division within the Highlands was that between the north and west crofting communities, with its characteristic (if not stereotypic) social structure of an upper layer of substantial estate owners with the mass of the population gathered in a single class of small-holders, and the smallholding farmers of the south and east, other divisions become apparent at smaller scales. In the south and east, for instance, small farmers formed the independent middle class missing elsewhere, whilst in Sutherland clearance was accompanied by 'a deliberate policy to create new employment for the displaced population', even if tenants were forced to rely on plots not designed for subsistence.[20]

Crofting; Community; Resistance; Reassertion

The refusal to firmly link crofting and community in the title of this section is, of course deliberate. It is the view taken here that actions within and motives for

18 Shaw, *Northern and Western Isles*, p. 118.

19 Withers, *Gaelic Scotland*, pp. 257, 317–18, and 412.

20 Richards, *Agrarian Change*, pp. 164 and 177; Withers, *Gaelic Scotland*, pp. 221-222; Tom Devine, *The Great Highland Famine: Hunger, Emigration and the Scottish Highlands in the Nineteenth-century* (Edinburgh, 1997), p. 3; Alexander Fenton, *Scottish Country Life* (Edinburgh, 1989), p. 129; Eric Richards, 'Structural change in a regional economy', *Economic History Review*, Vol. 26, No. 1 (1973): 63–76; Annie Tindley, *The Sutherland Estate, 1850–1920: Aristocratic Decline, Estate Management and Land Reform* (Edinburgh, 2010).

Highland disturbance after 1914 (and perhaps before) do not fully support the dominant view of the social evolution of the land working population as it moved through the crofting era; specifically the arrival of a singular sense of (regional) class consciousness and community. As will be demonstrated in subsequent chapters there is compelling evidence for the emergence of clear lines of fracture within the tenantry, and evidence too that the conflicts thus generated could lead to acts of protest which on first glance (by authorities at the time and in the historiography) could look remarkably like the actions of a unified community, but which do not look like this on closer inspection. Given the fundamental importance to protest in the Highlands of both the arrival of crofting agriculture and its social corollary, it is equally important to here sketch out what these looked like before turning to the detail of the reaction and opposition to socio-economic and cultural-ideological change.

The end of the Napoleonic wars brought a national agricultural depression exacerbated in the Highlands by the collapse of the kelp industry. This had the effect of increasing landlord and tenant indebtedness. For the former this only enhanced the shift to sheep farming whilst for the tenantry the continued gap between income and rent stifled all initiative and enterprise and re-emphasised dependence on the potato. The next stage in what have must appeared to be a decades-long crisis was famine occasioned by potato blight; first in 1836 which was then followed by the much more serious failure of 1846. That this Malthusian crisis did not result in mass mortality like its Irish counterpart, was due to greater (and more organised) charitable efforts which did not, however, prevent an acceleration of emigration.[21]

There is an inevitability to the fact that economic and demographic cycles would eventually drive a recovery of sorts, assisted by mass emigration and rising cattle prices. The consequent socio-economic stability and enhanced incomes during the 1860s and 1870s was, however, 'a prosperity founded on externally-determined price levels and wages' which compounded by 'a lack of tenurial security in law', was therefore highly vulnerable to external influence. Thus when agricultural and economic depression returned in the 1880s it once again had a twin impact. Sheep farming was now no longer returning significant profits and so, with the rise of Balmorality and the Royal family's popularising of the Highlands as sporting venue, estate owners increasingly converted sheep run to deer forest. Inevitably economic downturn for those who worked the land meant consequences more immediately life-threatening. The failure of the potato and corn crops in 1881, compounded by a poor season at the east coast fisheries brought a return to conditions reminiscent of earlier famines. Such cyclical fluctuations continued into the twentieth century when, for instance, the relative stability of the late 1890s gave way to a period of depression up to 1914.[22]

---

21 Flinn, *Scottish Population History*, p. 34; Hunter, *The Making*, pp. 34–49.

22 Trevor R. Pringle, 'The privation of history: Landseer, Victoria and the Highland myth', in Denis Cosgrove and Stephen Daniels (eds), *The Iconography of Landscape:*

Figure 1.1 Croft at Cheesebay, North Uist
Source: Author's photograph.

As has already been made clear these macro-scale economic cycles had distinct Highland manifestations. One critical aspect of this, indeed of paramount importance for shaping the reaction to clearance and associated processes and the later reassertion of a distinct way of life and landscape, was the reworking, over roughly the period already discussed, of the agrarian base to society into crofting agriculture. Elements of this and the socio-economic and cultural changes from which this emerged have already been sketched in but given the fundamental importance of the crofting (material *and* mental) landscape to protest performances it is equally important that we draw the principal elements together in one place.

The distinctive features of the croft as it emerged over the course of the nineteenth century were small arable plots with a share of common grazing, subsistence agriculture and an enforced reliance on part-time industrial by-employment for both a cash income and survival. In this way the land-working tenantry rapidly came to live *on* the land but not directly *from* it, often with long-term absences from the croft. Given this rapidity and the depth of feeling associated with clanship, it is unsurprising that older attitudes to land, here characterised as *duthchas,* continued to prevail amongst the tenantry. If the croft with its small

---

Essays on the Symbolic Representation, Design and Use of Past Environments (Cambridge, 1988); Hunter, *The Making*, pp. 50, 87–8, and 131–3; Devine, *Clanship*, pp. 180–82, 276, 200 and 206–7; Richards, *The Highlands, Vol. 1*, p. 242; Withers, *Gaelic Scotland*, pp. 248–52.

Figure 1.2 Borghaston township, Lewis
Source: by kind permission of Dr Mary MacLeod Rivett

amount of arable land often surrounded (as in Figures 1.1 and 1.2) by a "sea" of common grazing or arranged in linear townships, is the physical manifestation of the crofting landscape (a fishing boat would be another), then the continued importance of access to land (ideally land which had been worked by previous generations of the same family) for the ordinary Highlander is the sensing and affective manifestation of that landscape.

Alongside the crofter there were two further groups – the cottar and squatter (the similarity of terms with early formulations is no coincidence) – who lived on the croft or common grazing and were often related to the crofter. Such characteristics attracted (and continue to attract) much attention and analysis. For Geddes, for instance, crofting can be seen as a form of 'petty commodity production', occupying a transitional position between the pre-capitalist and capitalist modes of production. Encroachment of capitalism into the Highlands reduced the primitive mode of production to 'a degenerate combination of commercial surplus production by the lords, with an allied, debased peasant subsistence sector'.[23] This view is an echo of that held, perhaps slightly less polemically, by James Hunter in his magnificent *The Making of the Crofting Community* and is not too far away from that expressed in Eric Richards's equally influential two volume *The Highland Clearances*. Thus Hunter sees crofting as emerging from the socio-economic changes precipitated by the 'landlord's desire to make money by whatever means came to hand and whilst Richards's position seems to vary a little, he appears to firmly believe that the consequences of the sudden transformation of the economic status of the victims of the Clearances created a fully proletarianised labour force. Nevertheless he also

23 Michael Geddes, 'Uneven Development and the Scottish Highlands', Working Paper 17, *Urban and Regional Studies*, University of Sussex, 1979, pp. 16–27.

recognises differentiation within the tenantry with crofter/fishermen occupying a somewhat ambivalent status. Thus there would seem to be much accord between authorities over the nature of the crofting community although Fry is once again at odds with this consensus, seemingly suggesting that the 'old peasantry' simply evolved into crofters as a product of the deeply conservative society which pertained in the north and west and which retained a deep attachment to land at its core. Once again, however, it is Withers who has the more nuanced view when he cautions against 'attributing to an earlier Highland society a sense of unity it never in fact enjoyed' which then leads to an over-simplistic view of a society polarised between landowners and smallholders.[24]

It is with understandable caution, therefore, that we should approach the claim that the emergence of a crofting *mentalité* can be understood within the context of a series of shifting "axes", from that between chief and his clansmen, through that between landlord and tenant, to, ultimately, that between government and people.[25] What this perhaps most usefully does, however, is remind us that identity is neither fixed nor given; it is, rather, made and maintained through a series of relationships, associations and registers. In the Highlands especially, any crofting identity that emerged (a problematic claim discussed in greater detail in Chapter 5), the critical relationships were those to land and sea and to the flora and fauna which dwelt therein and thereon. Identity is also about relationships between people, whether they are between the tenantry and their landlords or within the tenantry. For Withers much of Highland identity is expressed in and through reactions against material change and to a variety of forms: 'language maintenance and religious revival, what may be called the "literary reaction", and the more evident incidents of physical resistance to eviction or protest against sheep farms and deer forest'.[26] These components lie at the base of the remainder of this and subsequent chapters but before turning to a discussion of protest attention must be given to the ambivalent impact of 'the myth of the clan past'. As discussed by Hunter, whilst this shows traits of all tropes of a "lost Golden Age" and contains much that is ahistorical, it nevertheless was based on the solid foundation outlined earlier. What this provided, moreover, regardless of any veracity, was a prism through which the tenantry could view their contemporary situation and which consequently compared highly unfavourably. From this what emerged was 'an effective if unsophisticated critique of the social and economic system … associated with commercial landlordism' which was expressed in forward-looking terms and 'in a language that all … could understand'. That this forward-looking critique and language emerged some time after the mental and material structures of landlordism were effectively in place is also related to this myth and to the tenantry's continued adherence to patriarchal beliefs in the power of

24 Withers, *Gaelic Scotland*, pp. 222, 255 and 257; Hunter, *The Making*, p. 30; Richards, *Agrarian Change*, p. 177; David Turnock, *Patterns of Highland Development* (London, 1970), p. 118; Fry, *Wild Scots*, p. 153.

25 Fry, *Wild Scots*, p. 243.

26 Withers, *Gaelic Scotland*, p. 332.

kinship relations up the social strata which is perhaps best evidenced in the Napier Commission evidence that 'if our landlord knew our circumstances well he would give us justice'.[27] Alongside the patriarchal remnant, and also carried forward into this *mentalité*, were important, albeit significantly modified elements of *duthchas* which may well be seen as the principle belief Highlanders were seeking to legitimate through protest. Underpinned by custom of both place and remembered occupance, by the late nineteenth century *duthchas* had become 'an ideologically-constituted *belief* in what the term stood for as a way of holding and inheriting land'.[28]

There is no doubt that from the late sixteenth century onwards Highland society, economy and culture underwent profound structural change as proprietors increasingly sought 'alternative material foundations to the Highland economy'. Typified as 'the gradual working-out of a conflict between two different ways of life', to all groups in society this amounted to 'a major re-working of material relationships towards land and social relations'.[29] In contrast to the Irish and English enclosure movements, however, physical removal of a population from the land also removed many of the layers of meaning, corporeality and the sheer need for the materiality of enclosure hedges and ditches.[30] In the Highlands the sign of removal from and barrier to the enacting of traditional ways of life became the eviction notice. It is for this reason that papers were frequently burnt and otherwise destroyed and their bearers deforced. It is to this and other reactions to the re-worked relationship to land and social relations by those most affected (and their descendants) that we now turn.

The Nature of Protest, 1782–1914

Any survey of the reaction to these major socio-economic and cultural transformations is forced to recognise significant variation in form, not least within protest typology. Before 1850, for instance, reactionary and spontaneous anti-clearance and food riots were the dominant form but after 1850 and especially after 1880, protest was more organised and aimed at recovering land previously expropriated (so protestors believed) under the drive to agricultural improvement or deer forest. The geography of protest largely replicates the geography of

27 Hunter, *The Making*, pp. 92–3.

28 Wither, *Gaelic Scotland*, p. 332. For an interesting and persuasive linking of the notion of *Duthchas* see A. Fiona D. Mackenzie, John MacAskill, Gillian Munro, Erika Seki, 'Contesting land, creating community, in the Highlands and Islands, Scotland', *The Scottish Geographical Magazine*, Vol. 120, No. 3 (2004): 159–80.

29 Withers, *Gaelic Scotland*, p. 222.

30 David Featherstone, 'Skills for heterogeneous associations: the Whiteboys, collective experimentation, and subaltern political ecologies', *Environment and Planning D: Society and Space*, Vol. 25 (2007): 284–306; Nicholas, Blomley, 'Making Private Property: Enclosure, Common Right and the Work of Hedges' *Rural History*, Vol. 18 (2007): 1–21.

improvement. At first most visible in the eastern Highlands, protest was later concentrated in the north and west.[31]

Resistance to Clearance c.1750–1879 Direct resistance to improvement can be said to have begun with attempts to prevent the introduction of sheep onto the Kildermorie estate, Easter Ross, in 1792. Here, with support mobilised across two counties, the aim was to drive all sheep belonging to the incoming graziers out of the northern Highlands. Lacking clear organisational structure, however, the resistance foundered in the face of military intervention. Kildermorie typifies what Richards recognises as 'sporadic but repeated eruptions of spontaneous resistance' to improvement clearly connected but not causationally-linked to the economic cycle, which, if we include riots against the induction of unpopular ministers, food riot, resistance to military recruitment and sheep mutilation, total nearly 60 incidents of opposition in the period to 1857. Within all protest up to 1860 Richards is able to recognise 'a recurrent, almost stylised, mode of action' which he is able to model as a four stage challenge to landlord authority (see Table 1.1).[32]

With the ending of large-scale clearances in the mid-1850s, incidents of resistance declined with few positive effects overall. Clearance, economic change and agrarian reorganisation were carried through in most areas with resistance serving only to slow down or ameliorate the worst excesses of these processes. Nevertheless, for Richards what this amounted to was a checking of the full exercise of landlord power and the garnering of public support which proved to be a resource in the much more significant events of the 1880s.[33] A further important resource in what has become known either as the Highland Land Wars or the Crofters War was popular memory and the remembered tradition attaching to landscape, whilst a further crucial difference between protest of the Land Wars and earlier disturbances was that events of the 1880s and later were essentially proactive. These were not acts of resistance or opposition to change – the Clearances had occurred and the re-worked landscape was largely in place – but were instead positive actions aimed at recapturing what was believed to be lost and reasserting landscapes that had passed. In all of this the oral tradition was central and can be seen to form the main device whereby claims to landscapes of customary behaviour and work practices were maintained and passed down the generations.

The Highland Land Wars c1880–1897 As already noted there was a relative economic recovery in the Highlands in the early decades of the second half of the nineteenth century. By the 1880s, however, this was over and downturn coincided

31 Kenneth Logue, *Popular Disturbances in Scotland* (Edinburgh, 1979), pp. 212–13; Withers, *Gaelic Scotland*, p. 358.

32 Withers, *Gaelic Scotland*, pp. 355–8; Richards, *Highland Clearances, Vol. 1*, pp. 250–81; Eric Richards, 'How tame were the Highlanders during the Clearances?', *Scottish Studies*, Vol. 17, No. 1 (1973): 36–9.

33 Richards, *The History*, pp. 329–30.

Table 1.1 Protest as a four-stage challenge to landlord authority

Stage	Characteristics
1.	Local law officer or landlord agent attempts to serve summons of removal. The first time he is turned away, the second subjected to some form of petty humiliation [usually termed 'deforcement'] – his papers burnt or stripped naked and chased off the land, or cast adrift in a boat – often by the women.
2.	Constables led by a sheriff and his assistants arrive. Real resistance follows with women invariably in the front line of defence. Sometimes men dressed as women involved. The authorities are usually repulsed. Appeals to a more distant authority often follow: the press or perhaps the landlord.
3.	Higher legal authorities and the government alerted. Local landowners make repeated claims that disturbance linked with outside agitators and 'Radicalism' which helps persuade authorities as to the necessity of military intervention.
4.	News of impending intervention usually enough to defuse the resistance; facilitated by mediation of the local minister.

Source: Richards *Problems*, pp. 39–40, *Highland Clearances, Vol. 2*, pp. 333–4; Withers *Gaelic Scotland*, p. 353.

with the return to disturbance, albeit on a much more significant scale than that hitherto experienced. These events properly began at Braes on the Isle of Skye in 1882 but there were important precedents, most notably the Bernera riot on the isle of Lewis in 1874. At first the characterising action of these events, perhaps influenced by Ireland, was the rent strike and during the autumn and winter of 1882 expressions of discontent spread firstly to other parts of Skye and then to other areas. Disturbance was at its most intense on Skye, however, and here seizures of land (which was to become the most significant protest form of this and later protest periods) and general disorder was so great that the Government were persuaded that only military intervention would quell it. For the immediate moment, however, troops proved to be unnecessary by the ultimate agreement of "the Glendale martyrs" to allow themselves to be taken to Edinburgh to stand trial. Despite the fact that they were sentenced to two months imprisonment this singularly failed to halt the impetus of the wider movement on Skye and elsewhere.[34]

An additional marked disjuncture with events of the earlier period was the level of wider public support which emerged for the tenantry's cause and which had two momentous consequences. The first of these took place in January 1883 when a group of radical Liberal M.P.s tabled a motion in the House of Commons calling for a Royal Commission of Enquiry into crofters' grievances. A reluctant government was forced to give way and in February announced the setting up of a commission to enquire "into the Condition of Crofters and Cottars in the

34 Hunter, *The Making*, pp. 131–45.

Highlands and Islands" under the chairmanship of Lord Napier. Partly in response to this and partly to ensure that agitation for change was maintained and more organised, the Highland Land Law Reform Association was established in the same month and held its first meeting in London. In less than a year the association had grown significantly, particularly in the crofting counties.[35]

The establishment of the Napier Commission temporarily halted the violence with which incidents of opposition had been increasingly prosecuted, but its slow progress meant that this soon resumed. In addition, terror tactics by the crofters both on property and towards non-participant crofters became increasingly evident as did the boycott, another tool in the protestors' toolbox imported from Ireland. The response of the authorities was, firstly, in September 1884, to arm the Skye police and secondly, to send gunboats and marines to the island. Neither did little to restore landlord authority.[36]

The Napier Commission published its report in 1884 and whilst the evidence it gathered now stands as a remarkable historical document in its own right, the report's recommendations failed to gather any significant support from either side of the conflict. Political momentum behind reform, therefore, was only maintained through ongoing violence in the Highlands combined with the fact of the elections of crofter M.P.s and ever-worsening conditions in the region. This ultimately led to the Crofters Act of 1886, its passage hastened through Parliament by the realisation that urgent remedial action was necessary. The Act was, however, based on solutions adopted for Ireland rather than those advocated by Napier and has provoked much discussion of its impact. The key absence in the Act was the lack of provision for the desires of the landless cottar. Indeed, such was the dissatisfaction with the Act amongst this group that it almost immediately provoked a new wave and intensification of unrest with an ever greater turn to land seizure as protest device. The response of the new Conservative government was to send troops to Tiree in July 1886, their reintroduction to Skye later the same year, followed by further deployments in 1887. This latter was largely in response to the Park Deer raid on Lewis, undertaken by some 700 men, mostly cottars, with the intent of driving out or killing the deer. This was rapidly followed by what was one of the most violent confrontations between the tenantry and the law, at Aignish, Lewis, in January 1888. Here about 1,000 people marched on the farms of Aignish and Melbost determined to clear them of sheep. They were met by a large force of troops and police. A violent confrontation resulted, with threats to burn down the farmhouse and steading leading to Aignish being placed under permanent military protection. This however proved to be the high point of this period of the Land Wars, nevertheless disturbances surrounding land remained numerous although events of seizure of land declined.[37] This notwithstanding, as the Sheriff of Ross-shire pointed out in 1891, the existence of a still-large and dissatisfied

35 Hunter, *The Making*, pp. 146–64.

36 Withers, *Gaelic Scotland*, p. 379; Hunter, *The Making*, pp. 137–41 and 150–53.

37 Withers, *Gaelic Scotland*, pp. 379–81; Hunter, *The Making*, pp. 174–5.

cottar population meant 'little hope of entire immunity from disturbance ... for many years to come'.[38]

Protest after 1897 Less evident in terms of motivation but more so in terms of the response to protest by the external political authorities, for some commentators protest of the period after 1897 is seen as constituting a new and distinct phase. Whilst an improving economy ensured that events did not reach the intensity of those of the 1880s, a new wave of land seizures commenced in 1900 occasioned by frustration with the evident failings of the Congested Districts Board (hereafter CDB); the first in a series of institutional attempts to tackle the problems of Highland landlessness and cottar grievances especially. The CDB was empowered to acquire and adapt land both for the enlargement of existing holdings and most importantly, for new holdings. In the fact that this was only enacted some 11 years after the Crofters Act, the Congested Districts (Scotland) Act fits well with the general pattern of Highland legislation – certainly that before 1914 – of being always reactive, never proactive. Moreover, the inherent weaknesses of the CDB, insufficient funding and cumbersome administrative procedures, set the pattern for subsequent legislation. For Leneman, such was the extent of these weaknesses that the CDB was largely ineffectual. Furthermore, the Irish model upon which this was based proved inappropriate for the Highlands as the tenantry did not want to become peasant proprietors (with one or two notable exceptions).[39]

Not only did protest resume but it seems to have become so habituated into social relations that 'raids and threats of raids on Hebridean sheep farms' became 'part of the accepted order of things' with events on Barra and Vatersay recognised as the model for what followed and having had a political influence above that of any other protest. Land on Northbay was seized in September 1900 and agitation then spread to other farms on Barra and to Vatersay with repeated seizures in 1902 and 1906. Ten raiders were jailed in 1908 but further seizures occurred in 1909.[40] This is only a bare outline of a complex and fluid set of events which makes it extremely difficult, if not superfluous, to isolate one moment and label it as somehow exceptional. It is hard, in other words, to draw support from either Barra or Vatersay for the argument which posits the significance of one event in determining the pattern of all subsequent events. Whilst it is important to pay close attention to the microspaces of protest this is less convincing when deployed as part of an attempt to link the particular to the generalised. It is more convincing to explore protest microspace as part of an

38 Quoted in Hunter, *The Making*, p. 181.

39 Donald J. MacCuish, 'Crofting legislation since 1886', *Scottish Geographical Magazine*, Vol. 103, No. 2 (1987): 90; Leah Leneman, 'Land settlement in Scotland after World War 1', *The Agricultural History Review*, Vol. 37, Part 1 (1989): 53. The Congested Districts Board was only ever able to acquire an extremely limited number of estates and at only one of those, Glendale on Skye, – interestingly, the catalyst for the intensification of the Land Wars – did the tenants go on to purchase their holdings.

40 Hunter, *The Making*, pp. 188–92.

attempt to understand the agency of local spaces and landscapes and the notion of geographical or chronological continuity attaching to that protest place. Chapter 6 will attempt just that in the context of three case studies.

Only with the establishment of the Board of Agriculture in 1911 did agitation start to subside once again, although such was the ongoing deep-seated and radical commitment to land amongst the tenantry that it was felt it took the outbreak of war to subdue 'a coming revolt'.[41] The Board was empowered with the redistribution of crofting and farm lands and was established by the Small Landholders (Scotland) Act which, along with its English corollary, marks for some the high point of the land reform movement in Britain. The 1911 Act allowed for the creation of crofts on privately owned farms with the new holders receiving financial assistance, security of tenure and their rents set by the newly-created Scottish Land Court. This latter was almost certainly the most successful aspect of the Act as the work of the Board of Agriculture, in the first instance at least, was held back by the costly and time consuming compensation procedures. The result was that many smallholding schemes were abandoned due to the fear of excessive compensation claims. Others, however, have argued that it was the peculiar circumstances of the war years which instead slowed settlement schemes.[42] It is certainly the case that there were a large number of attempts to enact settlement schemes during the war years but nearly all foundered. And whilst this may well support the alternative view of the problems associated with the 1911 Act it is surely significant that when protest exploded after 1918 it was felt necessary to draft new legislation in response to the situation.

A number of fundamental concerns underlay this post-war legislation: to increase, or at least retain, the population; to relieve congestion; to pacify the Highlands and thereby reduce the possibility of disturbance on the scale of Ireland and "Red Clydeside" but it took until 1919 before legislation was put in place that offered the possibility of a rapid amelioration of the situation. The Land Settlement (Scotland) Act 1919, introduced at a time when public opinion in favour of the tenantry's cause was maximised, brought significant new powers of effective compulsory purchase and a more realistic funding policy to progress the voluntary or compulsory breaking-up of large farms or estates into smallholdings via schemes of land settlement. Unfortunately, due to the perpetuation of administrative procedures from the 1911 Act and an underestimation of the costs

41 Hunter, *The Making*, p. 194.

42 James Brown, 'Scottish and English land legislation 1905–1911', *Scottish Historical Review*, Vol. 67 (1968): 35; Leneman, *Land settlement*, pp. 53–4; Ewen Cameron, '"Unfinished Business": The Land Question and the Scottish Parliament', *Contemporary British History*, Volume 15, Issue 1 (2001): 83–114; Ewen A. Cameron, *'Land for the People': The British Government and the Scottish Highlands, c.1880–1930* (East Linton, 1996); Ewen A. Cameron 'Setting the heather on fire: the land question in Scotland', in Matthew Cragoe and Paul Redman (eds), *The Land Question in Britain, 1750–1950* (London: Palgrave Macmillan, 2010), pp. 109–25.

involved, progress remained slow and it was not until 1921, when borrowing powers were increased, for the possibility of a satisfactory breaking-up of the land to become a real possibility.[43]

This notwithstanding, it was when it came to the definition of "smallholding" that the fundamental fault lines, both between the tenantry and landowners and agencies of government and (most significantly for the present volume) *within* the tenantry are revealed. To the Board of Agriculture a smallholding was an area of land sufficient to employ a man and his family; effectively a form of peasant proprietorship. This view found favour with crofters who, from the 1880s at least, had been consistently agitating for extensions to existing crofts to produce viable holdings. Cottars, on the other hand, took a significantly different and often conflictual view. Their aspiration was to become landholders and they often took a traditional and traditionally-informed view of the amount of land they required. For someone who is landless in a society and culture which valorises land and places it at the centre of identity, the acquisition of any amount of land is paramount. Cottar aspiration was for a croft and for land to live *on* if not necessarily entirely *from*. Underlying and underscoring this lay the desire to re-assert a particular way of life and landscape. It was this desire and view which brought cottars increasingly into conflict not just with landowners and agencies of government but also their crofter kin. The significance of these fault lines and conflicts has been somewhat underplayed in extant literature and was directly generative of acts of protest after 1914 and almost certainly before.

It is beyond doubt that the ineffectual and reactive nature of government policies towards the agitation for land both prolonged and exacerbated protest. With each successive government taking what amounted to 'a mild and incremental approach to land reform' from 1886 up to 1921, the inadequacies of each new piece of legislation inevitably gave rise to the next. This is, however, not to underestimate the significance of the wider context. A number of important intellectual currents emerge and coalesce across the last quarter of the nineteenth century and can be said to underlie land reform across Britain and the broader challenge to the landed interest of this period. Key here were the campaigns undertaken by Henry George and the wider "historicist reaction" to utilitarian doctrines. In both Ireland and Scotland this reaction was made manifest in the wider Celtic revival and provided a further link between the intellectual movement outwith the Highlands and the local leadership an excellent example of which was the *Celtic Magazine* edited by Alexander Mackenzie whose views were directly utilised to bring moral justification to the agitation.[44]

43 Cameron, *Land for the People*; Leah Leneman, *Fit For Heroes* (Aberdeen, 1989).

44 Cameron, *Setting*; John W. Mason, 'The Duke of Argyll and the Land Question in late nineteenth century Britain', *Victorian Studies*, Vol. 21, No. 2 (1978): 153; Clive Dewey, 'Celtic agrarian legislation and the Celtic revival: historicist implications of Gladstone's Irish and Scottish Land Acts, 1870–1886', *Past and Present*, Vol. 64 (1974): 42–55; Richards, *Highland Clearances, Vol. 2*, p. 78.

For some commentators each piece of legislation is also a milestone marking a new phase of protest, with 1897 perhaps the most significant of all. It is a principal contention of the present work, however, that such divisions undervalue both the extent and importance of acts of protest after 1897. It may well be more convincing to view post-1897 events as part of a continuum of protest from the 1880s at least. To do so would be to see the war years and the promise of land in return for war service as making events after 1918 almost inevitable and to see 1914–1918 as an important catalyst for subsequent events rather than hiatus. The implications and possibilities of this, in terms of both the rich detail of hitherto unused material and of the effect this period had on the typology of protest, will be discussed in subsequent chapters. The present work then, challenges the paradigm which separates Highland protest into semi-discrete chronological units and ascribes it to the manifestation of a single regional class consciousness. The more significant distinctions to be made are fine-grained and spatial. Protest spaces are active components in the shaping of the protest act with actions and motivations of crofters and cottars in land disturbances after 1914 evidently supporting the notion that there is a dynamic and constitutive relationship between landscape/environment/people and protest. In short, it is no longer sufficient to view protest spaces (and microspaces) as inert backdrops and frames for human action. This is a view, moreover, that can be applied not just to Highland historiography but also to the wider protest literature to which we now must turn.

Chapter 2
Protest Paradigms

> *It is perhaps time to reconsider the problem of machine-wrecking in the early industrial history of Britain and other countries. About this form of early working-class struggle misconceptions are still widely held, even by specialist historians.*

> *Acts of protest do not just happen. When read out of context, some protests may appear to be spontaneous, but even those events that do not have a clearly-discernible pre-history are necessarily a function of past events and experiences.*[1]

Historians and historical geographers have been as prone to work within dominant explanations as have their counterparts in any other academic discipline. It is the aim of this chapter to demonstrate that the study of events of social protest has been heavily influenced by this tendency and not always to the good.

The trajectory of these developments is well known and will not long detain us here. At first almost wholly ignored by the dominant "Whig" tendency (but subsequently taking on much of the character of that tendency), the study of social protest became absolutely central to the great paradigm shift that was "the new social history" and the history from below movement. Clear indication of this comes from the fact that Hosbawm's "machine breakers" was published in the first edition of *Past and Present* – the key journal of this paradigm. Whilst it is now widely acknowledged that some of the most important work on the study of class consciousness and conflict originated in concerns to explore the shape of protest passed it must equally be accepted that the influence of monumental writers such as E. P. Thompson, Eric Hobsbawm and George Rudé has been, if far from malign, something of a sheet anchor to progress and greater understanding.[2] Indeed, notwithstanding the efforts of the likes of Andrew Charlesworth, Adrian Randall and Roger Wells, it has taken upwards of 30 years (if not longer) for any new, convincing and coherent body of work to emerge. In what follows the intention is firstly to chart something of the contours of the study of protest passed, then to demonstrate the close links between the more general protest paradigm and that applied to protest in the Highlands of Scotland, before finally turning to a discussion of the most recent work – that which most closely parallels the interpretations applied here. It must be stressed, however, that the overriding aim

1 Eric J. Hobsbawm, 'The machine breakers', *Past and Present*, Vol. 1 (1952): 57–70; Carl J. Griffin, *The Rural War* (Manchester, 2012), p. 13.

2 Iain J.M. Robertson, '"Two steps forward; six steps back": the dissipated legacy of Captain Swing', *Southern History*, Vol. 32 (2010): 85–100.

here is to chart a course, with the aid of the lines of contour thus drawn, through the reefs and shallows of this by now considerable body of work. The argument will be developed that a turn to matters Highland in the arena of protest studies has been hesitant, limited and perhaps even more heavily shaped by the moral economy/class conflict paradigm than the more generalised counterpart. Thus the way is clear to take a fresh look and to do so in a context of a return to a broader, more conceptual approach which seeks to identify those aspects of the new thinking in protest studies which may stand up well when tested against the events of Highland disturbance after 1914.

The intent here is not comprehensiveness but rather to identify the mould from which the interpretation of Highland protest emerged. Inevitably key parts of the protest literature will be either fully or partially glossed over. The vitally important debate over the relative importance of overt and covert protest in the second half of the nineteenth century has, for instance, barely registered in the Scottish literature and will (regretfully) not feature here.[3] Similarly, questions of popular symbolism and violence get little attention and whilst the role of women in these events has been raised it generated little response.[4] These deficiencies notwithstanding, a significant literature on Highland protest has emerged and it is one which draws heavily on the foundational protest paradigm.

Establishing the Paradigm

Once the historiographical shackles had been broken it took very little time for the new, more sympathetic but ultimately constraining view to be established. Nevertheless an interestingly diverse range of themes within protest studies did emerge, bringing with it considerable insight into the méntalite and everyday worlds of the rural poor.

Perhaps the most obvious connection between the old and the new historiographies was that set of explanations which prioritised economic models of explanation. Known collectively as the "hardship model" commentators who advocated this perspective saw no direct relationship between absolute economic deprivation and protest but argued instead that disturbance was more likely to arise once economic recovery was underway and was thus the product of rising expectations confronting short-term economic declivities. Critiques of this model have averred to difficulties in quantifying the relationship and the ability to prove a direct link between economic condition and protest. For Andrew Charlesworth hardship was a necessary condition but was not sufficient cause to explain

3 For this debate see the collection of key articles and further discussion in Mick Reed and Roger Wells (eds), *Class, Conflict and Protest in the English Countryside, 1700–1880* (London, 1990).

4 Iain J.M. Robertson, 'The role of women in social protest in the Highlands of Scotland, c.1880–1939', *Journal of Historical Geography*, Vol. 23, No. 2 (1997): 187–200.

disturbance. To place the emphasis here may lead to what Thompson has seen as 'gross economic reductionism' with the protestor divorced 'from his social and historical context'. Thus economic explanations often conclude at the point at which they 'become of serious sociological or cultural interest' thereby failing to fully explain the typological similarities evident in much rural resistance.[5]

These early incursions were followed by attempts to identify and accommodate the chronological contours of changing protest forms. Popular here was the modernisation model and from this basic premise an analysis developed which allocated protest type according to a pre-industrial/industrial dichotomy with early industrial protest, "bargaining by riot", as a transitional form drawing characteristics from both earlier and later protest types. To make this less deterministic Geary argued that a chronological sequence is inappropriate and that the same group of workers could alternate between different modes of protest. This allowed Geary to suggest that pre-industrial protest remains evident in several European countries after the First World War.[6]

Criticism of this development has centred on its lack of an organising concept based on clear definitions and conceptualisation and an inadequate explanation of the transition from one stage to the next. Where continuity in crowd action is evident this was often explained either as the form of the action remaining constant whilst social content and function altered, or as the product of lags in socio-economic development caused by either arrested social change or times of rapid transformation; and yet both assume the retention of the pre-industrial/industrial dichotomy. More convincing may well be to see protest as but one function of crowd activity with other aspects as means 'of preserving communal identity or recasting it in the face of external pressure and underlying social change'. This ultimately leads to an approach which, as in Tilly's work on collective violence, subsumes the study of the crowd into the broader study of the social group or social activity involved.[7] Unfortunately, all this does is replace one dichotomy with another: that of reactive/proactive violence, and as such is equally flawed even if there is some utility in this for the understanding of the changing nature and chronology of Highland protest. Tilly identified three distinct forms: competitive – the competition between groups for physical and mental resources; reactive – where a group controlling a resource reacts to the prior claims of another; proactive – where a group lay claim to a resource under the control of another particular group and the members of the second group reacts to the claims of the first. Underpinning these changes in form was a shift from challenges to old claims

---

5 Andrew Charlesworth. 'Social Protest in a Rural Society: The Spatial Diffusion of the Captain Swing Disturbances of 1830–1831', *Historical Geography Research Series, Issue 1* (London, 1979): 30–31; Edward P. Thompson. 'The moral economy of the English crowd in the Eighteenth Century', *Past and Present*, No. 50, (1971): 77.

6 Dick Geary, *European Labour Protests 1848–1939* (London, 1981), pp. 26–8.

7 Robert J. Holton. 'The Crowd in History: some problems of theory and method', *Social History*, Vol. 3, No. 2 (1978): 219–31.

to disputes over new claims, the shift to the proactive form representative of the shift to the national area in which 'the bulk of the population were excluded from direct participation'. Collective action at this time it was suggested consisted of 'bids for places in the national structures'.[8] In avoiding the reductionist notion of protest as part of a linear progression to trade unionism Tilly's model has much to offer the study of Highland resistance. Nevertheless, in postulating a progression in form of collective action it cannot easily accommodate protest that is typologically different but undertaken for similar motives. Tilly's model also shares the weakness of all large scale theories, that of ignoring local variation.

This attempt to categorise protest is, in short, almost as much a conceptual blind alley as the other equally fascinating product of its intellectual time, Andrew Charlesworth's attempt to statistically infer the diffusion of protest, although it is important to recognise that he was never wholly in thrall to this methodology.[9] Charlesworth suggested that the origins of individual outbreaks of Captain Swing rioting may have had as much to do with the role of traditional forms of village sociability – kinship groups; the workplace; beershops; etc – as they had with influences from outside the immediate locale. He also emphasised 'local network of contacts between the militants' and 'small elites of village politicians' in generating the local spread of protest.[10] This view was echoed by Bohstedt and Williams in their study of the spread of riot in eighteenth century Devon but they went on to be amongst the first to suggest the existence of a "tradition" of riot amongst specific communities; a recognition which has great resonance for the study of Highland protest.[11]

In common with the study of rural resistance generally the more compelling protest narratives have looked to an underlying ideological base for their intellectual succour and conviction. It is for these reasons also that the classic position with regard to rural social protests as it emerged in the 1960s and 1970s, continues to carry both weight and relevance. This position draws on the study of agency and structure, with protest as expression of class relations; part of the complex nexus of relationships out of which the landscape has emerged. Modes of production were seen to determine class and 'class consciousness is the way in which these experiences are handled in cultural terms'. Class is relational and popular protest charts the development of antithetical relationships between and within classes in the countryside.[12]

8 Charles Tilly, Louise Tilly and Richard Tilly, *The Rebellious Century* (Cambridge, MA, 1975), pp. 259–64.

9 Charlesworth, *Social Protest in Rural Society.*

10 Charlesworth, *Social Protest in Rural Society*, pp. 31 and 48–51.

11 John Bohstedt and Dale E. Williams. 'The Diffusion of Riots', *The Journal of Interdisciplinary History* Vol. XIX, No. 1 (1988): 3–22.

12 Alan Baker, 'Reflections on the relations of historical geography and the Annales school of history', in Alan Baker and Derek Gregory (eds), *Explorations in Historical*

This however is only one, albeit the most important, aspect of a broader set of explanatory inputs. Indeed the origins of ideologically-based analysis lie in an understanding of protest in which groups were brought together by a "levelling" instinct of elementary social justice and a common desire to re-assert a disappearing socio-economic system (a complex of customary rights, paternalistic vertical networks and a moralistic and localised marketing system). Disturbance becomes understood as conservative, backward looking and often determined by the stage of development the capitalist system had reached. For Lewis, however, the principal backward-looking notion, an Arcadian vision of the traditional life of the countryside, more harmonious and basic than that of the city, was at the same time the principal means by which the central European peasantry accommodated socio-economic change. The traditionalist and anti-capitalist rhetoric of the various peasant parties was a product of their fear of change but also offered reassurance to the peasantry that even in evolving they remained a distinctive cultural group, thereby encouraging that evolution. The vision of an alternative Arcadian social order was utilised not to replace the existing social order but to gain entry into that order.[13] It is, however, equally important to note that despite their power these original explanations have come to be seen as both simplistic and generalised and when disturbances are anatomised on a localised basis, often inaccurate.

It is of course possible to suggest that all interpretations of protest are products of their time. Indeed that was partly the inspiration for the title of this chapter. This is clearly the case for the singularly most important protest perspective, that of Thompson's moral economy.[14] Indeed, such has been the influence of Thompson's thinking this view has leapt the spatial and temporal bounds of the original. The experienced reader will have to forgive the authorial indulgence but such is the importance and enormous reach of moral economy that a brief summary must remain an imperative.

Thompson convincingly advocated for a view which saw in almost every eighteenth century crowd action an underlying legitimising notion based upon the defence of traditional rights or customs which gave these actions consensus and continuity. Riot may have been prompted by short-term economic downturn but was drawn from 'a popular consensus as to what were ... legitimate practices in marketing, milling, baking etc', a consensus which was founded in moral assumptions of social norms and obligations.[15] A fascinating development of these precepts came from James C. Scott who argued for 'a norm of reciprocity' out of which protest would emerge rather than from 'frustration and relative deprivation'. Once the elite refused to recognise 'the peasantry's basic social

---

Geography (Cambridge, 1984), p. 27; Edward P. Thompson, *The Making of the English Working Class* (London, 1968), pp. 7–9.

13 Gavin Lewis. 'The Peasantry, Rural Change and Conservative Agrarianism', *Past and Present*, Vol. 81, No. 1 (1978): 119–43.

14 Thompson, *Moral Economy.*

15 Thompson, *Moral Economy*, pp. 78–131.

rights as its obligation' the path to breakdown in social relations was set. Defiance was then normatively justified and understood by Scott as an expression of local class interest. This in turn drew upon a network of informal social ties such as kinship, communal rights, religious sects, the local market and labour migration which came together to comprise a sense of moral economy.[16] Moreover, in the identification of these particular building blocks a clear link to Highland protest is established.

Criticism of the Thompson thesis has focussed on his lack of economic rigour (as well as his devotion to an economic explanation for the immediate onset of protest), his "romantic view" of pre-industrial society and for attempting to fit a generalised theory to essentially local events. More broadly, John Bohstedt has argued that the theory itself failed both to engage with an inconsistent recourse to protest amongst those threatened by the political economy and pay sufficient attention to the essentially local links between market and crowd action. Bohstedt initially identified these links as being a manifestation of local political negotiation but in his most recent, somewhat contentious work, he turns instead to an even greater emphasis on informal politics. In this Bohstedt is echoing much of the most recent and very exciting work on the ways in which power was negotiated in the early modern period. Here power is brokered and limited in everyday experience and through 'word, deed and gesture'. It is thus a quotidian politics in which a 'moral economy of expectations about food supply and marketing' may well exist but is but one component of the wider and more important politics of provisions.[17]

The second great pillar upon which the protest paradigm became based was Eric Hobsbawm and George Rudé's *Captain Swing.* As Adrian Randall has most recently claimed '*Captain Swing* remains a seminal publication and any new study of the riots still, perforce, begins with an acknowledgement of the debt owed to the book. After forty years, that remains a real achievement'.[18] The ideological genesis of this work was a lightly-worn, but still teleological Marxism, with the proletarianisation thesis much to the fore. What we can draw from this approach is a concern for the lives and livelihoods of the rural disposed alongside the appreciation of the need for fine-grained localised studies that pay close attention to the particularities of place and of the nature of social relations in-place. In recognising the centrality of the local economic, social and cultural milieu,

16 James C. Scott. *The Moral Economy of the Peasantry* (Yale, 1976), pp. 186–7; James C. Scott, 'Hegemony and the Peasantry', *Politics and Society*, Vol. 7, No. 3 (1977): 270 and 280–1.

17 John Bohstedt, *Riots and Community Politics in England and Wales, 1790–1810* (Harvard, 1983); John Bohstedt, *The Politics of Provisions* (London, 2010), pp. 6–15. One of the most significant works to explore the politics of negotiation is Michael Braddick and John Walter (eds), *Negotiating Power in Early Modern Society: Order, Hierarchy and Subordination in Britain and Ireland* (Cambridge, 2001).

18 Adrian Randall, '*Captain Swing*: a retrospect', *International Review of Social History*, Vol. 54 (2009): 419–27.

Hobsbawm and Rudé's work has played a significant role in the emergence of a rural history that aspires to rich and often very local contextualisation of change.

One of Hobsbawm and Rudé's principal concerns was to count and to categorise; in short, to adopt a quantitative methodology. Virtually ever since protest historians have variously either slavishly followed such approaches or railed against them.[19] The written record and the need to classify will only ever capture particular 'moments' within otherwise complex and fluid events. Thus, as Randall asserts, virtually every aspect of any event could change character and therefore fit uneasily within any attempt at compartmentalisation.[20] There was a perceived need, therefore, to move beyond the dominant paradigm and its essentially quantitative methodology. The legacy of *Captain Swing* is thus both inspirational and, in its ubiquity, something of a sheet anchor to further progress in our understanding of manifestations of social conflict. Alongside Thompson's moral economy thesis *Captain Swing* set the agenda for the study of social protest, ensured that rural riot would never more be written out of history, and placed protest more generally in a central position in the social histories of both early modern and modern England, a position, it was assumed, it would never relinquish. But we must also acknowledge that such powerfully defining moments, reflected in an inability not to begin any discussion of protest without an in-depth engagement with one or both, can hold back debate and the advancement of any protest theme. These two great works have become such a field of force in their own right that they have come to define what rural resistance actually *was*. There was thus a great danger (partly fulfilled) of complacency and stagnation within the study of both social protest and history from below.

Perhaps of more direct relevance to the ways in which Highland events have been understood hitherto has been Rudé's own subtle extension of notions of ideology in protest. It was his belief that popular opposition was the product of two elements, with only an inherent ideology – direct experience; oral tradition; folk memory – belonging to the popular classes. The second, no less important, element was that often more structured 'stock of ideas and beliefs that are derived or borrowed from others'. Interestingly, whilst he asserts that influence and input cannot be uni-directional, he nevertheless clings to the notion that ideology should necessarily remain a central concern. Ideology is, however, in essence an abstract. Consciousness does not explain fully how ideology is put into practice. The argument developed therefore, and was powerfully and convincingly deployed in a Highland context, that an alternative concept by which this linkage may be made is hegemony.[21]

19 Both approaches can, for instance, be found in the special volume of the journal *Southern History* dedicated to a consideration of the legacy of the book. See Steve Poole, (ed.) 'Captain Swing reconsidered', *Southern History*, Vol. 32 (2010).

20 Randall, '*Captain Swing*', pp. 424–7.

21 George Rudé, *Ideology and Popular Protest* (London, 1980), p. 22; Withers, *Gaelic Scotland.*

The domination of one class over another has generally been seen as "political rule". Gramsci, however, made a distinction between rule and hegemony. He saw the former as confined to directly political forms and times of crisis, and hegemony expressed in 'a complex interlocking of political, social and cultural forces'. Dominant and subordinate relationships are extended to include 'the whole substance of lived identities and relationships'. Hegemony is, therefore, 'a whole body of practices and expectations' from which the 'whole lived social process [is] practically organised by specific and dominant meanings and values'.[22] For Thompson such dominance can only be sustained by the constant exercise of skill, theatre and concession. Hegemonic control cannot impose an all-embracing domination upon the ruled. This allows alternative views and even resistance to be formulated. Critically for Withers's interpretation of Highland protest therefore, hegemony embraces oppositional forms, both residual and emergent and expressed either as alternative- or counter-hegemony. The former is associated with the rise to power of a new class but is only visible in an unrealised state. Once established it becomes a new hegemonic culture. Counter hegemony is any opposition to dominant hegemony. It need not be underpinned by an articulated class consciousness and can take both informal and organised forms. Thus mockery, foot-dragging, food riot or land seizure can all be recognised as counter hegemonic forms; to which Withers adds the retention of Gaelic, and the development of a poetry of opposition.[23] His work also demonstrates the way in which commentators worked with and within this original paradigm.

What has emerged from this first foray into the protest literature has been the identification of a series of contour lines which chart some of the most compelling engagements with history from below. Moral economy, class conflict and a turn towards custom, culture and locality-based studies serve to define these narratives. In conjunction with the social movements literature these serve also to frame what is here understood as the protest paradigm; most particularly the realisation that one aspect of this amounts to an ironic reworking of the Whiggish approach: the study *of* great men replaced by studies *by* great men. Here too what might be recognised as the geographer's perspective – land as disputed territory – is perhaps being embryonically felt rather than fully emergent. There is both great strength in and

22 Rudé, *Ideology and Popular Protest*, p. 22; Raymond Williams, *Marxism and Literature* (Oxford, 1977).

23 Edward P. Thompson, 'Eighteenth Century English Society: Class Struggle without class', *Social History*, Vol. 3 (1978): 133–65; Derek Gregory, 'Contours of crisis: sketches for a geography of class struggle on the early Industrial revolution in England' in Alan Baker and Derek Gregory (eds), *Explorations in Historical Geography* (Cambridge, 1984), pp. 110–11; Barry Reay, *The Last Rising of the Agricultural Labourers* (Oxford, 1991); Peter Jackson, *Maps of Meaning* (London, 1990), p. 53; Raymond Williams, 'Base and superstructure in Marxist cultural theory', in Raymond Williams (ed.), *Problems in Materialism and Culture* (London: Verso, 1980), pp. 31–2; Withers, *Gaelic Scotland*, pp. 327–401.

much that can be questioned with regard to this paradigm. This notwithstanding what one part of this amounts to is an ironic (and unconscious) reworking of the Whiggish paradigm: the study *of* great men replaced by studies *by* great men.

Flexing the Paradigm

Two important, more generalised points emerge from the writings and themes which fall under this particular badge of convenience. Firstly the "flexing" here comes from the fact that commentators more often sought to extend and shift the dominant paradigm rather than break it. Second, whilst much of the literature here has not been directly utilised to understand Highland protest, it clearly has much to say about these events. The exception, however, may well be those commentaries which turn towards cultural lives. The role of both popular religion and popular symbolism in protest acts became important foci but the question of greatest significance is undoubtedly that of land and kinship relations.

Here we find Hosbawm's classic "social bandits". Drawn from the rural surplus population, bandits were those peasant robbers considered criminals by the authorities but regarded by their people as heroes and fighters for justice. The transition from kin-based land holding patterns to capitalist rentier systems is crucial here. Reactive victims of circumstance, banditry tended to become epidemic in times of pauperisation and economic crisis. Individually bandits were not political or social rebels even if, they were often, however, the precursor of major peasant revolution.[24]

Hobsbawm used this model in his work on land invasions in twentieth-century Peru. He identified three types of occupations: where the land may belong to the peasant but may have been alienated in a manner disputed by them; where the land occupied did not belong to a private individual and was in fact public land; where 'the land may unquestionably belong to someone other than the invaders'.[25] Hobsbawm then moved to establish what he saw as the key characterising features of a typical land invasion. These were normally 'standardised [and] carried out by the whole community' in which collective and familial memory was the means through which claims to land were renewed and re-worked. The formalised and symbolic nature of the performance was enhanced by the fact that it was often preceded by a reconnaissance party and that the date of the invasion was often formally set and adhered to, with both women and children taking a prominent role. Crucially these were essentially local rebellions with any national aspirations decidedly secondary. Nevertheless, the impact of the event, suggesting their affective power, could be 'subjectively revolutionary' and if they took on such aspects their revolutionary character

24 Eric Hobsbawm, *Bandits* (London, 1969), pp. 17–31.

25 Eric Hobsbawm, 'Peasant Land Occupations', *Past and Present*, No. 62 (1974): 120.

was most often expressed in millennia terms or as a 'lost golden age'.[26] As will be demonstrated throughout the rest of this book, these characteristics, whilst perhaps a little too generalising, are those which resonate most clearly with Highland disturbances and, indeed, with pan-European land invasions. In southern Italy, for instance, as with Highland land invasions, those who seized land conducted themselves with great ceremony and acted in the belief that they were re-appropriating land that was rightfully theirs.[27]

In both Peru and southern Italy then, there is clear and important resonance (as will be made clear in the following section) with Highland events. Almost inevitably the same can be said for Ireland and Wales and also with the historiography of these events and on land issues in these areas more generally.[28] For Knott land is the focus to almost all Irish protest and it occupied a primary position in peasant consciousness, underpinned by consensual notions as to what were proper practices regarding the ownership, occupation and use of land. He begins from the traditional *udal* form of land holding in which the land "belonged" to the kinship group and was held in trust for his descendants by the current occupier. The maintenance of these traditional rights and customs in land, Knott believes, drew upon a 'system of norms and obligations' which was the basis of an Irish peasant ideology. It was this peasant ideology, Knott asserts, which shaped the whole character of the agrarian agitation – an analysis which seeks to expand the reach of Thompson's moral economy rather than break it.[29]

Attachment to the homestead and the community ties of kinship, religion and language were equally strong in Wales, with poverty and a rising population the immediate "push" factors behind disturbance, underpinned 'by a cultural and political divide between landowners and the rest of the farming community'.[30] Manifest as religious and linguistic differences between the English-speaking, Anglican landowners and Welsh-speaking Nonconformist land-working groups, this shaped, in the Tithe Wars of the late nineteenth century, an emergent and 'vague cultural and political nationalism'.[31] For others these disturbances can also be interpreted as the last attempt of a newly-proletarianised labour force to re-assert their claims in rights to the land. Partly in response to the emergence of tenant farmers as a distinct group and partly as a response to the failures of the Tithe Wars, rural labourers came to articulate their own class interests, a process

26 Hobsbawm, 'Peasant Land Occupations, pp. 121–49.

27 C., L. and R. Tilly. *The Rebellious Century*, p. 249; Frank Snowden, *Violence and Great Estates in the South of Italy* (Cambridge, 1986), p. 37 and 108.

28 John Dunbabin, *Rural Discontent in Nineteenth Century Britain* (London, 1975).

29 John Knott, 'Land, kinship and identity', *Journal of Peasant Studies*, Vol. 12, No. 1 (1984): 94–103.

30 David W. Howell, *Land and People in Nineteenth Century Wales* (London, 1978), pp. 9 and 62–3.

31 Dunbabin, *Rural Discontent*, p. 229.

which reached its climax during the Great War.[32] Once again, the parallels with Highland Scotland in a similar period are quite remarkable.

There are equally important connections to be made for a re-worked understanding of Highland protest with literature which turns to themes of popular symbolism, not least for the emphasis on the institutions and symbols of popular culture. Thus for Theunte the peasant world view was conservative, passive and fatalistic, with much of their song and poetry reflecting this. Whilst for Manning the use of customary symbols and rituals of festive misrule in protest signalled the limits of peasant opposition: to reassure 'that the protesters were not challenging the social or political order'.[33] For others, however, since rural protest sought to re-assert a threatened way of life and was a challenge to established social orders, symbolism was proactively influential. Leaders of the Forest of Dean riots in 1631 adopted the alias "Skimington". This character was a borrowing from popular culture where he led a loud and raucous procession designed to demonstrate communal disapproval of 'conduct considered scandalous or immoral'.[34] Utilisation of devices and techniques drawn from popular culture in protest performances, such as marching in a pseudo-military fashion whilst led by a musician, was, in part at least, an attempt to legitimise an illegal act. It was also the means by which Bossenden Wood rioters became aware of an incipient disturbance. In 1838, for instance, the battle of Bossenden Wood was preceded by a recruitment march led by a bugler, a flag bearer and a loaf of bread on a pole.[35] Perhaps even more importantly, Reay's work on the locale from which the rioters came, successfully linked Calhoun's claim that 'traditional communities were the crucial social foundation'[36] for protest, to Charlesworth's notion of the importance

32 David Pretty, *The Rural Revolt that Failed* (Cardiff, 1989), pp. 12–14, 20 and 45–63.

33 Mary Helen Thuente, 'Violence in Pre-Famine Ireland', *Irish University Review*, Vol. 15, No. 2 (1985): 131; Roger Manning, *Village Revolts* (Oxford, 1988), pp. 2 and 82.

34 Buchanan Sharp, *In Contempt of All Authority: Rural Artisans and Riot in the West of England, 1586–1660* (Berkeley, 1992), pp. 104–5, 164–5 and 175–8; Chris Fisher, *Custom, Work and Market Capitalism* (London, 1981), p. 175.

35 Keith Lindley, *Fenland Riots and the English Revolution* (London, 1982), pp. 110–12; Reay, *The Last Rising.* There is one letter to the Scottish Office in the post-1918 disturbances in which regret is expressed that the 'fiery cross' had not been carried round Highland townships: the traditional symbol for the raising of the clans. Protest has also been seen as an amalgam of rural revelry and crime – in the Rebecca riots for instance – and as such are an obvious discussion point here. As has already been made clear, however, the primary aim of this section is to point up points of intersection between the broader protest literature and Highland historiography. This particular topic has seldom been raised in this context and thus is confined to a footnote here. See, however, David W. Howell, 'The Rebecca riots', in Trevor Herbert and Gareth E. Jones (eds), *People and Protest in Wales 1815–1880* (Cardiff, 1990).

36 Craig Calhoun, *The Question of Class Struggle: The Social Foundations of Popular Radicalism during the Industrial Revolution* (Chicago, 1982), pp. xii-xiii.

of the breakdown of rigid social control, by observing that many of those who took part in the battle lived and worked together and drank in the same beer houses. Reay also put great weight on the importance of popular religion as one of the ideological bases to protest; reminding us once more of the under-explored connection between literature on popular beliefs in protest more generally and Highland disturbance more specifically. This was to be of profound importance in the breaking of the protest paradigm (see below).

In the context of the role of popular religion in revolt the work of Bak and Benecke is perhaps the most significant; in particular the view that this provided a system of moral values and 'eschatological promises of equality and justice' upon which to draw. They further argue that where the religion of the peasantry was different to that of the landowners, suppression only enhanced its oppositional associations. Finally religion brought a community-building function which provided the necessary association to develop an oppositional spirit.[37]

For both Hobsbawm and Nigel Scotland this was precisely the role taken by Primitive Methodism with Scotland emphasising the view that religious and secular radicalism evolved and drew together via a belief in the millennium. Echoing Bak and Beneke, Scotland believes that to the union activist 'the millennium was seen to refer specifically to the physical and material conditions of living'. The adoption of Primitive Methodism was 'often an act of open rebellion against parson, squire and farmer' and was essential to the development of a radical, religious ideology.[38] As will be noted below there are clear echoes of this interpretation to be found in the role of the Free Church in Highland disturbances.

It is perhaps dangerous and certainly artificial at best (although convenient) to divide up the protest literature in the way done here. In this however, the present work is not alone. For instance, in his most recent and paradigm-shifting work (*The Rural War)* Carl Griffin deploys a similar schema. As the focus of his work is on the Captain Swing riots, Griffin's second of three catch-all compartmentalisations is entitled 'the legacy of Hobsbawn and Rudé'. Nevertheless the guiding view is the same as that which has determined the current section: that protest literature of the decade after the mid-1980s falls into one of three approaches, all of which, as Griffin has it, 'tended to follow rather than lead the post-*Captain Swing* agenda'. In this tracking commentators perhaps sought to take one (as they saw it) under-developed aspect of the agenda and fully develop that. Alternatively they sought either to explore protest events over an extended time period or to engage with individual event in considerable detail. The final approach is that which proved to be one of the key signposts out of this conceptual blind alley. In the work of David Eastwood, Brian Short and Stephen Hipkin but perhaps above all in that of Roger

37 Janos M. Bak and Gerhard Beneke (eds). *Religion and Rural Revolt* (Manchester, 1984), pp. 2–9.

38 Eric Hobsbawm, *Primitive Rebels: Studies in Archaic Forms of Social Movement in the 19th Century* (Manchester, 1959), pp. 134–9; Nigel Scotland, *Methodism and the Revolt of the Field* (London, 1981), pp. 130–35.

Wells and Barry Reay, the focus in protest studies turned away from the national arena and towards that of the micro-geographical with an aim either to 'better understand the genesis, response to and aftermath of protest events' or to more easily explore new ways of thinking about protest.[39]

This critical mid-period, however, is not truly marked by innovative thinking and understanding but by a continued adherence to much of the established paradigm. These characteristics are also apparent in the study of Highland protest. Here too is the emphasis on moral economy, class conflict and ideologically-shaped actions. But here also is the curious absence of many convincing attempts to stretch and redefine the paradigm. For the Highlands, but also to a lesser extent for elsewhere, there have been few (if any) attempts to write explicit geographies of protest – especially the intra-regional geography of protest. Furthermore, whilst conflict has been seen to arise out of customary claims to land in the face of the capitalised commodification of ancestral holdings, the role of kinship has been undervalued. In studies of other protest events kinship is seen to provide both part of legitimation for protest and, as a significant component of a peasant ideology, central to the decision to protest. Further, the underlying legitimation of protest has been shown in part to be symbolic, drawing upon the institutions of popular culture: holidays, carnival and protest were often conflated "moments" in the countryside. Finally, protest has been shown to draw upon and even originate in a religious ethic, often of a millennial nature. Rural protest can be seen by some as backward-looking, drawing exclusively upon notions of a past society and social relations, yet by others as part of forward-looking claims to re-assert local views as part of new ways of doing, not as residual elements of past practice. Not all of this has impacted on the Highland historiographical consciousness in the way it perhaps it should have done. In turning to a discussion of the historiography Highland protest, therefore, the aim will be to engage with the detail and discussion but always with this attenuated context as framing device.

39 Key texts here would include: Reay, *The Last Rising;* John Archer, *By a Flash and a Scare: Arson, Animal Maiming and Poaching in East Anglia 1815–1870* (Oxford, 1990); Jeanette Neeson, *Commoners, Common Right, Enclosure and Social Change in England* 1700–1820 (Cambridge, 1993); Barry Reay, *Microhistories: Demography, Society and Culture in Rural England 1800–1930* (Cambridge, 1996); Adrian Randall and Andrew Charlesworth (eds), *Markets, Market Culture and Popular Protest in Eighteenth Century Britain* (Liverpool, 1996); David Eastwood, 'Communities, protest and police in early nineteenth-century Oxfordshire: the enclosure of Otmoor reconsidered', *Agricultural History Review*, Vol. 44, No. 1 (1996): 35–46; John Rule and Roger Wells (eds), *Crime, Protest and Popular Politics in Southern England 1740–1850* (London, 1997); Brian Short, 'Conservation, class and custom: lifespace and conflict in a nineteenth-century forest environment', *Rural History*, Vol. 10, No. 2 (1999): 127–54; Stephen Hipkin, 'Sitting on his penny rent: conflict and right of common in Faversham Blean, 1596–1610', *Rural History*, Vol. 11, No. 1 (2000): 163–77; Griffin, *Rural War*, pp. 18–21.

The Highland Paradigm

In reviewing the historiographical response to Highland protest and the various explanatory modes deployed two immediate points can be made both of which closely link this response to the broader protest literature. Firstly, here too we can see the influence of a limited number of hugely influential writers. Indeed, such was their influence that it can be plausibly claimed that the study of Highland protest has never fully escaped their orbit and remains under-developed at the very least. Second, it is equally possible to claim that the explanatory modes utilised for Highland protest have similarly remained dominated by the broader protest literature and that Highland historiography has failed to develop singular perspectives of its own. This is not to suggest, however, that there is a dearth of literature on Highland protest and what follows is not intended to be a review of its totality. Instead the aim is to point up the key areas of debate which will be carried forward into engagement with disturbance after 1914.

As with the wider protest literature it is possible to see economic decline as the immediate cause in determining the onset of protest. In the early 1880s, for instance, harvest failure and the worst attack of potato blight since the 1850s, was compounded by livestock disease and the failure of the east coast fishing. Exacerbated by earlier gains in living standards, the social effects of this relapse into economic uncertainty were such that it has been suggested that the disturbances of the 1880s were a revolution of rising expectations. Adding a further layer, Orr recognised in these early Land Wars a conjoint antagonism to the rapid growth of deer forests, economic decline and new wage regulations in the fishing industry.[40] This, however, is unconvincing as sole explanation. More convincing is the view which holds that economic downturn and motivation is the necessary backdrop to disturbance but that the more significant motivation lay elsewhere.

For Logue where the more significant set of motives might be found was in the moral economy and in attempts to preserve this against 'the new market economy of landowner and sheep farmer'. Drawing firmly on the Thompsonian paradigm, Logue saw moral economy emerging from folk culture and applicable to local farmers and meal sellers. It thus became a code which, if rejected, prompted direct action. Logue, however, was not content to stop there and, in the classic extension (if not over-extension) of the model, moral economy became applied to anti-clearance rioting. In this context Logue identified a 'moral economy of the clan' that was grounded in the values of a kin-based society in which the clan was the 'focus of all social, economic and cultural activity'.[41] His argument was that in attempting to retain use rights over land crofters were at the same

40 Hunter, *The Making*, pp. 131–2; Willie Orr, *Deer Forests, Landlords and Crofters* (Edinburgh, 1982), pp. 3–5, 46–7, 135; Richards, *Highland Clearances, Vol 2*, p. 343.

41 Logue, *Popular Disturbances*, p. 212; Kenneth Logue, 'Eighteenth Century Popular Protest', in Edward Cowan (ed. *The People's Past* (Edinburgh, 1985), pp. 119–21.

time attempting to re-assert this moral economy over and above the market-led decisions of landlord and sheep farmer. In common with much of the literature of the time Logue suggested that this appeal to a moral economy was 'backward-looking' albeit with some elements of 'forward-looking' notions in militia and induction riots. The connection between popular direct action and reforming/revolutionary politics was limited at best. Thus, as Eric Richards argued, much of Highland protest, being apolitical, unarmed, dominated by women and lacking effective leadership and ideology, appears to fit into Tilly's category of 'reactionary collective violence'.[42]

As with the broader protest literature, accompanying the desire to categorise, it is questions of the role of class and class consciousness which have, either explicitly or implicitly, dominated much of the discussion around Highland protest and, indeed, largely still do. Thus, for both Withers and Hunter the disturbances of the 1880s are predicated upon the emergence of a class consciousness amongst the crofting population perhaps from as early as the 1850s.[43] To Logue, however, whilst militia disturbances were the more obvious class conflict, anti-clearance riots were also characterised by class issues and thus the Land Wars were the culmination of a century long 'class war'.[44] This can be contrasted with Grigor's argument that realisation of common interests and objectives came after the early events of the Land Wars and in parallel with the activities of the Napier Commission. Along with Buchanan, Grigor sees this period, the three years after January 1883, as one of intense radicalism in which the act of giving evidence to the Commission was a 'profound psychological liberation, at both personal and communal levels'. This led directly to crofters recognising their common interests and creating a common identity.[45]

The final strands of this fascinating debate are those of questions of the relationship between Highland disturbances, and wider movements specifically with the Land League and the emergence of the Free Church. This latter has been alternatively seen as either the first Highland class conflict or a refuge into which passion was channelled away from overt opposition. Key here appears to be the role of the group of lay preachers (*Na Daoine* "the Men") who emerged with the Free Church. They undoubtedly had a negative impact on Highland culture but this has been interpreted in a positive light by James Hunter who argues that this revealed and confirmed to ordinary highlanders that landlordism had superseded clanship and in this way both The Men and the associated evangelical revival were a threat to all those whose interests lay in maintaining social and economic

---

42 Logue, *Popular Disturbances*, pp. 72, pp. 213–14; Eric Richards, *Highland Clearances, Vol. 1*, p. 141; Richards, *Highland Clearances, Vol. 2,* pp. 346–7.

43 Withers, *Gaelic Scotland*, p. 415; Hunter, *The Making*, pp. 87 and 94.

44 Logue, *Popular Disturbances*, pp. 214–15.

45 Iain Fraser Grigor, *Mightier than a Lord* (Stornoway, 1979), p. 70; J. Buchanan, 'Clearance, Conflict and Crofting', *Scottish Trades Union Review*, No. 32, 1986, pp. 4–5.

hegemony. Working with and from within Gaelic culture, the evangelical faith The Men promulgated became a base and means to counter hegemony.[46]

The debate which explores the extent of the influence of wider political movements is an equally fascinating strand of the discussions around the extent to which the Land Wars represent a significant disjuncture in Highland disturbance. Ewen Cameron for instance, has suggested that before the 1880s where land agitation occurred it was largely apolitical and isolated with little connection to wider politics. The 1880s, however, see a step-change in the nature and extent of these connections with the influence of the Highland Land Law Reform Association and (subsequently) the Highland Land League, coming to link Highland concerns to their migrant communities in Glasgow and Edinburgh and to left-wing politics in Scotland and Europe.[47] Perspectives such as these were extended by Withers through the use of the concept of hegemony to unite external and internal influences. The local Highland Land Law Reform Association branches are thus seen as means of counter-hegemony and the Association generally as the medium through which the ideas underlying protest could achieve political expression and become 'emergent features of a new social formation'. Central to this process was the support of the press and the expatriate Celtic and Highland societies which provided support for the infrastructure and political dimension of a protest movement generated from within.[48] This is certainly the view now taken of the influence of Ireland on Highland events. Here impact is now seen to have been at best limited with those agitating for land in the Highlands failing on the whole to adopt a nationalist ideology similar to that of their Irish counterparts. This meant

46 James Hunter, 'The emergence of the crofting community: the religious contribution', *Scottish Studies*, Vol. 18 (1974): 99–102 and 111–12; Withers, *Gaelic Scotland*, pp. 340–43; Steve Bruce, 'Social change and collective behaviour', *British Journal of Sociology*, Vol. 34 (1983): 568–9; Eric Richards, 'How tame were the Highlands during the Clearances?', *Scottish Studies* (1973): 41; Tom Smout, *A History of the Scottish People 1560–1830* (London, 1969), p. 464; W. Hamish Fraser, 'Patterns of protest', in Tom Devine and Rosalind Mitchinson (eds), *People and Society in Scotland vol. 1, 1760–1830* (Edinburgh, 1998), p. 272; John J. MacInnes, 'Religion in Gaelic Society', *Transactions of the Gaelic Society of Inverness*, No. 52 (19802): 239.

47 Ewen A. Cameron, 'Land agitation and reform in the Highlands and Islands', in Michael Lynch (ed.) *The Oxford Companion to Scottish History* (Oxford, 1974); James Hunter, 'The politics of highland land reform, 1873–1895', *The Scottish Historical Review,* Vol. 53, No. 155, Part 1 (1974): 45–68; Andrew Newby, 'Edward McHugh, the National Land League of Great Britain and the 'Crofters' War', 1879–1882', *The Scottish Historical Review*, Vol. 82, No. 213, Part 1 (2003): 74–91; Andrew Newby, 'Land and the "Crofter Question" in Nineteenth-Century Scotland', *International Review of Scottish Studies*, Vol. 35 (2010): 7–36; Ewen A. Cameron, 'Communication or Separation? Reactions to Irish Land Agitation and Legislation in the Highlands of Scotland, c.1870–1910', *English Historical Review*, Vol. 120, No. 487 (2005): 633–66.

48 Withers, *Gaelic Scotland*, pp. 385–9; H.J. Hanham, The Problem of Highland Discontent, 1880–1885, *Transactions of the Royal Historical Society*, Vol. 19 (1989): 19.

that key aspects of the land reform agenda could be taken up by radical Liberalism and thereby enter the mainstream of British politics in the early decades of the twentieth century.[49]

It is when Highland historians turn to discuss the underlying ideology which drove any class consciousness and unity amongst the land-working population that they come closest to establishing a distinct Highland interpretation of protest events. Here, for some commentators at least, is the ultimate foundation upon which protest was based. Both within the region and the Highland community at large, what were seen 'as rightful claims to land and methods of land management' were being re-asserted through (from the 1880s) acts of land invasion. For Withers, in combination, belief and protest performance formed the counter-hegemony of the Land Wars. Expressive of a regional class consciousness, this drew on '"inherent" notions of shared beliefs and consensus claims to land and of "derived" notions of class and class consciousness'. In this the importance of *duthchas* rests not on its reality as a tenurial claim but as 'an ideologically-constituted belief in what the term stood for as a way of holding and inheriting land'.[50]

It is at this point, in the early 1990s, that, depending on how it is viewed, the study of Highland protest either reaches full fruition or its growth is stunted. The work of Logue, Richards, Hunter and Withers in particular closely paralleled that of the more general paradigm. Here are Highland protest historiography's own "great men" and with Charles Withers's utilisation of Gramsci's hegemony, thinking behind the exploration of events of protest fails to develop much further. What all this amounts to is a "flexing" rather than breaking of the protest paradigm. And whilst the breaking of paradigms is not obligatory, much of our understanding of Highland protest remains somewhat under-developed. There is a need, for instance, for an extended discussion of the role of the institutions and symbols of popular culture in Highland protest and the use of disguise, cross-dressing and nocturnal attacks – all key aspects of protest elsewhere and widely discussed as part of attempts to extend and deepen the protest paradigm. Similarly, the extent to which cottars were integrated into any overall community of interests remains open to question as it has been rarely discussed in the extant literature.

This situation nevertheless amounts to something of a missed opportunity. Here was a chance to establish both a distinct Highland-based understanding of protest and through this to make a contribution to the development of protest studies more generally. Undoubtedly the most recent commentaries have sought to expand on this repertoire with consideration being given, for instance, to the role of women or the impact of World War One. Similarly, the increasing role of external political forces and internal socio-cultural mechanisms has been much scrutinised, but, to

---

49 Andrew Newby, *Ireland, Radicalism, and the Scottish Highlands* (Edinburgh, 2006).

50 Withers, *Gaelic Scotland*, pp. 331–2, 371, 413–15. This view can be contrasted with that held by Mitchinson. Rosalind Mitchinson, 'The Highland clearances', *Scottish Economic and Social History*, Vol. 1, No. 1 (1981): 4–24.

a greater and lesser extent, virtually all of this marks something of a return to established questions and foci.[51]

In protest studies more generally it is now widely accepted that whilst it would be incorrect to totally reject the grand narratives of moral economy and class conflict they must be viewed as part of a multiplicity of motivation. This certainly appears the case once the evidence from post-1914 disturbance is considered in some detail. Whilst, for instance, motives based on *duthchas* remain apparent, to this can be added causes unique to the era, such as the failure to keep the promise of land in return for war service and disturbances generated by conflict from within the tenantry. Indeed, issues surrounding land and rights to it bring continuity to a remarkable long-lived set of events. It is of course far from axiomatic that students of Highland protest should both automatically seek to place significant weight on events after 1914 and look for inspiration for their studies from the reinvigoration of the field that has taken place since 2006, but it is nevertheless interesting that neither opportunity has thus far been taken. As articulated by Griffin, where the most radical aspects of the latter are to be found is in the fact that such work has 'been attentive to the affective dimensions of environmental and material worlds' in shaping protest performances.[52] To look in this direction would be to look to protest as deeply and constitutively rooted in spatial configurations, drawing on a sense of place and landscape in which traditional rights to use and occupancy legitimated claims and validated attempts to recover land expropriated (in the eyes of the tenantry) in the creation of sheep run and deer forest. To attend to such considerations offers the possibility of a re-worked and more nuanced understanding of the protest cultures which underlay Highland protest. In order to do so it is first necessary to sketch in something of the detail of that most recent work which has served to break the paradigm.

Breaking the Paradigm

To view and explain actions in protest monolithically does both protestors and their diverse motivations a disservice. From this realisation the argument has developed that interpretations which rely on grand narrative are as much a liability as they are an asset. The need to take a fresh look at protest events is now widely accepted with an accompanying drive to find ways of approaching events more holistically. Protest historians have thus come to resist the easy dualisms of class

51 Perhaps the most important exception to this is the work of Annie Tindley on the Sutherland estates and Highland factory. See, for instance, *The Sutherland Estate, 1850–1920: Aristocratic Decline, Estate Management and Land Reform* (Edinburgh, 2010); Annie Tindley and Eric Richards, 'Turmoil among the crofters: Evander McIver and the "Highland Question", 1873–1903', *Agricultural History Review*, Vol. 60, No. 2 (2012): 191–213.

52 Griffin, *Rural War*, p. 22.

conflict in an attempt to reassert the protest studies agenda at a time when attention has drifted elsewhere. A good example of this comes from the work of John Walter. In an early study Walter drew on the Thompsonian perspective to explore grain riots in Maldon Essex, in 1629. His more recent work, however, is a radical departure. Any focus on riot is almost immediately dismissed as 'lazy shorthand for the complexity of crowd actions' which demand contextualisation into the broader "infrapolitics" of the ruled'.[53] In this there are elements of a broader trend in protest studies: away from the study of overt events and towards the work of James C. Scott and what Michael Braddick and Walter term in their introduction to the same volume 'the tactics by which the relatively powerless seek to defend their interests'. The problem, however, with such an approach is one they themselves recognise. To move away from overt protest forms may result in producing histories of power 'without victims'.[54] In stressing the negotiating and vitiating power of hidden transcripts and everyday resistance Braddick and Walter come close to arguing for the mediation of power relationships. In turning the focus away from crowd actions and conflict they come close to denying the reality of power inequalities in social relationships. That they draw back from this position is to their credit but any turn away from the material realities of social conflict is to be regretted. Whatever analytical model is applied, it is difficult to deny that to study popular protest is to study the victims of unequal power relations.

If we are thus to build new and more convincing interpretations of disorder these must admit both complexity of cause and the fact that protest could be generated as much by conflict from within as it could consensus. This position is by now thoroughly embedded into the protest literature, as the work of Steve Poole (amongst others) testifies. In his study of a single act of rural incendiarism (in its singular focus itself a perfect example of the new agenda in protest studies) Poole suggests that the monolithic explanation he is grappling with – that of a "war" between labour and capital – is 'unhelpfully reductive' and that full understanding will only emerge from paying much closer attention to local specificity, to the theatre of protest and to a history of protest from above as well as below.[55] In so doing Poole is not only seeking to break with old shibboleths but is also drawing explicitly on the tenets of Andrew Charlesworth's "agenda" for the study of British rural protest.

53 John Walter, 'Grain riots and Popular Attitudes to the Law', in John Brewer and John Styles (eds), *An Ungovernable People* (London, 1980), pp. 47–84; John Walter, 'Public Transcripts, Popular Agency and the Politics of Subsistence in Early Modern England' in Michael Braddick and John Walter (eds), *Negotiating Power in Early Modern England* (Cambridge, 2001), p. 123.

54 Michael Braddick and John Walter, 'Introduction' in Braddick and Walter (eds), *Negotiating Power*, pp. 7, 41.

55 Steve Poole, 'A lasting and salutary warning': incendiarism, rural order and England's last scene of crime execution.' *Rural History*, Vol. 19, No. 2. (2008): 163–77.

In the context of the arguments just deployed it is especially unwise to ascribe to one scholar and to one paper the role of catalyst for a sea-change in the way in which historians approach a topic, but in protest studies if any relatively recent paper deserves that accolade it is Charlesworth's. It is not his fault, moreover, that it has taken so long to effect the paradigm shift he so obviously desired. Under the guise of a discussion of three variably effective texts, and with characteristic insight and precision, Charlesworth produced a comprehensive "state of the nation" report on the health and future direction of protest studies and identified key future areas for endeavour, some of which we have already encountered in Poole's article. Up to that point, Charlesworth asserted, historians had been too reductive in their understanding of what constituted protest and called for greater attention to be paid to Scott's everyday forms of resistance. Interestingly, whilst this is a call that has been widely echoed in the more recent protest literature a full working through of the implications of Scott's approach remains unrealised. Here too Charlesworth has the answer as he suggested that rural labour historians were fully occupied with documenting the major episodes of protest.[56] And whilst for England much of this documentation could be said to have been done that is certainly not the case for the Highlands of Scotland and absolutely not the case for protest after 1914. The immediate focus of what follows, therefore, will necessarily be on the documentation of overt disturbances whilst freely acknowledging the inevitably incomplete nature of this exercise.

This concern for the regional is one shared by Charlesworth and Poole and if the latter, through his focus on one event in one place, has rather backed away from fully carrying through this concern this must not be allowed to detract from the utility of his work. In effect, what Poole has achieved is a thoroughly convincing study of the microspaces and micropolitics underpinning one particular act of arson – a much neglected indicator of social relations in nineteenth century rural England. Poole convincingly suggests that such events were far from mono-causal expressions of discontent and draws attention to the theatrical and performative elements which inhere to such actions once their full complexity is revealed. Most importantly, Poole gives full weight to the role of local authorities and local labouring non-participants in the fire at Kenn and clearly shows that protest historians neglect such roles at our cost. Finally, Poole is able to point to the symbolic geography which often underlay traditions of protest in particular places and indeed, the association of particular places with protest in the popular and hegemonic minds.[57] This is an agenda for study the current work aspires to match.

Through this close attention to the importance of place Poole's work is redolent of the call made in the editorial 'Rethinking the Idea of Place' which Felix Driver and Raphael Samuel wrote for the *History Workshop Journal* in 1995. Driver and Samuel argued that, notwithstanding *HWJ's* best efforts and the ongoing

56 Andrew Charlesworth, An Agenda for Historical Studies of Rural Protest in Britain, 1750–1850, *Rural History*, Vol. 2, Issue 2 (1991): 231–40.

57 Poole, *A lasting and salutary warning*.

radicalisation of local history, there remained an urgent need for historians to think again how best they could represent the history of the local. Their belief was that this project would be best served by 'opening up lines of communication between historians and others concerned with places and their pasts' and they specifically identified 'geographers, anthropologists and archaeologists' as likely partners. Essentially what they were calling for was a distinctively spatialised history viewed through the lens of 'the idea of place'.[58] It is a matter of regret that an explicit response to this call has been somewhat limited, caused, perhaps, by their choice of place as a framing device since this has distinctly geographical connotations. A more convincing meeting ground between the three great disciplines identified by Driver and Samuel may well be that of landscape.

An additional reason perhaps why mainstream history has failed to take up this challenge has been that it has developed its own form of spatialised history: that of microhistory. This mode of historical enquiry has perhaps found its best (certainly most spatialised) expression in the work of the Italian micro historians but such approaches have also proved particularly fruitful to historians of rural resistance. Key here has been two of the other texts foundational to the most recent thinking on protest, that of Barry Reay's study of the Courtenay rising in Kent in 1838 and of Roger Wells's work on the links between crime and protest in Burwash (Sussex) in the first half of the nineteenth century.[59] Despite their varying foci there is much common ground between the two which can be summarised as firstly a concern to witness how wider processes, the impact of the 1835 Poor Law Amendment Act in particular, play out in specific landscapes. From this a broader concern was to document, often in minute detail, local instances of crime, conflict and other manifestations of local power relations underpinned by the recognition of a broad spectrum of protest with an emphasis on everyday forms of resistance. Finally, there is strong reliance on key sets of evidence and methodologies.

These are both works of significance and they shape key aspects of the approach taken here. In particular, both pay close attention to the local environments of protest, to the lifespaces of individual protestors and to their associational networks. Reay, for instance, claims to have produced 'a detailed study of the rank-and-file of an insurrectionary movement of a kind ... never attempted in any study of popular protest in Britain'.[60] He went on to establish important kinship-based links between rioters, to point to their close physical proximity to one another and to particular beershops. Finally, Reay asserted that poverty was another bond of shared experience and suggested that, notwithstanding a lack of evidence, it was his belief that the uprising offered a rare actualisation of a latent belief system: the

58 Raphael Samuel and Felix Driver, 'Rethinking the idea of Place', *History Workshop Journal*, Vol. 39, No. 1 (1995): vi.

59 Roger Wells, Crime and protest in a country parish: Burwash, 1790–1850, in John Rule and Roger Wells (eds), *Crime, Protest and Popular Politics in Southern Britain* (London, 1997), pp. 169–54; Reay, *The Last Rising*.

60 Reay, *The Last Rising*, p. 130.

Scriptures. There is, of course, much here that is echoed in Highland protest; as is one of Reay's key assertions as to the utility of the microhistorical approach: that it allows us to appreciate that individual motivation was different and occasionally contradictory.

Inspiration for a re-worked understanding of Highland disturbances can also be found in the turn towards the linguistic and to those two great eponymous "Captains" of protest movements: Swing and Ludd. Here the discussion has centred on the rhetorical construction of the Captain and on what may be said to bring coherence to the 'disparate set of discourses which constituted protest across time and space'.[61] Such creations represent the visible tip of a protest mythology and a psychological need to reflect unity both from within the movement and in the way it was understood by external authorities, and as means to focus 'fear and disapproval'.[62]

Overall, what we appear to be seeing is a turn towards protest's cultures. As with so much of the more recent innovative work on protest this began with the early modernists and with a focus on the position of local customs in protest, latterly integrated into an understanding of the local politics of negotiation.[63] For students of nineteenth century protest amongst the early adopters of this shift of focus were Kevin Binfield and Malcolm Chase, with the former exploring the linguistic tropes adopted by the Luddites and the latter focussing on the symbolic power of places and spaces to protest events. This work was drawn on by Navickas to suggest that the nineteenth century crowd's use of moors, fields and routes was both symbol and spectacle with landscape given meaning by crowd action as not only passive host but as also constitutive of both everyday activities and the resistance performances that emerged from them.[64]

Given that the phrase is his, it is unsurprising that perhaps the most powerful advocate of the concern for protest's cultures has been Carl Griffin. In a series of important and varied contributions, Griffin has consistently sought to move forward the protest agenda and, most significantly for the present work, address past geographies of the interconnectedness of nature/culture. What this culturally-inspired approach to protest's performances amounts to is a strong move away

61 Peter Jones, 'Finding Captain Swing: Protest, Parish Relations, and the State of the Public Mind in 1830', *International Review of Social History*, Vol. 54, No. 3 (2009): 436.

62 Katrina Navickas, 'The Search for General Ludd: the Mythology of Luddism', *Social History*, Vol. 30, No. 3 (2005), 281–95; Jones 'Finding Captain Swing', 442.

63 See, for instance, Braddick and Walter, *Negotiating Power;* Steve Hindle, *On the Parish?: The Micro-Politics of Poor Relief in Rural England c.1550–1750* (Oxford, 2004); Andy Wood, 'Subordination, Solidarity and the Limits of Popular Agency in a Yorkshire Valley', *Past and Present*, Vol. 193, No. 1 (2006), pp. 41–72; Andy Wood, *Riot, Rebellion and Popular Politics in Early Modern England* (London, 2002).

64 Kevin Binfield, *Writings of the Luddites* (Baltimore, 2004); Malcolm Chase, *Chartism: A New History* (Manchester, 2007); Katrina Navickas, 'Moors, Fields, and Popular Protest in South Lancashire and the West Riding of Yorkshire, 1800–1848' *Northern History*, Vol. 46 (2009): 93–5.

from compartmentalisation and categorisation accompanied by the recognition that the non-human must be understood as an equally dynamic agent in giving meaning to space.

When these perspectives are viewed as a central element and catalyst in the recent revival and reinvigoration of protest studies what we may be witnessing is a near-irreversible turn away from the approach which seeks to uncover master narratives of rural resistances. The emphasis must, instead, be grounded in the understanding people derived from their everyday interactions and associations in local environments. In turning to the Highland landscape we can identify a physical space that had been fundamentally re-ordered as part of deep-rooted ideological shifts. For the Highland landlord, drawn into southern society and adopting the viewpoint of the market economy, the main purpose of landownership came to be the production of an enhanced cash income. Throughout the region tenant populations were increasingly confined to small plots on the coastal margins. Here was a population physically uprooted from their spatial context and re-ordered into this new landscape which of itself co-constitutively created a new social and cultural order. In their everyday lives crofters and cottars were reminded on a daily basis of this re-ordering the landscape it had created. Popular memory merely reinforced this as it simultaneously made landmarks (in the sense deployed by Maurice Halbwachs[65]) out of past protest spaces. For crofters and cottars, therefore, it would have been a relatively easy task to draw together the spectacle and the everyday. It can be no wonder that Highlanders turned to the spectacular as they gave shape to their grievances. In this way their actions after 1914 were no different to those taken by their counterparts in the 1880s. But as the following chapter will show, in a number of other ways protest performances after 1914 were significantly different. The old paradigm would not allow for this variation.

65 Maurice Halbwachs, *On Collective Memory* (Chicago, 1992). See also Andy Wood, *The 1549 Rebellions and the Making of Early Modern England: The 1549 Rebellions and the Ideology of Popular Protest* (Cambridge, 2010).

PART II
Highland Social Protest After 1914: Detail and Debates

The FACHRS project suggests that the quantifying approach of Captain Swing remains ascendant. Indeed, we can see this model clearly informing the work of Charles Tilly and his followers. However, such an approach brings with it assumptions which might obscure as well as reveal. Roger Wells, in an early challenge to the "quantifying" spirit, had warned historians of the dangers in seeking to draw meaning from the quantification of riot since the sources were deficient, deliberately so in many cases. Moreover, categorizing "events" into one typology – "machine-breaking", "wage meeting", or "robbery" – risks missing the importance of a changing context as incidents developed. Many Swing actions began peacefully enough but changed character as farmers resisted, as different groups joined in, or as drink, levied or freely given, took hold. The composition of a Swing "mob" might change only a little in the course of a day's "mobbing", their "mental world" staying the same, but their mood and actions shifting according to events. Quantification brings a clearer sense of dimension but carries with it the risk of compartmentalisation.[1]

The three chapters which comprise this Part take an in-depth and empirically-based approach to the delineation of post-1914 land disturbances. The principle aim here is to quantify and categorise protest events and draw attention to what amounts to a significant (and largely successful) challenge to authority. There are obvious reasons why this challenge took until 1919 to fully emerge but it is equally obvious that the potential to mount the challenge was in place by 1914. Further, in the period between 1900 and 1914 there is evidence of many of the characterising features of subsequent protest even if these are somewhat underplayed in the extant literature thereby suggesting considerable continuity between events of the earlier and later Land Wars.

It would nevertheless be incorrect to understand events of the earlier Land Wars as prelude or *mise-en-scène* for those post 1914 and if the preceding chapters have created that impression that was not the intention. It would be facile to deny the importance of either the earlier events themselves or historians' interpretations of them. Disturbances after 1914 simply could not have happened in the way they

1 Randal, *Captain Swing*, p. 426.

did without the existence in the collective memory of the earlier Land Wars and governmental reactions to them. Precisely because they were so important this must serve also to give greater weight to the assertion of the importance, breadth and depth of the events these chapters begin the process of examining. The focus here will almost entirely centre on protest performances: their typology; chronology; geography and how we might understand them. The chronology of any set of disturbances is obviously (and rather simplistically) important to establish. It should be the first action of any student of protest and yet, for the Highlands after 1914 this has only been partly achieved. The general outline has been established but such is the variation from this outline that a return to consideration of the chronology of events in the level here undertaken is warranted. Similarly, there is clear evidence for a wider protest repertoire and of significant variation in the geography of disturbance than suggested hitherto. In particular the *threat* to raid emerges as a separate protest performance, alongside others which together gives rise to the suggestion that the geography of events after 1914 may be better understood less as manifestation and representation of a single, region-wide class consciousness, but more convincingly as a number of different, albeit interleaving geographies.

It follows, therefore, that one of the principal motives for pursuing protest events to the level of detail essayed here is the belief that this is both necessary and rewarding. Where other less focussed works are compelled to generalise and therefore to ignore forms and occurrences of protest, attention to such level of detail reveals a significantly less homogenous set of events made apparent in terms of chronology, typology, and geography and in explanation. It is essential therefore, to view the following three chapters as components of an inter-communicating whole, driven by a singular focus which ensures a comprehensive uncovering of a set of disturbances (a meta-, if not actual movement) which was to radically reshape the Highland landscape (at a local level), tenurial arrangements and, ultimately, patterns of land ownership. From this the argument is made that in their emphasis on the period 1882–1886 commentators have underestimated and underplayed the importance of events after 1914. Moreover, in so doing important expressions of motivation have been set aside which lead to different and more convincing ways of interpreting these events and from this, perhaps, social protest more generally.

Central to this re-working is a concentration on disturbance alone which permits interrogation and understanding at a level hitherto impossible. Thus it becomes apparent that in the performing of protest a fascinating combination of ritual, formalism and near-anarchy is revealed – often in the same event. The protestor clearly knew how to behave and what was expected of him or her and would often undertake this performance with remarkable formalism. In the main protest type – the land seizure – participants would often begin with a written threat; people would assemble at a pre-arranged (and often symbolically significant) place, march to the land in question and proceed with a formal declaration of possession. They would also often enlist the help of sympathetic lawyers and other local authority figures including Members of Parliament and church ministers (from *both* the Free Church and Church of Scotland). All of this they did in order to legitimise their actions. This interplay between protest actants is reminiscent of Charlesworth's "stately gavotte" found in eighteenth century food riots in England. As Griffin asserts, most food riots were tightly choreographed but with rioters well aware 'that their "dance" needed to be vigorous. Riot was a performance, a staging of a demand, a playing out of a right, but above all it had to be assertive.'[2] This further reminds us that these were powerfully affective and illegal undertakings which, in an otherwise law-abiding actor, call from that actor a considerable depth of commitment. Protest could involve considerable opprobrium and conflict from both outwith and within the tenantry, and could involve court appearances and jail sentences. Whilst the nature of the performance might of itself involve symbolic elements they were beyond question underpinned with serious intent.

On other occasions a different set of protestors (and on occasion the same set) could ignore all of this. In these circumstances protestors may well resort to what is identified here as the informal occupation of land. Essentially involving the *ad hoc* utilisation of land these events could be remarkably long lived and reflect very local contexts that on occasion point to a near collapse of established social arrangements. Perhaps most interestingly, however, whilst these certainly lacked the characteristics of the more easily recognisable overt activities, they should certainly not be identified as covert forms of protest.

There is much merit in the micro-focussed exploration adopted here. Nevertheless, there are obvious dangers in this approach, not least that of lack of relevance to any understanding of events of protest from a different time and/or place. This, however, is not a criticism that can be levelled at either of the two great microhistories of social protest: Reay on Bossenden Wood; Wells on Burwash[3] and whilst a similarly comprehensive microhistory is not attempted here the aim in focussing down on the local and particular is to make clear how complex and multi-faceted these events were and through this, as did Reay and Wells, to make a contribution to the understanding of protest more generally. In a Highland context this becomes both an essential tool to full understanding and means to overcome the problems associated with quantification so vividly described by Adrian Randall in the opening quotation. It is nevertheless with these caveats firmly to the fore that we proceed to quantify protest after 1914.

2 Andrew Charlesworth, 'From the Moral Economy of Devon to the Political Economy of Manchester, 1790–1812', *Social History*, Vol. 18 (1993): 205–17; Griffin, Affecting violence, 140.

3 Reay, *The Last Rising*; Roger Wells, *Crime and protest in a country parish.*

Chapter 3
Performing Protest

'The raiding is all part of a concerted action ... in the north of Scotland'.

'I have taken an interest in the subject for years but have never known the spirit of the people so determined to get reform and in some places in particular they are very near to a state of mind in which they could seize the land.'

'In time I expect the Government will be compelled to utilise all available land for smallholdings and enlargements.'[1]

This chapter takes as its point of departure the fact that the broad outlines of events of protest in the post 1914 Highlands have been long established. Land disturbance has become a central part of the story of the twentieth century Highlands and have been used to reinforce dominant interpretations of Highland protest more generally. Governmental responses have also been subject to much scrutiny and important interpretations have emerged. Thus both Leneman and Cameron have concluded that the 1919 Land Settlement (Scotland) Act was 'perhaps the most efficient piece of legislation' attempting to address issues surrounding access to land as it built and simplified procedures introduced in the Small Landholders (Scotland) Act of 1911 and had a profound impact on the lives of many within the crofting tenantry.[2] As with events of protest, it is nevertheless vital, as Cameron asserts, that we view the success of the post-war legislation in the context of the failures of that from before the war, not least the Congested Districts (Scotland) Act, 1879 which gave rise to the Congested Districts Board. Moreover, in recognising this it is hard to disagree with Cameron when he argues that far greater attention should be paid to the period after 1886 instead of treating it 'as an unimportant addendum to the more important and interesting events of the 1890s'.[3] It is to Cameron's credit that he goes some way towards redressing this imbalance. Legislation from 1886 is revealed as manifestation of the tensions between two competing and ideologically

1 Scottish Government, Rural Payments and Inspections Directorate, Estate Management Section, Edinburgh Scottish Ministers Land Settlement Estate files (hereafter R.P.I.D.), local Member of Parliament to Chair of Board of Agriculture, 24 December 1918 (please note that on the request of the Scottish Government, Rural Payments and Inspections Directorate all names have been withheld from these files); The National Archives of Scotland, Crofting Files (hereafter N.A.S.), AF83/786, Sir Robert Greig to Scottish Office, 1 July 1925.

2 Leneman, *Fit for Heroes?*; Cameron, *Land for the People*, p. 2.

3 Cameron *Land for the People*, p. 9.

derived views over how to solve the land issue in the Highlands. The first of these was developed by the Liberals in Ireland and applied in much greater depth in Scotland, was that of 'dual ownership'. Alternatively, for the Conservatives the solution was that of land purchase and proprietorship. The 1919 Act, on the other hand, introduced in the important circumstance of a coalition government was, for Cameron, 'an honest attempt … to construct a non-ideological approach to land settlement and was, in the Highland context certainly, perhaps the first such attempt.[4]

Ideological or not there can be little doubt that legislation after 1886 was significantly more reactive than proactive. To acknowledge this must be to acknowledge also that a reaction requires something to react against. Across the whole of the Land Wars period (early and later) what successive governments were reacting against was not the problems of crofting tenure as encapsulated in the land issue more generally but these self-same problems viewed through the lens of acts of social protest. This is, of course, not a new or original claim but it has rarely been articulated quite so directly. In every case where commentators have engaged with events in the post 1914 Highlands protest events take centre stage. Nevertheless, and for very good reasons, that stage has always been a shared one. Even Fraser Grigor,[5] with his singular perspective on *Highland Resistance* fails to differentiate between protest types identified here, and consequently downplays the significance of the frequency with which members of the crofting tenantry resorted to acts of protest. These are serious omissions which, when attended to, significantly alters our understanding of post 1914 events.

Attention is, however, turned only to what has been called overt protest forms. Given that covert Highland protest consequently still awaits its historian an engagement with the totality of protest after 1914 remains tantalisingly distant. This singular focus thus serves to perpetuate the false division which inheres to the overt/covert dualism and does not permit a full discussion of everyday forms of resistance. In a chapter which discusses protest typologies it would nevertheless be remiss to fail to note those moments when covert protest forms became folded into the more overt. Perhaps the most common of these was fence breaking. Often conducted at night these activities equally often gave way to protest types which are the focus of this chapter. In June 1921, for instance, following agitation for a raid on Galson farm, Lewis, a turf dyke was broken down. This was subsequently escalated into land seizure. On the mainland approximately four miles of fencing was destroyed in July 1937 in Glenganisp deer forest during the course of agitation to gain land there. The following year fires were deliberately set in the forest. In a further example, the oral tradition of protest at Elgol, Skye, preserves an incident from the late nineteenth century, although the exact date was not recalled. Here, crofters determined on gaining access to grazing denied them decided to break

4 Cameron *Land for the People*, p. 193–4.

5 Iain Fraser Grigor, *Highland Resistance: The Radical Tradition in the Scottish North* (Edinburgh, 2000).

down the boundary fence. They arranged themselves along the fence and placed a blind man in a chair on a prominent spot. The crofters were blindfolded to prevent anyone knowing who took the first action. At a signal from the blind man the fence was uprooted.[6]

Fire setting and fence breaking fall into the category of covert activity and the anonymity of the above actions reinforces this. Yet it is also important to note the near total absence of disguise or anonymity associated with protest elsewhere and from earlier periods.[7] For Thompson

> The anonymous threatening letter is a characteristic form of social protest in any society which has crossed a certain threshold of literacy, in which forms of collective organized defence are weak, and in which individuals who can be identified as the organizers of protest are liable to immediate victimization.[8]

Anonymous letters were symptomatic of a society where dominance was near total. They were vital precursors to more democratic forms of organisation. This is not the case for Highland Scotland. Here control was not total, proletarian democratic organisations already existed and land raiding did not signify a lack of organised defence. It is more convincing to see the few occurrences of anonymous letters and other such forms of protest in the post-1914 Highlands as products of the recognition within the crofting community of forms beyond normative behaviour to protest. As will become very apparent, the rhetoric and theatre of protest was clearly understood by all parties (with, perhaps, the exception of Lady Gordon Cathcart and Lord Leverhulme).

Similarly, and to briefly return to Elgol, once this event is explored in more depth (the *raison d'être* of this and subsequent chapters) a more nuanced understanding emerges. Fence breaking here was a collective act, conducted in plain sight. Our ability to categorise this hybrid event is made yet more difficult by what happened next. The landlord accepted the situation and crofters' cattle continued to graze alongside the proprietor's cattle, free of rent.[9] This was now an informal utilisation of the land, an activity which cannot be seen as covert. It may be more convincing, therefore, to abandon the covert/overt dualism; to move away from the study of protest "movements" and towards complex protest performances. These manifest a variety of form that have been hitherto largely overlooked or downplayed. Taken

---

6 N.A.S. AF83/190 Solicitors to Board of Agriculture, 7 April 1920; AF67.158 7 July 1923; AF67/331 Sub-Commissioner Wilson to Board, 3 July 1921; R. I. P. D. 12973/c/1 Tormore and Gillen, 13 April 1926; 38609, Glencanisp, Board report 10 July 1937; interview, Lachlan Macintosh and Roderick Nicolson, Elgol, Skye 2nd October 1991.

7 The use of the blind man at Elgol must be explained by the fact that this was from an earlier era.

8 Edward Thompson, 'The Crime of Anonymity' in Douglas Hay, et al. *Albions Fatal Tree* (London, 1975), pp. 255 and 271–2.

9 Lachlan Macintosh and Roderick Nicolson, *interview.*

together with a detailed exploration of the temporal distribution of disturbance this begins the process of deep interpretation of Highland protest.

The Range of Protest Performances

Table 3.1 Protest types evident in the Highlands after 1914

The threat to raid
The land raid
The refusal to hand back land gained under the Defence of the Real Act
Organised squatting
The informal occupation of land

As illustrated by Table 3.1 one of the central claims made in this chapter is for the recognition of new protest forms. Most significantly, the case will be made for the threat to raid as protest device in its own right, at times separate and distinct from and deployed differently to the actual act of land seizure. In addition, the recognition as protest of the refusal to hand back land given temporarily under the Defence of the Realm Act demands reappraisal of previous views on the geography of protest on the mainland. Finally, a closely related action – the informal occupation or utilisation of land is held here to point to an understanding of protest as firmly rooted in the populations involved, not as externally-motivated events. This variance in type notwithstanding, it is undeniable that the land raid remained the most potent and central protest form, not least in terms of the effect such actions had on public opinion and governmental response.

The Threat to Raid

> The whole thing is a farce from beginning to end simply fooling innocent individuals, making them believe that [the Government] have intentions of distributing land for smallholdings. We now for the last time ... warn the Board we are not going to tolerate this treatment any longer ... You can deem Glenshiel deer forest in our possession from 1st day of August 1920. We have been promised land, and an Act has been passed to give us that land ... but the Board are not inclined to do that.[10]

The foregoing encapsulates much of the complexity encapsulated in protest form. "Threat" was both the beginning of a process leading to an act of land seizure and a protest device in its own right, as demonstrated by the above threat to seize land in Glenshiel deer forest. Here applicants did not carry out their threat and it is clear that their intent was primarily to ensure that the Board of Agriculture

10 N.A.S. AF 67/65 25 May 1920.

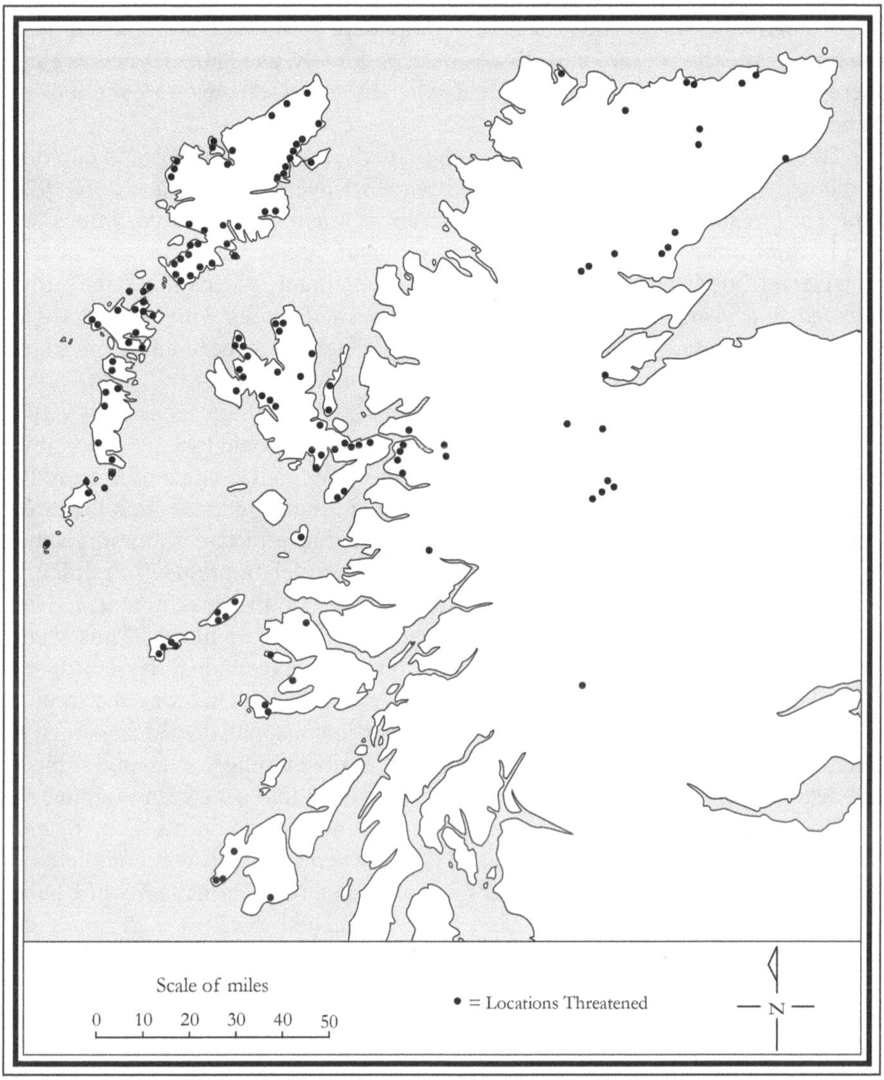

Figure 3.1 Locations of threats to seize land

continued through with its land settlement plans rather than to actually seize the land. The threat was deployed as a protest device in its own right. The complexity inherent in the threat to raid comes also from the fact that at other times raid did follow threat, with this being undertaken by either the same group which issued the threat or, as at Glenshiel, by unconnected parties. This sense of raids and threat representing different events (or very different "moments" within the same event) is given greater weight by the fact that there was often a clear disconnect between the occurrence of threat and raid as both individual events and, more generally, at the time of year these were most likely to occur. Finally, as Figure 3.1 makes clear, there is a broad distribution to the threat, whereas actual seizures were more likely to be confined to the islands.

Threats to seize land were made both by individuals and groups and could be made once or repeatedly. On Vatersay between November 1917 and July 1920, repeated threats to raid Eoligarry came from at least three separate groups and singly from other individuals. On the other hand threats could be separated by considerable periods of time, as at Lairg (Sutherland) where the same group allowed five years to pass before issuing a second threat. Similarly, the only written threat to raid the glebe lands at Keose, Lewis, was received by the Board in October 1929. Stock was not placed on the ground until 1931.[11] It is difficult to ascertain why there should have been such lapses although on occasion it was in response to Board of Agriculture suggestions that they would take no action until the time of a break in the lease. Keose does, however, indicate that to achieve the desired effect pressure did not need to be constant. It also indicates that the threat was recognised by both protesters and government as effective without recourse to the raid. The threat therefore cannot be seen as solely a prelude to raiding. It was both warning and means to increasing pressure on the government. Indeed, there are very many examples of this from all areas of the Highlands. Thus events in the Waternish peninsula of Skye were by no means exceptional. Here post-war formal agitation began in Geary township in March 1919. This took the form of a simple written threat to raid but was to evolve into a sophisticated campaign of letter writing and petitions that was ultimately involve virtually every township in the district. Very little of this pressure was translated into actual land raiding but the Board of Agriculture felt compelled to react as if it would be. They opened negotiations for a significant scheme of land settlement which was completed in 1926.[12] This, therefore, was the power of the written threat. The actuality of it being carried through to seizure was unknowable. Mandated to effect land settlement schemes and anxious to minimise disturbances the Board felt compelled to respond as if each was an advance warning of a raid. There is no recorded instance of a threat failing to result in at least the consideration of a smallholding scheme precisely because on many occasions the threat was a warning of seizure later realised in fact. It is this fact in particular – the full effectiveness of protest – that commentators have significantly underplayed.

The length of time often taken to implement a scheme where only threats were forthcoming is however indicative of the limited effectiveness of this device. The pressure applied ensured that the area continued to be under consideration but a raid always commanded more attention. Consequently the Board of Agriculture often carried forward a scheme which their predecessors, the Congested Districts

11 R. I. P. D. 1164/m/1 Eoligarry, 19 November 1917, 12 November 1919, 2 February 1920; 7 July 1920; R. I. P. D. 40917 Keose; N.A.S. AF 83/591; AF 83/592.

12 N.A.S. AF 67/155; AF67/65 19 May 1920.

Board, had originated. Balephetrish farm on Tiree was one such, which, as a result of threats to raid in December 1912, the Board reconsidered for a scheme. Alternatively, where a scheme had been investigated but rejected prior to the Great War, the acceleration and intensification of agitation after 1919 often led to reconsideration. At Forsinain, Sutherland, a scheme was first considered and rejected in 1914. In 1915, however, the Board's local representative reported that he was being 'inundated' with applications for land and the decision was made to reconsider the scheme but this was once again abandoned. On the 3rd November 1919 Donald Fraser wrote 'It is now quite a well-known fact in this district that if the farm is not given to the boys who have fought for it there is to be serious trouble there soon, as we are to go and take possession of the place.' The Board of Agriculture's local officer was instructed to investigate a scheme.[13]

It is clear, therefore, that threats were made verbally as well as in written form even if rarely preserved in the archive.[14] This is a regrettable deficiency as they speak much of the important local context of social relations as inscribed in protest. Perhaps of greater significance is the fact that as well as being a device to maintain pressure externally the written threat reflects also pressure from within. On the islands especially demand for land always exceeded the amount of land available. This of itself was generative of tensions between claimants but these were exacerbated by the kin-based, past-inheritance beliefs which underlay the claim to land. Protestors primarily saw their rights to land as deriving from the belief that previous generations of their family had lived and worked that particular land. This is what legitimated their actions in their eyes. Claims to land could be very specific and competed over if rival descendants felt they had rights to the same piece of land. These are conflicts which emerge clearly in the nature of the threat to raid. In March 1922, for instance, a group of landless applicants from the township of Torlum on Benbecula wrote to the Board of Agriculture complaining at the preference being shown to those who were applying for, and likely to get, extensions to their crofts. They went on to write that they had

> resolved, (unless the Board ... shall by return of post faithfully promise us that they shall hold back from their present scheme of these enlargements, from the

13 N.A.S. AF83/328, May 1914 scheme first investigated, 23 January 1915 Board's decision to abandon, 17 July 1915 decision made to re-open scheme, 1 November 1915 abandoned; AF83/329 10 January 1916, Board meeting endorses decision to abandon, 9 January 1919 applications for holdings renewed.

14 Just one verbal threat is preserved in the archive – at Lingerbay on Harris in February 1921 – and this only because the estate factor reported it in writing to the Board of Agriculture. When interviewed in April 1990 Murdo MacCuish from North Uist was able to recall local crofters threatening to seize land in the area. There is an inevitable lack of precision over this recollection and is much more likely to be a reflection more of the memory of general tension rather than threat to a precise location. N.A.S. AF67/146 21/2/21; Oral interview, Murdo MacCuish, Sollas, North Uist, 9 April 1990.

> one and only farm in Benbecula, available for settling landless ex-soldiers, and that without delay to settle us and any other ex-soldier or soldiers, as you shall think fit on the said Nunton Farm) we shall avail ourselves of the land.[15]

In this instance the threat was made by a group but it was just as likely to come from an individual and often, as with the Torlum group, as part of an explicit attempt to pre-empt and thwart the claims of others. And whilst on at occasion an alliance between rivals could emerge or threat could lead to seizure, it often did not. The threat was often sufficient and meant as an expression of discontent in its own right. It functioned as gesture and signal of intent (this is not to deny its affective weight, however), registering the correspondents' interest in and commitment to the land in question. Where we might also find the power of the threat is in what Griffin has identified as the 'affecting violence' of the protest performance. For Swing protestors this came from the potential for violence suggested in their actions rather than the actuality of physical violence.[16] In protest performances in the Highlands after 1914 the recourse to actual violence was as rare. The consequences of such action on the body politic was by then very well understood and only rarely needed playing out. In the rituals of liminality attaching to Highland protest, then, the fear engendered by both physical violence more generally and the threat to seize land (in a violent manner), was psychosomatic, a fear manifested in the body of bodies unseen and in the fear of land violated in the act of seizure.

In short the threat could function as separate protest device – as much against rivals from within as against dominant landscape constructions. To ignore the threat to raid or to simplistically and automatically draw them into the land raid is to diminish the efforts of those who turned to the threat as means to protest and is a denial of the reality of the chronology and geography of Highland disturbance.

The Land Raid

When considering the forced seizure of land in the Highlands after 1914 there is no need to proselytize for this as a hitherto unrecognised and important protest form. This was by some measure the most significant protest type in the period under consideration and the multiple and wide-ranging manifestations of the raid are much delineated and discussed in the literature. It is important, however, to assert once again the belief that in none of this literature is the full range and depth of raiding ever fully articulated. This book is, of course, an attempt to put this right.

---

15 N. A. S. AF67/154, letter Roderick Wilson and four others to Board of Agriculture, 4 March 1922.

16 Carl Griffin, 'Affecting violence: language, gesture and performance in early nineteenth-century English popular protest', *Historical Geography*, Vol. 36 (2008): 139–62.

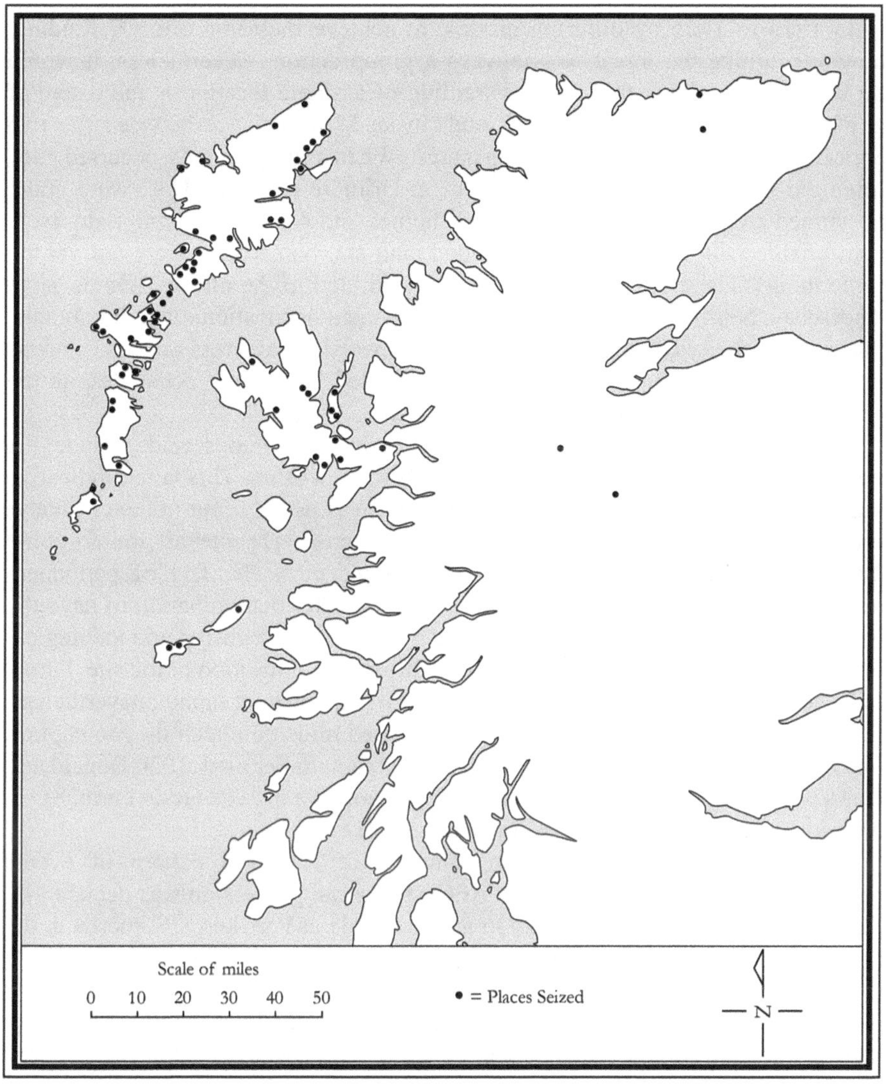

Figure 3.2 Locations of land seizures

Figure 3.2 indicates that there is a clear and distinct geography to the occurrence of the land seizure – something that can be said for all protest forms identified in this chapter. What, however, mapping form cannot reveal is the fact that, and similarly to the threat, land raids were a complex mixture of single event and repeated actions, the latter not always undertaken by the same groups. Thus, for instance, the raid which re-established the southern-half of Raasay as crofted land occurred just once by one cohesive group, whilst Coll was raided annually from 1919 to 1921 by differing groups, to achieve the same effect.[17] Raiding, however, unlike the threat, was always a group action. Nevertheless, it would be wrong to conclude that multiple raiding of a single location is indicative of any greater determination to gain land. Instead, the balance between the two appears a reflection of local circumstance. When multiple raids occurred they often did so because the participants, as at Drimore on South Uist, were under no immediate pressure to abandon their homes and so, where appropriate, were comfortable with moving between raided land and home (they were not yet the same thing). The close proximity of the raided land to the raiders' homes, as at Cheesebay, North Uist, also ensured that permanent occupation often did not take place. Nevertheless, where overcrowding was worst, as at Gress on Lewis, house building and permanent occupation of the raided land could occur despite the proximity of the township from which the raid took place.[18]

Other pressures which could force a single continuous raid include the unsuitability of such homes or pressure from the township. This latter, indicative once again of important tensions from within, was usually (but not exclusively) pressure from crofters on cottars to quit the croft. Despite all the forgoing qualifications it is undeniable that in some instances the fact of permanent occupation of a raided site seems to indicate a greater determination to have the land. As at Raasay this called for a degree of endurance, hardship and ideological commitment beyond that of the more straightforward utilisation of the site. Direct links between type of raid and determination to gain the land cannot, nevertheless, be made. For instance, some single non-repeated raids do match the assumption that they were minor events in comparison to others. In February 1920 Donald and Charles Stewart and Neil Lockhart took possession of a field on Gesto Farm, Skye. No further actions in protest survive in the archive.[19]

Despite these differences even minor raids shared a pattern of events recognisable across time and space. At Gesto formal possession was declared by pinning a notice to the field gate. On a larger scale at Portskerra, Sutherland, the raiders were preceded by a piper and once formal possession had been declared a dance was held in celebration of the action. Raiding, as Reay has pointed out for other incidents of social protest, was firmly based in the institutions of plebeian culture. Raiders would often assemble at a well-known location and march to the selected farm. On one level this reflects the military training many had undergone both before and during the war. On another, it also reflects how stylised and ritualistic such incidents could become. Thus at Keose, Lewis, in June 1931, those demanding land went onto the site 'and, as a gesture, each turned up a sod'. Nothing further was done by way of cultivation.[20]

17 N.A.S. AF67/149; AF83/363; AF83/331.

18 N.A.S. AF83/207; Oral Interview, Peter Morrisson, Berneray, 7 April 1990; S.R.O. AF83/363.

19 N.A.S. AF83/363.

20 R.I.P.D. 40917, Keose Glebe, 15 June 1931; 40917/c/1, 13 January 1932.

Table 3.2 The "model" land raid

1. The land raid is preceded by written threat which often specifies the exact date on which the raid takes place. Occupation would be formally declared: in writing; verbally; or both.
2. The landlord begins the legal process. The police and Sheriff's Officer are resisted at the first attempt to arrest the raiders. Peaceful arrest follows. The raiders are jailed.
3. Higher authorities become involved. The Board of Agriculture feels compelled to act and to enter into negotiations with proprietor and tenant to gain access to land for applicants from the raided area. Appeals would be made on behalf of the imprisoned raiders from both within and without the crofting community. National and regional newspapers take a prominent role.
4. On release from jail, raiders re-occupy the land. Proprietors agree to "open up" the land. Most, and often all the raiders are eventually settled on the raided land.

As made clear in Table 3.2, the response of landlord and government was similarly well established. Raiding was a civil offence and it was the responsibility of the landowner to seek legal redress. This took the form of an interdict, an order preventing the persons named on the order going onto the land. If breach of interdict took place and those in breach failed to appear to answer such charges, this then became a criminal offence. The Sheriff's Officer and the police would then have the responsibility of ensuring those in breach appeared in court. A jail term was the inevitable result. Release before the end of the term could occur if the raiders promised not to return to the land. This promise, whilst made, was rarely kept. Institutions of central government, principally the Board of Agriculture and Scottish Office, respectively saw their primary responsibility as enacting schemes of land settlement and the maintenance of law and order. These duties ensured that, certainly once a raid had occurred and usually well before this, a settlement scheme on the land in question had at least been considered.

Whilst the legal process was underway the Scottish Office often attempted to prevent the spread of illegal acts and to bring the incident to an end without force or imprisonment of raiders. Coupled with the responsibilities of the Board of Agriculture to effect smallholding schemes, this led landowners and, to a lesser extent, government bodies, to believe that action from below was controlling governmental response. Thus, at the time of raiding on the Strath Halladale Estate, Sutherland, in 1923, the Board noted that 'the effect of a successful raid of this nature is to practically compel the Board to finance the result of the action.'[21] It was, however, rarely politically expedient to publicly admit this connection. Thus in 1928, in response to a parliamentary question, the Board noted that whilst they 'have in some cases promoted schemes on raided lands it is not the case that scheme has followed on raid as effect on cause, but rather the raiders disturbed

21 N.A.S. AF67/65, 7 July 1920 Board to Scottish Office; AF67/158 4/6/23 Board to Scottish Office.

a situation which was tending towards solution.'[22] This was palpably not the case. A scheme followed virtually every raid and certainly those which generated publicity resulting from the jailing of ex-servicemen. For some of these schemes negotiations concerning the break-up of the farm only began after it was raided. The position of the Board with regard to raiding is made clear by their response to threats to seize land on Aline farm, Lewis, in 1930 'To proceed with a scheme now would probably prevent an outbreak of raiding, which ... might, as in previous cases, lead the Government to proceed with a scheme as a means of pacification.'[23]

As much of the forgoing makes clear, similarly to the way in which Richards adopts a four-stage challenge to landlord authority for earlier protest the regularity with which participants from all sides of a raid behaved makes it possible to model such behaviour (see Table 3.2).

Nevertheless, we should not imagine that actions after 1914 either wholly mirror those of the earlier Land Wars or that they were anything other than more than representational. As with every model the reality of events of raiding (and their aftermath) was significantly messier than this implies and undertaken with considerable affect. And even if violence to both property and person, which to Withers is one of the characteristics of earlier protest, is not evident on the same scale after 1914 there can be no doubt that these were affectually violent; causing psychological hurt without any need of recourse to the physical action. And when protest was accompanied by violent behaviour as at Balranald, the wider community appear to have viewed violence to person, if not to property, to be outside what had become the boundaries to acceptable behaviour in conduct of a land seizure. The consequences of this are both practical and conceptual. Deforcement – the forceful prevention of the Sherriff's Officer from serving official papers, a potent symbol of the protests of the 1880s – seems to have occurred just the once, at Kilbride on Skye in 1923. In this instance arrest of the raiders was only completed by a 'large force' of police officers; again reminiscent of the 1880s.[24]

It is perhaps perverse that comparatively little space has been devoted here to this most significant of protest forms. The reason for this is, it is hoped, obvious. There is nothing contentious about the raid as protest and its structure and implications are generally well known. Where discussion does lie (and with all protest forms identified here) is with motivation, meaning and interpretation. These have not been the foci of this chapter, however. Here the concern has been with typology and the argument that there are significant implications of the fact that commentators have been unable to engage with the range of protest types here delineated. It must be acknowledged, however, that one of the dangers of structurally separating out protest types is in the implying of fixed boundaries between forms. This is the

22 R.I.P.D. 49751 Land Seizures General, June 1928.

23 N.A.S. AF83/378, Boars memorandum to Secretary of State for Scotland, January 1930.

24 N.A.S. AF67/152 14/2/21 and 21/2/21; AF67/157 letter from Neil MacLean to Sir Arthur Rose, 20 July 1923 and 20 August 1923.

exact antithesis of the Highland situation. Protest events were remarkably fluid and often made up of manifestations of multiple forms. Further, while perhaps not wholly contingent – the land raid was clearly the central form – protest events do nevertheless reflect local and temporal circumstance and context to a significant degree. The forms where this is most clearly seen are those which have hitherto been completely ignored in any discussion of Highland protest. The remainder of this chapter will therefore begin the process of addressing this lacuna.

The Informal Occupation of Land

The informal occupation of land is here understood to mean the utilisation of areas of land by crofters or cottars for which they paid no rent and to which they had no legal entitlement. It is distinguished from "raid" by the fact that formal possession was never declared and by a certain degree of connivance from the landlord/tenant. Despite this it is clear that such unofficial utilisation could be a form of protest, albeit a passive rather than active form. Fixing the precise location (and distribution) of this somewhat fluid, if not amphourous protest form is not easy to achieve. Nevertheless some attempt has been made to do that here, as Figure 3.3 reveals (see below).

The informal occupation of land only becomes formally "known" (present in the archive) when no longer acceptable to the landlord/tenant. Once unacceptable informality could move to a more formal act of protest. It is, moreover, entirely possible that such shifts were actually reversions with the origins of the informal event being found in protest, although some caution must be attached to this assertion. In 1922, for example, it was reported that the Drumuie crofters had free grazing on Scorrybreck Farm, Skye, 'for a long time'. Similarly, it was reported in 1914 that stock from Inver Alligin had been allowed to graze in Torridon Deer Forest 'without question' from 1887.[25] In both cases the answer to what provoked such arrangements is uncertain but the fact that 1887 was when the earlier Land Wars had reached a peak must point to a link between other protest forms and informal occupation.

Such links become much more obvious in other informal occurrences. The area around Sconser on Skye, for instance, was a much disturbed one and land in the deer forest was seized in 1917. This was one of the rare occurrences when both the Board of Agriculture and the propriety tenant failed to respond. Local crofters and cottars continued to utilise the land and by 1939 local opinion had it that the MacDonald Estate had agreed to the grazing of cattle free of rent. There is no evidence that this was the case; a suspicion reinforced by the change in propriety tenant in that year with the new tenant immediately interdicting local

25 R.I.P.D. 5863/c Scorrybreck report from sub-commissioner, April 1922; 11150, Torridon, report of sub-commissioner, 30 November 1914.

crofters and cottars to put a halt to the illegal grazing.[26] Situations such as this one also gave rise to allegations that acts of protest were encouraged by landlords or sitting tenants to enhance the value of any compensation that often accompanied a scheme of land settlement with the compliance of landlord/tenant being signalled by their willingness to ignore informal utilisation of their land.

This close connection between informal occupation and protest event emerges in a variety of ways and different places. At Barvas on the island of Lewis for instance, for two years after 1920 the local crofters had grazed their stock on the glebe lands without the agreement of the proprietor or minister. To both the Board of Agriculture's local officer and the minister, the land had been raided, although no formal declaration had been made and the 'raiders' had not communicated with the Board of Agriculture. Furthermore grazing began as a result of the inspection of the land by the Board's officers prior to negotiating a scheme. Finally, neither those grazing the land, the proprietor, minister nor government were prepared to take further steps to resolve the situation. The crofters and cottars continued in their utilisation of the land without paying rent.[27]

Directly or indirectly, perceived or in reality, and as at Barvas, the Board of Agriculture played a central role in protest performances. One key aspect of this role was that its actions or inactions (again perceived or in reality) could prompt an act of protest or, indeed, the informal utilisation of land. Further, if informal occupation developed out of the frustrations engendered by the procedures entailed in establishing a smallholding scheme. In this case occupation was rarely with the agreement of the proprietor or tenant. At Aline, Lewis, the proprietor reported in January 1932 that smallholders' stock had been present across the whole of the estate for at least two years and had been placed there as a consequence of the (then) Department's decision to acquire the land. There was no formal declaration of seizure here even though the scheme had been initiated in response to local agitation for land and threats to raid. On Eigg in an attempt to avoid an overt act of protest the proprietor offered enlargements to the island's crofters following a threat to seize the land. The crofters' response was to immediately place their stock on the land in question and to refuse to pay any rent for the additional grazing.[28] Effectively this was an act of protest.

In other instances the Board's local representative intervened in an attempt to alleviate the local conditions and arrange for access to land for those in greatest need. When these short-term agreements ceased, those given land often refused to hand it back. In 1917 in order to prevent raiding on Tolsta Farm (Lewis) the Board of Agriculture's sub-commissioner, Colin Macdonald, came to an informal

---

26 R.I.P.D. 17725/1 Sconser; 1611 Sconser, letter from Sconser crofters to M. P., 25 February 1939.

27 N.A.S. AF83/748, letter from (church) minister Norman Laing to M. P., 15 May 1923.

28 N.A.S. AF83/668 Sub-Commissioner Duncan Stewart to Board; AF83/378 A. Macrae to Board of Agriculture.

arrangement whereby 40 cottars from the local area gained access to one acre each on Tolsta farm. In March 1919 they were asked to quit but refused. Two years later they were still in possession. In addition, their stock was straying across the remainder of the farm thereby placing the tenant in an impossible situation. Here again there was no overt expression of any intention to gain possession of the land but Tolsta was one of the centres of agitation for the recovery of the farms of Coll and Gress and surplus stock in the area was readily grazed on these two farms.[29]

Within the informal utilisation of land therefore can clearly be seen the potential for protest and means to protest in its own right. The Board were aware of this and often acted formally to establish crofters or cottars on the land if it appeared that the informal arrangement was breaking down. In 1937 the Board noted that since 1914, due to a sympathetic proprietor, crofters had been putting stock in Glencanisp Deer Forest, Sutherland. 'In 1921 there were approximately 1000 head of sheep...in the forest. Later reports state that the number...had gone up to 1500.' In 1936 the Estate was sold and the new proprietor announced his intention of clearing the forest. As a consequence the crofters renewed their application for enlargements. The Board was keen to meet this in order to prevent a resumption of overt disturbance. A similar situation developed in Harris.[30]

A variant on the informal occupation of land is evident on Lewis. Here, such was the extent of the overcrowding on the crofting townships that squatting was a common occurrence much later than in other areas. In the Highland context squatting could take place either on the common grazing or on crofts, but always with the agreement of the township crofters. After the First World War at times this became more organised and took on aspects of protest. Groups of squatters commenced house building on the common and at the same time wrote to the Board asking them to legalise their situation. They were, in effect, attempting to coerce the government into acting by force of numbers, although squatters could also make individual threats. In December 1922 one such individual wrote that he was 30 years old, living on another man's croft with his mother and two sisters. His hope was that 'you will do for the landless people here in this village as you do in other districts'. When such assistance was not forthcoming his correspondence became more forthright, expressing his frustrations that 'we are patiently waiting for the Board to come and set out the allotments on the west end of Leurbost which was measured by your surveyor … a few weeks back … it is high time now you were coming to do so or we will have to take possession on our own'. It took until 1927, but here, as in every case where there was similar pressure applied, squatters were ultimately successful.[31]

---

29 N.A.S. AF83/532, Report from Thomas Wilson, 31 March 1919.

30 R.I.P.D. 38609 Glencanisp, Board memo 15 March 1937; 61110 Borve, Sub-commissioner to Board, 1 November 1929; Board minute 28 September 1932.

31 R.I.P.D. 118777/L/S/1, Lewis Housing, letters 2 December 1922, 3 March 1923; 40959 Lewis Squatting. By the 1930s the position had changed and the estate owners (the island was no longer owned by one person), in an attempt to end the squatter problem,

The movement of squatters onto the common found support from crofters. In October 1922 seven cottars from Gravir wrote that with the agreement of the township's crofters they were preparing houses on the common. On the one hand such acts of support cut across any uncritical assumption of increasing crofter/cottar tensions but even here these were all too readily apparent. As late as 1936 Tolsta Farm remained troubled. The Lewis estate owners were attempting to regularise the position of the island's squatters by adopting the same feuing/letting tactic used by the Board of Agriculture a few years earlier. This met with a generally positive response apart from at Tolsta where crofters threatened resistance if the scheme went ahead. Indeed, tensions were still apparent in the 1950s when, at a public meeting on the island to consider legalising the squatters' situation, objections were made on the grounds that this was a threat to crofters.[32]

This, of course, did not make such squatting any less legal. Moreover several factors mean we should typify such squatting as protest: actions were collectively based and organised; were preceded by letters stating the intentions of the cottars to carry out such actions and were followed up by calls for the Board of Agriculture to effect a legal solution. In short, organised squatting matches closely with behaviours in land raiding. Squatting of this type was clearly a means of putting pressure on the Government and often occurred in areas where other expressions of protest are evident both before and after the squatting, as such it is very reminiscent of Wood's and Bohstedt's local political negotiation.[33] Further, those who participated in such events linked their actions with other acts more readily seen as protest. One of the Gravir cottars had previously threatened to raid Orinsay, whilst at Leurbost threats 'to take possession on our own' were carried through in the form of organised squatting on old peat workings.[34] At times inter-changeable with other forms of protest, particularly the land raid, organised squatting was a localised form of social protest which reflected the unique pressures of continued overcrowding on Lewis and serves to further reinforce the assertion of the importance of local context. There was, in short, a complex local politics at play in protest performances. A point which is given further emphasis by what follows.

The Defence of the Realm Act and the Refusal to Surrender Land

These local contexts are no less important for understanding the implication of the deployment of the Defence of the Realm Act for Highland protest. The challenge

---

regularised their position. Squatted land passed into the legal possession of the squatters and although this involved a loss of common grazing it meant that squatters now paid rent and rates

32 R.I.P.D. 118777/G/S/1 Lewis Housing, letter 13 October 1922; *Glasgow Herald*, 20 April 1936; John A. Burnett, *The Making of the Modern Scottish Highlands, 1939–1965* (Dublin, 2011), p. 261.

33 Bohstedt, *Riots and Community Politics;* Wood, *Riots, Rebellion.*

34 R.I.P.D. 118777/G/S/1 Lewis Housing, letter 13 October 1922.

Table 3.3 Deer Forests opened up under the Defence of the Realm Act

Forest	County	Date of Expiry of Tenancy
Scorrybreck	Inverness	1920
Inverlochy	Ross & Cromarty	1920
Maxwells	Ross & Cromarty	1920
Dundonnell	Ross & Cromarty	1920
Balmacaan	Inverness	April 1920
Eredine	Argyll	Whitsunday 1920
Bochyle Grazings	?	2nd May 1920
Inverailort	Ross & Cromarty	2nd July 1920
Attadale	Ross & Cromarty	1st November 1920
Kintail	Ross & Cromarty	28th November 1920
Mingarry	Ross & Cromarty	1921
Eileanreach	Inverness	30th March 1921
Strathcarron	Inverness	April 1921
Alladale	Inverness	23rd April 1921
Ledgowan	Inverness	28th May 1921
Glenfinnan	Ross & Cromarty	1st August 1921
Chorrie Island	?	28th May 1921

?=County not found in archive or elsewhere.

Source: Compiled from the following: R.I.P.D. 34315/1; 22955/1; 35809/1; 40928; 5863/1; 74141; N.A.S.AF83/607.

to *laissez faire* has been identified as 'one of the salient and enduring features of the domestic history of the First World War.' In this the Defence of the Realm Act (hereafter DRA) was of importance; 'not for the substance of the Act but that it permitted various collectivist impulses and organisations to build up'.[35] In the Highlands the Act was of importance because it was utilised, although not always openly articulated as such, as part of attempts to temporarily satisfy the agitation for land when other legislation proved inadequate. One key aspect of DRA was the recognition that maximisation of food production may involve an element of central control and compulsion. The intention was to encourage an increase in productivity, in both areas under cultivation and in stocks held. For the Highlands this was often interpreted by the local Agricultural Executive Committees, who were charged with implementing DRA under direction from the Board of Agriculture, as the means by which areas within deer forests could be returned to agriculture. This was further seen as the means by which the land working population could be given access to land which existing legislation was largely unable to touch and for which they had been agitating. Based on the justification

35 Arthur. Marwick, *The Deluge* (London, 1969), pp. 163–9.

that it was inappropriate for the landlord or sporting tenant to be compelled to turn to agriculture and to bring in an agricultural tenant from outside would be unsatisfactory, either voluntary or compulsory agreements resulted which gave grazing or cultivation rights to local crofters and cottars. Unfortunately archival evidence for the full extent of these agreements appears not to have survived but it would seem that at least nineteen deer forests were opened up in this way (see Table 3.3). It is also clear, as at Eoligarry on Barra, that the Board of Agriculture were prepared to directly sponsor DRA schemes on tenanted farms in particularly disturbed areas.[36] As such this was a thinly-veiled attempt to address issues of overcrowding, land hunger and the tensions caused by these and the legacy of earlier socio-economic and cultural upheavals. This proactive approach is perhaps one of the strongest arguments why 1914 can be said to mark a significant break with the nature of protest of an earlier period.

In acting in this way the Government's principal ambition appears to have been the maintenance of law and order, enhanced by the fact that the country was at war and facing rebellion in Ireland. The DRA provisions, as with Kintail Deer Forest in Glenshiel, were viewed as a way of temporarily relieving escalating tensions. This particular forest had been the subject of near constant agitation since the 1880s. Threats to raid were equally prevalent and peaked in 1913 with one correspondent citing the frustrations generated by the failures of the 1911 Act, which, he claimed to have returned from Canada as a consequence of. Later the same year the Board was presented with a petition from the area threatening a mass raid to which they responded in their usual manner by considering a scheme. Here however, as in many cases, a combination of war-time conditions and landlord obstructionism caused the scheme's postponement with the inevitable consequence of further agitation. In 1917 the Board turned to a DRA scheme as a temporary solution.[37]

Tenancy arrangements were for three years. There was therefore only one period of tenancy, the Act ceasing with the end of the war. It is at this point that DRA intersects ever more closely with protest. Whilst some tenants agreed to relinquish their holding and some proprietors continued with voluntary agreements, at other forests the tenants refused to return the land. This was the case at Glenmore in Strathcarron. The lease here expired in April 1921 but a year later the crofters' stock was still in the forest. Their view was that they had no choice as without this grazing they were over-stocked but such was the poor condition of their sheep that selling the surplus was impossible. Technically actions such as these, as with the informal occupation of land noted in the previous section, were not land seizures. They were, nevertheless, unauthorised and illegal. As such, as a reflection of the local context and as an expression of the desire to regain and retain land, these were undoubtedly protest actions.

36 N.A.S. AF67/143 T. Wilson to Board 7 November 1917; Board of Agriculture memo to Scottish Office 5 March 1918.

37 N.A.S. AF83/336.

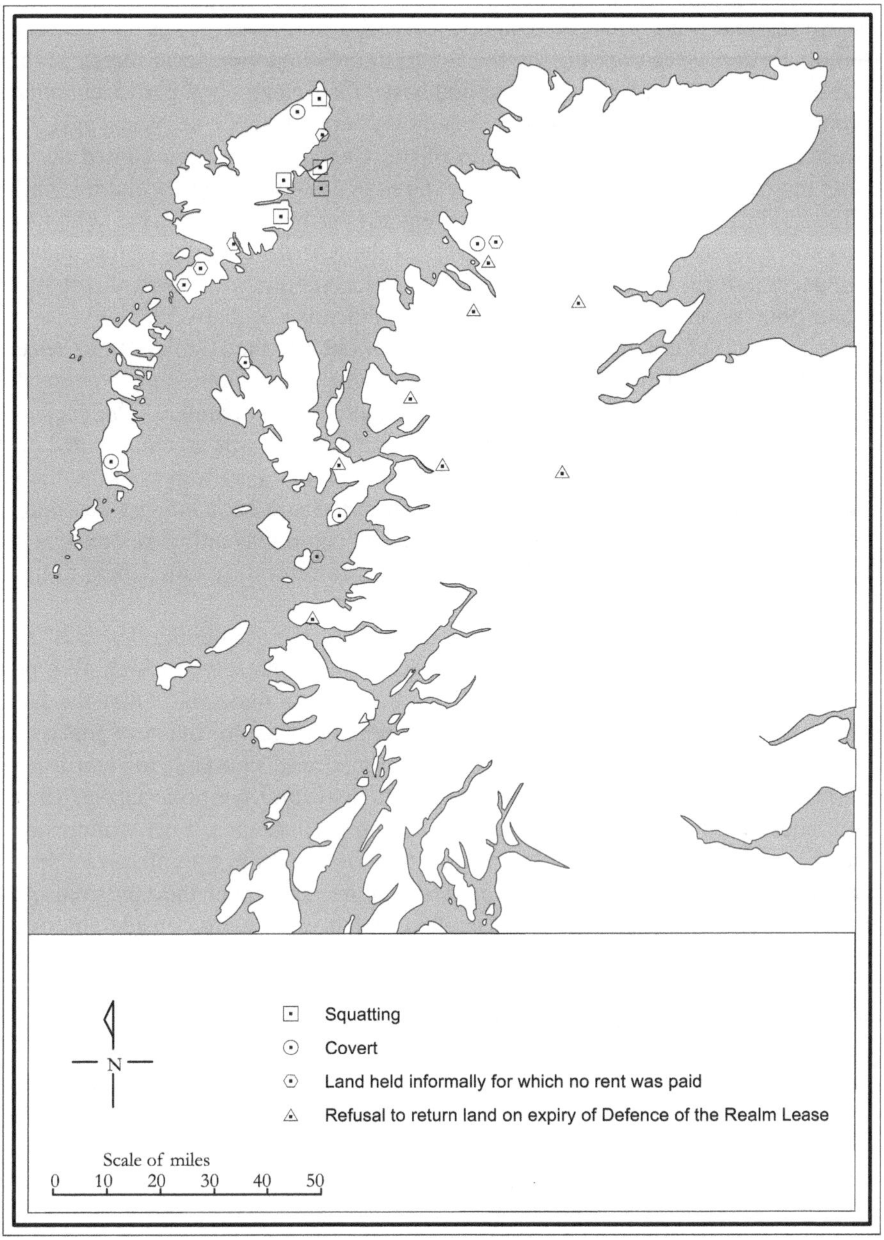

Figure 3.3 Locations of other protest types

In a further clear parallel with the informal occupation and reinforcement of the identification of the refusal to return land gained under DRA as an act of protest, such refusals often both firmly fit within local continuities of disturbance repertoires and were expressed in the language of protest. Thus the Western Bunloit crofters were pressurising the Board to break up their local forest, in this case Balmacaan, from before the war and based their claim upon past occupation: 'From time immemorial until the Deer Forest era of about 60 years ago, our ancestors held as grazing ... a portion of the Deer Forest.' They gained access under the Act, but when the agreement expired in 1920 refused to withdraw. Only in 1922 did the proprietor attempt to prevent any further utilisation, but with little success. Frustrated with the slow progress of the Board's attempts to formulate a permanent agreement, the crofters wrote in 1923, via their solicitors, threatening to take possession. Negotiations failed again in October of that year.[38]

Assessment of the effects and importance of DRA to the Highlands have been somewhat muted. This was perhaps the first time when Government policy to alleviate the problems of landlessness was not exclusively reactive. The decision to open up the deer forests to crofter and cottar tenancies was an enlightened one that encouraged acquiescence amongst the population at an important moment. This was, however, only temporary. The refusal to hand back land gained under these tenancies clearly indicates that pressure for land was only suspended with the onset of war and that the willingness to turn to protest to gain access to land was, if anything enhanced after November 1918.

As will shortly be demonstrated, what occurs almost contiguous with the War's end was an exponential increase in incidents of protest in which all types identified here were of significance. It is nevertheless undeniable that the land seizure remained the most potent protest weapon, not least for the newspaper and public attention it often attracted, although the fact that it is possible to identify key characteristics of this form suggests that its ritualistic and symbolic aspects (from both sides) were becoming more central to the performance. Such conclusions must be treated with caution, however, as they detract from the affective impact and emotional engagement acts of protest require. To model the land raid also removes protest from its vital local context which went some considerable way to determining the form disturbance took from the repertoire available to protest actors. This view is given additional weight and the importance of the local context emphasised, by the fact that at certain times and in certain places "normal" social relations appear close to collapse. This starts to look less like limited and ritualised political negotiation and more like the "war" of the 1880s. Key to this view is the identification of the prevalence (and we can confidently speculate that the archive records only a minority) of informal and *ad hoc* land utilisations. These actions were part protest and, in that authorities often ignored such utilisation, part prevention of protest. This hybrid form connects that which has been previously recognised as distinct: everyday forms of peasant resistance and overt protest. These important insights alone reveal the need for the discussion undertaken here

38 R. I. P. D. 40928, Balmacaan, 13 January 1922 Copy letter sent by solicitor, 3 May 1923 letter from solicitors to Board.

but this also sets the important typological context for the detailed discussion of the chronology of disturbance.

The Chronology of Protest

Inevitably, disturbance surrounding land after 1914 cannot be wholly removed from the context of events prior to that date. It has already been demonstrated how, on Hebridean sheep farms especially, land raids and threats to raid had 'become a part of the accepted order of things' and it should be assumed that, notwithstanding the fact that protest was at a low level, some, but certainly not all, of the varying typologies of post-1914 protest were evident in the first decade of the twentieth-century. During this decade the recourse to protest was maintained by the frustrations engendered by legislative weaknesses in dealing with the problems associated with land hunger and lack of access to land. By 1913 emotions amongst the crofting tenantry were such that one newspaper was able to see 'ample evidence of a coming revolt'. It was this revolt which was delayed until the war's end with, Hunter argues, discontent among the Highlanders being 'submerged in the wider and more awful violence of the European war'.[39] It will be strongly asserted in Chapter 5 that this delay served only to amplify the magnitude of the outburst of protest which took place after November 1918, the contours of which are clearly outlined in Figure 3.4.

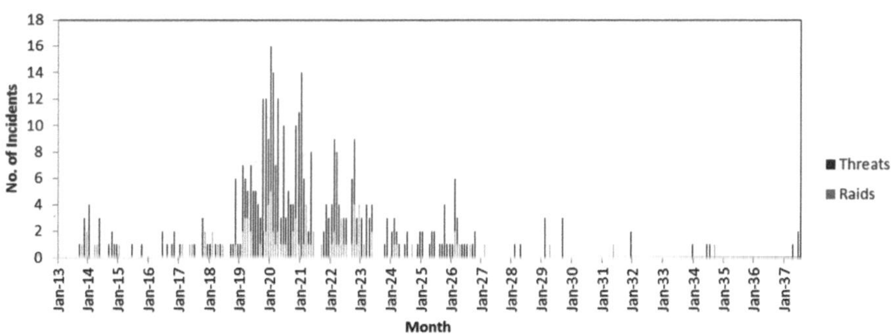

Figure 3.4 Performing protest after 1914

By 1914, then, the Highlands had experienced over 30 years of virtually continuous protest, albeit fluctuating in both intensity and geography. During this period there had been a number of flawed attempts to address the underlying issues. The principal weakness of such legislation was a continual failure to provide adequate mechanisms to address the desires of the land-working population to re-assert a particular way of life. Whilst the position of crofters was somewhat ameliorated

39 Hunter, *The Making*, pp. 192–5.

by government actions, the failure to break up the large farms and deer forests created in the shift to the market economy meant that little could be done for the landless and ensured that protest continued. This has given rise to the argument that participation in twentieth-century protest was dominated by cottars and squatters. And yet the concerns of crofters for enlargements to their holdings were only diminished by state action and not removed. Moreover, many crofters either wanted replacements for their existing, worked out, crofts or were agitating to return to what they saw as *their* land. And even if they did not actually participate in particular land seizures their opposition to the continuing presence of cottars and squatters in the township and utilising the township grazing was, on occasion, one of the key motives behind seizure. Crofters, therefore, retained a significant presence in post-1914 protest performances.

In the same vein any emphasis on war as hiatus is equally misleading as whilst there were relatively few overt incidents between August 1914 and November 1918 there can be little doubt that the potential for disturbance remained. As already noted, this is clearly demonstrated by the Board of Agriculture's enthusiasm for the use of the Defence of the Realm Act as means to diffuse this.[40] This tactic notwithstanding, neither the patriotic feelings engendered by war, nor the fact that a large percentage of the menfolk were absent on war duties, prevented raiding taking place during the war years. Indeed, those events which did occur had great significance both for their location and for the maintenance of continuity with earlier events. During the first eight months of 1914 raiding took place on Lewis, Tiree, Barra and Taransay. Further raids were threatened in Barra, Lewis and Harris whilst land at Reef (Lewis), that had been first occupied in November 1913 was still being cultivated. This situation was causing tension between the Board and Scottish office as they had diametrically opposed views over how to respond. The Board were in favour of attempting to settle the raiders on the ground whilst the Under-Secretary for Scotland was not afraid of direct actions. He feared encouraging 'similar raids in other places if this was attempted'. The proprietor obtained an interdict against the raiders and in March 1914 eleven of them were sentenced to six weeks in gaol for breach. This gained much public sympathy both within Lewis and in the country as a whole and, as a result of questions in the House of Commons, the Scottish Secretary announced an enquiry into the incidents. On their release the raiders resumed agitation but this was not sustained as the local feeling was to suspend action until after the war, a decision probably not unconnected with the estimate that three quarters of the applicants for holdings in the Board's schemes had been called up.[41]

Here then, very early in the period under consideration, is the classic land protest set of actions which accord very closely with the model as proposed earlier (see Table 3.2). In addition, Reef stands as an example of the complex longevity

40 Marwick, *The Deluge*, pp. 168–9,and 267–8; R.P.I.D. 106117 Deer Forests and Land Settlement.

41 N.A.S. AF67/61; S.R.O. AF67/62; S.R.O. AF67/143; S.R.O. AF67/144.

of incidents of raiding. The cottars based their claims to be taking legitimate action in the fact that Reef farm had been 'cultivated for [i.e. by] smallholders' until the clearances of the 1850s whilst the Board of Agriculture also recognised the importance of the collective memory of past events to protestors. In a note to the Under-Secretary for Scotland it was stated that agitation at Reef in 1884 resulted in the sending of a gunboat to the island, an action which had not been forgotten in the area and which 'may not be without influence upon the future acts of the present generation of cottars'.[42]

There can be no doubt that whilst the war acted as a brake to protest the power of that brake weakened rapidly through the war years. There is an evident incremental increase in acts of protest, culminating in 1917 with them spreading to both Mull and Tiree, hitherto peaceable. Nevertheless there were very few recorded incidents of protest on the mainland with just one land seizure, at West Garty in the clearance township of Portgower in Sutherland. Here it is not without significance that of the ten reported raiders four were women.[43] It is also important, perhaps even more so, to recognise the latent power of the demand for land in the fact of the rapid rise of disturbances on the mainland after November 1918.

Seemingly inevitably, with the end of the war the number of incidents of protest rapidly increased throughout the Highlands (see Figure 3.4). The principle exception to this was the island of Lewis. Here it is impossible to avoid the conclusion that the sinking of H.M. Yacht *Iolaire*, on the 31 December 1918, had such a profound impact on the community that it must have limited the recourse to protest on Lewis throughout 1919. On board the *Iolaire* were a large number of demobilised navy ratings. The boat struck rocks and sank just outside Stornoway harbour with the loss of approximately 200 local men (there is some divergence over the exact figure). For John Macleod the cultural impact of this awful event touched every township on the island and helped to destroy a way of life.[44] Indicative of the impact this must have had, is the story told by Màiread in *Children of the Black House*.

> My Aunt Marion's husband was known to everybody as the "Boyken". He and Aunt Marion had a family of four boys and three girls ... My immediate duty was to sit with the youngest children and entertain them ... It was no easy task! Kate and Alice were so excited that they wanted only to talk about the present their father might bring them in his kit-bag ... Sandy and Uilleam, the eldest boys were out building the Ard bonfire at the Ruba Deas ... Neighbours were back and fore from the house with gifts of cuddies, treacle bread and crowdie for the Boyken, everyone curious to know if Marion had heard any news ... I remember sitting near this blazing peat fire some time after two o'clock in the morning ... I must have been awakened by the chill of the room. The fire

42 N.A.S. AF67/61, Memo from Under Secretary for Scotland, 4 December 1913.

43 N.A.S. AF83/287, March 1917; AF83/250, December 1917; AF67/64, May 1918.

44 John Macleod, *When I Heard the Bell* (Edinburgh, 2010).

> was all but dead and the wick of the paraffin lamp turned down … the clothes-horse had been moved away from the inglenook and also the pots of broth and stew … Marion was sitting back and forwards, on her milking stool rocking backwards and forwards … I rose from my chair and turned up the light. Her voice choking with emotion, Marion said, "The light has gone out of my life!" "Has the Boyken arrived?" She did not answer. … "The Boyken will never come home child, I am a widow." … Though I had briefly nodded off in my chair, I was certain that nobody had opened the outer door to bring my aunt ill tidings … There was more consternation … when it was discovered that Marion was unable to speak … She regained her speech some weeks later, but, for the rest of her life, she was afflicted like that when the days of the dying year reminded her of the disaster … The bonfires on the hill remained unlit that day … They remained on the hilltop disintegrating and decaying – sombre memorials to the 205 men who drowned on the blackest night in the history of our island.[45]

Whilst for many families the consequences of this blow was to hasten the decision to emigrate, others, like Màiread's, continued to be driven by a strong desire to remain. Many too continued to believe that the only way this could be achieved would be through greater access to land and turned to protest when this was not forthcoming.

The first major post-war incident occurred in South Uist in December 1918. Here, Angus and Alexander Campbell were interdicted from illegally building houses on Glendale farm. The Campbells were old men and Lady Gordon Cathcart's refusal to grant them a site for a house on any of her estates brought the case notoriety and was in the words of the Board of Agriculture's commissioner, 'an intolerable situation'. The outcome was that the proprietrix agreed to a settlement scheme on Glendale albeit for high compensation.

Generating much publicity, the South Uist case was merely the harbinger of the explosion to come, evidenced by the fact that in the following year even areas hitherto more associated with acquiescence, Tiree and Caithness for instance, became disturbed. Nevertheless, it was on the islands where protest was at its most intense with the views of the Borve crofters being typical. In 1920 they renewed their demands for the grazing rights on the Torogay Islands with the argument that 'it is a very small compensation we ask in return for fighting .... we shall not be any worse off in Prison than in the trenches of Flanders'. Sheep were placed on the islands in May.[46]

Taking the Highlands as a whole, when all forms of protest are added in and threats to raid recognised as separate events on occasion, 1920 was the most

45 Calum Ferguson, *Children Of The Black House* (Edinburgh, 2003), pp. 167–71. Please note that Màiread was the author's mother and the recollection noted here does not come from a formal interview or recorded oral history but is instead what has emerged from Màiread's stories and reminiscences.

46 N.A.S. AF67/146; *The Scotsman* 11th December 1918; N. A. S. AF67/145; AF67/155, letter to Scottish Office 18 March 1920.

disturbed of all the post-war years (see Figure 3.4). This is further evidenced by the fact that, unlike most other years, disturbance continued at a high level throughout the summer. The following year, however, saw no events of protest during August and September even though a number of new forms to protest became fully apparent. A significant number of DRA leases expired in 1921 and the Board of Agriculture was faced with refusals to return the land to the proprietor. Organised squatting also became evident on Lewis.[47] The intensity of feeling apparent in such episodes is made further evident by the fact that land seizures were becoming, if not commonplace on the mainland, certainly significantly more frequent and still present in areas hitherto relatively undisturbed in this post-war period. An important consequence of this escalation for the Board of Agriculture was that it was being forced to concentrate its efforts on the more disturbed areas, ignoring the more peaceable. In response to a petition from Port Ellen on the island Islay, for instance, it was noted that

> For various reasons the Board has been unable to carry out any land settlement in Islay since the war with the exception of two small schemes of single holdings. There are upward of 150 qualified ex-service applicants ... in Islay and of these thirty are from the neighbourhood of Port Ellen where the demand for land is clamant.[48]

It was admitted internally that one of the reasons for the Board's comparative lack of effort on Islay was that overt protest actions there had been minimal.

Agitation and disturbance remained at a high level throughout 1921 and 1922, from early 1923, however, through to 1926, there was something of a decline. Nevertheless, when raiding did occur it was with all the determination of the immediate post-war years. This was especially true in South Harris and Lewis, in places such as Scaristaveg, Melbost and Laxdale. The belief that those born in the area had a right to the land also remained strong, as did the idea that war service brought an entitlement to land. In April 1924 Hector McInnes from Caligarry (Skye) wrote that 'there is plenty of land there on Tormore.... and why should we not have it. We have fought for it and we will have it'. In March 1928 the Board received a letter from those taking part in the agitation for Borve Farm, Harris to the effect that 'there is to be a raiding party organised in the course of a few days and then we will have our share of our own Native isle'.[49]

For the first time since 1916 there would appear to have been no raiding in 1925, although threats continued, some of which were carried through to actual raids the

47 R.P.I.D. 118777/G/S, Gravir; 34315/1, Eileanreach Deer Forest; 118777/K/S, Gravir.

48 R.P.I.D. 33496, White Hart Parks, petition from 12 ex-servicemen, 8 October 1922.

49 N.A.S. AF67/158, H. McInnes and others to Scottish Office, 16 April 1924; R.P.I.D 61110, Borve.

following year. Agitations such as these could be remarkably long-lived. On the Waternish estate on Skye, for instance, the same land had been subject to agitation since at least 1919 and probably much earlier. Threats to seize were issued in 1919, 1921, 1923 and 1925 and always by the same group. Despite the regularity of the correspondence and hence (we must surmise) the seriousness of their intent, it took nearly a decade for them to obtain access to this land – a further indicator of the relative power (or lack of power) of the threat without seizure. Nevertheless, a more rapid move to break up land could generate its own frustrations. At Nunton on the island of Benbecula, for instance, dissatisfaction with the way in which the land had been broken up (in January 1925) was generative of threats to new seizures. This was one of the areas where disturbance was at its most intense and here threats to seize land were made as part of the more general campaign to ensure only ex-servicemen were included in the scheme. At Eoligarry on Barra, perhaps even more contested than Nunton, those who had failed to obtain holdings under the scheme regularly threatened to take possession of unoccupied holdings. In October 1924 one correspondent, who had been applying for land since demobilisation, wrote that he had 'Taken Charge' of one such holding and in June 1925 a group of applicants wrote that they were 'taking possession of unoccupied holdings at Eoligarry'.[50]

Land disturbance intensified again in 1926, with the focus very much on the conjoined islands of Lewis and Harris. In response to this, and to fears of extensive raiding in the spring 1926, the Board of Agriculture moved to break up a number of farms, one of which had raiders in occupation. This in itself generated threats as there were more applicants than potential holdings and there was a perception amongst applicants that 'the man in possession has a greater chance' of gaining a legal holding. Elsewhere the campaign for land on Waternish continued and at Tobson, Lewis, cottars who had lost a Land Court decision on their eligibility to remain on the township issued a number of threats to seize land at Bosta in the belief that 'we deserve a bit of the land which we have been fighting so hard for'. They continued their unsuccessful agitation until 1929 at least.[51]

In the closing years of the 1920s protest was increasingly confined to Lewis and Harris with what might be understood as the last successful raid taking place at Laxdale in 1934. This does not mean that protest came to a halt, as it continued up to the outbreak of World War two and resumed in the late 1940s (albeit at a hugely reduced level) with at least one celebrated incident of seizure.[52] These

50 R.P.I.D. 26509/M/1, letter 8 October 1924, letter 20 June 1925; N.A.S. AF83/668; AF83/669.

51 N.A.S. AF83/790; AF67/66; AF83/794; AF83/795; AF83/800; R.P.I.D. 61110, Borve; 38453/1, Boreray; 26509/M/1, Waternish; N.A.S. AF67/60, 26 August 1926; AF83/805; 7 September 1926 and 2 October 1926.

52 See, for instance, Ewen Cameron, '"Unfinished Business": The Land Question and the Scottish Parliament', *Contemporary British History*, Volume 15, Issue 1 (2001), pp. 83–114; Fraser Grigor, *Highland Resistance*.

incidents notwithstanding it is clear that much of the intensity and affective power of the post-World War One agitation had largely dissipated by the third decade of the twentieth century. In the first 14 years of the century whilst there were some signs of an incipient revival in protest, events had not come close to reaching the intensity of that of the 1880s. Between 1919 and 1923, however, and again after 1925, that intensity was matched and perhaps even surpassed. Indeed, something similar can be said for the Government's response. Driven in part by public sentiment (shaped as ever by newspaper opinion) and, indeed, by a greater level of sympathy from within, the Scottish Office moved proactively to both introduce legislation which proved reasonably effective in attempting to address the land issue and to act on that legislation. Coupled with the revival in mass emigration in the post-war period this goes a long way to explaining why the intensity of protest was only sustained over a comparatively short period. Nevertheless, to discuss the chronology of protest in the way undertaken here lends a certain linearity to our understanding which at times can rather undermine important local contexts and the appreciation of the micro-spaces of protest performances. Events at Sconser on Skye are a good example of this. In 1939 a dispute arose over grazing rights in the forest with those who were allowing their cattle to trespass on it being seen as 'in effect raiders' by the (then) Department of Agriculture. Applications for grazing rights had been with the Board since at least 1912 and raiding had taken place in the area in 1917 with a DRA agreement being put in place shortly after. It was this agreement which led to the situation only being addressed in 1939.[53] Events here therefore encapsulate every protest form evident in the post-1914 Highlands (and, no doubt, other forms which might be understood as covert, everyday resistance) and demonstrate the pitfalls of a strictly chronological approach. For this reason alone it is vital that events of the second decade of the twentieth century be approached from a place-based perspective (see Part III). There remains, nevertheless, a number of themes within this broad chronology which demand exploration.

The Seasonality of Protest

One of the most significant trends to emerge from a close and chronological reading of the available evidence and from Figure 3.5 is the fact that protest did not occur evenly throughout the year. This is particularly the case for both the threat to raid and the raid itself. All other protest forms were either numerically insufficient to reveal meaningful pattern or else their nature, as in the informal occupation of land, meant that a start date is impossible to establish accurately.

A comparison of these two protest forms reveals a significant difference in the principle periods when they occurred. There is a peaking of land raiding between the months of March and June, whilst the period of greatest intensity for the issuing

53 N.A.S. AF67/66, 26 August 1926; R.P.I.D. 1611, Sconser, July 1939, Internal Board memo.

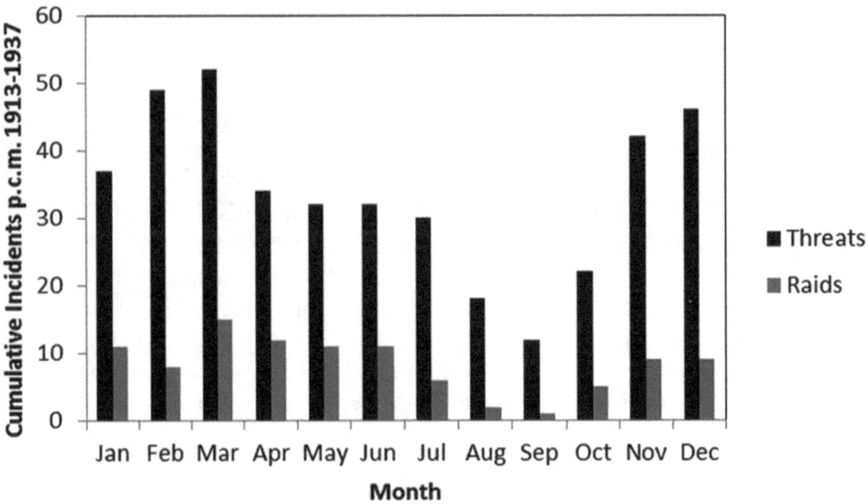

Figure 3.5 Cumulative monthly occurrences

of threats to raid was between November and March. In addition, threats could be issued throughout the year whilst there are no instances of raids taking place in either August or September. At first glance this pattern suggests support for the view that threat was nothing more than prelude to raid: the former coming earlier than the latter. A deeper look, however, suggests otherwise and that the threat was something different. Both the geographical distribution of threats and the fact that they could be made during, whilst, and after the occurrence of a raid is strongly suggestive of diversity and lack of connection.

This rejection of any automatic link between threat and raid is given further weight by when the bulk of threats were made on the mainland. Here the distribution of threats was of isolated peaks within an otherwise even pattern. In other areas of the Highlands the winter month peaking is both more pronounced and consistent. This lack of uniformity across the region does not suggest an unbreakable link between threat and raid. In addition the raid appears much more closely connected to the agrarian cycle than does the threat with the concentration of that in the winter months explained more by climatic and diurnal limitations than by any connection to a subsequent seizure. In the winter the days were simply too short and climate too poor to accomplish much outdoor activity. Letter writing is best done indoors and was usually the work of an individual; the winter was, then, the period when individuals were most likely to be at home, fully resident in the township and with time available to write.

The actual raid was most often a group activity and most often undertaken during the late spring/early summer period. This was the raiding "season", recognised as such by local and wider authorities. Thus if a raid were to take place in the summer months this would be 'more of the nature ... of a demonstration than a seizure'.[54] Undoubtedly spring was the time when pressure for land was at its most intense. The Leverhulme estate factor reported in April 1924 that threats to seize part of Linshader farm had been made 'at this season every year since he has been in the Lews'. Similarly the Board's official on Harris in September 1925 was surprised by threats made that month as he 'did not expect threats of raiding till early spring'. In January 1926 the prospective raiders renewed their threat and wrote that they were 'compelled by circumstances to take possession of the said farm on or about 1st February'. They did not but wrote again delaying the raid until the 1st March. This was their final date as spring work had to be started by then. They carried out their threat on the day specified.[55]

Protest, then, was undoubtedly seasonal but we should not see this seasonality as wholly reflective of economic motivations and the need for sustenance or as a purely pragmatic set of actions that reflect the practically of protestors' needs. Discussed in much greater depth in Chapter 7, this seasonality was also and perhaps primarily, the manifestation of deeply-rooted cultural practices in relation to land and landscape. Work tasks as practice within the crofting tenantry reflected a local, vernacular and moral attitude towards land and the use of land. This in turn impelled protest events as attempts to re-assert those attitudes and ways of work in the face of the values (and sporting needs) of the political economy.

The Diffusion of Protest?

Consideration elsewhere of the spread of nineteenth-century Highland protest has usually seen it as the product principally of 'face-to-face' contact and of one group of crofters following the example of others. In wider protest discussions diffusion is often seen to be influenced by route-ways and smaller market towns.[56] Whilst there is some evidence to suggest the presence of these influences in Highland protest after 1914, the most influential factor in appears to have been the precedent of earlier events – whether in the same location or more generally.

Unlike the influence of earlier events in the same place, direct evidence of contemporaneous events elsewhere having an influence over the decision to protest is largely confined to the threat to raid. On occasion, as at Killin, Perthshire, the precedent was the success of raiding more generally rather than any specific locale. It was, nevertheless, the Lewis disturbances which were most often referred to, as at Kishorn on the mainland – despite the fact that the Isle of Skye was closer and therefore the most logical precedent. Similarly applicants near Thurso wrote, 'We don't want to take it by force as they did in Lewis. But it looks as if we will have

54 N.A.S. AF83/287, 17 March 1917; AF83/378, 30 June 1930; AF67/150, 7 June 1920.

55 N.A.S. AF67/152, June 1921.

56 Charlesworth. *Social Protest*; Bohstedt and Williams. *The Diffusion of Riots*.

to if nothing will be done.'[57] This influence may be explained by the reporting of the events in the newspapers. The *Stornoway Gazette* was one of the two leading Highland newspapers and, being based on Lewis, reported events there in more detail and more frequently. Disturbances on Lewis also more often attracted the attention of the national press a fact reflecting the ongoing "modern" turn of events of land disturbance and not passing unnoticed by protestors. The press then, may well have become a tool of protest. In December 1919, for instance, the solicitors for the South Uist Estate reported a raid on Askernish farm. They believed that the aim of this was not to gain land but to attract press attention.[58]

On Lewis, perhaps even over and above the more celebrated incidents at Coll and Gress, the link and fulcrum between the earlier and later Land wars can be seen to be the 1913 land seizure on Reef farm on the far west of the island. Reef is recognisable as both model and mnemonic because it was long running, as intense as those at other places on the island, and was recognised by all sides as shaped by earlier events in the same location. Thus the Secretary for Scotland, Robert Munro, was able to write that 'any action which the executive might take in regard to the Reef raid is likely to be very carefully watched in the Highlands and islands.' He further drew attention to the fact that the 1884 raids on the farm occasioned open resistance to authority and the consequent stationing of a gunboats off Uig and believed that 'this story is doubtless a well-known tradition in Uig and may not be without influence upon the future acts of the present generation of cottars.' Agitation resumed in 1908 but plans for a Congested Districts Board scheme broke down (like so many others) and made further disturbances almost inevitable. By 1913 the Board of Agriculture was advising against a scheme on the basis that responding to seizure in this way would only encourage others. And whilst this policy was not to hold for very much longer (if in fact it had ever held), the Reef raiders withdrew from the land and did not resume agitation until 1920.[59]

Crofters and cottars clearly in fact required very little encouragement but perhaps the way in which an earlier act of land seizure was most directly influential on a subsequent threat of seizure was to increase the number of participants in the subsequent event, as at Drimsdale, South Uist. Nevertheless, those agitating for land were certainly aware of the benefits raiding brought. In 1922 applicants for land from Aird, Benbecula wrote 'we have come to the conclusion that raiding brings the break-up of farms', a sentiment which was echoed by the solicitors for the Lady Gordon Cathcart, the landowner of much of South Uist. Skene, Edwards and Garson argued that the Board of Agriculture, faced with a determined group in possession of land, would respond in a way that allowed the group to remain in

57 N. A. S. AF67/65, 3 February 1920; AF83/660, 16 February 1925; AF67/176, 30 June 1920.

58 Finlay MacLeod, *Crowdie and Cream* (London, 1982), p. 96; N. A. S. AF83/19, 23 December 1919.

59 N. A. S. AF67/61, memorandum from Robert Munro, 4 December 1913.

possession and that this was recognised in the crofting community. Consequently, 'the Glendale incident, following on the precedent of Vatersay, was regarded as conclusive proof that all that was necessary to enable the people to get the land was to raid it.'[60]

There would seem to be little consistency to the evidence of agitation for land being inspired by the actions of others. Indeed, it would further seem that past behaviour in the same location, the continuity of protest in a specific place, was of more importance to the decision to seize land. Claims such as these have become commonplace in protest literature, particularly in relation to large-scale periods of protest such as the Captain Swing riots in the south of England in the early 1830s. Here there has been much discussion around questions as to whether Swing can be understood as a widespread protest "movement". In considering the importance of continuity of protest in a particular place to these riots Griffin is hesitant in any conclusions he feels able to offer. Despite an exhaustive archival search in very few locations does a discernible and consistent connection emerge and such is the complex spatial patterning of Swing-related events he feels unable to support the notion of a relationship between 'forms of agrarian capitalism ... past protest practices [and] ... Swing's form and diffusion' That connection, however, is more discernible for the later Land Wars and more appealing too, is Jones's identification[61] of the operation of "meta-movements" within diffuse protest events.

Discussion: An End to Protest

To recognise any form of movement for land in the post-1914 Highlands demands a concomitant recognition of countervailing processes even if we were to find common cause with Burnett who suggests that it was the period after 1939 which was critical to the full working out of socio-economic and cultural change for ordinary Highlanders. It is nevertheless equally important to recognise that these processes date back much earlier into the first decades of the Twentieth century with, for Hunter, the full integration of crofting society into the money economy. For Leneman, moreover, one critical disjuncture between the old world and the new came at the very end of 1926 when the Board of Agriculture were allowed for the first time to treat non ex-servicemen on the same basis as ex-servicemen when it came to allocating holdings.[62] This was also the last year of widespread land disturbance in the Highlands and is therefore perhaps a hinge-point, although the claim must be treated with some caution. What all this amounts to are threads in the important but little-discussed question over the ending of protest and the

60 N. A. S. AF67/152, 8 January 1920; AF67/151, 18 October 1922; AF83/245, 13 October 1922; S.R.O. AF67/152, July 1920; AF83/190, 8 January 1920.

61 Jones, *Finding Captain Swing*; Griffin, *Rural War*, p. 179;

62 Burnett, *The Making*; James Hunter, *The Claim of Crofting* (Edinburgh, 1991); Leneman, *Fit For Heroes*.

aftermath of that ending. Emigration offers another possibility but it was at the same time an expression of protest. In Skye this was articulated as an alternative to obtaining land. On Mull the threat to emigrate replaced that to raid. We must nevertheless be cautious of uncritical assumptions that this type of threat was of the same magnitude as that to raid.

Time and socio-economic change appears to have eroded radicalism if not levels of demand. As the 1920s gave way to the 1930s, and in the islands especially, a growing emphasis on the younger generation obtaining a full education, combined with significant improvements in communication and transport, increased and diversified employment opportunities. This weakened traditional reliance on the land and caused applicants to opt only for crofts likely to return a profit. At Cheesebay on North Uist, for instance, it took almost a decade to put a land settlement scheme in place, by which time demand was far more 'discriminating' that it had been when the scheme had been first proposed. Nevertheless, across the Highlands applicants continued to strive to gain what they saw as viable land. In 1926 the Scottish Office accepted that applicants 'see patches of land scattered throughout the forests of a character that they would be quite content to have and agitation for them will continue'. In 1928 the 3785 outstanding applicants were contacted by the Board of Agriculture over their intentions: 1315 replied that they still wanted land.[63] It would seem that geography – in the form of land, the crofting landscape and the tasks to be performed within it – continued to matter. Indeed there is a case to be made that the more rewarding perspective to take on the post-1914 disturbances is a spatial one. It has already been noted how a strictly chronological approach does a disservice to the nature of the enduring opposition in some places and there are important exemptions to the cessation of intensive land agitation after 1926. There is a need, therefore to take a second look before any firm conclusions can be confidently asserted regarding the nature of protest after 1914. It is necessary, in short, to turn to an intra-regional geography in order to deeper our understanding and make clear what was happening in this critical period.

---

63 R. I. P. D. 26814/CB/1, Cheesebay, report by sub-commissioner, October 1923; N. A. S. AF78/17, 17th Report of the Board of Agriculture, p. 20.

Chapter 4
The Geography of Protest: Regional and Intra-regional Perspectives

The concern of this chapter is with the geography of protest, and specifically with the straightforward spatial distribution of location. This somewhat limited perspective is adopted here for two reasons. Firstly, because the nature of our understanding of these Highland events demands it; as the previous chapter indicates, the historiography of post-1914 protest has paid insufficient attention to the diversity and numerical intensity of the pressure for land. While we may agree with Adrian Randall[1] that counting events is notoriously both a fraught and a flawed process and that this does not axiomatically demonstrate significance, it nevertheless adds an important layer to our understanding, particularly when a full delineation of the scope of these protests has not as yet been achieved. Withers, for instance, does pay close attention to the geographical perspective when discussing the long-run transformation of the Highlands more generally and of events of protest in particular, but his concern is with a 'culture region' and he consequently does not seek to fully address the intra-regional variations revealed here.[2] This chapter confines itself to a straightforward consideration of the distribution of disturbances because these events demand that we do so. It is more than a concern for dots on a map – as important as this is – but it enables us to plot the situation of events "on the ground" in the important mental and material contexts which gave rise to them. These are, moreover, contexts which only fully emerge from the *raison d'être* of the current work: a monocular perspective on protest performances alone and new approaches to its interpretation. The second key reason why the concern of this current chapter is solely that of the spatial arrangements of these Highland events is that protest culture is, initially at least, more appropriately considered in its own right.

Finally this approach represents the continuation of a recent trend. Buchanan, for instance, has taken Lewis as her sole focus whilst, in *Aimhreit an Fhearainn*, both the islands of Skye and Lewis are covered.[3] In both instances, however, the time period under consideration is broader than that drawn on here and this is inevitably reflected in the consequent narratives. Buchanan, for instance, begins with the 1874 Bernera riot and considers only 'four of the crucial episodes in the history of our island' in any detail and ignores a number of other equally important

1 Randall, Captain Swing, pp. 419–27.

2 Withers, *Gaelic Scotland.*

3 Joni Buchanan, *The Lewis Land Struggle* (Stornoway, 1996); The Islands Book Trust, *Aimhreit an Fhearainn* (Stornoway, 2012).

Figure 4.1 Highland land agitation, 1914–1939

disturbances such as those at Reef or Uig.[4] It must be acknowledged, however, that this was her brief when the book was commissioned.[5]

The Geography of Protest

As with the chronology of post-1914 events, a focus on the regional geography of protest adds little to the already-established understanding of Highland disturbance. Cross-regional patterns have, moreover, been established in the context of the delineation of the timing of protest events. When, however, comparisons are made between specific areas of the Highlands and when new protest forms are admitted, different and hitherto unexplored patterns emerge. Drawing on, for instance, the patterns revealed by Figures 4.1 and 4.2 clear differences emerge in the timing and distribution of protest events between (and within) the islands and the mainland. The impact of the recognition of new protest forms on the latter has already been noted but what is further revealed is the continued (from before 1914) shrinking back of the most intense expressions of resistance into the Gaelic heartland: the islands of the Outer Hebrides. This formulation must be used with caution, for, as Burnett has acknowledged, there are a number of ways in which the *Gàilhealtachd* can be understood. For the period with which he was dealing Burnett suggests that it was utilised culturally 'as "the land of the Gael" as opposed to "the Gaelic-speaking area"'. Here, however, in part in the hope of avoiding Blaikie's critique of Burnett's work, namely that it is difficult to establish 'just where the essentialism ends and constructionism begins', the "heartland" is understood linguistically. Nevertheless, and even more pertinent to the present work, this notion of a shrinking back to a Gaelic heartland is further challenged by the identification of new protest forms, some of which interestingly appear more prevalent in areas where recourse to the land raid was much reduced. To the areas which Burnett identifies as the *breac- Gàilhealtachd*, in other words.[6]

4 Angus Macleod, 'Foreword' in Buchanan, *Lewis Land Struggle*, p. 5.

5 *The Lewis Land Struggle* was commissioned by *Cuimhneachain Nan Gaisgeach* as one part of their attempt to memorialise the land struggle on Lewis. Even though the intent behind the memorials that they created at the same time (see Figures 6.5 and 6.6) was to link with wider events, inevitably this has become focussed on Lewis solely. The Angus Macleod Archive, Ravenspoint Centre, Kershader, Isle of Lewis, Series B, Files C1-6, Section 5.

6 *Breac- Gàilhealtachd* is defined by Burnett as 'the "speckeld Gaeldom that now constituted the vast majority of the terrain of the Highlands, the wide spread of parishes and communities where a sense of undeniable Gaelic past and identity lingered but the number of actual Gaelic-speaking residents had dwindled to a few speckles on a map of Gaelic's linguistic retreat as the natural speech community of everyday life.' Burnett, *The Making*, pp. 17–18; Andrew Blaikie, review of *The Making of the Modern Scottish Highlands, 1939–1965: Withstanding the 'Colossus of Advancing Materialism'* (review no. 1238), online: http://www.history.ac.uk/reviews/review/1238, [accessed: 6 April 2013].

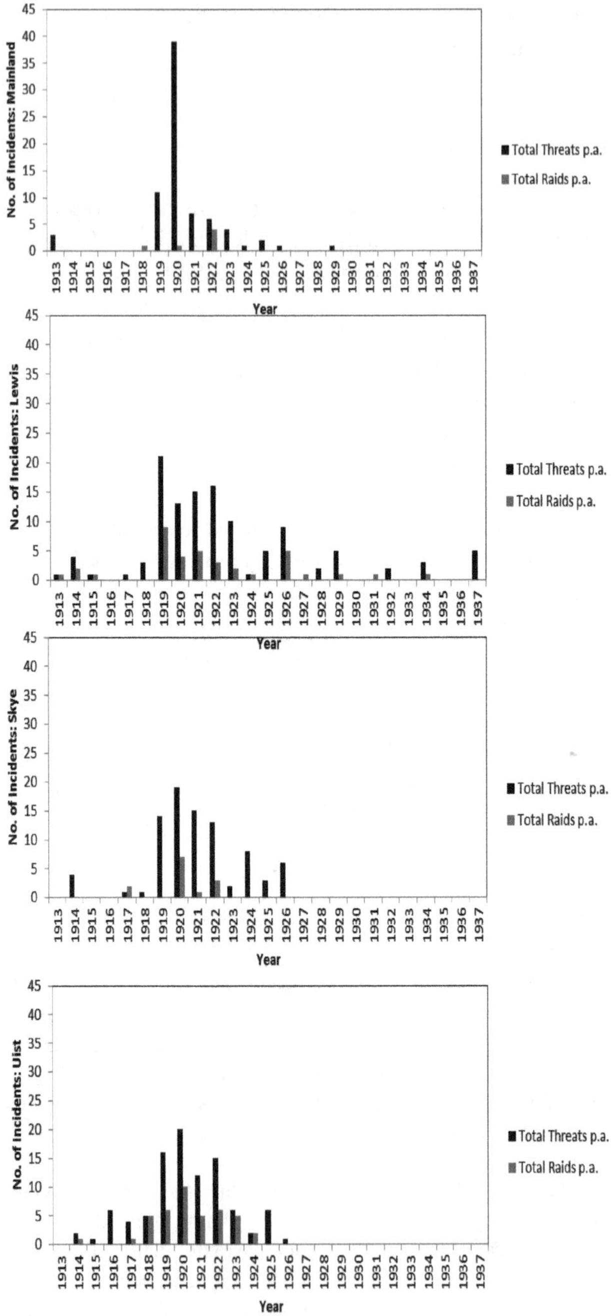

Figure 4.2 The chronology of protest by area

Different places therefore turned to protest in different ways and at different times. Very little of this variation has been discussed in the academic literature hitherto and this approach significantly changes our understanding of the nature of post-1914 protest. There is therefore much to be gained from a focus on the intra-regional geography of Highland protest and from a consideration of what was occurring in those discrete areas which appear broadly and most obviously homogenous; always accepting that there is a certain artificiality to such categorisations and that a focus on an individual event may ultimately be the most convincing lens through which to view the dynamics of the various cultures at play in the protest performance. Nevertheless it is to the intra-regional geography of protest that we now turn and, given the significantly different pattern exhibited by the mainland and southern islands, it is appropriate that we turn to these first.

The Mainland and the Southern Islands

Here what is immediately apparent is that, with both the threat to raid and the refusal to hand back land leased under Defence of the Realm agreements emerging as separate and distinct means to protest, earlier studies have underestimated the nature and extent of disturbance in this area. This was the case even though the geography of protest in this area was far from homogenous. While threats to raid were evident across the area, actual acts of seizure were confined to a few locations. The associated processes of agricultural change were equally inconsistent spatially. In Sutherland crofters were pushed to marginal land, either on the coast or to the boundaries of their old townships. On the coast especially the plots were insufficient for subsistence but in both cases the result was land hunger – the desire to extend the existing areas of cultivation. On Tiree raiding was more a function of overcrowding on those crofts created in an early attempt to accommodate a rising population without recourse to clearance.

The only agitation on the mainland during the war years came from the Ross of Mull. In November 1914 applicants for land from Bunessan issued a general threat to raid. The Board's sub-commissioner believed that it was 'quite possible the threat .... will be carried out' and his senior reported that 'we have had much trouble .... in this district' believing that the local minister was responsible. This threat was repeated in December and January and again in 1917. At this time the Board's correspondent (not the minister) wrote that 'As one who has had a great deal to do with recruiting and persuading Parents to let their sons join the Colours, I feel bound to call attention to this dilettanteism by which these noble and self-sacrificing parents may suffer hunger and deprivation.' Applications resumed in 1919 and were almost exclusively peaceable.[7]

Whilst raiding did not occur in the Ross of Mull, a similar combination of Board inactivity and war service brought about raiding in Tiree. This agitation

7 R. I. P. D. 11077, Ardachy, Argyll; N. A. S. AF 83/287, letter from A. R. Campbell (J.P.) to Board of Agriculture 17 March 1917.

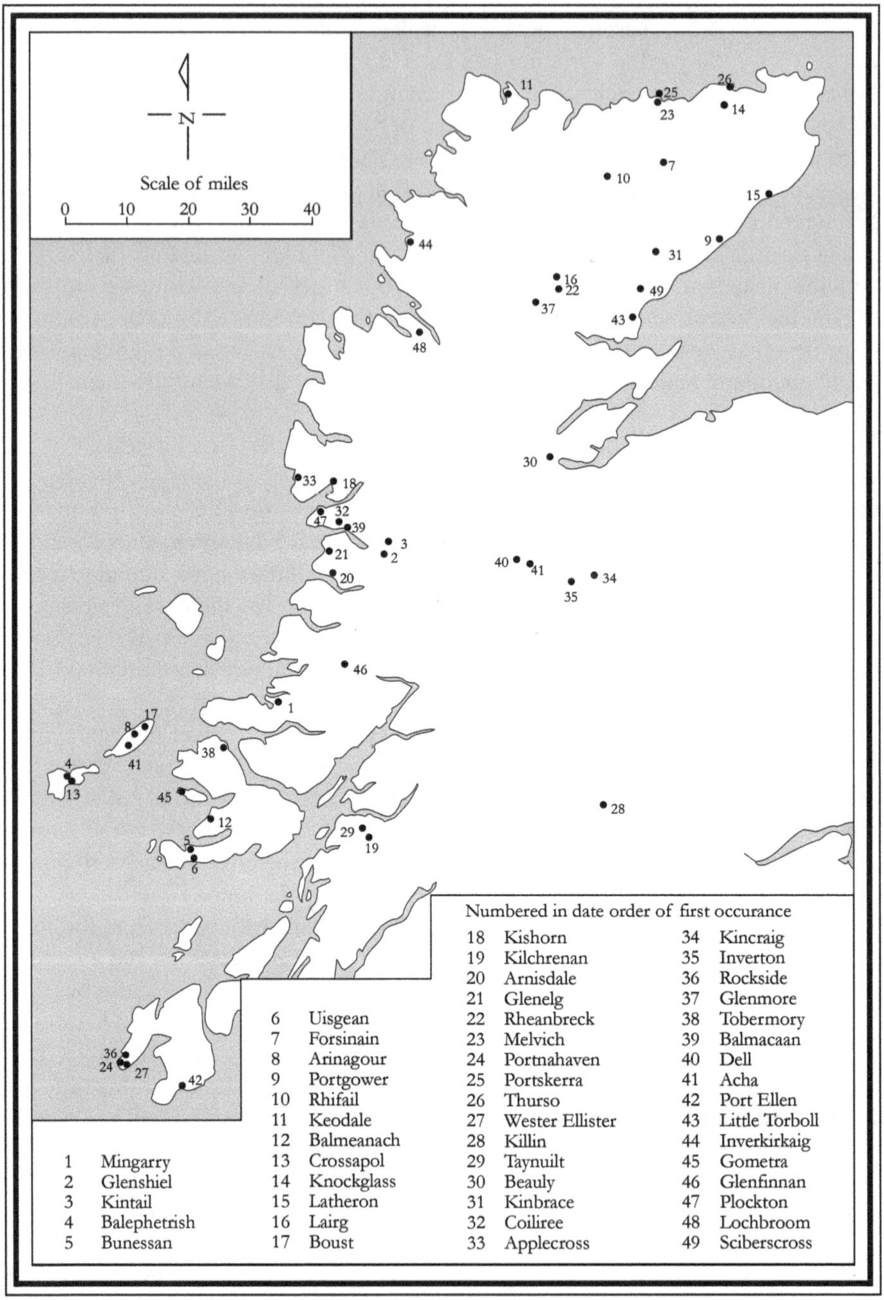

Figure 4.3 Locations of protest on the mainland and southern islands

was centred on a number of farms, was complex and long-running and involved a combination of illegal and more peaceable activities. Proposed schemes of land settlement originated with the Congested Districts Board and, in December 1912 in response to a threat, these proposals were revived. Repeated threats ensured urgent action and, in 1914, the Board received official approval to put the scheme into operation, a decision which was made known in the area. Due to the size of the compensation award the Board unfortunately decided to withdraw. However, this decision came too late to prevent the utilisation of holdings already marked out and in June of that year the Board received a letter expressing both surprise that the holdings were not officially in the possession of those working the land and stating the determination of these individuals to continue with their cultivation. Peaceful agitation resumed in March 1916 but the same compensation issues still prevented the Board of Agriculture from acting, although they did consider a scheme for potato ground. Peace did not last long and, in December 1917, that part of Balephetrish that had been marked out by the Board for lots was forcibly occupied by nine cottars from the district. The raiders were interdicted and, in April 1918, they were sentenced to ten days imprisonment for breach. On release they re-occupied the land. There was much bitterness between tenant and raiders but finally, in July, the tenant agreed that the raided land should be included in a Defence of the Realm scheme.[8]

With the end of the war the proprietor, the Duke of Argyll, in anticipation of renewed agitation with demobilisation, offered the farms of Balephetrish, Reef and Crossapol as smallholdings at the expiry of the lease on Whitsunday 1922. Whilst the majority of applicants acquiesced, the delay did bring a number of threats, particularly from cottars. Towards the end of the lease another difficulty became apparent. The scheme removed the potato plots given to the cottars under the earlier agreement as the proprietor preferred large holdings. The capital required to obtain this type of holding meant that few of the cottars gained access to the farms. Once again the majority appear to have acquiesced, although some threats were made to seize the land.[9]

What this micro-study of agitation on Tiree reveals is that the agitators appeared ready to move between protest and more peaceful activities almost at will; a clear indication of the sophisticated nature of the tactics of local negotiation deployed in their attempts to win the land. This study further reveals that land agitation events on Tiree did not end in a clear-cut way. This too is of wider significance.

Despite the fact that the land had been broken for smallholdings on Islay cottar dissatisfaction with the way in which this had been done continued to manifest itself until 1926 at least and caused conflict within the local community.[10] The literature on protest elsewhere tends to ignore the impact of such an event on a

8 N. A. S. AF 83/249; AF 83/250; N. A. S. AF 67/165.

9 N. A. S. AF 83/250; AF83/251; AF83/252; AF83/267.

10 N. A. S. AF 83/250; AF 83/267, 3 December Archibald MacLean and 15 others to Board of Agriculture for Scotland.; AF83/267, 14 June 1921 J. McInnes and eight others to

location or group once it had ceased. As with work on Tiree this is an important omission.

The longevity of much of the agitation for land is both a remarkable testament to the tenacity of those who desired land and to the power of land and landscape as a motive to protest. The cultural depth of this is further revealed in the disturbances on the island of Coll. Here, in June 1918, six applicants from Arinagour wrote that 'Our Fathers had this farm Sixty Two years ago and the landlord took it from them, and we are going to take charge in the beginning of October'. Here, as in other places in the southern islands, the pattern was of initial applications bringing about the consideration of a scheme and then, if progress was slow, reminders by way of threats to seize would be forthcoming albeit with rare recourse to actual seizure. A scheme for the whole of Arinagour was agreed in May 1922.[11]

On the mainland only in Sutherland is there evidence of agitation for land during the war years and even there raiding did not take place until 1918. In May six men and four women took possession of land on West Garty farm. They were rapidly interdicted and, remaining in possession, were arrested in July for breach of interdict. The men were eventually sentenced to ten days in jail and the women one. Hunter believes that the women were given an equal term: this is not so. Since they had little support in the area the raiders did not re-occupy the land on their release and they failed to coerce the Board into breaking up the farm.[12]

Demobilisation saw an increase in agitation, most especially in Sutherland where the ex-service crofter applicants of Durness began two years of agitation for land at Keodale. The Board eventually purchased the estate after receiving many letters and threats to raid. In the same area, both Armadale and Forsinaird farms came under threat during 1919. The former was rapidly purchased to prevent a raid whilst the Board decided not to interfere with the latter because it was held by six crofters as a club farm. Despite this, Forsinaird was raided in June 1922.[13] This action by cottars against crofters clearly brings into question the notion of a supposed unity within the crofting community and the over deterministic assumptions of class conflict between tenantry and landowners upon which this putative unity was seen to rest. As will be discussed in much greater depth in the following chapter, these events of protest once again reveal that conflict in the Highlands and Islands was significantly more complex than hitherto believed and any explanation of them therefore needs to acknowledge this.

Board of Agriculture for Scotland.; AF67/165; R. I. P. D.49751 Land Seizures General, 9 April 1926, reports seven applicants to raid Scarinish Farm.

11 R. I. P. D.2731/C/1, Arinagour, Coll; R. I. P. D.2731/M, Arinagour, letter from six applicants at Arinagour31 June 1918; R. I. P. D.2732/B, Acha and Kilbride, Coll; N. A. S. AF67/167; Malcolm Kennedy and Kenneth McKinnon to Scottish Office, 16 December 1920.

12 N. A. S. AF67/166, general threat of raid, 23 March 1920; AF67/64, Duncan Carmichael threat to Geisgeir farm, 8 February 1923; James Hunter, *The Making*, p. 196.

13 R. I. P. D.25910/1, Keodale. R. I. P. D.46841/1, Armadale; N. A. S. AF67/65.

Indicative of this complexity and of the gestures written into it is the sequence of seizures which began at Kirkton Farm in Sutherland. Here, on 28 May 1920, fourteen men from Portskerra marched onto Kirkton, proclaimed possession and marched home. They repeated these formalities two weeks later. On both occasions the raiders informed the Board of their intentions without gaining a response beyond warnings of the likely consequences of their actions. Given the public sympathy that this engendered and the fact that they were mandated to instigate schemes of land settlement, Board members found it difficult to justify their inaction in this case. In addition, the numbers of those working the ground was increasing. The result was a reluctant compromise in which the 'raiders were agreeable to remove the stock from the farm on getting an undertaking that the Board would make the land available.'[14]

Across 1919 and 1920, even if actual land seizure was limited by the standards elsewhere, agitation and protest events became apparent in other Highland counties including Caithness – which was not always seen as a crofting or protest location. As elsewhere farms were being broken up as a result of protest actions, particularly, as at Barcaldine in Argyll, if the protesting group was a large one, and the numbers and incidence of these events continued to increase into 1921. It was during this year that the majority of the leasing arrangements carried out under the Defence of the Realm Act began to expire. This inevitably generated tensions. At Glenelg and Strathcarron the crofters refused to remove their stock and the pursuit of a scheme for permanent holdings ensued. At Balmacaan a deadlock was reached with the crofters refusing to remove stock, the proprietor unwilling to take legal action to remove them and the Board of Agriculture feeling unable to bring in a permanent scheme. Stock were still illegally grazing the forest in 1924.[15]

Agitation on the mainland declined earlier than was the case in the Hebrides. Nevertheless threats continued to be regularly received by the Board until 1929 which ensured that they continued to act with a caution which events continued to justify. In October 1926, for instance, the decision by the Board to re-sell Eriboll Farm, Sutherland, caused sufficient feeling to necessitate a police presence at the valuation.[16] The Board also had to continue to face a variety of protest forms. As with the Defence of the Realm-based events, the more informal protest device (which often followed the ending of a Defence of the Realm agreement) was most common on the mainland. At Glenganisp, as with Balmacaan, the proprietor had tolerated the illegal grazing of crofters' stock in the Deer Forest for more than a decade prior to 1936 when ownership changed. The new owners were not so tolerant.[17]

---

14 N. A. S. AF67/65.

15 R. I. P. D.34315/1 Eileanreach Deer Forest; R. I. P. D.35809 Glenmore; R. I. P. D.40928 Balmaccan Deer Forest.

16 R. I. P. D.26788/2/2, Eriboll, Sutherland.

17 N. A. S. AF 67/156, R. McLeod to Scottish Office, 12 June 1923; R. I. P. D.38609 Glencanisp.

In many respects what occurred at Glenganisp typifies events of protest on the mainland. Clearly they lacked the intensity of those elsewhere and the range of motivation. Only rarely, it would seem, were there the overt and direct expressions of ideological and conflictual views of the sort expressed by Alexander Murray who threatened to seize land on Sciberscross farm because 'my people were ever on it'.[18] Even here the ideological underpinnings lack the depth of those found much more frequently in other areas. This and the fact that overt expressions of the ideology of landholding were largely confined to the Western Isles parallels related shifts in the earlier geography of protest and the causal agencies which gave rise to expressions of resistance. Perhaps as a function of landlords' lack of concern to protect their property; perhaps as a function of the amount of land encompassed by mainland estates, protests in this area more easily and more often (comparatively speaking) metamorphosed into its informal form. The commitment to protest was clearly there; it simply took the most contextually appropriate form. Once again, the need to investigate protest in its local context and through the locale is clearly demonstrated.

Skye

For Skye, the key local contexts were the negotiations between the Board of Agriculture and the MacLeod estate over the purchase of a number of their properties and threats of illegal action being generated by the Board's behaviour. An early example of the latter was an enlargement scheme at Monkstadt, in June 1914. On its completion, groups of those who failed to gain inclusion in the scheme threatened raids and complaints were received from those whose summer grazing had been taken over by the scheme, highlighting once again the fact that the resolution of protest events could be generative of further conflict. Agitation re-surfaced in 1922 and peaked in October with the partially successful threat of a rent strike; an important echo of a key early protest device[19]

As in all other areas, once the War began land seizures on Skye were limited being confined to just two places, Kyleakin and Sconser. Both were prompted by disputes over access to land, the former with the proprietor's agents, the latter with the township's crofters and this continued until 1939 at least. A similarly long-running agitation occurred in Waternish. From March 1919, groups of crofters from the townships of Geary, Hallin and Gillin (spelling varies; Gillen on Figure 4.4) threatened land seizures. Eventually, and as a result of a public meeting, the crofters of Waternish decided to act as one group. Further threats were received in 1921 and 1923 during which time the Board was negotiating a scheme but in 1925 a change of proprietor meant that negotiations had to begin again. This caused the

18 N. A. S. AF83/403, letter Alexander Murray to Board of Agriculture, 8 March 1929.

19 R. I. P. D. Monkstadt, 6204/B, letter to Board of Agriculture for Scotland; 10 October 1914.

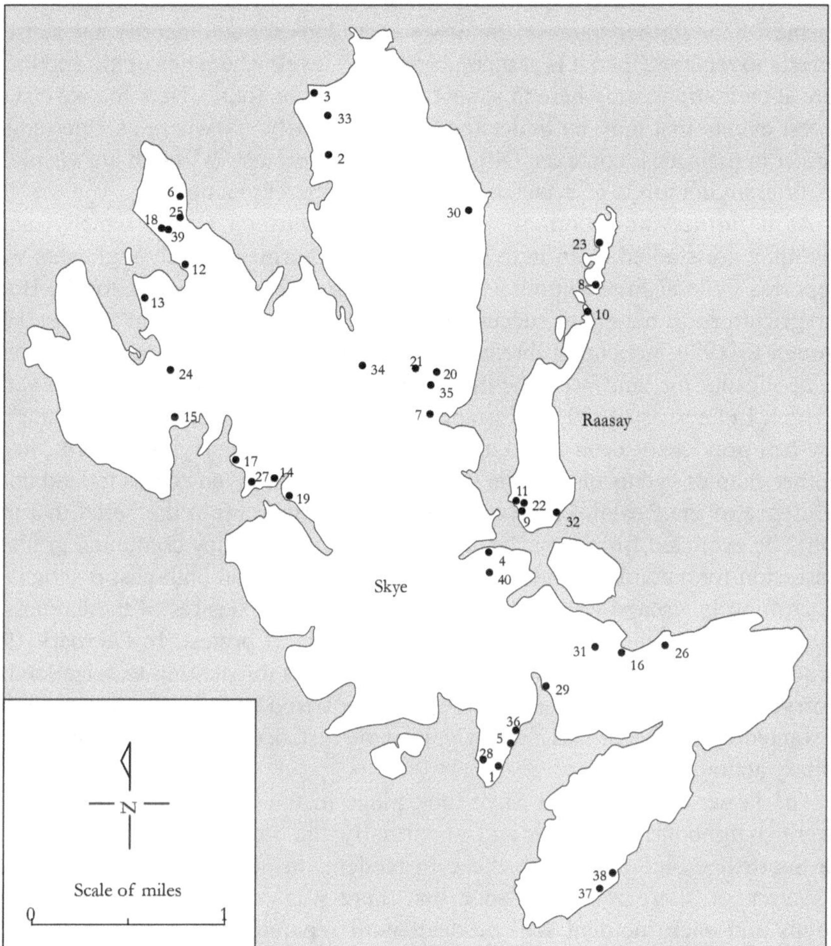

Numbered in date order of first occurance

1	Glasnakille	11	Clachan	21	Scorrybreck	31	Swordale
2	Totscore	12	Lusta	22	Home Farm, Raasay	32	Fearns & Eyre
3	Bornesketaig	13	Claigan	23	Dry Harbour	33	Kilmuir
4	Sconser	14	Bracadale	24	Dunvegan	34	Skeabost
5	Drinan	15	Orbost	25	Gillen	35	Achachork
6	Geary	16	Broadford	26	Breakish	36	Kilmore
7	Portree	17	Ebost	27	Ullinish	37	Tormore
8	Rona	18	Hallin	28	Elgol	38	Calligary
9	Inverarish	19	Gesto	29	Kilbride	39	Dunhallin
10	Kyle Rona	20	Scorrybreck	30	Lealt	40	Sconser Deer Forest

Figure 4.4 Locations of protest on Skye and Raasay

crofters to send a series of threats to raid and the Board to prepare a compulsory scheme.[20] This further suggests that if we are to look for and identify any sense of protest movements, then it is at this sub-regional level, where ties of kin and locale were at their strongest, where this most often might be found. Here too we can see protest events that may be understood homogenously elsewhere as emerging as distinct in their local contexts. Different targets of protestors' wrath are visible, as are different durations of events and the use of different tactics.

As a further indication of the differences between events which emerge once they are studied at an individual level, in Duirinish parish applicants were supported by their Free Church Minister. Here too, the time it took for the Board of Agriculture to negotiate successfully with the proprietor, from at least 1919 through to 1924, generated threats to raid as reminders of the serious intent of the applicants for land.[21] Furthermore these threats could be extended to actual seizures. In February 1920, for instance, six men from Portree seized the land that they had previously been given as potato ground. On Scorrybreck Farm, in yet another echo of events elsewhere, those who had been given access to land under a Defence of the Realm Act scheme, refused to give it up in the belief that they would be excluded from the scheme under negotiation. They continued in illegal possession for a number of years. It is clear, therefore, that both past practice and the crofting landscape were crucial formulations in the desires of the landless to obtain land and that these also drove forward acts of protest. In February 1921 Farquhar Macrae sent the last of a number of letters threatening to seize land on Scorrybreck in which he stated that the holding offered by the Board was too large; he wanted four acres or less.[22] Clearly, in some instances, overt protest could be a solitary action.

The larger land raids on Skye took place in the vicinity of Broadford, on several neighbouring estates and at virtually the same time. The Board and the Scottish Office dealt with these in tandem. In contrast to what happened at Waternish, there is no evidence that there was collusion between the two groups and each incident will be dealt with separately here, as far as this is possible. The origins of the Strathaird raid lie with the failure of the applicants to gain holdings on Glasnakille (spelling varies; Glasnakillie on Figure 4.4) and Drinan when they were created by the Board in 1918. Written threats to raid were not received until October 1920 and, at first, were aimed at any part of Strathaird but they were later concentrated on Romaston. A public meeting, held on 11 November 1922, decided that Romaston should be raided on 5 December. This raid was carried out by seven men from Elgol. The proprietor

20 N. A. S. AF67/299; R. I. P. D.1611 Sconser; AF67/155; AF67/156; R. I. P. D.2659/M/1, Waternish.

21 N. A. S. AF67/146; AF67/147; R. I. P. D.27011, Bracadale. R. I. P. D.27011 Bracadale..

22 N. A. S. AF67/147, Farquhar Macrae to Board of Agriculture for Scotland, 5 February 1921; R. I. P. D.5863/M, Scorrybreck; 5863/1, Scorrybreck; 5863/C, Scorrybreck.

obtained an interdict but this was ignored. In February 1923 the raiders were summoned for breach of interdict. Their agent, Donald Shaw, spoke for them in words which have a wider resonance: 'Cottars in Skye and other parts of the Highlands have never considered themselves as being in breach of any moral law in laying claim to cultivate some of the lands held by their forefathers.' And yet, from conversations held in Elgol, it would seem that this statement cannot be strictly applied to the raiders. Their primary motivation was not to reclaim land perceived as rightfully theirs but was the result of the new proprietor failing to give them Romaston, which had been promised to them by the previous landowner in return for their war service. By contrast, the archival evidence points to a deeper attachment to land and to strong anti-landlord sentiments. On 29 January 1924 John Grant, one of the raiders, wrote to the Scottish Office complaining about their failure to break up the estate which was 'the property of an English Capitalist who only visits ... for a few months in the Year and keeps it purely for Sporting Purposes'. He expected to be offered land on the estate 'where we and our People have been reared' and failed 'to see why, In order to Please any Sportsman, we should be removed from our own territory and separated from our own people here'. The raiders were sentenced to six months imprisonment but national politics intervened. Facing a parliamentary debate on the incident, the government reached an agreement with the opposition by which the raiders were to be offered land on Skye by the end of 1924, in return for an opposition agreement not to press their case. This result proved unsatisfactory to the raiders who issued further threats, although they took no further direct action and only two, John Grant and Alexander MacKinnon, took up the offer of crofts.[23]

Raiding on Kilbride followed similar lines. A scheme for enlargements and new holdings, first proposed in 1913, was abandoned due to the war. Demand for land resumed in 1919 and, given the local feeling that promises of land had been ignored, the first threat to raid came, via the local United Free Church Minister, in December 1920. Having been persuaded by the Board's local officer to abandon plans to raid in 1920, seven men from Torrin and Kilbride informed the Board of their intention to begin cultivation in March 1921. This time they carried out their threat. In July the Board's Land Committee gave permission to re-open negotiations. These proceeded slowly and in December 1921 and March 1922 further threats were made. This was followed by a letter to the Scottish Office stating that they would again take possession in two weeks. This time the raid led to the Board's decision to suspend negotiations until the raiders withdrew. They did not; in the spring of 1923 the raiders were interdicted with a summons for breach issued in June. Before this could be served the Board made it known that, in the light of the decision to reinstate the Strathaird raiders to the list of applicants for land, they were considering re-opening negotiations. The serving of

23 *Dundee Advertiser* 28 February 1923; N. A. S. AF16/158, John Grant to Scottish Office 29 January 1924; AF67/158.

the warrant nevertheless proceeded but this was resisted and the Sheriff's officer was deforced. Once they had been successfully arrested the raiders were tried and sentenced to 25 days imprisonment. They apologised to the court, were re-instated on the list of suitable applicants and gained holdings on Kilbride.[24]

A similar pattern of commitment to the cause, resistance beyond what became the norm for events after 1914 and much public, parliamentary and governmental attention (both official and unofficial) is evident in the events which led up to the purchase of the island of Raasay in 1922. This much-celebrated set of disturbances will be discussed in some detail in Chapter 6; it only remains here to suggest that the events on the island are indicative of one part of what we might identify as the transitional Skye pattern. In common with the mainland and with the other islands of the Inner Hebrides, seizures on Skye were confined to a few celebrated locations with threats to raid and informal utilisation of land comprising the bulk of the protest incidents. Nevertheless, where seizure did take place it was often undertaken with a level of intensity and commitment redolent of protest on the outer isles, to which we now turn.

The Southern Hebrides

Whilst there are a number of similarities in the expressions of protest (and most importantly in their ownership contexts) there is sufficient difference between the manifestations of protest on the conjoined islands of Lewis and Harris and those on the rest of the Outer Hebrides to justify a separate discussion of these areas.

As suggested by Figure 4.5 the islands from Barra and Vatersay in the south, through South Uist, Benbecula and North Uist, to Berneray in the north, comprised an area of almost constant agitation from 1907 (and earlier) until 1925 and these events exhibit patterns and depths to protest both rarely articulated in the extant literature and only apparent when investigated at this sub-regional level. Equally importantly, whilst the seizure of farms on Barra and Vatersay was seen as a focal point of disturbance before 1914, agitation after the onset of World War One, on Barra especially, was no less intense and significant.[25]

Agitation and disturbances over Eoligarry, the last large farm on Barra, was one of the most fraught and celebrated protests of any that occurred after 1914. The causes of this protest were multiple and complex but they centred around the fact that, notwithstanding a general fall in numbers, population remained high on the island, and that there was considerable over-crowding and consequent

24 N. A. S. AF67/157; N. A. S. AF67/157; R. I. P. D.5809/A Kilbride; N. A. S. AF67/151, 30 January 1923 Board of Agriculture for Scotland memo; R. I. P. D. 5809/C Kilbride; D.5809/C/1, Kilbride, letter from Free Church manse 7 December 1920, letter from seven correspondents from Torrin 28 February 1921, decision of land committee 7 July 1921; N. A. S. AF67/157, police report of raid 18 March 1921, police report of second raid 29 November 1922.

25 James.Hunter, *The Making*, p. 192; L. Leneman, *Fit For Heroes*, p. 106.

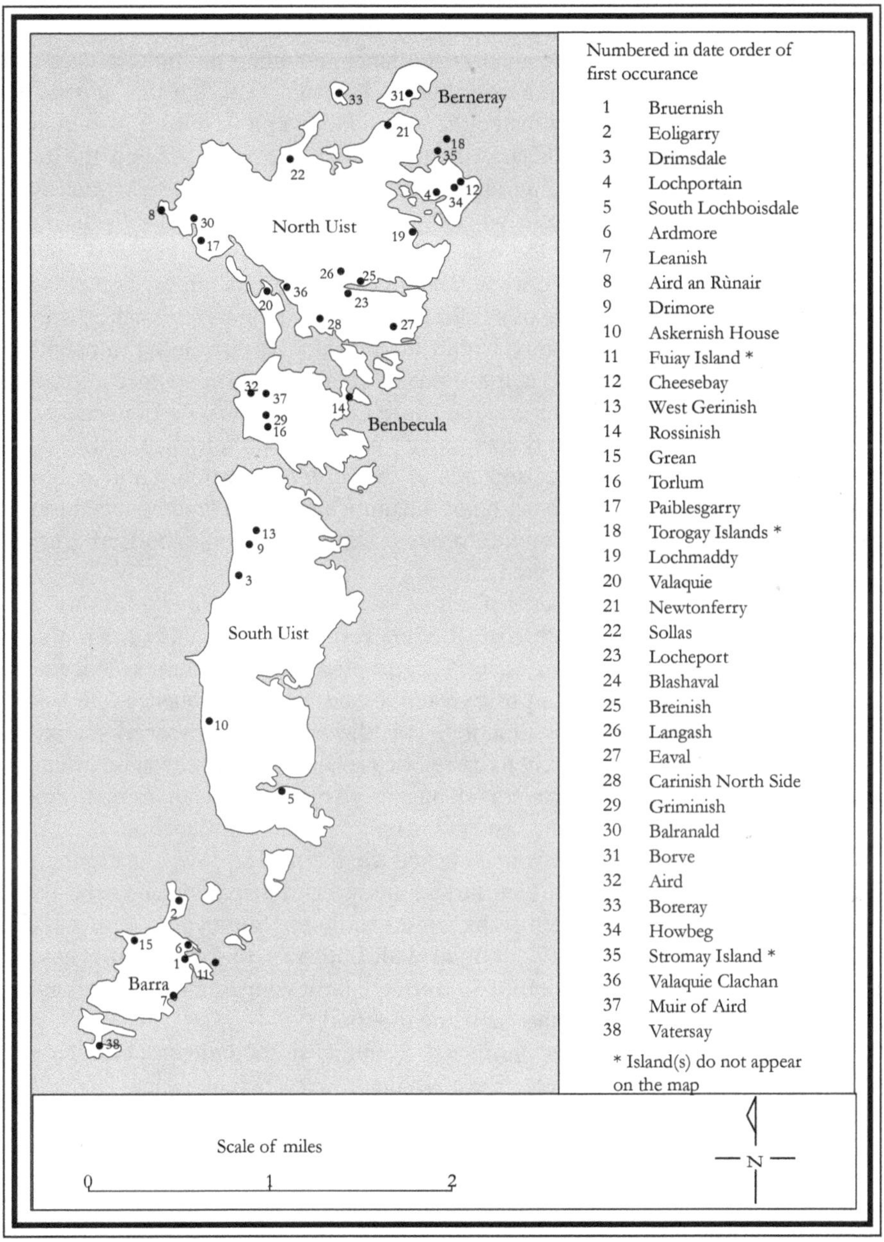

Figure 4.5 Locations of protest on the Southern Hebrides

land exhaustion; all of which underpins the final significant causal factor, that of crofter/cottar tensions. After much disturbance including multiple raiding and house building, the Board acquired Eoligarry Farm in 1919, but this appears to have served only to have exacerbated the situation. Over a year after its purchase the land had not been fenced, large numbers of cattle were grazing the farm and the numbers of those raiding and house building had increased. Moreover, critical divisions within the land working tenantry had emerged with the farm ultimately being divided along these fault lines between those cottars who wanted new, small crofts and those who wanted enlargements to existing crofts.[26] As with protests elsewhere, this writing of conflict into the landscape raises other, deeper questions over assertions of unity within the tenantry. It also failed to calm the situation and did not meet sub-commissioner Thomas Wilson's expectation that this purchase would 'bring to an end the Barra Land Problem'. Portions had been held back for the (locally hugely unpopular) farmers and their shepherds but all that this prompted were further seizures of the reserved portion. Ultimately the Board were forced to take the position of the more aggressive landowners through the interdicting of one of the raiding groups. Despite this, unauthorised grazing continued and further threats were issued.[27]

A remarkably similar pattern of cause, actions and sentiments during and after protest is evident on South Uist. Raiding resumed early in 1918 at multiple locations and often more than once. The proprietrix of the farms concerned, Lady Gordon Cathcart, took no positive action and, as a consequence, the Board were compelled to legalise the situation. This did not always proceed smoothly, however. At Askernish agreement to carry out a scheme was reached and holdings were allocated by ballot. The raiders felt aggrieved by the inclusion of non-raiders and the pre-allocation of holdings and at the ballot 'when Mr MacKinnon ... came forward ... some person or persons knocked the hat upside down, scattering the contents ... The ex-servicemen then turned around and marched round the Farm ... and pulled up all the wooden stobs put down by the Surveyors.' A successful ballot took place in February 1921 but, as with Eoligarry, this did not prevent the unsuccessful raiders from continuing to work the farm with grazing disputes again characterising the immediate post-settlement period.[28]

As was the case on other farms on South Uist, raiding at Drimore and Drimsdale was an annual event. Because these were neighbouring farms, the Board of Agriculture tended to treat them as one although there is actually very little evidence to suggest concerted action or the mingling of groups. Events of protest, both here and more generally, were more often primarily the actions of

26 R. I. P. D.1164/C. Eoligarry; N. A. S. AF67/145, letter from Secretary for Scotland to Board of Agriculture for Scotland, 15 November 1917; AF67/157; N. A. S. AF67/143.

27 R. I. P. D.1164/C, Eoligarry; 1164/RA Eoligarry; N. A. S. AF67/145, Thomas Wilson to Board of Agriculture for Scotland, 7 November 1917.

28 N. A. S. AF67/146; AF67/152; AF67/147; AF83/190; AF83/191, report from N. MacLean to Board of Agriculture for Scotland, 8 October 1920; AF83/200.

discrete groups who had intentions towards very specific parcels of land, often connected to (or to a belief in) past occupation and clearance. Once again, a sense of a wider social movement beyond that of Jones's 'meta-movement' is hard to discern. Nevertheless raiding occurred contiguously on both farms in 1919, 1920 and 1921. Moreover, in each instance a similarly complex set of motives were expressed. Raiding was the product of the breaking of war-time promises of land; the success of the Askernish raiders; and the possibility that the farm might be given as enlargements when the raiders wanted wholly new holdings. Unusually, however, the raiders withdrew from these farms once land division schemes had been agreed upon.[29]

On North Uist (which is separated from South Uist by Benbecula) raiding resumed in 1918 when the Ard an Runair and Paiblesgarry portions of Balranald farm were seized in March. These proved to be relatively short-lived incidents and the next significant event did not occur until May 1920 when prospective raiders wrote to the Board of Agriculture expressing their determination to recover land 'which was taken from them about 1920' and which 'they look on as their own to the present day'. On the 3rd December 'led by Donald Ewen McDonald on the pipes we headed for Paiblesgarry and started dividing Paiblesgarry into plots'.[30] From this point forward the actions taken by raiders highlight a difference within protest that only becomes apparent if these are studied at the local level. It is clear that on the Uists, Benbecula and Barra emotions within the tenantry were at a significantly higher level than in other areas. Here a reversion to the level of confrontation and resistance of the 1880s can be seen and the response to their actions by the landowners was equally retrograde. Each side followed key aspects of the model as laid out by Eric Richards for the earlier period.[31] Thus the raiders at Newton forcibly prevented the proprietor from working the land and, in January 1921, were interdicted. When the Sheriff's Officer came to serve the formal papers they were seized and burnt. As a result of this the raiders were sentenced to 30 days imprisonment but, when the police arrived to arrest them, this was prevented by a large crowd assembled for that purpose. They were ultimately arrested in August but were released (and here we meet with the one factor which perhaps most often and most directly differentiates post-1918 protest from that which preceded it) in time to be included in the ballot for holdings. Despite their law-breaking they retained a chance to secure land. Driven by popular sentiment throughout Scotland and by their legislative obligations, the Board of Agriculture had moved to reach agreement over a settlement scheme with the proprietrix. That this was successful

29 Jones, *Finding Captain Swing*; N. A. S. AF67/152; AF83/207; AF83/208; N. AF83/209; AF83/212; AF83/213.

30 N. A. S. AF67/152; R. I. P. D.8185/C/2, Balranald.

31 See Table 1.1 and Richards *Problems*, pp. 39–40, *Highland Clearances Vol. 2*, pp. 333–4; Withers *Gaelic Scotland*, p. 353.

is testimony to the changed atmosphere of the post-war era. Nevertheless post-settlement tensions remained evident until 1923 at least.[32]

The underlying pattern of land tensions in this area was remarkably consistent. Schemes did eventually emerge although overcrowding continued and continued to generate frustrations. These were exacerbated by the general perception that the Board of Agriculture moved slowly and reluctantly to carry out their responsibilities whilst, on their part, the Board felt the frustration of being opposed by intransigent landlords and their agents. To imagine protest embodying anything other than the highly complex context in which it occurs is to do it a disservice. We must not, for instance, ignore the complexities and affectual force added by war service. Thus the formal taking of land at Lochmaddy Parks in January 1920 began with a meeting at The Comrades of the Great War clubroom from whence a group marched in a military formation onto the ground. After their claims were pegged out the men danced 'a Scotch Reel'. Approximately eight acres was seized and, in December, this land was still being worked by nine of the raiders.[33] Here too we must note that the actions which signified the continuation of the occupation were work tasks. This fact has significant implications for how we might continue to interpret Highland protests.

The early 1920s were the period of most intense disturbance on North Uist. Very many letters threatening seizure were received by the Board of Agriculture and the Scottish Office during this period with a significant raid occurring at Newton and more minor incidents recorded at Breinish, Blashaval and Langash.[34] It is, nevertheless, important to acknowledge the presence of a different response to the frustrations and circumstances which generated the protests, that of emigration.[35] Whilst this process has been extensively discussed elsewhere, the connections between emigration and protest have been explored less often. On the outbreak of war emigrants would, on occasion, return to join a Highland regiment and would, less frequently, use the threat of having to return abroad as leverage to obtain land. Similarly, the occasional correspondent would write in threatening terms from abroad. Presumably in instances such as these, the proxy actant would be a family member or friend in the area. In addition, and in more significant numbers, correspondents of both the Board of Agriculture and the Scottish Office

32 N. A. S. AF67/150; AF67/151; R. I. P. D.268814/2, Locheport. R. I. P. D.26814/M/1, Locheport, letter to Board of Agriculture for Scotland, 18 January 1922; R. I. P. D.26814/1 Newton; R. I. P. D. 26814/M/1 Locheport.

33 N. A. S. AF67/148, police report 10 January 1920 and 21 January 1920.

34 N. A. S. AF67/150; AF67/151; R. I. P. D.268814/2, Locheport; 26814/M/1, Locheport, letter to Board of Agriculture for Scotland, 18 January 1922; 26814/1 Newton; 26814/M/1 Locheport.

35 Harper Marjory, *Scotland No More?: The Scots Who Left Scotland in The Twentieth Century* (Edinburgh: Luath Press, 2012); Harper, Marjory, and Evans, Nicholas, J. 'Socio-economic Dislocation and Inter-war Emigration to Canada and the United States: A Scottish Snapshot', *The Journal of Imperial and Commonwealth History*, Vol. 34, No. 4 (2006): 529–52.

would draw together the two processes. In 1922 correspondents from North Uist suggested that 'we do not want to leave the land of our forefathers but ... I see nothing else desirable but Emigration'. The Board of Agriculture used this, and other actions, as reason to move to purchase Newton Farm.[36]

The island of Benbecula is located between South and North Uist and disturbances there reveal similar patterns to those elsewhere in the Outer Hebrides. Threats to land and actual raids occurred early and frequently. The proprietrix, Lady Gordon Cathcart, or her representatives, reacted with hostility, intransigence and recourse to the law. The raiders were equally stubborn and, in their refusal to yield the ground that they had seized, they virtually forced the Board of Agriculture (as they conceded) to attempt to introduce a scheme. This proved difficult to achieve and failed to both satisfy the demand for land and to halt the protest. As the then Chairman of the Board, Sir Robert Greig, reported to his counterpart in the Scottish Office: 'Uist is in the same position as Lewis was, viz. more applications for land than there is land to subdivide. In time I expect the Government will be compelled to utilise all available land for small holdings and enlargements.' This was in 1925 when, according to Greig, Langash was the only 'farm remaining in North Uist not settled by us.' It was broken up for enlargements in 1926.[37]

There is no record of any written threats to Langash although it is clear that local crofters had kept sheep on the ground (illegally) 'for years'.[38] This absence of any new protest event mirrors the experience of those on Benbecula and the Uists as a whole. After about 1924 incidents of protest declined exponentially, but, indicative of the enduring power of the desire for land, of the utility of the sub-regional perspective and of the particular manifestation of these processes on North Uist, land raiding reappears here well after the end of World War Two. In June 1951 crofters from Balmartin wrote to the Department of Agriculture stressing their need for enlargements to their existing crofts. The local sub-commissioner recommended no action, partly on the grounds that it would generate agitation for land elsewhere. The Department took his advice. In 1952, however, Balelone bordering on Balmartin, came up for sale and the Department considered making a bid but, once again, the advice they received was in the negative. Inevitably, a move such as this would have become known in the locality and, when no offer was forthcoming, would have generated frustration amongst the applicants. This generated the first threat to seize land on the 18th November. This was subsequently postponed until the 28th to allow the local M.P. to intercede but this time there was no postponement and, on the appointed day, four men, with the support of the Presbytery of South Uist, took part in a very public demonstration of their intention to have the land. They subsequently

---

36 R. I. P. D.26814/M/1, Locheport, letter to Board of Agriculture for Scotland 18 January 1922.

37 N. A. S. AF83/238; AF83/245; AF83/246; AF67/154; AF83/786 letter from Greig to Rose, 1 July 1925.

38 N. A. S. AF83/786, report from (sub-commissioner) James Coull to Board of Agriculture, September 1925.

signalled their intention to take no further action until the publication of the Taylor Commission report. According to Angus Macleod, who took a central, active role in the Commission, the submission of this report was looked forward to throughout the crofting counties. In the case of Balmartin, despite the perceived inadequacies of the solutions proposed by Taylor, a positive outcome was eventually reached. The newly-established Crofters Commission reported on this issue in 1957 in favour of breaking up part of Balelone farm for extensions to existing crofts. The Department of Agriculture acquired this land by compulsory purchase in February 1959. This was the last successful land raid and, as such, exists as a small challenge to the current view that, post-1945, Highlanders were predominanftly 'disorganised, demoralized and lacking in conviction that crofting life could be sufficiently improved to entice a younger generation.'[39]

It was of course on behalf of this generation (as well as their own) that the land agitators were acting. Whether their actions were sufficiently nuanced to allow for the recognition that there was no further land available for sub-division (always a contentious claim), whether the emigration of the 1920s reduced demand or whether they simply ran out of energy (or a combination of any or all of the above), is unclear. Whatever the cause, there can be no doubt that, by 1923, the intense wave of post-war disturbances in this area had broken. Protest continued, mainly in the form of threatening letters, and was indeed resumed after 1945, but at a much reduced level. This pattern was different to that on Lewis and Harris.

Lewis and Harris

Alongside the holdings of Lady Gordon Cathcart, Lord Leverhulme's proprietorship of Lewis and Harris stands as the most powerful reminder of the inherent complexity, best characterised as the heterogeneous antagonistic associations, which underlay and generated local protest. On Lewis and Harris, alongside the ongoing overcrowding of the hugely restricted crofting townships, the most significant factor in terms of agitation for land was Leverhulme's development plans. Furthermore, whilst the local population declined after 1921, overcrowding remained a problem well into the 1930s. This produced sustained pressure on land and caused the Board's official to comment that 'It does not surprise me that they broke the law ... what does surprise me is that they kept the law so long'. It is unsurprising therefore, that protest began early here, with raids in a number of areas and on the island of Taransay in April 1914.[40] Notwithstanding this upsurge, which

39 Fraser Grigor, *Highland Resistance*; R. I. P. D. 115549/1 Balmartin; personal correspondence Angus Macleod, 4 December 1992; Angus Macleod, *Crofter Fishermen*, unpublished article, Angus Macleod Archive, Kershader, Isle of Lewis, Series G, File 4, Section 31; Commission of Enquiry into Crofting Conditions, *Hansard*, 25 April, 1951; Hunter, *Claim*, pp. 72–3.

40 R. I. P. D.5549, Reef, report sub-commissioner to Board of Agriculture for Scotland, 13 April 1919; N. A. S. AF67/144.

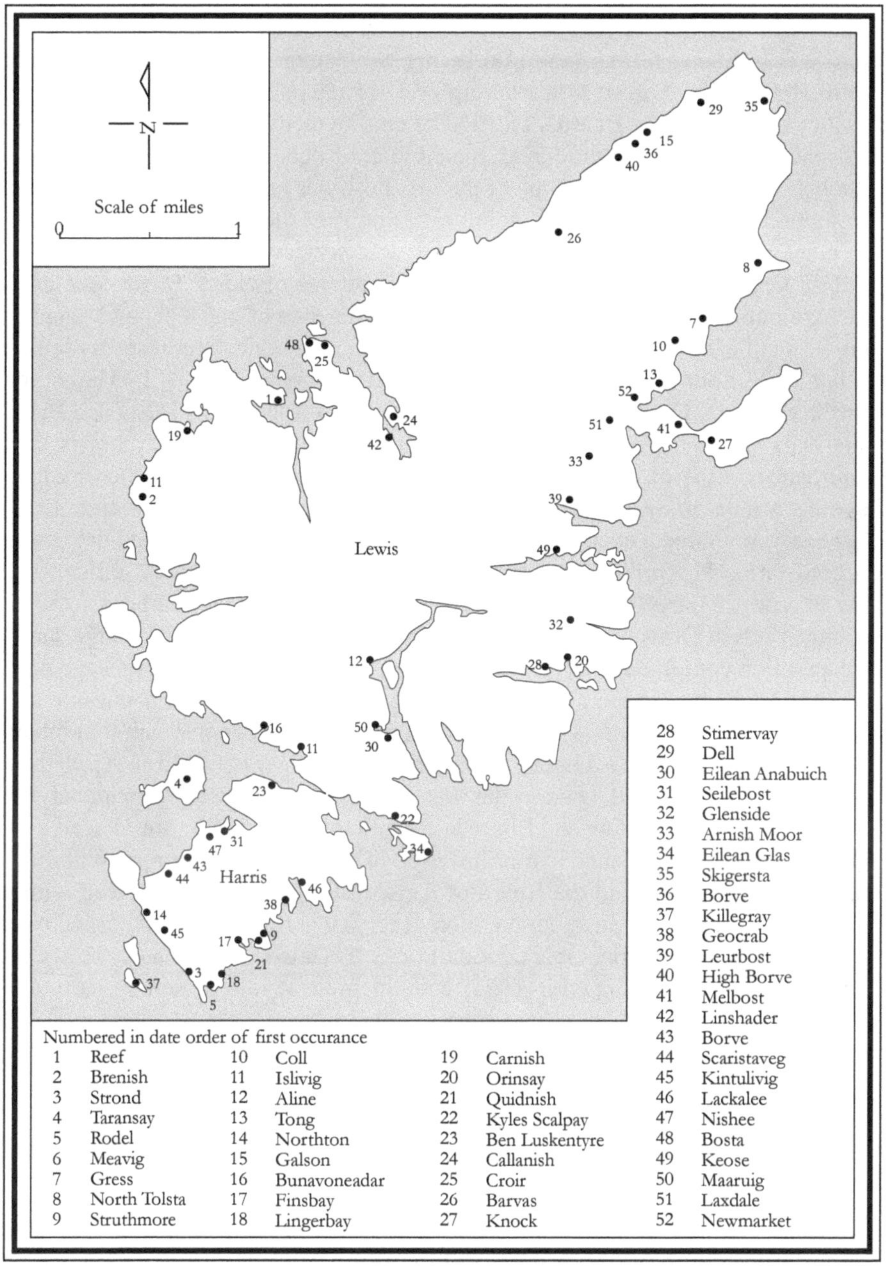

Figure 4.6 Locations of protest on Lewis and Harris

points to Lewis and Harris as the most disturbed of the areas under consideration, there was only one further land raid before November 1918, at Meavig, part of North Harris Deer Forest, in the spring of 1915. Here too a combination of the absence of support, the Board's creation of employment in road building and the call-up of the raiders into the forces, meant that the occupation was not sustained, although Meavig experienced one of the first post-war raids, in May 1919.[41]

Agitation in Lewis resumed within a fortnight of the armistice and, as noted for other areas, the motives included both war service and inherited claims to land. In February 1919 a petition from 57 inhabitants of North Tolsta concluded that 'We ourselves and our sons have fought in defence of our King and country, and we shall also fight to get the land if steps are not soon taken to see us settled on the land of our ancestors which we consider is ours by right.'[42] In March, the farm in question, Gress, was raided by a large group from North Tolsta and Back. This marked the beginning of the most celebrated of the post-war Lewis land disturbances – the often interconnected raids at Gress and Coll and ones which have been memorialised on the island (see Figure 6.6). Again, in March 1918, Coll Farm was subject to an inspection by a large group with cultivation beginning on both farms in April. By the end of the month the Board's local officer was able to report 84 crofts marked out at Gress, twelve of which had been worked, separate raids at Orinsay and Aline, and people at Tong preparing to do the same. The agitation continued to develop across the island: 'at Coll, 34 crofts have been marked and 10 have been planted ... at Tong 16 men were given about one and three-quarter acres on a grass park ... but 4 of this number together with four others took possession of the remainder of the farm'. Galson was raided in April from the Barvas township and again in the first week of May, when approximately 50 ex-servicemen from Shader and Borve laid claim to parts of the farm.[43] Faced with such widespread disturbance it must have felt to the proprietor, his representatives on the island and off, and the Board of Agriculture that they were faced with a near-uprising. This was an agitation, moreover, that carried with it the capacity to be sustained over a considerable period of time. At Galson, for instance, as at Coll and Gress, agitation resumed in 1921, with attempts to raise a raiding party and the breaking of a turf dyke to gain access to the grazings. Threats were repeated regularly through to 1923 when the farm was finally broken up.[44]

As with that of Lady Gordon Cathcart, Leverhulme's response played a central role in the shaping of the protest. Neither fully trusted the Scottish Secretary not to release any jailed raiders. Consequently both were reluctant to undertake legal

41 N. A. S. AF67/145; Personal correspondence Cathy Morrison, Meavig North Uist, 30 December 1992; N. A. S. AF67/146.

42 N. A. S. AF83/363, Petition from North Tolsta to Board of Agriculture for Scotland, 8 December 1918.

43 N. A. S. AF83/363 (supervisor) R. Graham to Board of Agriculture for Scotland, 27 April 1919; AF67/331.

44 N. A. S. AF83/363; AF67/331; AF67/391.

proceedings to remove the raiders. The result was that those in possession often remained so for a considerable time, although this was not the case at Coll and Gress. Occupation here followed the agricultural cycle and remained on a cultivation basis, although house sites were marked out. Pressure built up again in the winter of 1920 and raiding resumed in February 1921. After considerable negotiation, smallholding schemes for the farm were finally agreed with Leverhulme in 1922, although he attempted to exclude the raiders. In response to pressure from the districts, the Board ignored this, stating for Orinsay (to be settled at the same time) that, as there had been continual occupation for three years, 'to select holders other than the raiders .... would be useless' because they would be unable to remove those in occupation. Force appears not to have been considered. The creation of smallholdings at Orinsay but not at the adjacent Stimervay, brought about raiding from the disappointed applicants for the latter and both actions produced a threat to raid at Crowmore. The Stimervay raiders were interdicted but proceedings were never brought against them. Remarkably, these entirely illegal plots were still in limited occupation in 1940.[45]

Although they are significantly less celebrated today, on the island or in the literature, the disturbances on the west coast, most noticeably on Bernera and Uig, could match the intensity of those on the east coast. Here too Leverhulme was forced to make a number of farms available for smallholdings with any delay in the scheme often prompting at least a threat to seize. Things went a little further at Barvas when, in October 1921 '3 horses, 52 cattle and about 200 sheep' were on the ground, a situation which continued at least until May 1923.[46]

Only rarely did the Board of Agriculture reject all possibility of a scheme on an eligible farm. One such was Dell Farm where the cause was the presence of a mill which meant that 'it is in the best interest of the local community that the farm should remain as at present held'. Applicants for land replied that

> It is certainly to the benefit of the community that the mill be retained but there is no connection whatever between the mill and the farm. The mill was built and certain fields attached ... long before the farm was formed by forcibly ejecting the crofters from their holdings ... What we desire to have broken up ... is that park unjustly grabbed from our ancestors.[47]

The Board held firm, the farm was not raided and remained as a single unit. Elsewhere, whilst raids and threats to raid declined, 1922 was the year in which

---

45 N. A. S. AF67/326. N. A. S. AF67/331; N. A. S. AF67/151; N. A. S. AF67/292; Bob Chambers, *Life On The Edge* (Stornoway: 2011).

46 N. A. S. AF83/358; AF83/359; AF83/478, report 23 October 1921 and 15 May 1923.

47 N. A. S. AF67/151, W.Campbell to Board of Agriculture for Scotland, 14 January 1922.

the majority of organised squatting took place. The incidence of protest therefore remained high.

On Harris, agitation was often long-running and complex. Part of the reason for this was that fact that those undertaking acts of protest met with more opposition from within than did their counterparts elsewhere. Since much of the detail of this will be covered in the following chapter discussion here will be confined to a simple narrative in order to demonstrate the nature of protest on the island. Inevitably this dates back to earlier clearance. Thus, according to a solicitor from North Uist engaged by crofters from the neighbouring island of Berneray, Borve Farm (on Harris) was created from a township cleared in 1853. Agitation for the Torogay islands, which had been attached to that township, had been a near constant since then and, in January 1920, 18 out of the 24 crofters from Borve (on the island of Berneray) placed 509 sheep on Torogay. A year later the raiders were granted grazing rights on some of the islands through the Board of Agriculture's intervention, but this was not enough for some of them. A smaller number refused to remove their stock from those islands over which they had not been given rights. In this instance the Board refused to contemplate regularising the situation, arguing that 'the applicants are not in need of this land' and that this was nothing more than 'wanton Breach of the law.' Nevertheless, and in yet another reminder of the clear differences between the situation which pertained in the 1920s and that of the 1880s, the proprietors would often fail to seek legal redress and have the raiders removed. This was the case for the remaining Torogay islands and the Berneray crofters continued to graze their sheep on areas to which they were not entitled until 1926 at least.[48]

At Lingerbay agitation resumed almost as soon as the war ended with threats to raid, followed by the symbolic marking out of land and a subsequent formal raid in April 1921. Leverhulme took little action over this. By December houses had been practically completed on the land but, in July 1922, the raiders were jailed for 40 days for illegal removal of a fence. On release they returned to Lingerbay. They were still in possession in 1925. Earlier, in January 1923, Killigray Island, which was attached to Rodel, had stock placed on it by six men from Geocrab, while a separate attempted land seizure was thwarted by men engaged on Leverhulme's schemes at Leverburgh. In March 1926, in what begins to look like a concerted campaign, land was seized at Seilebost. Indeed, a near-anarchic situation appears to have developed in this area of west Harris with successive reports of 'extensive trespass on the forest area' being made to the Board of Agriculture by their local officer in 1927, 1929 and 1932. In the course of the last report it was noted that neither threats to raid nor actual raids had occurred in the area 'in recent years' due to the fact that 'the present owner is not keen on stalking and has shut his eyes to trespass'. In July 1933, due to fears that a new proprietor (Leverhulme had sold his estates some time before) would take a more traditional view and prompted also

48 N. A. S. AF 67/66, Board to Under Secretary for Scotland, 22 June 1921; R. I. P. D. 61109/1 Scaristavore, Board of Agriculture report.

by a parliamentary debate on the situation, the estate was purchased by the Board of Agriculture.[49]

The level of desire to break up western portions of Harris for smallholdings is all the more remarkable given the fact that, in mid-1919 at a public meeting, Leverhulme had managed to obtain the agreement of many of his tenants, to refrain from such activity.[50] The west coast was, however, where the best land was to be found and was the area from which people had been cleared to the vastly inferior east side. Thus, Scaristaveg and Scaristavore, located between Borve and Rodel, were subject to the same pressures and patterns of disturbance with very similar outcomes. On Scaristaveg the most celebrated incident has also been discussed in some detail in the Introduction and will be returned to in Chapter 7. Here therefore, all we need note is that the post-war agitation began in 1925, involved both informal and formal land occupations, disputes between those who went to war and those who did not and friction between townships and cottars and crofters. At one point as many as 35 raiders were illegally working the land and here too raiders had to serve multiple jail sentences. Ultimately, those who persisted in their law breaking were given holdings on Luskentyre.[51]

This late revival of agitation and land seizure was attributed, by the Board and Estate officials, to the final abandonment of Leverhulme's schemes in the previous year. In November 1925 the Estate Factor wrote: 'I am afraid that unless some settlement is arrived at there will undoubtedly be raiding next Spring, and it will be next to impossible to control without resorting to force.' The Board's views were similarly bleak 'Since the cessation of the late Lord Leverhulme's development works ... the demand, for small holdings has become acute and there is every indication that, unless measures are adopted to meet this demand raiding will take place on an extensive scale in the early months of the year.'[52] Harris is, moreover, the classic example of the new realities with regard to land agitation as they pertained after November 1918. War service, awakened public opinion, new legislation and the willingness of government to act on the tenantry's behalf, all combined with a grudging acceptance amongst landowners of these new realities

49 N. A. S. AF 83/164, anonymous letter to Board, 1 May 1914; AF 83/170, J. MacDonald to Board, 2 December 1918; AF 67/146 letter from A. Maclean and others to Board of Agriculture; 14 April 1921; AF83/170 Police report, 20 July 1922; AF 83/790 letter from (sub-commissioner) J. Coull to Scottish Office, 13 November 1925; AF67/156; AF67/148; AF67/65; AF 83/800; R. I. P. D.40911, Scarristavore Islands; Police report, 26 March 1926; R. I. P. D. 61110 Borve, sub-commissioner reports 9 March 1927, 1 November 1929, 28 September 1932 and 4 July 1933.

50 N. A. S. AF 83/1665, report from sub-commissioner to Board of Agriculture, August 1919.

51 N. A. S. AF67/66; AF83/796; AF83/797; AF83/800.

52 N. A. S. AF83/787, copy of letter from factor Norman Robertson to estate agents, 19 November 1925; AF83/790, Board memo to Scottish Office and treasure, 21 December 1925.

to ensure that, providing an appreciable demand was present, protest once begun nearly always led to one conclusion: the acquisition of the land by the tenantry.

On Lewis too, protest almost everywhere led to the breaking up of land for new crofts or extensions to existing crofts, either by agreement with the proprietor or via the purchase of the land by the Board of Agriculture. Here, however, protest was even more long-lived than on Harris and derived more from the consequences of overcrowding and the appalling local housing conditions. By 1929 Leverhulme had long abandoned his schemes on Lewis, sold large portions of his estate and given the rest in trust for the benefit of the island. This did not, however, prevent the Trust from behaving like most other landowners and only giving way to pressure for the break up of farms most reluctantly. At Melbost, for instance, the Trust refused to consider the possibility of a scheme and continued to let the farm. It was raided in May 1929 and a scheme to turn a portion of the farm into fishermans' holdings was approved in March 1931. This pattern was repeated at Keose between 1931 and 1933 and at Laxdale between 1934 and 1937. Laxdale and Melbost were close to Stornoway and in both instances the main motive appears to have been the extremely poor housing conditions that pertained in some parts of the town. At Keose there was a heavy squatter presence, also indicating overcrowding.[53]

Nowhere, however, has the connection between acts of protest and the break-up of large estates been more clearly stated than was the case for Aline farm, on the border between Lewis and Harris. In the post-war period, the farm was first raided in 1919 and although the raiders withdrew, threats were again issued in both 1920 and 1922. Correspondence between the Board of Agriculture and those agitating for land continued for some considerable time but no further threats were made until 1929. This deer forest had been amongst the earliest considered for a scheme by the Board in 1913 when a report noted that, notwithstanding the fact that it once held up to 18 crofts, it was unsuitable for a smallholding scheme being agriculturally very poor and lacking in communications. This did not prevent ongoing pressure for the breaking up of this land. In 1929 this pressure was increased through direct threats to seize land and the active involvement of the local M.P. Following a second full report, the senior sub-commissioner (Duncan Stewart) felt that since there were now competing 'gangs of applicants' from both Lewis and Harris for this land 'it is likely seizure will result'. He felt that a scheme was now inevitable. The (by then) Department reported to the Secretary of State for Scotland that 'To proceed with a scheme now would probably prevent an outbreak of raiding which, if it were to occur, might as in previous cases lead the Government to proceed with a scheme as a means of prevention.' The decision was a matter of policy but Sir Robert Greig, the Permanent Secretary to the Department of Agriculture, argued that pre-emptive action was the best course.[54] It was responses such as these which

53 R. I. P. D. 61147/1 and 61147/2 Melbost; 40917 and 40917/C/1, Keose Glebe.

54 N. A. S. AF 83/363, report of sub-commissioner, 14 April 1919; AF 83/378, report by Duncan Stewart, 22 January 1930, response by Sir Robert Greig to Department report, January 1930.

distinguished the post-1914 disturbances from the earlier Land Wars. In the earlier period the response was slower and was always reactive and limited. There is no doubt that there were clear connections between the actions of the 1880s and those of the immediate pre- and post-war periods, with important precedents being set on both sides of the conflict. Nevertheless, what distinguishes the post-1914 period is the proactive nature of much of the governmental response (this altered little, even with changes of government) and the success of the protests occasioned largely by this more (and wider) sympathetic attitude. In response to the threats to the farm a scheme did go forward at Aline. But, in a further demonstration both of the benefits which derived from the singular focus adopted here – on the detail, manifestations and implications of protest alone – and of the fact that scheme did not automatically lead to the normalising of the situation, the owner of Aline reported to the Department in January 1932 informing them that immediately the decision had become known two years previously that a scheme was to go ahead 'the Smallholders have had their stock overrunning the whole' of the farm. Remarkably it took a further two years to make the fence between the smallholdings and the rest of the farm fully stock-proof. But even more remarkably it was reported, in July 1946, that no rent had ever been collected for these new holdings.[55] Clearly, therefore, whilst the benefits from paying close attention to both the geography and the chronology of protest are very apparent, what is also obvious, and what has received little attention in the wider study of acts of popular protest, is that equal attention needs to be directed towards the consideration of the aftermath of such events. The standard assumption is of a return to something approaching a normative state, albeit significantly altered for the individuals concerned. This Chapter has demonstrated that this can be far from the case and that even a successful protest event can be generative of further disturbance.

Discussion – The Power of the Monocular Perspective

At first glance, both the chronology and geography of the post-1914 land disturbances appear straightforward and closely match the view which has prevailed for some time. There would appear to have been a rapid expansion of protest events from November 1918, with an almost equally sharp decline a few years later. This was paralleled by a shrinking back of disturbance into its Hebridean heartland. On the mainland, only Sutherland approaches the protest levels evident on the islands. First glances, however, are nearly always fleeting, superficial and erroneous. The rewards of a more sustained, focussed and in-depth exploration are clear – enabling, at the very least, a near exclusive concentration on the breadth and depth of the land agitation. What has emerged is an enhanced understanding of the significance and importance of these events and the realisation

55 N. A. S. AF 83/378, A. Macrae to Department of Agriculture, 11 January 1932; AF83/380, letter Stewart Rule and Co, to Department of Agriculture, 6 July 1946.

of a greater breadth to the types of protest performances which together amount to a re-working of the chronology and geography of Highland disturbance.

The protest events after 1914 were spatially and temporally variable in ways that have hitherto passed largely unnoticed; one key example of this is the fact that protest endured on the mainland for longer than has hitherto been imagined. Similarly, to recognise the threat to raid as a protest performance in its own right reveals a distribution of protest greater than and at variance to that previously recognised. There is also significant variation across the region to be considered which, when all these factors are added together, suggests that the regional perspective may not be the most helpful for our efforts to understand Highland protest. Exploration of any supposed continuity to and categorisation of land disturbances is best conducted at an intra-regional level. Local geographies of protest should be seen to both underlie and cut across the idea of a single regional geography and a unitary regional class consciousness.

Understandably, given its larger population, it follows that the area where protest endured at its most numerous and intense was the islands of Lewis and Harris. More interesting, however, is the fact that there is little evidence to suggest that, despite this level of occurrence, protest reappeared on these islands in any significant way after World War Two. Seizure of land at Knoydart, on the mainland, has often been celebrated as the last land raid but, as has been demonstrated here, that honour actually belongs to Balmartin in North Uist. And it is in the Uists where protest seems to have been at its most intense, regular, and most reminiscent of that of the earlier Land Wars period. The cause of this remains something of a matter of conjecture but it must have been connected to the fact that the proprietrix of a large part of the area, Lady Gordon Cathcart, was, along with Lord Leverhulme, the most intransigent of the landowners in the face of pressure for land from the tenantry.

Pressure for land, then, was not equally evident over time or space. The explanation for this differing pattern lies, in part, in contemporary landlord behaviour. It is also founded on historical factors, principally the differential implementation of improvement. At one level, protest replicates the late arrival of improvement to the north and west but, when change within the area is considered, the prevalence and longevity of protest on the Uists and Lewis and Harris can be seen to be the product, in part at least, of the implementation of improvement there. The kelping industry allowed the maintenance of high population levels. Whilst kelp had, by the 1920s, long ceased to be of significance, population levels remained high and overcrowding became a cause of attempts to increase access to land. Coupled with the complex nature of protest, this suggests that a more complete understanding of the protest phenomenon may only be achieved when analysis is conducted at the level of the locality.

Nevertheless, some common, and hitherto often overlooked, factors do emerge from this typological, chronological and regional perspective. There was a clear and obvious, but by no means automatic, connection between the threat and the actuality of land raids. Such actions often mirrored (and were inspired by) those of an earlier period, albeit with significantly more success. This, however, should not detract from the fact that these were transgressive acts of considerable complexity, often involving internal as well as external conflict. Finally, it has become very clear that there could be significant aftershocks emanating from any protest episode, the nature and implications of which have, once again, been largely excluded from the historiography of Highland disturbance.

To take a singular view then, to focus on the detail and dissection of Highland land disturbances permits a much more convincing understanding of the importance of the post-1914 events in relation to those of the earlier Land Wars. Flowing from this, the weight of evidence now available to us permits a much more nuanced analysis of these events which both challenges the dominant paradigm and suggests new ways of looking at these events of rural resistance more generally. It is the aim of the third of these predominantly empirically-based chapters to begin this process of in-depth re-working.

Chapter 5
Testing the Protest Paradigm

'I fear, we should never submit tamely to what our Forefathers did.'

This chapter is principally concerned with the causes behind Highland social protest after 1914 and it will consider these events in the context of the issues identified in earlier chapters and raised in relation both to social protest generally and to Highland Scotland in particular. Attention will also be given to the impact of the Great War (and war service) and, from this, to the question of whether the period 1914 1918 marks such a significant discontinuity that it renders untenable the notion that the disturbances that occurred after 1914 were part of a longer protest tradition. From a focus on short term economic causation and a discussion of the supposed ideological underpinnings to protest, the argument will be made that it is impossible to isolate any one explanation or, indeed, set of explanations of the decision to protest and that we should accept that the various protestors undertook such actions from a multiplicity of motivations. Nevertheless, it is possible to see much of what was occurring during and after World War One as being based in and drawing inspiration from the crofting landscape – a landscape made meaning*full* by work tasks. This is a major departure from all other interpretations of Highland protest and it is inextricably linked to the suspicion that such was the impact of the Great War on the nature of these events that we can no longer talk of a tradition of Highland protest.

The Effect of the War

In the Highlands the war's impact was felt on a number of different levels and in a number of distinct ways. However, as the impact of national public (and governmental) opinion has already been noted, discussion in this section will be limited to that of the impact of war service (directly or indirectly) on the post November 1918 revival of land disturbance.

Having said that it is important to note that one of the key reasons why the impact of war service on disturbance was so profound was because recruitment had been so successful. This was particularly the case in the early months of the war, even if we now must discount the over-romanticised notion of a 'rush to the colours'. A key part of this success was that, because the long tradition of viewing the Highlands as a distinctive recruitment area had persisted, the call to arms could be thus based upon a strong appeal to locality and past loyalties, and to a vestigial clan tradition. This appeal was further reinforced by the fact that those doing the recruiting were often drawn from the traditional land-owning families.

Even though the traditional role of landowners and landownership had been under threat in the Highlands since the 1870s, in the second decade of the twentieth century they still had latent powers of political and social leadership. In this way, moreover, recruitment and recruiters served to maintain the well-established link between military service and land, and, from this, to aid in the further maintenance of the crofting tenantry's "traditional" belief in their entitlement to land.[1]

For the many who went to war (whether in the army or the navy) this shared experience and mutual support demanded by war service created what has become known as 'primary groups'.[2] These small informal and functional groups were the basis of the comradeship which, for many, was the most intense and important product of their war. Critically, for the Highlander the solidarity created by war service was broader than that based on the township and it removed much of the residual deference evident in Highland society before the war. Thus, in April 1919, Finlay MacLeod wrote on behalf of a group of applicants for land from the Northton township on Harris that 'Our dispositions are...changed somewhat since the war began and, I fear, we should never submit tamely to what our Forefathers did.'[3] Sentiments such as these, often repeated in letters to the Scottish Office and the Board of Agriculture, do much to explain the explosion in protest in the immediate post-war years and indicate that the level of agitation during this period was the near equivalent of that of the 1880s. At the very least war brought a lessening of the fear of the consequences of raiding. In March 1920, the crofters of Borve, on the island of Bernera, wrote to the Scottish Office as part of their long-running campaign to regain possession of the Torogay Islands. Prior to the War this campaign had been entirely peaceable and without reward. War service appears to have utterly changed their attitude and they now felt that 'It is a very small compensation we ask for in return for fighting ... We shall not be any worse off in Prison than in the Trenches of Flanders.'[4] Notwithstanding the fact that their agitation had one or two further twists and turns to go through (see below), they were to be ultimately successful.

Further aspects of the relationship between war and protest became apparent through a number of different registers: upon the participants directly; upon the recruiters; through the belief in a promise of land in return for war service; through the martial inheritance of the ordinary Highlander. This latter – the land 'gained

1 Ewen A.Cameron, and Iain J.M. Robertson, 'Fighting and bleeding for the land: the Scottish highlands and the Great War', in Elaine Macfarlane and Catriona Macdonald (eds), *Scotland and the Great War* (East Linton, 1998), pp. 81–102; Ian F.V. Beckett and Keith Simpson (eds), *A Nation in Arms: a Social Study of the British Army in the First World War* (Manchester, 1985); Ewen A. Cameron, 'The Political Influence of Highland Landowners: a reassessment', *Northern Scotland*, xiv (1991), 27–45.

2 Guy L. Sebold, 'The Essence of Military Group Cohesion', *Armed Forces & Society*, Vol. 33, No. 2 (2007), pp. 286–95.

3 N. A. S. AF83/165, F. MacLeod and others to Board of Agriculture, 22 April 1919.

4 N. A. S. AF67/155, Borve crofters to Scottish Office, 18 March 1920.

for the Chiefs by the power of the sword'[5] – gave partial rise to the belief that fighting for the land entitled an individual to hold a share in that land. It was also, following on from the increased integration of the Highlands into the British space economy, easily translated for the combatants into fighting for "your country".

Whether their country actually made the promise of land in return for war service is something of a moot point; but it remains the most significant aspect of the relationship between protest and war service. At a national level there can be no doubt that something resembling a promise was actually made and that it was clearly made at times in the region as part of the recruitment drive. Whether it was universally made is more debatable but the critical fact is surely that applicants for land *everywhere* in the Highlands appear to have believed that it had been made and the perceived failure to honour this supposed commitment became a key motive in their protest. Moreover, it appears to have mattered little who the protestors believed had made the promise and to whom. Thus, at Torrin in Skye and at Lairg in Sutherland for instance, the promise cited was that issued to the country at large (and was therefore little better than propaganda in many instances). At Lochmaddy on North Uist, however, there is evidence of something more direct and specific.[6] According to Donald MacLeod 'it was on account of the direct promise made to him by Captain Beaton, of land, in the Schoolhouse that he ... joined up, that he is now here since hostilities ceased and has got nothing.' MacLeod went on to restate his determination to remain in possession of the land that he and eight others had seized.[7] The process of recruitment, moreover, appears to have had an impact on the social sympathies of the recruiters both towards the landless and more broadly. In March 1917, for instance, A.R. Campbell wrote complaining at the inactivity of the Board and stated that

> As one who has had a great deal to do with recruiting ... I feel bound to call attention to this dilettantism by which these noble self-sacrificing parents may suffer hunger and privation ... As a Justice of the Peace I must warn you of what the consequences will be if these people are made desperate by hunger.

For the veteran land campaigner J. G. Mackay, 'Highlanders at home and abroad had shown themselves to be loyal citizens of the Empire and had answered the call. The bitterest opponent of land reform could now see the injury done to the country by denuding it of its peasantry'.[8]

The War further appeared to have galvanised the crofting tenantry even in the traditionally more quiescent areas of Argyll and Caithness. This was apparent both

5 Interview Murdo MacCuish, North Uist, 9 April 1990.

6 N. A. S. AF67/65; AF67/157.

7 N. A. S. AF67/65, D. MacKay and others to Board 2 March 1920; AF67/157, 16 December 1921.

8 N. A. S. AF83/287, A.R. Campbell to Board, March 1917; *Inverness Courier*, 11 February 1916.

to the region's M.P.s and in correspondence received by the Board. In December 1918 the M.P. for Argyll, wrote that he had 'never known the spirit of the people so determined ... It is apparently one of the results of the War and it will be intensified when the men come home from France.' In October 1920 the secretary of the Dunbeath (Caithness) branch of the ex-servicemen's organisation, The Comrades of the Great War, wrote to the Scottish Office threatening to raid Knockglass farm unless the farm was rapidly broken up.[9]

It would seem, therefore, that such was the impact of war service – even on those who did not serve – that it may have served to rupture any former tradition of protest. It would be wrong, however, to wholly abandon this perspective of continuance since there is significant evidence to suggest that protest was reviving anyway in the second decade of the twentieth century. It was the view of sub-commissioner Wilson, for instance, that the war had served only to postpone efforts at reclaiming land although he did concede that, as a result of the War there was 'a determination to cast aside legal methods, and by force of seizure, obtain what they deem their rights'.[10] Nevertheless the effect of the War was undoubtedly important and the ideological hardening which followed the war led to a reinforcement of the already existing aims and nature of protest. War brought a renewal of protest and created a climate of opinion receptive to the tenantry's aspirations, which found a new expression in their refusal to remove themselves from the deer forests which they occupied. As will be seen, however, their decision to protest continued to be based on the traditions of protest evident in particular locations.

Stretching the Paradigm: Economic and Ideological Motives

Alongside the impact of the war, economic reasons can be advanced to explain both the immediate decision to agitate for land and the differences between townships in their participation in such agitation. Generally, agitation for land was given immediate impetus after the war by the failure of the herring fishery, thereby removing one of the sources of external income upon which crofting depended. The national economic depression of the 1920's removed a further source. In South Uist, for instance, a season's failure in the fishing in June 1914 provoked an early crisis.

> This year has proved a failure in the fishing industry here and now we have nothing to lay our hands on except the small patches of potatoes we planted ... on other people's crofts. The most of the applicants are jammed in the corners of their neighbour's houses ... and can't get even a place to build a house.

9 R. I. P. D. 25912/1 Sunart, Argyll, 24 December 1918; N. A. S. AF67/61, 16 October 1920.

10 D.A.F.S. 8185/1, Balranald, North Uist, 8 October 1918; N. A. S. AF67/143, November 1917.

During the year local crofters began to cultivate part of Glendale Farm, a circumstance which continued throughout the war years and, as with many other such 'informal' protest events, it was not until houses began to be built that the proprietor recognised this as a "raid".[11]

A variety of basic economic causes were expressed by those agitating for land. At Gillin, Skye, the crofters paid an annual rent for peat but, in 1919, their supplies became exhausted. When they applied to use a new area the landlord increased their rent from 5s to £2. They refused to pay and called on the Board to grant them the ground or else they would take it. In 1923, the failure of the Waternish crofters to gain seasonal employment in the south caused them to agitate for more land. A similar sequence of events pertained in 1926 and, at both times, they threatened illegal action. Their alternative was clear to them: we 'must make a living for ourselves and families someway, and we are confident, if the Estate of Waternish was broken up ... it would enable a great many men to live in their native land, otherwise we must emigrate.'[12] As has already been noted, this was far from the only instance when emigration or land seizure was presented to the authorities as the only alternatives available to the crofting population.

Similarly, on Lord Leverhulme's estates on Lewis and Harris, the outbreaks of protest appear closely related to his schemes to improve the islands' economies. For Lewis, it is generally recognised that the popularity of Leverhulme's development plans was, in part at least, a function of how physically distant people lived from them. Leverhulme had a tendency to focus upon the east coast, on the main town of Stornoway and its immediate hinterland. Despite the fact that protests on Coll and Gress were intensive and large-scale in nature, it was continually claimed that support for protestors' actions in the east was minimal. This divergence may well be the product of Leverhulme's drive to fracture communal coherence, largely conducted through the pages of the *Stornoway Gazette* and the provision of lavish hospitality in the form of large-scale fetes in the grounds of Stornoway Castle. He was aided in this by the belief amongst the general population that, because his schemes offered the possibility of greater economic stability, they could function alongside a crofting economy – notwithstanding Leverhulme's clearly stated opposition to the retention of a crofting way of life. This paradox may well offer tangential support for the views of the Board of Agriculture's sub-commissioner

11 N. A. S. AF83/145, A. Campbell and others to Board, 19 June 1914; *The Scotsman*, 14 December 1918.

12 S.R.O. AF67/155, D. McRaild to Board, 21 December 1920; AF83/668, Sub-Commissioner J. Elliot-Scott to Board, December 1925; D.A.F.S. 26509/M/1 Waternish, Geary crofters to D. Shaw (forwarded to Board), 18 April 1923; AF/83/669 M. MacDonald, K.C., M.P. to Board enclosing copy letter, further letter 22 November 1926; AF83/769 Sub-Commissioner C. MacDonald to Board, 20 December 1923; AF83/790 Board memo, 20 December 1925.

on the ground – Thomas Wilson.[13] He stated that, whatever people from Stornoway might have said publically, 'at heart they are all of the opinion the people should get the land, and they tell me so'.[14]

When raiding did occur on Lewis Leverhulme's initial response was to dismiss those men from his employment who were from 'districts where farms had been raided'.[15] This proved to be extremely divisive and there is a body of (largely overlooked) evidence of tensions within the tenantry resulting from this. At large public meetings and through a similarly sized petition, support for Leverhulme's schemes was voiced and land raiding denounced. These initiatives were met by a counter-petition from many of the more radical districts. In the immediate post-war years, however, anti-raider sentiment appears to have triumphed; in October 1920, a whole series of resolutions from public meetings undertook 'for at least ten years not to take part in the illegal raiding of any farms in Lewis'. Whatever the motive behind these actions, genuine or otherwise, the Scottish Secretary, Robert Munro, was convinced and agreed to Leverhulme's request for a ten year moratorium on the compulsory acquisition of land for crofting.[16]

Effectively this amounted to a total prohibition on any further schemes on Lewis since Leverhulme was highly unlikely to offer any more farms voluntarily (he had already reluctantly agreed to the breaking up of some). This could not be sustained, however. Leverhulme was experiencing financial difficulties and was forced to abandon his development plans for both Lewis and Harris. The response from within the tenantry was to resume raiding. This obliged the government to consider, once again, plans to break up farms on both islands. Dialogue was resumed and, even though Leverhulme's negotiating position was significantly weakened, he still proved an intransigent opponent. He was also convinced that both the Board of Agriculture and the Scottish Office, in the form of Robert Munro, firmly favoured the views of the crofting tenantry as opposed to those of the landowners with incidents such as that at Galson Farm appearing to vindicate this view. Here Leverhulme's manager[17] on Lewis suggested that, whilst there had been annual threats to the farm for a number of years, those made in 1922 were more likely to be translated into actual seizure as a consequence of the production

---

13 It is a matter of some regret that the historiography of this period has largely overlooked the important role of the Board's local officers.

14 Nigel Nicolson, *Lord of the Isles* (London, 1960), Buchanan, *Lewis Land Struggle*, p. 100.

15 Buchanan, *Lewis Land Struggle*, p. 107.

16 Buchanan, *Lewis Land Struggle*, p. 116; Nicolson, *Lord.*

17 There is a significant body of correspondence between Leverhulme, his representatives and various government bodies preserved in the archive. See, for instance, N. A. S. AF67/331. It is, however, a matter of some regret that, as with the Board of Agriculture's sub-commissioners, the role of the factor/agent has been sadly neglected in the wider historiography, notwithstanding Tindley's most welcome interventions. See especially: Annie Tindley, 'They sow the wind, they reap the whirlwind:' estate management in the post-clearance Highlands, c. 1815–c. 1900', *Northern Scotland*, Vol. 3 (2012), pp. 66–85.

of a circular letter from the Board asking those who had applied for land if that was still their ambition. This had led the local population to believe that the farm was to be broken up and engendered frustration when this did not occur. Secretary of State Munro's view was that that crofting and industrial developments could co-exist, that the expressed desire of the population to retain access to land should be respected and that the Board of Agriculture were mandated to meet the demand for land. Notwithstanding the nuanced nature of this response, the raising of expectations (and the subsequent frustration when these were not fulfilled) consequent upon government action was a common theme in Highland affairs from at least the 1880s. This is evident in the responses to the Napier Commission, to the creation of the Congested Districts Board, to the Deer Forest Commission of 1892 and to the Land Inquiry of 1912.[18]

Such frustrations were equally evident on Harris, even if (as suggested by popular memory) the Harris tenantry were generally in favour of Leverhulme's plans; perhaps a consequence of the fact that 'there was never a time in the history of Harris in which they were so much dependent on their proprietor ... in earning their livelihood.' When raiding threatened to provoke Leverhulme into halting his development schemes, a public meeting of 'nearly all the townships throughout the Parish of Harris' was held at Leverburgh on 30th May 1921. At this meeting a determination to prevent raiding was clearly expressed as otherwise 'ourselves and our children to suffer serious hardships'. At that time there was significant agitation over the Lingerbay portion of the estate which serves as further reminder of the fact that the tenantry were not automatically and universally supportive of land seizure. One of the outcomes of the May public meeting was the despatch of a deputation to those aiming to seize land on Lingerbay with the aim of preventing the planned raid. They were unsuccessful and, when the raiders were goaled for the removal of a fence, letters supporting their action were sent from the district.[19]

Lingerbay was not, however, the only example of tensions on the island between those in favour of Leverhulme's plans and those who were strongly committed to more traditional taskscapes. In January 1923 'men engaged on the Works at Leverburgh' prevented a land seizure on Rodel Farm. What these examples also show is the diverse nature of the role played by economic considerations in the land agitation. It is insufficient to identify these protests as a "knee-jerk" reaction to economic downturn, although we must not rule this out as immediate catalyst. Additionally, economic considerations lay behind some crofters' decisions to oppose land invasions from within and to work with proprietors in developing estates. Tenants' fears of economic catastrophe may also explain the resumption of intense agitation following the collapse of Leverhulme's schemes on Harris.

---

18 N. A. S. AF83/207, 12 July 1919; AF83/328, 9 October 1925; Nicolson, *Lord*; Andrew G. Newby, *Ireland, Radicalism, and the Scottish Highlands* (Edinburgh, 2007).

19 N. A. S. AF83/245; Letter Alexander MacLeod, Leverburgh to John MacDonald, Finsbay. I am grateful to Mr. D. Morrison, Harris for allowing me to use this material. N. A. S. AF83/170 various letters of support July 1922, solicitor letter to Board, 3 February 1922.

As with the vast majority of protest performances, agitation began with threats to seize disputed land but it was clear that 'unless measures are adopted to meet this demand, raiding will take place on an extensive scale.' What this illustrates, therefore, is the depth, power and fundamental nature of the belief in land as the prop and basis to Highland culture and the accompanying belief that the land and croft endure when all else fails; a view that remains clearly evident within the crofting community to the present day.

Land Ideology and Popular Politics

Similarly diverse manifestations are apparent once the relationships between land, ideology and protest are explored in any depth. The primary concern here will always be with the belief in rights to land: whether this was evident in the post-1914 period; and whether it existed as motive for protest in the manner and depth established during the earlier Land Wars. Nevertheless attention will also turn to concerns related to this perspective and to the ways in which the ideology of rights to land may be said to provide the link between (and an influence on) the actions of the tenantry and wider political movements; most specifically the Highland Land League.

Land, The League and wider political movements Unquestionably it was during the early decades of the twentieth century when questions of land reform moved into the mainstream of British politics.[20] Paramount here, as it had been since the last quarter on the nineteenth century at least, was the Irish question. In the context of Scottish land disturbances the key question has always been that of the influence of Irish tactics and radical politics over Highland events. For Hunter, this connection was as much practical as it was ideological, while for Newby the disconnection between Ireland and the Highlands was more important.[21] Newby asserts that, apart from a few radical pockets in Skye and Sutherland, the tenantry did not generally support Irish solutions to their problems. This attitude tended to remove the taint of nationalism from their reform demands and thereby enable aspects of these demands to be taken up by radical Liberalism in the early decades of the twentieth century.[22] Moreover, in the context of protest events of this period, there is little evidence that the government recognised any links between Highland and Irish protest (they were more concerned about possible links between the Highlands and Red Clydeside). On the ground, however, the perception was somewhat different. The tenant at West Garty, for instance, felt that

20 See, for instance, Ewen A. Cameron, 'Communication or Separation? Reactions to Irish Land Agitation and Legislation in the Highlands of Scotland, c.1870–1910', *English Historical Review*, Vol. 120, No. 487 (2005), pp. 633–66.

21 James Hunter, 'The Gaelic Connection: The Highlands, Ireland and Nationalism, 1873–1922', *The Scottish Historical Review*, Vol. 54, No. 158, Part 2 (1975), pp. 178–204.

22 Newby, *Ireland*, p. 196.

the raid there represented 'Ireland in Sutherland' while, in 1921, the factor for the South Uist estate felt 'that the Sinn-fein [sic] element is pretty strong' there. This was, however, denied by the local police inspector. Nevertheless other, radical political allegiances were similarly noted. Thus, to the Rhifail Estate factor, those taking part in the agitation there were 'practically communists', whilst to those opposed to his threatened raid on Lingerbay, John MacDonald was a 'hair brained redlag socialist'. Once again there are continuities here with earlier events. In 1889, for instance, the Tongue factor on the Sutherland estate wrote to the Duke's secretary that 'There are a number of young fellows about Bettyhill who go away for summer work in the States and return in winter bringing with them all sorts of democratic, even communistic views. I am a bit anxious about these fellows.'[23]

Of greater import appears to have been the politically less radical Highland Land League. Reconstituted in 1909, the League entered a new period of relevance and success in the Highlands and there are some indications that they had an influence on the agitation of the first two decades of the twentieth century, perhaps drawing this into a wider social movement for land. For the agitation after 1914, the evidence of direct connection between the League and these Highland events is nevertheless slight. The seizure at West Garty in Sutherland directly followed a League meeting while the Board of Agriculture strongly suspected the locally-influential figure in disturbances on Raasay – Murdo Macleod – to be a conduit between his locale and the League. Other evidence for such a connection is more tangential.[24] For Nicolson, if less so for Newby, much of the agitation for land on Lewis was influenced by the Highland Land League and other radical groups, but perhaps the strongest connection is found in the figure of Donald Shaw. He was a solicitor and a member of the League and his firm was engaged to represent both raiders in their court cases and groups of applicants to the Board of Agriculture. In his representations Shaw often articulated a moral, ideologically-based argument, basing the tenants' claims to land on expropriated "ancestral" holdings. In this way, ideological beliefs from within the local culture and society were linked to wider political aims. In addition, the use of such language by prominent League members may well have been one way in which the traditional beliefs in rights to land were maintained and continuity with earlier periods sustained.[25]

23 N. A. S. AF67/64 W. Sutherland to Board, 29 May 1918; AF67/152 John MacDonald to Board, 27 January 1921; AF83/595, 6 February 1921; Copy letter to Lord Leverhulme from Leverburgh, 2 June 1921. I am grateful to Mr D. Morrison, Harris, for the loan of this material. National Library of Scotland, Sutherland estates papers, Acc. 10225, Factor's Correspondence, 1484.'John Box to Henry Wright, 13 February 1889. I am very grateful to Annie Tindley for her permission to use this reference.

24 N. A. S. AF67/67, the meeting was held on 27 March 1918 and the farm raided the following day; AF67/149; Interview Murdo MacLeod, Raasay, 30 September 1991.

25 See for example R. I. P. D. 26509/M/1, Waternish, Skye, 1 June 1925; *Dundee Advertiser*, 28 February 1923, as part of his defence of the Strathaird raiders Shaw stated

It is however, only with the associations of ex-servicemen – principally The Association of Die-Hard Soldiers and Sailors and The Comrades of the Great War (the latter intriguingly set up by a group of conservative M.P.s worried about possible subversion)[26] – do we get to direct connections between wider political movements and land disturbances. Operating on a purely local level but evident throughout the Highlands, branches of the Comrades acted to support individual members or groups of members in their agitation. In June 1920, for instance, the Brora branch wrote in support of the Portskerra raiders 'that the treatment meted out by the Board of Agriculture to ex-service men who apply for land is only fostering a spirit of unrest and rebellion in these parts.' Individuals also utilised the threat of enlisting the help of these associations in order to put extra pressure on the Board, although only occasionally would a branch be directly involved in an agitation. On Berneray, Roderick MacLean, the local Comrades branch secretary, as part of their long-running agitation to reclaim land on the Torogay Islands, wrote to the Board of Agriculture threatening to put sheep on them while the Dunbeath branch also threatened a raid in Caithness. This latter was in support of their secretary, whom the Estate had tried to exclude from a scheme that had been proposed there. On North Uist the raid at Lochmaddy in January 1920 was supported by the local branch of the Comrades from whose clubroom the raiders marched (headed by a piper).[27]

Before the war it was the Land League who had been most influential in the area of national politics. Increasingly, however, the region's M.P.s appear to have taken over this role. The influence of the League seems peripheral therefore, although the links with non-resident Highland communities remained important in the land struggles and the League's role in this, along with that of the Independent Labour Party, were significant. Despite this, and through the activities of groups such as The Comrades of the Great War, politically-based agitations seem to have remained local affairs. If, therefore, we are to look for ideological bases for these protests we must look to older ones.

The ideology and land and landholding There is much evidence that protests during this period were strongly rooted in claims to previously expropriated holdings; the foundations of which were both embedded in Highland cultural beliefs and were transmitted through proverbs such as: 'By right of blood and sweat the land is the peoples' and

---

'Cottars in Skye and other parts .... have never considered themselves as being in breach of any moral law in laying claim to cultivate some of the lands held by their forefathers'.

26 Nick Mansfield, 'The National Federation of Discharged and Demobilized Soldiers, 1917–1921: a view from the Marches', *Family and Community History*, Vol. 7 (2004), pp. 19–32.

27 N. A. S. AF67/65 Comrades of the Great War, Brora Branch to Scottish Office 1 May 1920; AF83/143; AF67/148, 18 March 1920; AF67/161, 16 October 1920; AF83/430 Report by Sub-Commissioner J. Coull; AF67/148.

Taomannach an t-iasg
Teugmhalach an t-sealg
Ach am fear a dh'aitcheas am fearann
Chad'fhag e duine falamh riamh

(Translated as)

Uncertain is the fish
Hazardous the hunting
But the man who cultivates the land
It never left anyone empty.[28]

Evident in and underpinning much protest activity, these beliefs were expressed as 'this being the land of our forefathers' and authorities were informed that 'we shall also fight to get the land if steps are not taken to see us settled on the land of our ancestors which we consider is ours by right.'[29]

Such sentiments could be expressed both individually and as a group but rarely were they articulated as directly as at Gress, Lewis, where, in December 1919, the secretary of the ex-soldiers and sailors organisation wrote to the Board threatening to raid Gress 'Because its [sic] our land that was taken from our forefathers by bad law'. Similarly, in March 1918, a group comprised principally of Hougharry crofters seized land on Balranald Farm, North Uist, of which they believed their 'ancestors were wrongly deprived'. They therefore considered it 'a matter of right and justice' that it should be restored to them. The response of the proprietor was to justify his own occupation in similar terms and to offer the raiders land for potatoes. They took up his offer and ceased the occupation. This arrangement only temporarily ameliorated the situation and in the following year the Hougharry group again began agitating for land. In March 1920 they wrote to the Scottish Office that, as 'The land Bill is passed now ... there is no obstacle in the way to hinder progress'. They went on to complain at the Board's inaction and to state their claims to that land: 'It adjoins the Township and formerly belonged to it … We are convinced that we are acting right when we take possession of the land from which our ancestors were wrongfully driven.'[30]

---

28 Colloquial. I am very grateful to Dr Donald Meek and Dr John MacInnes for their advice on this usage.

29 Interview *MacCuish*; Interview L. Robertson, Elgol, Skye, 2 October 1991; N. A. S. AF 83/363m Petition from North Tolsta, Lewis to Board of Agriculture for Scotland, 8 February 1919.

30 N. A. S. AF67/147 John MacDonald to Scottish Office, 11 December 1919; D.A.F.S. 8185/1 Balranald, North Uist, 30 March 1914; Hougharry crofters to Board, 30 December 1918; N. A. S. AF67/152, Alexander MacDonald and 11 others to Board, 2 March 1920.

At about the same time crofters from (mainly) Knockintorran resumed their agitation for land on the southern portion of the farm. In May 1920 they wrote that

> All the crofters in the said township have decided – owing to the scarcity of fodder and poor pasture – to take possession of the part of Paiblesgarry (about 150 acres) which was taken from them by James MacDonald, tenant of Paiblesgarry and Balranald ... at that time the people were ignorant about laws and rights and the powerful and wealthy did very much as they choosed [sic] ... why did we send our sons to fight for this country if it wants to deprive us of our existence ... they look on the land that was treacherously taken from them as their own to the present day.

As expressed here, land was both past claim and, as their means of existence, present right. It should be noted, however, that there were other applicants who were rivals for land at Balranald, most notably a group of cottars from Sollas and Hougharry, but who did not legitimate their desires by this rationale.[31]

Nevertheless a sense of attachment to a specific piece of land was frequently prominent and this was often as clearly expressed as it was by Malcolm Morrison and his fellow cottars from Islivig (Lewis) who were aiming to regain the 'land from which our forefathers were cleared to make room for sheep and deer … we must have the land to live on. The land is there. We cannot live without it.' This also reveals the presence of a forward-looking element within the notion of land-holding, as identified by Withers for an earlier period: crofters and cottars desired land 'to live on' and to remain in the area.[32] Such sentiments are also evident at Reef (close to Islivig) where, in December 1913, those who had seized part of the farm wrote to *The Scotsman* explaining the rationale behind their raid

> The farm of Reef was for ages cultivated by smallholders before the clearances about sixty-five years ago, when the Gaelic tenants were evicted and forcibly driven out of their land and homes and thereafter forced to exist ... elsewhere … For many weary years we tried in vain for land to help us to exist in our own native country.[33]

While the cottars of Valtos and Kneep did not explicitly lay claim to Reef on the basis that it was their ancestors who had held it, they nevertheless expressed the notion of land as a local birthright. Underlying this claim was the belief that past cultivation of a specific piece of land brought a present right to reclaim that land

31 N. A. S. Malcolm MacDonald and 16 others, Knockintorran to Board, 17 May 1920; R. I. P. D. 8185/M Newton, cottars from Sollas, 9 March 1922.

32 N. A. S. AF83/359, Malcolm Morrison and others to Board, 4 February 1920; Withers, *Gaelic Scotland*, p. 396.

33 *The Scotsman*, 31 December 1913.

for cultivation. There is therefore an important and hitherto unnoticed relationship between work tasks, the land and actions of protest.

Within this land- and task-based ideology there is a further reminder of the kin-based nature of much of Highland cultural formations. In expressing their ideological claims, claims were made to the ancestral, and to past landscapes of inheritance. Thus, in June 1919, Angus Smith wrote in application 'for the croft that belonged to my grandfather in the southernmost end of Galson ... and was ousted to give place to the farm mentioned'. In April of the same year an identical sense of legitimation, it is 'my father and grandfather homes we wanted', was extended to and formed the basis of a threat to raid the land.[34] In this and in many other ways, the respect with which crofting society treated prior generations was made material in their attachment to the ancestral family crofts. This desire to return to an ancestor's holding was at the same time, then, an individual expression of ideological claims to land and part of a collective memory and community consciousness.

At first glance, the disturbances at Borve on the island of Harris support all the bases of claim enumerated above. Land on the estate was seized by at least three separate groups, two of whom legitimated their actions in the ideology of their rights to the land. However, research into the genealogy of the families from the Bays district of Harris (where the raiders originated) reveals that the land which they seized had not been cultivated 'by the forefathers of those who seek to possess it'. And yet, in many respects, this is unimportant. It is the *belief* of those undertaking the agitation which is crucial. They believed that they had an entitlement to a 'share of our own native isle', a 'claim for our own land'.[35] In the Bays, it is significant that this was not expressed as an entitlement to a specific piece of land but drew instead on the notion of land as a birthright: being born on Harris gave a right to a croft on Harris. Similar sentiments were apparent across the crofting counties. At Drimore, South Uist, correspondents justified their threat to raid in terms of their inability to 'get a smallholding in the place where we were born and brought up'. Similarly, those who seized part of Forsinain Farm, Sutherland, wrote 'we maintain we are the rightful heirs to this place ... as we were born and brought up practically on the farm'.[36] The notion that a stake in the land was virtually a birthright was amongst the most prominent manifestations of the ideology of land-holding at this time perhaps indicates a weakening of the belief in rights to a named piece of land.

It would seem, therefore, that what has been considered to be the 'expressed collective belief in the inalienability of land' was central to the ideology underlying and motivating the later Highland Land Wars. For many incidents of protest 'the sense of land as their land, an inherited occupance, a physical setting with which

34 N. A. S. AF83/774, 19 June 1919; AF83/363, 10 April 1919.

35 Interview with Bill Lawson, Harris 15 November1992; N. A. S. AF83/800, Police report 25 March 1926; D.A.F.S. 61110 Borve, Harris, 1 March 1928.

36 N. A. S. AF83/207, 12 July 1919; AF83/328, 9 October 1925.

Highlanders were indissolubly tied through continuity of social and material practices'[37] inspired the decision to raid and reaffirms the view that protest after 1914 must be understood as closely connected to the long tradition of Highland land disturbance. Furthermore, and although it is outside the main area of this study, it is important in this context to note that protest was on occasion legitimated in much the same way in the Shetlands. There are a number of possible reasons for this, not least the possibility of direct influence from the Hebridean agitation, but it nevertheless behoves us to be aware that this may well question the supposed specifically Highland basis of this ideology of landholding.

What also appears to have occurred is that expressions of this ideology became less specific as the links to expropriated land weakened over the generations. This trend gave rise to a belief in a more generic birthright to the land, a notion underpinned by a similar sense to that articulated above but expressed less specifically. Perhaps even more critically, these overtly expressed ideologically-derived motives were never evident in isolation. They were always associated with other motivational impulses and were on occasion absent from some incidents of protest. This means that it now seems difficult, if not impossible, to sustain the argument for monothetic explanations of protest – we must break the paradigm in other words. All the evidence suggests that, for Highland protest after 1914 (if not earlier), most incidents can be fully understood only when it is recognised that a combination of motives, social and economic; long-term and short-term, are evident in the onset of these protests. Furthermore, the individual participants did not necessarily enter into protest for identical reasons. Highland protest is therefore rooted in a complexity of cause.

Breaking the Paradigm?

This shift away from a singular causational viewpoint is acknowledged in most major works on Highland protest. Nevertheless, few seem able to pursue the recognition and delineation of the complexity of cause which emerges when the evidence is examined in the depth undertaken here. Of equal importance in this challenge to the Highland protest paradigm is the fact of conflict *within* the tenantry which, of itself, was also generative of protest.

Complexity of causation was evident in the agitation for land on Lewis. At Dell Farm agitation was aimed at 'that park unjustly grabbed from our ancestors' – a clear expression of claims to land based on past occupation. At the same time, however, correspondents also cited the failure of the authorities to fulfil their wartime promises of land reallocation ('About seven eighths of the farm ... has been uncultivated for years and yet for this fallow land we have bled') and complained that 'the lawbreakers [have]... possession of what they desired while we have not benefited by abiding the law'. Similarly squatters on the west coast

37 Withers, *Gaelic Scotland*, pp. 389–90.

of the island justified their threats to seize land on the basis of the failure of war promises coupled with references to their ideology of landholding.

> We will never be content until we get what was promised, what we suffered for freedom for ourselves and others ... We pray to God that something will come about soon that will give us freedom, land and a home for our families at a fair rent.[38]

In both these examples the archive fails to point to a preliminary motive; and this is perhaps correct. In virtually every incident after 1914 evidence emerges of protestors entering into protest for a combination of motives. Lewis was no exception. In addition to the protest triggers noted above, here we find hints of the conflicts within the tenantry which make land disturbances of this era so distinctive. Nevertheless, and indicative of the need to understand land-based tasks as the underscoring leitmotif for Highland conflicts, when expressed within the protest performance its expression varied. Thus expropriated land could be basis to ideology but was also expressive of and equated with freedom; both individual and economic. Land could also represent home, belonging and entitlement; by past occupation or war service or both. Complexity, then, is apparent within the spectrum of motivation to protest but also within the individual behaviours which came to comprise that spectrum.

An additional element here was the frustration engendered by the often lengthy delays between initial decisions to investigate the possibility of a scheme and the land being broken up for smallholdings (if it ever was). On Skye, at the farms of Kyle and Lussa and as one example amongst many, there can be no doubt that the Board's deliberations were protracted. At Melbost Farm on Lewis, agreement to break up the land for smallholdings was close but then broke down in the face of Leverhulme's announcement that he wanted to convert the farm to dairy production (milk was extremely difficult to obtain on the island at that time he argued). As a result, the Secretary of State ordered the abandonment of the scheme. The farm was immediately raided and, in time, broken up for crofts.[39] An appreciation of the complexity to motivation must now be unavoidable. What must be much more open to question is the extent to which motives other than those based on land can be said to have been a primary driver of protest. They may well have been the motor but they were rarely the ignition system.

> ... you have now kept us about two years in daily expectation of a Final Settlement ... I would ask you if you consider it fair or reasonable as a Board set up ... to do justice – to turn round after about two years Correspondence and tell

38 N. A. S. AF67/151, letter W. Campbell and others to Board of Agriculture, 14 January 1922; R. I. P. D. 25912/1 Sunart, Argyll, 24 December 1918; AF67/61, 16 October 1920.

39 N. A. S. AF67/150, 12 December 1920; AF 83/145.

> us you are not going further with your Scheme... you are just bringing troubles upon yourselves.[40]

Conflict in and through Protest

The current dominant explanation for Highland protest rests on class conflict and events such as those at Melbost and Kincraig have unquestioningly been interpreted as the product of an 'emergent class consciousness from within'. There is evidence to support this hypothesis in events that took place after 1914.[41] At the same time, however, there is also evidence to support the notion that the emergent class consciousness that we may see in these events was not that of the crofting community in its totality but those of cottars and crofters separately.

The division between crofter and cottar over access to land emerged as each recognised distinct and opposing interests based on their competing needs: those of crofters to gain enlargements to their existing crofts; those of cottars to obtain land for a croft. For crofters this may be interpreted as an individual act designed to maximise income or as an attempt to maintain a viable presence on the land, given the nature of their croft. While the external economic conditions of the time would appear to support the former view, crofters never justified their agitation in terms of economic ambition but rather in terms of economic necessity and survival. Both crofters and cottars characteristically based their actions on an ideology of land-holding which was at once both relational to specific locations and collectivist in its origins and impulse. This collectivist impulse was undoubtedly rooted in the strong kinship links that provided an important base to Gaelic identity, even if we must recognise that direct action by groups was not necessarily confined to those solely comprised of kin. It is a recognition of their shared interests that linked these groups although it is clear that this impulse did not always cross the growing social gap between cottars and crofters. When it is unpicked in the detail that is possible here, the agitation surrounding land at Balranald Farm on North Uist is revelatory of both the complexity and the tensions adhering to protest performances when the land under threat was very specific and finite. The presence of the ideology of rights to land as a key motive in these events has already been noted. Also significant here is the presence of groups competing for the same land but divided by location and social grouping. It was crofters from Knockintorran who based their claims to land at Paiblesgarry on past claim and present right while the cottars from Sollas and Hougharry did not (at least in writing). The sense of tension between these groups – based in part in this difference – was heightened by the claim made by the proprietor that the unstated aim of those seizing the

40 N. A. S. AF83/609, D. MacIntosh to Board of Agriculture 22 December 1920.

41 R. I. P. D. 8185/1, Balranald, North Uist, 8 October 1918; S.R.O. AF67/143, November 1917.

land was to gain enlargements to existing crofts only. To this end cottars had been purposefully excluded from the raiding groups.[42]

Something similar was evident on the Trotternish peninsula on Skye. In April 1922 a public meeting of ex-servicemen and crofters from within the area was called to protest against 'servicemen or others from outside to get [sic] any part of this land from which our forefathers were cruelly evicted.' They called on the Board to restore 'the lands of our ancestors to us'.[43] Both the Balranald and Trotternish examples demonstrate tensions *within* the crofting tenantry which caution against any presumption of uncritical unity and reveal instead something close to an ideology of opposition from within. At Nunton, Benbecula, sub-letting by raiders who had gained holdings prompted complaints that this, rather than working the croft, had been the raiders' original intention. If correct, their actions question the expressed desire of the raiders for land in order to survive. In this case, however, the accusation that this had been the real intent behind the seizure appears more a function of conflict between applicants as it was made by those who had failed to obtain their own holdings. Here too, the conflict was additionally between ex-service (or their kin) and "civilian" applicants and this division continued even into the allocation of holdings. In 1925, in order to ensure that only ex-service applicants obtained land, a threat was made to resume illegal seizures. The Board of Agriculture appeared to give in to this pressure.[44]

Furthermore, a significant number of land seizures and threats to seize were the product of crofters no longer content to have others on their crofts. In January 1921, cottars from Tobson (Lewis) wrote threatening to raid Croir farm as they were 'warned by the Township [sic] Crofters to clear off our stock'. Some seven months later the crofters wrote setting out their own position. In the township there were as many squatter families (twenty) as there were crofter families.

> that means heavy Congestion on poor Crofters. These squatters has got more [sic] stock than many of the crofters … we can't put up with them any longer upon us ... I am requested by the crofters to ask you to remove the squatters … before the end of September ... or else we shall pay no rent or tax ... The state of our Township will be sent to the Prime Minister. Poor crofters widows and orphans ruined to poverty by Ex-servicemen heaped upon them.[45]

42 N. A. S. AF67/147 John MacDonald to Scottish Office, 11 December 1919; D.A.F.S. 8185/1 Balranald, North Uist, Board of Agriculture memorandum, 30 March 1914; Hougharry crofters to Board, 30 December 1918; 8185/M cottars from Sollas, 9 March 1922; AF67/152 Alexander MacDonald and 11 others to Board, 2 March 1920; AF67/152 Malcolm MacDonald and 16 others, Knockintorran to Board, 17 May 1920.

43 R. I. P. D. 5863/C Scorrybreck, Skye, 6 April 1922.

44 N. A. S. AF83/245, Nunton, letter 21 April 1924 from five applicants from Griminish; AF83/246, threat to raid made 20 January 1925.

45 N. A. S. AF67/152 6 April 1918; AF67/157, 24 January 1921; AF83/751, letter from Tobson township clerk, 9 August 1921.

Two points of significance emerge from this. Firstly, it must now be apparent that war service could be a point of tension and conflict as much as it was a unifying and radicalising factor. Second, differences between groups appear also in nomenclature. To the crofters, the additional people on their crofts were 'squatters' while the landless perceived themselves as 'cottars'.

In this instance, the priority given by the Board of Agriculture to settling ex-servicemen only added to the tension, which continued despite the creation of Croir township and the re-location of some cottars there. In 1926, the Tobson cottars threatened to seize the old township of Bosta, by then part of Tobson's common grazing. Furthermore, what was created from the farm did not match the cottars' expectations or needs. Indicative of the planning errors which could occur when the authorities were under pressure, the new township was set up without summer grazings. In July 1930, the Croir township clerk wrote to the Board that

> We have been asking you to give us Summer Grazing … since the Settlement was formed nine Years ago ... We fared better as cottars … only for the Bernera crofters allowing our stock to their moor .. [or] ... we would have no stock at all … we are notified by the Bernera holders that this is the last year we will get our stock to the moor.

The Croir township therefore petitioned the Board of Agriculture for either a moor of their own or holdings elsewhere; failing both they threatened a rent strike, interestingly repeating the threat deployed by their Tobson counterparts a decade earlier.[46]

Furthermore, it is clear that it was not just crofters who were proactively asserting their interests. On Tiree, for instance, where the Board proposed to give crofters enlargements away from the coast, cottar applicants for the same land wrote that 'When there was fighting to be done we had first chance to be shot; not your precious crofters. Likewise when there is land set out ... we shall have first share of it, or there will be trouble. In fact we shall have it all, with no crofter companions.'[47]

The complex conflicts generated by competing claimants, their beliefs in rights to land and the finite nature of the available land were all apparent on the west coast of Harris in 1925. Northton, Scaristaveg and Scaristavore ran conjointly from south to north. Northton was a crofting township, established by the Congested Districts Board early in the twentieth century. Scaristaveg was a cleared crofting township and Scaristavore an existing township. Elements of the complex nature of the land agitation in this area have already been discussed in both the Introduction and previous chapter. Full understanding, however, can only rest with a consideration of Scaristaveg in the context of attitudes, actions and

46 N. A. S. AF 67/66, 11 Tobson cottars to Scottish Office, 26 August 1926; AF 83/751, Croir township clerk to Board of Agriculture, 28 July 1930.

47 N. A. S. AF83/267, letter from Balephetrish 24 March 1922; AF67/154.

tensions emanating from the other two townships. With the compliance of the proprietor, Northton cattle had been able to range freely across the three townships but the prospect of new holdings on Scaristaveg threatened this. Consequently, Northton crofters applied for enlargements. When these were not forthcoming they threatened a raid on Scaristaveg. These actions revealed socially divisive tensions within Northton. In November 1925 cottars from the township threatened to raid the same land. They repeated this threat in March 1926, arguing that new holdings should have preference over enlargements. On the morning of 25 March this cottar alliance informed the Board of Agriculture that they had carried out their threat. That afternoon a second telegram from the Northton crofters informed the Board that they had 'made these three raiders stop'. In early April the cottars wrote again, stating that they were still in possession and arguing that, because they were without crofts, they had 'a right to take possession of the land and ... the Northton crofters, who already have crofts, have no right to interfere'.[48]

It was not just the Northton township crofters who were interested in Scaristaveg. As already noted, cottars from Scaristavore had seized land on the farm shortly before the Northton tension became apparent. This move was prompted by their belief that the Scaristavore proprietor was working with the local crofters to ensure that the farm was broken up for enlargements. Once in possession, the cottars were given help to maintain and extend their occupation by the Northton crofters.[49] This is a remarkable tale of the heterogeneous antagonistic associations at work in this complex protest performance.

Events on the north-west coast of Harris add a further strand to the complex nexus of alliance and fracture evident in these acts of protest and surrounding access to land. Neither written records nor local popular memory indicate why the Northton crofters acted as they did but this was not a conflict over scarce resources – there was sufficient land to satisfy the demands of the two different groups. The suspicion remains, therefore, that the Northton crofters were supporting the Scaristavore cottars as means to suppress the ambitions of their own cottars (to whom they were likely to be related). The Northton crofters wanted a specific block of land and acted to maintain that claim. They did not take up an oppositional stance to cottars generically, just to those cottars who threatened their own claim. But, whatever the reason, conflict between crofters and cottars emerges very clearly here. Nevertheless, in this case there is also evidence of a wider underlying tension within the social structure of the land working community. This was reported by

48 N. A. S. AF 83/800, John MacCuish and two other cottars to Board of Agriculture, 16 November 1925; Angus McQueen to Board of Agriculture on behalf of Northton crofters, 31 December 1925; John MacCuish and others to Board of Agriculture, 22 March 1926; telegram John MacCuish to Board of Agriculture, 25 March 1926; telegram McQueen to Board of Agriculture on behalf Northton crofters, 25 March 1926; John MacCuish and others to Board of Agriculture, 8th April 1926; John MacCuish to Board of Agriculture, 9 May 1928.

49 N. A. S. AF 83/795, D. Stewart to BoA, 15 March 1926 and 18 March 1926.

the senior sub-commissioner for the area. 'Mr McLeay has been Keeper, Farm Manager, Farmer ... and now Proprietor at Scaristaveg. He has had success and his activities have brought him necessarily into direct conflict with the Community.'[50]

Clearly this tension between crofters and cottars was most evident in areas of overcrowding but, given that crofters and cottars were often close relatives, the tension was also created by the feeling that past occupation and inheritance gave both equally valid claims to the land. At Scorrybreck (on Skye), claimants of land 'from which our forefathers were driven' objected 'to servicemen or others from outside' getting 'any part of this land from which our forefathers were cruelly evicted'. When the Board proposed to create crofts rather than enlargements, the Scorrybreck crofters wanted the Board 'to reconsider their scheme so that justice be done in restoring the lands of our ancestors to us' and threatened a raid if the Board did not do so. The same arguments were used in disputes over Quendale links in Shetland.[51]

As first suggested by Withers, the conflicts within crofting society as revealed by land protests suggest that to present such events as manifestations of a class conflict that existed solely between a homogenous crofting community and their landowners is no longer tenable.[52] It may be possible to recognise, for instance, the emergence of a hierarchy within the crofting tenantry, largely as a result of crofters gaining enlargements onto potentially profitable land. This may suggest the emergence of a proto-middle class from within, subsequently coming into conflict with proletarianised cottars. We can counterpoise this perspective, however, with Lord Leverhulme's reported view that 'I must have control of my factory hands! How can I have that in the case of men who are in the independent position of crofters?' This quote suggests a greater accord with Reed's view of nineteenth century English rural protest.[53] He believes that what is evident here is a fluidity to the class structure, based on transient alliances and oppositions. If we follow Reed, what we may be witnessing within Highland protest are the normal and complex processes of negotiation, confrontation and fracture within a class. Neither position, however, can encompass the fact that the actions taken by crofters and cottars look, at times, like the actions of separate and opposed classes. The period after 1914, when cottars agitated as an exclusive group is significantly underplayed in the established literature and it would appear that they did so, in

50 N. A. S. AF83/795, D.Stewart to Board of Agriculture, 18 March 1926.

51 R. I. P. D. 5863/C, Scorrybreck, Letter from public meeting of Stenscholl to Lealt Eastside ex-servicemen and crofters, to Board of Agriculture, 6 April 1922; N. A. S. AF 83/695, letter 9 ex-servicemen to Board of Agriculture, 8 October 1921.

52 Withers, *Gaelic Scotland.*

53 Buchanan, *Lewis Land Struggle*, p. 118; Gerald M. Sider, *Culture and Class in Anthropology and History* (Cambridge, 1986), pp. 7–8 and 170–71; Mick Reed, 'Class and Conflict in Rural England: Some Reflections on a Debate', in Mick Reed and Roger Wells (eds), *Class, Conflict and Protest in the English Countryside 1700–1880* (London, 1990) p. 23.

part at least, on the basis of the distinctiveness of their concerns from those of the landowning and crofter classes.

There is, however, a strong element of contrivance in any recognition of these supposed class divisions to the extent that it becomes imperative to examine those forces and alliances which run counter to the processes of class. The existence of such forces and alliances mean that it is very difficult to construct generalities over what was occurring in the Highlands in the early decades of the twentieth century. Events of protest were strongly determined by local contexts and were highly fluid. Kinship links could cut across supposed cottar/crofter divisions and there is plentiful evidence of groups of agitators being comprised of both strata. Notions of class conflict further fail to explain how fracture and alliance could be visible at the same time, and often in the same event (as on the west coast of Harris in 1925) and are further challenged by the fact that the protestors drew support from other layers of society, most notably, but far from exclusively and often inconsistently, from both Church of Scotland and Free Church ministers. Other supporters included a Justice of the Peace on Mull and, at Portskerra in Sutherland, the main correspondent was also the local merchant.[54] There is a view, therefore, that we should perceive such actions as frequently drawing on whole communities, although the plentiful evidence of growing internal divisions perhaps stretches the notions of unity beyond breaking point. It is more persuasive to recognise this set of events as highly complex, contingent and fluid in nature. Further, the vast number of events of protest which took place after 1914 and the varied range of protest types utilised in these actions suggest that to admit all of this into any monothetic interpretation attempted thus far blurs and attenuates such thinking to such an extent that it is unable to bear the weight that the significance of these events demands. There is a need and an opportunity to take a fresh look; to expose Highland protest to the most recent thinking in protest studies. In so doing, we must return to the fundamental physical, emotional and quotidian bases of Highland culture. Land, landscape, and a moral sense of resource utilisation were the forces which drove protest forward.

The multi-layered nature of these protest events is further demonstrated by the attitude of some prospective raiders to their landlords which was based less on conflict than on what Hunter has recognised for the 1830s as 'residual deference' – a belief that a higher authority would act to ameliorate the situation once alerted to the fact. In March 1917, Peter Stewart expressed his frustration at being unable to get land and felt that 'if the case was Properly laid before the Mackintosh. He would do something for me'.[55] Paternalistic Highland society, or at least paternalistic Highland belief systems, rested on such reciprocal arrangements of authority and paternalistic concern. Authority was legitimated by tradition: on the expectation of behaviour handed down from the past. The early abandonment

54 N. A. S. AF67/65; AF67/161.

55 Hunter, *The Making*, p. 215; Eric Richards, *A History of the Highland Clearances, Vol 2*, pp. 333, 346; N. A. S. AF83/609, 27 March 1917.

by Highland authority of such concerns was largely concealed by the crofting tenantry's retention of such pre-capitalist attitudes. In part at least such attitudes were later amalgamated into and helped to underpin the ideology of protest and continued to be evident in unrest after 1914. Nevertheless, the "authority" increasingly referred to in events of protest was the local M.P. Correspondents attempted to gain the support of their M.P.s in every stage of the agitation process and often utilised the threat of writing to their M.P. in attempts to provoke the Board of Agriculture into action.

Protestors were not alone in retaining seemingly archaic attitudes and views which had association with the attitudes of nearly a century earlier. These could also be found amongst local authorities in the 1920s. In April 1924, for instance, the Rhifail Estate Factor wrote that he had

> never met MacKay [but] from what I hear he is a disturbing effect in Strathnaver. In several of his letters he said he was not a coward like some of his forebears who were burned out of Strathnaver, but it is a pity that the last dregs were not burned out at the same time.[56]

Undeniably, both sentiments of residual deference and the desire to retain such deferential and servile positions were strongly present in the Highlands in the early decades of the twentieth century. From below, the obstruction (and therefore the strata of society which was perceived to have changed the most) was where it is always found in such expressions of frustration at the workings of a paternalistic society – with the middleman. In the context of the twentieth century Highlands that would be the Factor (and, we might speculate, the gamekeeper and his ghillies). His position was never easy but attitudes such as that from the Rhifail Estate (and this was just the most extreme of a range of similar views) which stretch back into the agitation of the 1880s, could not have helped. With the advent of the Congested Districts Board, the Crofters Commission, and the ever-increasing presence and proactive role of the Board of Agriculture's local officers, a further layer of complexity and "noise" was added to the (perceived) relationship between the tenant and his landlord. Indeed, in some instances, the Board became the landlord. Undeniably, local representatives held a variety of attitudes towards the processes that they were administering and to the populations that they were dealing with – although there is no extant evidence of the type of views held by some members of the factory. Some, Thomas Wilson for instance, were believed to have moved too far in the opposite direction. We ignore the role of such actors from above in these protest performances at our peril.[57]

Undeniably sentiments of residual deference remain strong within older generations of the present-day crofting tenantry. These may well inform the

56 N. A. S. AF83/595, 16 April 1924.

57 I am very grateful, once again, to Annie Tindley for her most useful promptings towards this discussion.

popular memory which points to the encouragement of seizure by landlords and tenant farmers to enhance subsequent compensation awards. Such actions, it was suggested, were based on the premise that the Board would inevitably utilise their powers to allow the raiders legal access to the land.[58] More importantly, Government and landowners were often in genuine conflict. This was particularly the case on the estates of Lady Gordon Cathcart and Lord Leverhulme. In 1920, Cathcart's solicitors wrote that, following on from raiding on Askernish farm, and acting under the influence of panic, the Board were coerced into allowing the raiders to remain in possession and were 'thereby directly encouraging raiding'. They additionally felt that such action by the Board confirmed to those agitating for land that 'all was necessary ... to get possession of the land was to raid it'. The same solicitors, this time acting for the proprietor of Eoligarry, Barra, again wrote to the Board accusing them of frustrating the cottars into raiding by instigating the procedure to create smallholdings and then delaying doing so almost indefinitely.[59] The fact that the same solicitors expressed the same view, albeit on behalf of different owners, is surely noteworthy.

The hugely controversial position adopted by Lord Leverhulme regarding the breaking up of farms on both Lewis and Harris, in opposition to the views of the crofting tenantry and of the Board of Agriculture and the Scottish Office, has been discussed earlier in this chapter. Worth noting here, however, is the fact that there appears to have been something of a history of such intransigence on the part of the local landowner. According to Buchanan, 'fraught negotiations between the Board' and the previous proprietor, Major Duncan Matheson, meant that the Board's plans to break up the farms that were subsequently raided had to be suspended due to the onset of World War One.[60]

Undoubtedly other landowners took a more conciliatory position and supported the Government's attempts to manage the situation. Thus, in 1922 and in order to facilitate a scheme being carried out on raided land, Lord Lovat wrote to the Board that 'I consider the action of the crofters ... constituted a simple trespass and not a raid' meaning that all parties were able to ignore the fact of the raid.[61] Had they been unable to do this, those who has seized the land would have been prevented from obtaining it by the Munro bar (see below) and the successful breaking up of the land in question could have been impeded. Such flexibility notwithstanding, the very nature of the legislation under which such proceedings took place ensured confrontation. Since raiding was a civil offence, and the desire of the Government was to maintain order, proprietors could characterise the Government as inactive, vacillating and supportive of the tenantry. It was thus more common for landlords

58 Interview Mr and Mrs D. MacLean, South Uist 12 April 1990.

59 N. A. S. AF83/190, Skene, Edwards and Garson to Board, 8 January 1920; AF67/143, 19 September 1917.

60 Buchanan, *Lewis Land Struggle*, p. 98.

61 N. A. S. AF83/731, 12 April 1922.

(and their representatives) to adopt a position closer to that of Lord Leverhulme than that of Lord Lovat.

In part as an attempt to limit such conflict and in part also as a response to landlord criticism, the Scottish secretary announced, in December 1921, that future raiding would act 'as an absolute bar to land settlement'. That this policy was unsuccessful was the result of the problems brought about by the resolution of the raiders' claims, and the fact that there were often 'more applicants, apart from raiders, than can be accommodated by any scheme that the Board could frame' and because of the statutory obligation on the Board to provide land. Political expediency therefore often meant that this bar was not enacted. After the bar was put in place in virtually every case of raiding in which the raiders were imprisoned and then returned to the land they were eventually settled on it. The attitude of such raiders was evident at Melbost, Lewis where it was noted that, while 'It has been announced that the Secretary for Scotland has said that no raiders would benefit by raiding, ... it is generally realised that it would be worth it, even to help others to benefit by it'.[62] This is perfect encapsulation of both the communal crofting *mentalité* and a signifier of the inevitably of conflict in the post-World War One Highlands (and, indeed, before). What all these separate and conjoint conflicts amount to is a fundamental challenge to the view which sees conflict in the Highlands as simply class conflict. It was both wider and more fine-grained than that. What we might need to recognise here is an emergent tri-partite, if not quadri-partite conflict of interests.

Discussion: Motives; Conflicts; Movements

This chapter must be viewed in conjunction with the two which precede it. While those concentrated on a close, empirically-based reading of the chronology, geography and typology of these disturbances, the current chapter has drawn on further examples of the extensive evidence and historiography now available to us to consider those themes first identified as central to an understanding of, at first, protest more generally but then brought into this Highland context. Evidence of underlying economic and ideological motivations seems to accord with what is understood from earlier protests but, when this is investigated in greater detail, a more nuanced analysis emerges which questions many assumptions and re-emphasises the power of the monocular perspective utilised here.

In terms of this relationship between the earlier and the later Land Wars there is strong evidence to support the assertion that World War One marks a significant disjuncture in Highland protest. Important here was the impact of the war on the attitudes of the local and national authorities, and, indeed, on public opinion towards the crofting tenantry. The broken promise (whether this was perceived or

62 N. A. S. AF67/153; AF67/151, 30 January 1923; D.A.F.S. 61147/1 Melbost, Lewis, Sandwick crofters to Board, 26 May 1923.

made is largely irrelevant) of land in return for war service revived and enhanced the agitation for land in the immediate post-war years. Nevertheless, there is evidence to suggest that such agitation was reviving anyway and, since the decision to protest continued to be based on the traditions of earlier protests, this suggests that continuity rather than hiatus may be the more important characterising attribute here. At the very least, this rhetorical continuity serves to remind us that protest is inevitably and inherently complex; and that our interpretations must therefore reciprocate.

This continuity comes, particularly, from the evident economic, political and ideological motives underlying the decision to protest. Undoubtedly the ideological motivation is the more significant and the evidence supports the view held by Charles Withers of an 'expressed collective belief in the inalienability of land' underpinning the decisions by crofters and cottars to retake land that they viewed as their own.[63] Both this belief, and the social and material practices from which it was derived, were maintained until well into the twentieth-century.

There is a need to go further, however. The underlying ideology of a right to land was not simply collective. The transmission and maintenance of this ideologically-constituted belief was via individuals and between generations and also drew on landscape and on the tasks performed within it. For an individual, the expression of ideological claims to land could take the form of a desire to return to an ancestral holding. This desire was, at the same time, an essential component of collective memory and community consciousness. The importance of these kinship links on one level often determined the composition of the raiding party and, on another, sustained the attachment to the family croft which, when the family was disassociated from that croft, impelled and maintained the desire to reclaim it. The collective expression of this desire became the legitimating notion for land seizure. In this way kin, land and landscape were intimately connected.

Once more, however, we should be aware of fracture and disjuncture within this 'challenging collectivity'.[64] Most significant is the distinction between crofter and cottar. To recognise its existence is perhaps to depart most radically from the established narratives of the events of the Highland Land Wars. It is hard to move beyond the perception that what was occurring in the Highlands from the 1880s onwards was a form of warfare. Where the events after 1914 raise serious questions is over whether it is possible and desirable to maintain the view of Highland disturbance as a class war (or wars) driven by a growing consciousness of class. The view taken here, and substantiated by the evidence, is that, at best, we should now view class conflict as one register of disturbance amongst many. Greater emphasis needs to be placed on an understanding of these events as fluid, uneven and ever-changing skirmishes which may have class as a referent; while acknowledging that class consciousness could lead also to internal divisions within the tenantry (which were also motives to protest) and was far from the

63 Withers, *Gaelic Scotland*, p. 389.

64 See Samuel Clark, *The Social Origins of the Irish Land Wars* (Princeton, 1979).

only motivating belief. And, if we are to see this as a conflict driven by groups, alliances and antagonistic associations, then we now need to view it as a tri-partite, if not quadri-partite conflict. This view must also raise serious questions over the existence of any sense of homogenous purpose and community within the land working population. At the same time, we must also recognise the potential for kin-links to work in opposition to these divergent forces. In this, and with this detailed unpicking and understanding, Highland events would seem to align much more closely with views developed most recently in protest studies more generally.

This approach also resonates with one key aspect of the current most fertile area in new protest studies: that surrounding the Captain Swing riots in rural southern England in the early 1830s. Here a strong case has been made that close attention to events in particular places reveals much more of the reality of protest performance than is possible from a more Olympian viewpoint.[65] The disturbances in the post-1914 Highlands were similarly far from clear-cut and were neither wholly ritualistic nor gestural. They were, in actuality, affectively powerful, drawing on a desire for land which went beyond the purely economic and the need to subsist. It is critically important, therefore, that we recognise the depth of emotional commitment required to plan and carry through a protest performance of whatever form. For too long consideration of the emotional underpinnings to crowd action has been absent from the study of social movements. This was a consequence of the adoption of resource mobilisation theory which meant that scholars took a rationalist perspective on such movements and treated protestors as rational actors largely devoid of emotion. With the turn to culture, however, and with the subsequent shift to non-representational theory, emotion has been readmitted to our analyses on the grounds that it is 'part of the "stuff" connecting human beings to each other and the world around them'; functioning both to motivate and to channel action.[66]

Within this it is equally important to recognise that events of protest have serious repercussions and post-existences. The impacts of these largely successful actions on landowners, farmer-tenants, shepherds and sportsmen and their implications for wider governmental and social policy are obvious and have been much discussed elsewhere.[67] Less obvious are the consequences for the tenantry of the land settlement schemes that almost inevitably followed from any land seizure of remotely serious intent. When they have been discussed elsewhere, these schemes have generally been portrayed as beneficial and, clearly, there were significant long-term benefits for those who achieved a new holding or an extension of their existing holding. But, in the short-term, and as indicated by the post-scheme threats, actual land seizures, and by grazing and other disputes noted here, the legacy for the local community was often one of conflict and ongoing

65 Jones, *Finding Captain Swing*.

66 Jeff Goodwin, James M. Jasper and F. Poletta (eds), *Passionate Politics* (Chicago, 2001) p. 10.

67 See, for instance, Burnett, *The Making*.

tension. What, then, seems to have been left behind once the land disturbances reached some sort of conclusion is a little-studied endgame. These aftershocks were clearly not new counter-hegemonic expressions and neither were they proto-movements, although elements of both are clearly present within them. They serve instead to further remind us of the affective underpinnings of acts of protest and reveal the breadth of conflicts and tensions around land which must feed into 'the stresses of unresolved issues' that continued to be played out in the period after World War Two.[68]

Whether the more visible and conclusive protest events in the Highlands constituted a social movement is also an important consideration, as it has been for the body of Captain Swing literature. For Peter Jones in *Captain Swing*, Rudé and Hobsbawm established a model of addressing popular protest in a way that has become virtually standard in the protest literature. This takes the form of brief narrative case studies contextualised into wider structural frameworks. Contained within this there is, in Jones's classic phrasing, 'an almost irresistible impulse to find "moments" of popular protest as existing within "movements" of the labouring poor'.[69] This impulse is perhaps more evident in the study of Highland protest than it is in the study of protest almost anywhere else. For Jones, however, this is problematic at best because very little attempt seems to have been made to define the key terms in this literature. This failing is coupled with an inability to identify the one "special end" to which all the protestors were supposed to be working ("the land" is probably not a sufficient end point for Highland protest). Furthermore, alongside the recognition of protest movements, sits uneasily the parallel recognition, by the same authorities (on Swing), of the lack of any features which might give any movement coherence. Jones argues that it is far more convincing to reverse the paradigm. He believes that the investigation of one incident in depth and then the location of that incident in a 'wider frame of reference' permits a perspective which accords much more closely with that of the reality of a situation and of its participants: his preferred focus is therefore 'the overwhelming influence of economic and social relations in the locality'. From this reasoning emerges his assertion that the Swing events are best conceptualised as 'meta-movements ... composed of a series of interrelated incidents and events ... individually defined but played out across a broad canvas'.[70]

In the study of Highland protest the symbiotic factors of (re)gaining access to land and the rise of class consciousness and conflict are recognised, implicitly at the very least, as lending this disturbance the coherence of a wider social movement, the political manifestation of which was the Highland Land League. In addition, the adoption of the collective title of either "The Crofters War" or "The Highland Land Wars", perpetuated in the present volume, perhaps lends a near metonymical validity to an understanding of these events as amounting to the expressions of a

68 Burnett, *The Making*, p. 15.

69 Jones, *Finding Captain Swing*, pp. 429–58.

70 Jones, *Finding Captain Swing*, p. 434.

social movement that may otherwise be more convincingly seen as expression of a varied set of discourses, diffuse across both time and space.

At first glance, these are powerful and persuasive perspectives. The whole thrust of this volume is, however, to look at the Highland disturbances at least for a second time and in greater depth. This is certainly what Andrew Newby has done for the role of the Highland Land League in forging and maintaining a wider political movement.[71] The outcome of his work has been to raise serious questions over the impact of these movement-building attempts in the Highlands and from within the region it is equally important to question both the importance of class to protest and its ability to bring to this phenomenon the over-arching coherence of a protest movement. While the weight of numbers and the geographical range of the disturbances may suggest otherwise, it may well be more persuasive to follow Jones and to suggest that, rather than seeing it as a social movement, it would more convincing to view these disturbances as a meta-movement: 'a series of events coherent and tangentially connected in terms of their concerns and the manner of their progress, but having no guiding principle or special end outside the localities where they occurred.' To move with Jones, in other words, towards a focus on the local and the particular since this was the arena in which this protest, neither pre-political nor archaic, was actually played out. Such a shift is given added weight by the fact that, no matter which way the archive is interrogated, no firm and explicit evidence of coherence across both time and space emerges, aside from landlord, local authority and (occasionally) governmental paranoia. A social movement can only emerge, it would seem, through inference from above.

It is, however, possible to take a more sympathetic view of the idea of a general movement to reclaim land underpinning protest if one draws deeper inspiration, as has Carl Griffin, from the social movement literature. Griffin looks for 'solidarities' underpinning events to show that these were not individualistic actions and he finds that these are often drawn from socially criminal activities such as smuggling and deer stealing. Discipline and organisation came with the ex-soldiers often drawn into protest, but, for Griffin, the most potent template for solidarity in protest was communally-based work practices.[72] Virtually all of this construction has strong echoes in Highland society and culture. In particular, the suggestion has been made here that it is in the reassertion of traditional work practices that the means, motives and outcomes of Highland social protest can be found. This argument will be developed further in Part Three; there too the benefits to be gained from a focus on the micro-spaces (and places) of protest will be revealed. In drawing together protests at the individual level and popular memories of places and events, and a sensitivity to the dynamic and constitutive role of kin, land and

71 Andrew Newby, 'Edward McHugh, the National Land League of Great Britain and the 'Crofters' War', 1879–1882', *The Scottish Historical Review*, Vol. 82, No. 213, Part 1 (2003): 74–91; Andrew Newby, 'Land and the "Crofter Question" in Nineteenth-Century Scotland', *International Review of Scottish Studies*, Vol. 35 (2010): 7–36.

72 Griffin, *Rural War*.

landscape, space emerges as something more than passive setting. Nature/culture is similarly seen not as a passive/active binary (paralleling that of landscape/body) but as co-constitutive; shaped and shaping. In these environments of co-presence, space, as is too often the case in protest historiography, must be recognised as more than backdrop; something more than the arena in which protest occurs or the boundaries (on whatever scale) which delimit disturbance. Rather, space can be seen to be of itself an active agent in the making of acts of resistance and the reassertion of transgressive landscapes. What this further demands is much greater sensitivity to the microspaces of oppression, resistance and proactive protest. In the context of events of Highland protest, greater sensitivity to these microspaces is best achieved through close and culturally-informed attention to individual events and through the utilisation of a range of evidences; not least the collective memories of these events. What emerges from this is a realisation that the Highland land disturbances are perhaps most convincingly understood as constituting a meta-movement aimed at the reassertion of the crofting taskscape.

PART III
Protesting Bodies Performing Tasks in Place and Space

> This is not a manifesto for the study of dead bodies; … Instead, it is a manifesto for taking the historical geographies of embodiment seriously. Neither do we intend that this introduction, or the essays that follow, should be read as attempts to make the bodies of past geographical protagonists live through the vicarious medium of archive, theory and print. … Our bodies – and those of the authors' subjects – are instead seen as staging points in a series of interactions with all sorts of matter that make up the world. … Furthermore, the human actors so central to the writing of most history are important – but not as the sole agents of change, that which is after all the *locus classicus* of social history. Human actors instead should be understood as archival vectors – we feel the term conduit too strong, too suggestive of elemental historical truths – of the past. To again paraphrase Thrift, actors, whether human or non-human, are but "ongoing arrangement[s] of objects and symbols within a field involving the body." The embodied historical geographies, the embodied practices that we wish to promulgate are generous in their allowing for an infinite array of worlds in which the agency of all things is allowed for in truly democratic ways.[1]

This book was born out of the realisation that there were two significant issues within Highland protest after 1914 which demanded attention. First, these events were of considerably greater significance than has been allowed hitherto. Second, stemming from and paralleling the first, came the realisation that as a consequence of the issues exposed by and the questions raised by an enhanced understanding of protest after 1914, it now no longer seems tenable to pursue grand narratives of class and hegemony by way of interpretation. This is by no means an isolated epiphany. It fits exactly with the trajectory of protest studies more generally. As recently articulated by Katrina Navickas, in our new histories of protest class is by no means abandoned it is simply made more nuanced, recognised as complexly manifest in protest, and accepted as but one possible register of identity amongst many others.[2] The search for greater nuance and the embracing of complexity

1 Carl Griffin and Adrian Evans, 'On historical geographies of embodied practice and performance', *Historical Geography*, Vol. 36 (2008), pp. 9–10.

2 Katrina Navickas, 'What happened to class? New histories of labour and collective action in Britain', *Social History*, Vol. 36, No. 2 (2011): 192–204.

therefore characterises the following two chapters, with the primary objective of offering a deep reading of the character of Highland protest as delineated in Part Two. Taken together what follows can be understood as partly an endpoint to which the three preceding chapters have been leading and partly a departure from the spatial breadth indulged in in those chapters. In Part Two the discussion has roamed widely across the region and even when concerned with sub-regional geographies individual examples have been deployed to support a broader focus. This was certainly also the case when discussion turned both to the identification of the breadth of protest typologies evident in post-1914 Highland protest and to the explication and interpretation of the motives which can be said to have underlain these events.

In that Chapter 5 engaged with established analyses and interpretations it stands as something of a bridge between the two main parts of the book. It nevertheless took empiricism as its principal frame – as means to critique the aforesaid analyses and interpretations. In the following two chapters whilst empirical evidence is readily turned to it is deployed in service of wider tropes; of space, place and landscape, and through this a consideration of protests' cultures.

In a Highland context it would be remiss at best for any exploration of protest culture to ignore popular memory given the still extant significance of this to Highland culture more generally. In what follows the argument will be made that notwithstanding the historiographical and methodological issues surrounding oral histories, this remains a powerful aid in the search for deeper understanding which lies at the heart of this part of our discussion. In that popular memories inhere to particular places, spaces and landscapes it is entirely appropriate that the chapter in which the popular memory of protest events is most deeply drawn on is that which takes the individual event as its framing device. Here once again the inspiration is the trajectory much of protest studies has taken almost ever since the very earliest interventions – towards an ever-richer understanding of the importance of the local context and the everyday. In the interweaving of archival and oral sources, individual and collective memory, and past and present social processes here attempted, the aim is to essay a more contextualised understanding of Highland disturbances which might also act as foundation and testing ground for new ways of looking at and interpreting protest more generally.

In many respects Navickas's 2011 paper in *Social History* noted above is a close relation of Charlesworth's "agenda" published in *Rural History* some 20 years earlier, although the journals in which they were published betray something of the differences between them. Both are "state of the nation" pieces and both identify ways forward. One of the significant differences between the two is that the more recent paper is able to be far more optimistic than the former. Alongside a number of important new perspectives Navickas identifies environmental history as 'offering great potential for these new histories'.[3] It is this potential, particularly when enhanced by efforts to make the nature/culture binary more problematic –

3 Navickas, *What happened*, p. 201.

the "stuff" of the best environmental history – which these closing chapters seek to help to bring to fruition. Here too, the individual event is utilised as springboard from which to launch a discussion of new ways of seeing Highland protest – as underpinned by vernacular environmental beliefs, by a dynamic and formative sense of place/space and by work tasks performed in an imaginative taskscape. In all of which the popular memory of past spaces and events – maintained in and through kinship links – is recognised as one of the binding threads.

Chapter 6
Placing and Anatomising Protest

This and the following chapter are both partly endpoints to which the three preceding chapters have been leading, and partly a departure from the regional focus adopted in those chapters. In this chapter we are concerned with individual event. In previous chapters the discussion has roamed widely across the region and even when concerned with sub-regional geographies individual examples have been deployed to support a broader focus. The aim of this chapter is to move the discussion on, through a concentration on place and the detailed discussion and contextualisation of individual events, to, in the following chapter, a consideration of new ways of thinking about the relationships between space and protest.

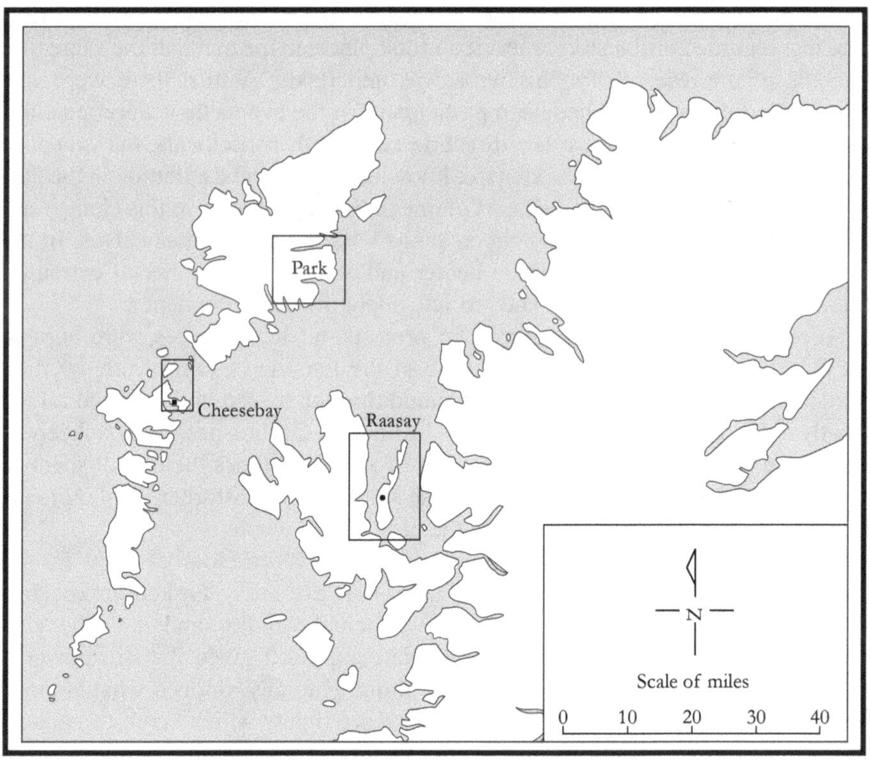

Figure 6.1 Case study locations

The limitations of the few attempts there have been to engage with individual Highland events have already been discussed and will not detain us here as, in turning to discussion of protest in three particular places, the aim is, following Peter Jones, to essay a more nuanced understanding of particular "moments" of protest in the locality.[1] This chapter will therefore move forward from the recognition of the crucial importance of economic and social relations in the locality and, in part at least, use this springboard from which to launch a discussion of new ways of seeing Highland protest. Central to this discussion, it is suggested, must be the recognition of the role of popular memory of past spaces, events and landscapes.

In this chapter popular memories of protest past are deployed with a view to casting greater light on various aspects of the cultures of Highland protest both in the past and how it is understood and recalled in the present. Memory attaches to particular places and spaces; in so doing transforming them into psychic terrains which serve as anchors and mnemonics for landmarks of identity at all spatial scales. Here, then, the aim is to interweave this story of individual event with the popular memory of that event. Certain aspects of these invaluable sources have already been discussed in the Introduction. It is nevertheless appropriate here to note that recorded oral history interviews took place, in the main, at the same time the bulk of the research for this work was undertaken. Whilst there were very few people left alive who had been participants in the events they were recalling, virtually every interviewee was a direct descendant of participants, the exception being Angus Macleod, whose extensive knowledge of the land agitation in the Park district of Lewis both sits at the heart of one of the case studies in this chapter and was assembled from his direct conversations with the raiders themselves. In this way Angus was himself a tradition bearer and alongside a number of extremely detailed conversations we also entered into a lengthy correspondence.

Directly reflecting the geography of protests, all interviewees were born on the Outer Hebrides, although at the time of the interviews some were, by then, resident elsewhere. Interviewees were found through a "snowball" methodology, greatly aided by the help on every island of native Gaelic-speaking gatekeepers. Their help was invaluable and in the case of John MacInnes the month spent on his croft on Cheesebay (see following case study) was transformational, not only to my work as an oral historian but to the project as a whole.

Time and circumstance alter memory. To mine oral sources only for the "facts" which can be extracted from them is an extremely limited approach at best. Nevertheless oral histories can have factual validity, and it is the view taken here that this is an entirely appropriate approach given the still-powerful role of the oral tradition in Gaelic culture more generally.[2] Indeed what emerges from the interviews conducted for this work are inputs which serve to enhance our understanding of protest after 1914, if not more generally. More detail of

1 Jones, *Finding Captain Swing*, pp. 429–34.

2 See, for instance, Ferguson, *Children.*

individual events emerges, the possibility is opened up for a greater sensitivity to, and enhanced role for local landscapes as motives for protest; opportunity arises to engage with discussions surrounding the leadership role in protest. Popular memory is, in short, a powerful aid in the quest for enhanced understanding of protest's performances in a Highland and local context.

The wider methodological inspiration and context into which these interviews will here be placed is that of the microhistorian, and Samuel and Driver's call to rethink 'the idea of place'.[3] As discussed in Chapter Two the microhistorical approach is one that offers much to the protest historian (and historical geographer) interested in the power of space and place to shape protest. It is not the intention here to produce a full microhistory – that is beyond the scope of the evidential base – but its ethos: 'the conviction that detailed observation and analysis will not only reveal "new meanings" in structures, processes, belief systems and human interaction, but sometimes even ... render macrohistorical analyses irrelevant' is shared here.[4] In the interweaving of archival and oral sources; individual and collective memory; past and present social processes, the aim is to (by the end of the following chapter) reach a more rounded understanding of Highland disturbances in which a sense of place and landscape is seen as protest-shaping. One consequence of the adoption of these perspectives will be the opening up of post-1914 agitation to new explanations which draw on vernacular environmental relations. A further intention of this focus on the individual is to point to the variation from the 'model' land raid proposed earlier. At times, for instance, the land broken up was not the same as the land that was raided. In addition it often only took one term of imprisonment to achieve success. The first of these variations from the model is of particular significance when ideological motives were prominent. The offer of different land was invariably unsatisfactory and at the very least led to contemplation of continuing occupation. At Strathaird in Skye, in 1923, political considerations meant that the raiders were offered land whilst still in jail. This was explained by the Under Secretary for Scotland:

> we were informed that Mr D. Shaw, The Land League, and similar people, are out to exploit this case ... It was therefore thought expedient to come to terms with the opposition before they were got at during the week-end ... the raiders are to be offered holdings in Skye next year ... The offer of holdings ... may mean a larger concession ... but the public disapproval by the opposition of raiding justifies ... the price paid.

3 Samuel and Driver, *Rethinking.*

4 Reay, *Microhistories*, p. 260.

The raiders were not offered the land they had raided, Camusunary and Robaston, but land on an estate distant from their homes. This involved an unacceptable separation 'from our own territory and ... our own people' and the agitation continued.[5]

The behaviour of the Strathaird raiders otherwise conforms to that norm identified above. Elsewhere the performing of protest was undertaken with violence untypical of the general pattern. At Balranald, South Uist in 1921, when 'Captain MacDonald ... started sea weeding ... we approached them and overturned all the carts. The next day they returned ... and so did we! Captain MacDonald thinking he would frighten or deter us, came on horseback. We sent the servants back to Balranald.' This account minimises the extent of the confrontation out of which breach of peace charges arose. Those charged failed to appear in court and when the police went to arrest them, due to the threatening nature of the crowd they were unsuccessful.[6]

Violence also occurred when holdings were allocated to non-raiders, thereby excluding raiders. At Askernish, South Uist, a ballot was held as applicants (including raiders) far exceeded the number of holdings created. However

> when Mr MacKinnon ... came forward with the hat ...some person or persons knocked the hat upside down scattering the contents on the road. The ex-servicemen then turned about and marched round the Farm ... and pulled up all the wooden stobs ... marking the different boundaries of holdings.[7]

This incident typifies the post-war experience of violence: aimed mainly at property with personal violence at a minimum. Despite this, the level was such that it sustained a fear amongst authorities of the potential for violence in raiders' actions, a fear compounded by the fact that most raiders were militarily experienced.[8]

The foregoing demonstrates the variation apparent within the normative model established earlier. A significant element of this chapter will, therefore, be devoted to a close reading of just three events of land seizure. This protest form has been chosen partly because it is generally recognised as the characterising action of the Land Wars period, but also because it leaves behind the richest archival traces. Nevertheless the events focussed upon – Cheesebay on North Uist; the island of Raasay; the Park district of Lewis – have been chosen neither because they have left particularly rich traces (although they have) nor because of any notoriety at

5 N. A. S. AF67/158, 1 June 1923; N. A. S. AF67/158, letter from John Grant, Elgol, to Scottish Office, 29 January 1924; Interview with Lachlan Mackintosh and Roderick Nicolson, Elgol, 2 October 1991.

6 Account of the Balranald raid by Angus MacAulay in 1975, in Comann Eachdraidh Uibhist a Tuath (collective authorship), *Croft Histories: Balranald and Paiblesgarry* (Stornoway, 1988), p. 9; N. A. S. AF67/152, Police report 14 February 1921.

7 N. A. S. AF67/147, Police report 9 October 1920.

8 N. A. S. AF67/152, Police report 25 February 1921; AF67/154, Police report 24 January 1923.

the time (Raasay) or subsequently (Park). Rather these raids have been chosen as exemplars of what emerges when a longer perspective than that taken for the rest of the book is adopted, because they represent differing motivations of economic necessity, ideological commitment and overcrowding, and because the close connection between land, landscape and environment clearly emerges from these sets of disturbances.

Cheesebay

One of the most important contexts that earlier chapters have been unable to address has been that of the Governmental response to agitation in the area before 1914. At Cheesebay on North Uist, a part of Newton Farm since the Clearances, the first attempt to draw up a land settlement scheme appears to have begun in 1913. At that time the area of the farm was approximately 7000 acres and the proprietor was Sir Arthur Orde. Neil and Angus McCaskill each paid £11 per annum for the grazing of 80 sheep on Cheesebay, but there were outstanding applications for land on the farm from Bernera, Boreray and townships in North and South Uist. Ongoing demand for land, principally from Bernera and other islands in the Sound of Harris, was prompted by overcrowding and a lack of peats on those islands, coupled with the good harbour and land at Cheesebay (see Figure 6.2).[9]

The report for the 1913 scheme stated that Cheesebay comprised 'very rough and broken moorland – mostly low lying of poor quality.' Most of the area had 'at a remote period been occupied and cultivated ... and is now mixed heather and grass – capable of being brought back to cultivation by spade work.' In addition the bay made an excellent harbourage and peat and water were plentiful. The scheme, which was mainly to accommodate migrants from Harris, was for forty new fishermen's holdings plus enlargements of the peat ground for local townships. It also stands as an excellent example of both the ambition and somewhat limited vision of these land settlement proposals. A Church and School were to be built at Ruisgarry, a canal was to be cut at Stolie to avoid using a particular hazardous section of The Minch but the path into the new settlement (a sizable population) was only to be a turf track with the main form of communication remaining that of boat. The Board decided in favour of this proposal notwithstanding the estate's counter-proposal of just eleven new holdings. In May 1914 it was the Board's scheme which went before the Land Court although extensive delays in the procedure prompted Angus MacQuarrie to write on behalf of applicants for land, saying that they were becoming impatient and were considering illegal action.[10]

9 N. A. S. AF83/385, Report on Cheesebay by T. Wilson, 29 September 1913; Interviews with Neil McIllop, Glasgow, 28 June 1990, Peter Morrison, Bernera 10 April 1990 and Alistair MacLean, Bernera, 10 April 1990.

10 N. A. S. AF83/385, Wilson, Cheesebay, 29 September 1913; AF83/386; AF83/387. A. MacQuarrie to Board, 15 November 1915.

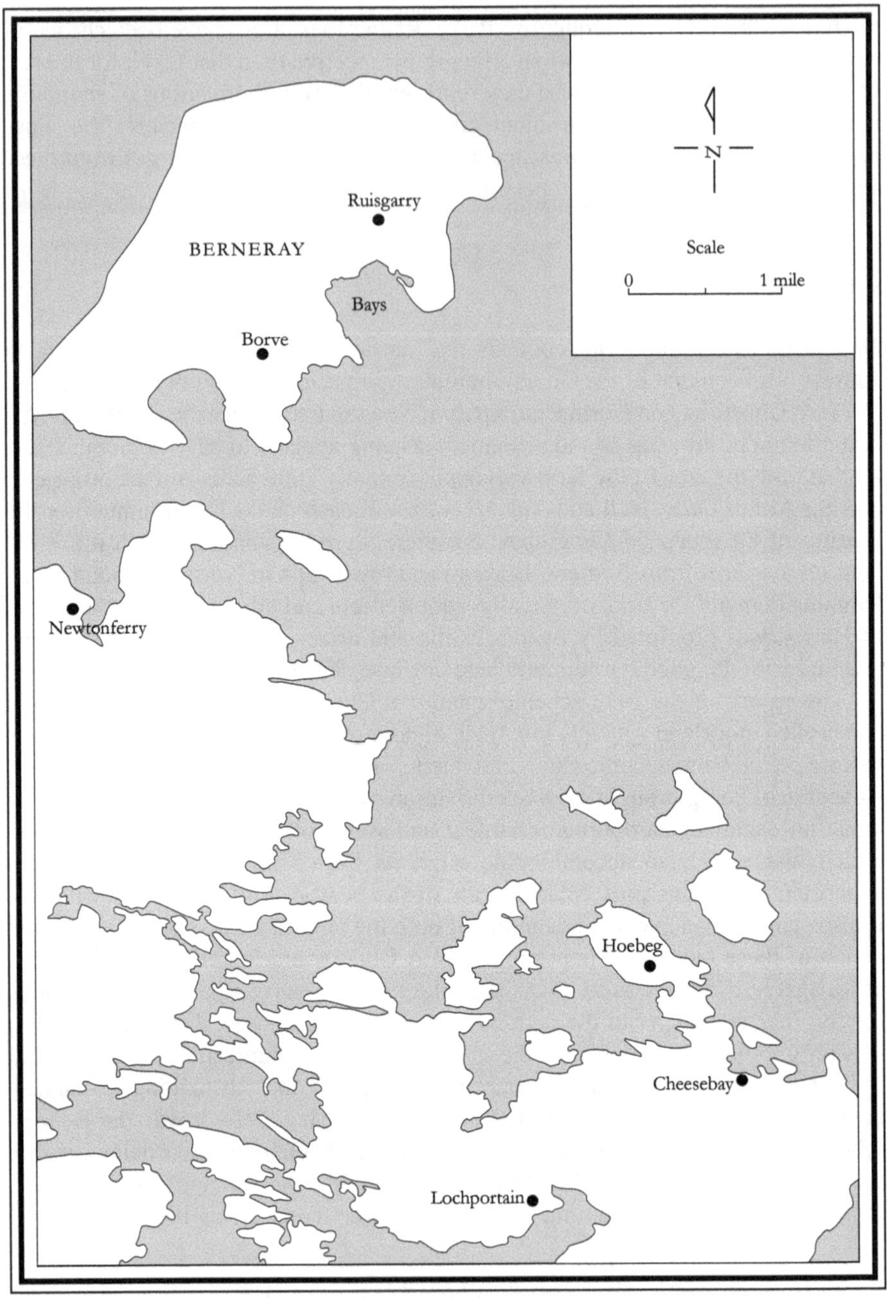

Figure 6.2 Cheesebay

The Land Court finally approved the scheme in December 1915 but, as with many other estates, due to financial difficulties and the war, the Board took it no further. In February 1917 the decision was made to advance the scheme, but it was not until the following July that compensation to proprietor and tenant was fixed. Such was the amount of the award that the Board again decided on abandonment. Prior to this the Board had considered a scheme for potato ground under the Defence of the Realm Act. This was also rejected.[11]

The response of the local community was, at first, slow. Not until August 1919 did Angus Macaskill and other cottars threaten a raid, with agitation intensifying over the course of the following year. Thereafter those agitating most strongly for land formed themselves into groups whose membership was interchangeable. These both threatened raids and undertook small-scale raiding. Thus, in November 1920 Angus Macaskill, Norman Macaskill, Neil Macaskill, Angus MacDonald and Donald Macrae wrote threatening a raid on the farm as 'such employment we can obtain is far from significant ... and we have nothing to look for employment and livelihood but the land.' In June 1921 Peter MacDonald, Neil MacDonald, Donald MacDonald and John MacDonald from Boreray wrote threatening a raid, whilst in October 1922 Peter MacDonald joined with Donald Macrae and Ewen Macaskill threatening 'to enter on possession of the plots we marked out some time ago.'[12] This was the first written indication that anything approaching a formal seizure had taken place.

Larger raids at Cheesebay, took place in 1922 and 1923. The written record reveals five separate occupations of land between 1920 and 1923 and at least thirteen written threats to raid. Of these, nine came from areas or families unconnected to any of the seizures. Moreover, the connections between the various raiding parties would appear slight. Only one person from the earlier raid took part in the 1922 occupation and when house building commenced in January 1923 only half of those taking part had been previously named as raiders. This, however, is to ignore important kinship links between participants, non-participants and those formally identified as "raiders". Drawing on these links and on what is recalled about the various groups, participation and participants in raiding appear almost interchangeable, with connections between raiders being based on kin and with family members taking part as representatives of the wider family. Other indications of the fluidity of these events from within popular memory include hints that raiding both began earlier and was more frequent than the written record suggests. On the other hand, the collective memory supports and underscores archival evidence that part at least of the disorderly activity at Cheesebay was prompted by conflict within the land-working tenantry. In March 1923, for instance, those who had begun house-building in the area wrote to say

11 N. A. S. AF83/388. The decision taken to abandon came on 8 August 1918.

12 N. A. S. AF67/150, Angus Macaskill, et al. to Board 22 November 1920, Peter MacDonald, et al. to Board 2 June 1921; AF67/151, Peter MacDonald to Board October 1922.

that they had cut peats at Howbeg (spelling varies; Hoebeg on Figure 6.2), as Bernera crofters were preventing them from doing the same on their home island. This action was actively resisted by other raiders at Cheesebay.[13]

The often rich remembered record usually complements archival evidence and is best utilised when working at the level of individual event. In this way more detail can emerge which offers the possibility of a widened understanding of the nature of the event. One example of this would be raiding in the North Harris Deer Forest in 1915. The oral tradition of the raid identifies all participants and shows that the raiders cultivated two distinct areas on both shores of Loch Meavaig, where the written record does not.[14] Similarly, at Cheesebay there is evidence of larger numbers going on to the land. Neil McIllop, for instance, believed that up to thirty people in two boatloads went across from Bernera whilst the police reported seventeen. The fact that the raiding group could vary in size and that there was competition for the land in question has been verified within the local community. Confirmed too has been the independently captured recollection of both McIllop and Peter Morrison that once they had left school they joined their respective fathers as members of these fluid groups. Neither son is recorded in police reports as raiders and neither were the two young girls taken, it was suggested, by the Raasay raiders to help with domestic chores.[15] Whilst this does not wholly exclude the possibility that informants were (independently) remembering themselves into a heroic event, what these recollections clearly achieve is to demonstrate the close connections between protest performance and the wider community in which they were based and recalled. Recollections of a larger and more gender varied number of participants reveal the need to maintain and reinforce this in the present.

Other recollections of the raiding at Cheesebay by descendants of participants suggest both that there were more visits from Bernera but that the initial seizure took place later than the archive suggests. This earlier date falls before Neil McIllop would have left school – the point he recalled at which he became eligible to join a raiding party. Similarly Neil McIllop's father is not recorded as one of the house builders, and yet the shelter that McIllop assisted his father in building is one of his clearest memories. It is nevertheless important to be equally cautious over the reliability of the written archive. In this instance, unlike many other protest incidents, information of when raiding took place did not come directly from the raiders themselves but from the local Police Inspector who received his information via a third party.[16] The possibility of visits passing un-observed and un-recorded is thereby enhanced and further reinforced by the fact that such

---

13 R. I. P. D. 26814/M/1, Newton, letter to Board of Agriculture, 5 March 1923; Interview *McIllop*, Glasgow, 28th June 1990.

14 N. A. S. AF67/145, Police report 4 February 1915; Personal correspondence, Mrs Cathy Morrison, Harris, 30 December 1992.

15 Interview McIllop Peter Morrison, Bernera, 10th April 1990; Interview Callum Mackay 30 September 1991.

16 Interview, *McIllop*; R. I. P. D. 26814/M/1, Newton.

visits were rarely overnight. Even if McIllop is here imagining either himself or his father into a more heroic/central position than either actually occupied this clearly indicates the ongoing importance of these events to identity constructs on both individual and communal levels. As part of this, and as a hitherto much-underplayed part of the protest performance, the position of the local police force and their relationship to the tenantry must be acknowledged at the very least. They certainly lived alongside crofters and cottars and could be related to them.

The number of visits is important when the motivation behind the raid is considered. If the visits were infrequent and the raiders withdrew at the request of the Board of Agriculture, raiding at Cheesebay could be considered more of a demonstration to show the continuing intent of Bernera cottars to gain land. However, if Cheesebay was continually utilised, then the intent of the Bernera people was more serious. It was recalled that shelters and turf houses were built on Cheesebay and peats cut. Minor cultivation took place and the raiders took steps to prevent others utilising the area they were occupying.[17] All this indicates that the raiders had serious intentions towards Cheesebay specifically, rather than a general determination to obtain land; although it would be incorrect to assume from this that they had an ideological commitment based on rights to land. Confirmed in conversation with John MacInnes from his own discussions with some of those who took part, it may be possible to infer that, even in those raids where the connection between raider and land seized was seemingly absent, those seizing land had a serious and specific intent towards a specific piece of land. Oral testimony, then, can be of great assistance in the building up of a more resonant context for protest – both in the past and present.

What is remembered additionally serves to re-emphasise the complexity of cause as virtually every interviewee expressed in some sense the belief that protest drew on a sense of entitlement to land, even those who deny that this was influential in the decision to raid. It was passed down to Norman MacLeod, for instance, that there was not axiomatically any 'great desire to return to the exact location ... from which their forebears had been evicted' but there was a belief that lands from which people had been cleared were 'their own.'[18] Similarly, George Stuart did not believe that the desire to return to land that their ancestors had occupied was an important motive in the Coll and Gress raids on Lewis. This was despite some of the Gress raiders being descendants of those originally 'chased' from their old settlement. John Stuart, however, felt that alongside the desire for a home and their belief in war time promises of land, the Gress raiders did feel that the land was rightly theirs. 'Because they were born and brought up on it generations ago ... they made it'.[19] This sentiment, which will be argued below

17 Interview, *McIllop*.

18 Personal correspondence, Norman Macleod, Harris, 11 February 1993.

19 Interview, George Stewart, Coll, 7 November 1992: 'When I was a boy and herding and carting over there [Gress] there was ruins of houses in four or five places. They weren't like a street at all. They were just ruins together about five or six of them ... grouped

is expressive of and underpinned by an imaginative taskscape, is close to but does not directly equate with that expressed by some of those who undertook the raid and identified in earlier chapters as amongst the clearest expressions of the ideology of landholding.

Popular memories of protest events – either direct or inherited – offer the possibility of the extension of our knowledge of the post-1914 agitation for land and both supports and question the written record of such events. Whilst we must be aware of the limitations inherent in oral material, the same can be said for the written record. Issues notwithstanding, what is recalled of these events would seem to offer the possibility of more firmly placing them in the context of the community from which they arose and in which they are remembered. The material provided allows such events to be considered from a different perspective and further questions our ability to fit protest into normative categories. In addition such material can assist in addressing questions not easily addressed from the written record.

The response of the Board of Agriculture to the raiding at Cheesebay was to re-open negotiations with the proprietor. These were complete in January 1923 but resumption of raiding caused the Board to withdraw. Unofficially they felt the scheme too far advanced to halt and that raiders could be excluded but this would mean the possibility of further trouble. The Board was faced with an excess of applicants for any possible scheme and thus 'abandonment of negotiations would penalise the law abiding applicants for the illegal action of a few.' The decision was made to proceed with purchase, as once they were proprietors the Board had the power to eject raiders. Officials felt that this was 'not a pleasant prospect' but such action would show that the 'intimation as regards raiding and it's [sic] consequences on those who raid, really meant business.' The new proprietors were never forced to demonstrate their determination and, in fact, installed some of the raiders as new holders using the fact that the raiders were not resident to circumvent the general bar on raiders gaining holdings.[20]

Finally, three points may be made concerning motivation for seizure of land at Cheesebay. Firstly, whilst the intention of the Board was to break up the land, the speed at which it proceeded and the ease with which the proprietor was able to delay the break up engendered much frustration and directly influenced the decision to raid. Underlying this were other long-term structural motives, principally economic necessity and the poor conditions pertaining in the raiding townships (mainly lack of peat and overcrowding). Finally, the Government's reaction, conditioned by political considerations, caused much frustration and exacerbated the tendency to illegal actions.

---

together and they were just there ... That's where the people at Back came from. People that were chased from Gress.'; Interview John Stuart, Gress, 5 November 1992.

20 R. I. P. D. 26814/2 Newton, Board of Agriculture memo 19 January 1923; N. A. S. AF67/151, note by C. Weatherill, 30 January 1923

Raasay

The origins of post-1914 events on this island lie in the ending in 1912 of an informal grazing agreement between crofters from Oskaig and the island's proprietor. This group were subsequently successful in a bid to gain enlargements to their crofts but failed to obtain an arable park adjacent to the township they were agitating for. In 1915, due to an imminent break in the lease, the same families renewed their agitation for this park and this prompted the Board of Agriculture to consider a wider scheme – the first time they appear to have done so. Lack of progress, however, meant that in the autumn of 1916 agitation for land became a more general movement from the north of the island (and from Rona) aimed at the one-time arable land in the south. Unlike Cheesebay very little detail either of the first set of proposals for a scheme of land settlement or nature of the ground in question survives, although it is generally accepted on the island today that the area targeted was steep but fertile. This was tacitly acknowledged by the Board of Agriculture in 1917 when consideration was given to the setting up of a Defence of the Realm Agreement, although this was rejected on the grounds that the land that was most easy to return to cultivation was too far from current habitation.

This rejection notwithstanding a more limited Defence of the Realm scheme, in a different location, was set up. When this particular scheme ceased with the war's end, the cottars who had gained land, and then lost it, resumed their agitation. When no more land was forthcoming they returned to the ground and cultivated it in the spring of 1919 and 1920. This, their return and cultivation, was only the most visible point of a much more widespread agitation from both Raasay and its neighbouring island of Rona which caused the Board to persuade the proprietors, a firm of ironmasters, not to pursue an interdict.[21]

The Board further attempted to revive its scheme on the grounds that 'It would be difficult to justify this proposal on other grounds than the conditions of the applicants is necessitous, and so urgently in need of amelioration that disorder is inevitable unless steps are taken to remove the trouble.'[22] This was an entirely accurate summation. Numerous threats to seize land were received, particularly from Rona, with correspondents from this island being additionally motivated by the belief that they were trying to recover land expropriated from their ancestors. This pressure notwithstanding, negotiations between the Board and the proprietors broke down in August 1920 prompting threats such as that from Rona stating 'there is great unrest prevailing among us here, owing to the slowness of your Board in dealing with our applications ... we are now determined to fight and shed

21 In this instance the first illegal cultivation preceded any threat. When the Board did receive threats they were made by different groups and individuals than those in occupation. R. I. P. D. 14113, Raasay; N. A. S. AF67/149, Report by T. Wilson 11 May 1920.

22 R. I. P. D. 14113, Raasay, 12 December 1919.

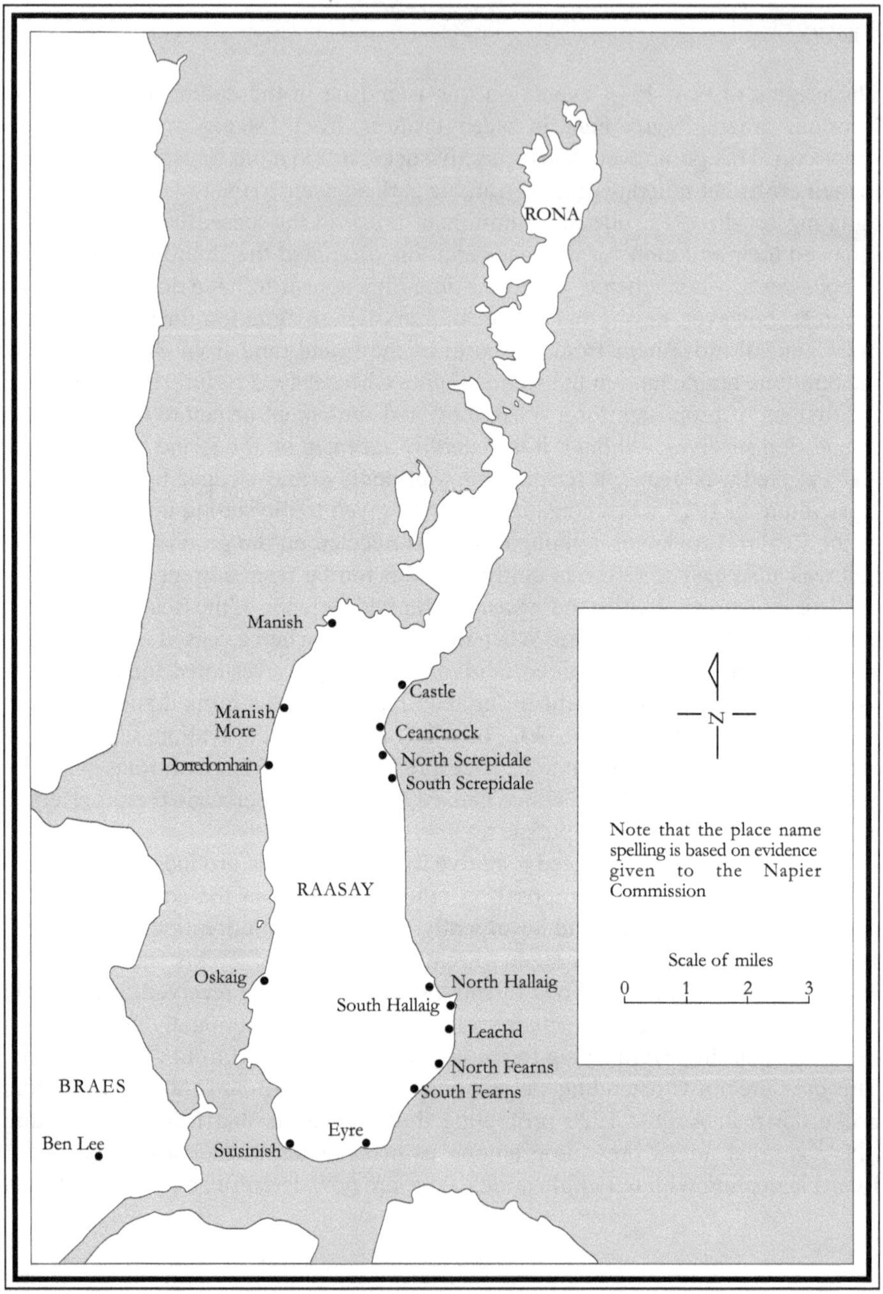

Figure 6.3 The islands of Raasay and Rona

our last drops of blood ... for our liberties at home' thereby revealing, once again, the close connection between protest and military service.[23]

On Raasay the shoemaker occupied a prominent position both within the community and in popular memory. For instance, it is recalled (by more than one informant) that groups attempting to gain land often sought the advice of the Shoemaker whose response was consistent: if illegal acts were decided upon they needed to be carried through resolutely.[24] As a result of one such conversation the Rona people decided to raid and, in February 1921, wrote threatening to raid the south end of Raasay on the 15 March with it actually taking place six days later. The men inspected the site and, forced by the weather to stay overnight, rebuilt some walls for shelter. When they returned on the 4th April they marked off plots and commenced planting. Callum Mackay adds that whilst building houses they first erected a bothie which they called 'the Company Lodge'. They were immediately interdicted.[25]

The proprietors were determined to halt the raid, the Director of Land Settlement believing that Bairds felt 'nothing for public opinion or for the fate of the raiders' and that they were prepared to demolish any houses built. Opinion within the Board was consistent with the earlier agitation: given the determination of the raiders and the conditions on Rona, a scheme was inevitable. Thus 'it is for every reason desirable that the island of Raasay should be acquired and settled without delay.' In 1921 the official position was that the Board of Agriculture (supported by the Scottish Office) would not contemplate a scheme whilst land was subject to illegal occupation. Nevertheless at Raasay, as with a number of prominent raids, unofficial negotiations for purchase were instigated.[26]

Across the early autumn of 1921 attempts were made to arrest the raiders but with little success as the police did not have a boat and, as confirmed by the Chief Constable, 'all local Boat owners are more or less in sympathy with the raiders.' Other Government departments with boats were reluctant to get involved and even when transport was obtained the raiders would always be warned well in advance of their arrival. All of this was exacerbated by the fact that the authorities were very worried by the close links between Raasay and Skye and the strong likelihood (supported by popular memory) that Skye men were willing to help the raiders

23 R. I. P. D. 14113/M, Raasay, 19 February 1920 and 21 January 1921.

24 Interview Murdo James Macleod, Raasay, 30 September 1991. Other interviewees felt that The Shoemaker may have been more influential and acted as catalyst for the seizure.

25 R. I. P. D. 14113/M, 25 February 1921, 2 April 21 and 4 April 1921; Interview, *Mackay*; N. A. S. AF67/149, 26 April 1921.

26 N. A. S. AF67/149 Letter from Sir Arthur Rose to Scottish Office 27 September 1921 and 17 October 192, letter from Charles Wetherill to Sir Arthur Rose 30 November 1921, 10 October 1921 secretary of State for Scotland publishes instructions 'that in future land raiding is to operate as an absolute bar to land settlement, and that persons taking part in such raiding shall be removed from the Board's list of approved applicants for small holdings.'

resist arrest. In addition the number of those in illegal occupation and living at the south end continued to grow, with as many as 47 there by the end of the year.[27]

It was the Shoemaker who obtained advanced warning of the arrival of the police. The raiders would leave

> their houses and they went on the hills and were watching the police at a distance ... There was an uncle of mine ... he was very ... an ex-navy man ... exposing himself too much and one of the policeman spotted him and he made after him and John Mackay would go a wee bit and ... he would say to the police "you needn't come further you'll never catch me and even if you did I wouldn't go on that boat ... I would put my foot through it" he says "and sink the Boat. "You would be drowned yourself" says the policeman "Not at all" he says "I was in the Navy I would swim the Channel" [laughter] ... so there was a hillock there where he was standing and the police was a bit away from him and we called it *cnoc a phoileasmain*, the hillock of the policeman. [laughter].[28]

A successful arrest was made early in the morning (perhaps as early as 2 a.m.) after the raiders had been to Applecross on the mainland to Communion in the Free Church. When this became known, the people of Braes in Skye who were

> very much in favour of the raiders ... quite a few of these gallant men of Braes, some of whom were ex-servicemen, came across ... so they went to the pier ... at about four o'clock ... there was a crowd of Braes people ... prepared to make a stand ... to stop the police ... they said what they would do if the police showed any resistance they would put them off the pier. But the raiders didn't like to make any noise and said they were prepared to go quietly.[29]

After imprisonment, and after refusing to resume living on Rona, the raiders returned to Raasay. On arrival they were met by a crowd led by a piper from Portree (on Skye). He piped them around Raasay House, where the officials of the Board of Agriculture were staying, and across to Fearns and Eyre.[30]

The return of the raiders to the seized land compelled all other parties to realise that prison would not force abandonment of seized land. In January 1922 the Chairman of the Board of Agriculture wrote to the Under Secretary for Scotland that

27 N. A. S. AF67/149, Letter from Chief Constable 22 August 1921, letter from Procurator Fiscal's Office 28 September 1921, letter from Sir Robert Greig (Board of Agriculture) to Scottish Office 6 December 1921; R. I. P. D. 14113 Raasay, report from T. Wilson.

28 Callum Mackay *Raasay*.

29 Callum Mackay *Raasay*.

30 Callum Mackay *Raasay*.; R. I. P. D. 14113, Sub-Commissioner to Board of Agriculture 17 December 1921.

> £20,000 is more than the Estate would bring in the open market and under ordinary circumstances I do not think the purchase of Raasay is justifiable. The circumstances however are quite exceptional and the case is parallel to that of Eoligarry [Barra] where we had no alternative. Here also I think we have no alternative ... I recommend the scheme because our hands are forced and the proposal is the better of two bad courses.

The Estate was purchased the following month for £16,000 and the raiders, including those from earlier incidents, were settled on the land. Their success continued to inspire those less successful to threaten raids until at least 1929.[31]

As already apparent, a strong oral tradition has built up around these events which points to considerable additional detail and a wider range of motivation to that maintained in the archive. Here, as elsewhere, those undertaking acts of protest were frustrated by the failure to fulfil war-time promises of land, but there were also locally specific socio-economic motivations. Roderick MacLeod, brother of a raider, recalled the inconvenience of living on Rona as motive. To get goods in and cattle out use had to be made of ferries to Raasay and then Portree on Skye. Fearns and Eyre were chosen partly because they were close to Raasay pier. Similarly, Callum Mackay pointed out that the area chosen was near to a school. Nevertheless all informants held the belief that the predominant reason behind the choice of the south end of the island was that this was the area from which their people (both MacLeods and Mackays) had been removed and to which the raiders felt entitled.[32] This is a belief, moreover, which was openly articulated to the Napier Commission:

> Q 7837 'I don't remember the first removing, but I remember Mr Rainy about thirty years ago clearing fourteen townships, and he made them into a sheep farm ... Castle, Screpidale, two Hallaigs, Ceancrock, Leackd, two Fearns, Eyre, Suisinish, Doirredomkain, Mainish ...
>
> Q 7857 Have any people been evicted at any time from Rona?
>
> No. The people were not living in Rona at first at all. They were sent to Rona'
>
> Q 7858 Did the people out of these fourteen townships ... go of their own accord?
>
> No, not at all. The people were very sorry to leave at that time. They were weeping and wailing and lamenting. They were taking handfuls of grass that was

31 R. I. P. D. 14113, 2 January 1922; 14113/3, letter from Board of Agriculture to Scottish Office, 16 February 1922; 14113/M, letter from Rona, 28 January 1929.

32 Interview Murdo James Macleod, *Raasay*; Interview Roderick Macleod, Ose, Skye 5 October 1991.

> growing over the graves of their families in the churchyard, as remembrances of their kindred.[33]

Theirs was a view of land that would not have been recognised by the landowners but equally it was not shared at Cheesebay, either at the time of the Napier Commission or subsequently. Why should this be? Answers may lie with the effectiveness of the earlier agricultural re-organisation. At Raasay some inhabitants were removed to the borders of their old settlement. This meant that kin links could be maintained and claims to the land from which they had been removed sustained over time and over generations. Importantly, the land remained in sight. Retention of an ideological view of land and hence the desire to regain access to which people believed they had a right was, in part at least, the product of a deeper proximity than at Cheesebay. In this instance the earlier removal appears more thorough and a core population of ex-inhabitants did not remain. It is important to recognise, then, the important role played by landlords, who were themselves reacting to broader socio-economic processes. Thus, as will be seen in the final case study, raiding in the Park district was in part a reflection of the Lewis problem of overcrowding; a factor elsewhere but which only appears as an explicit primary motivation in protest on that particular island.

Raiding on Raasay was carried out under the immediate impetus of the failure to gain promised land and the economic and social conditions prevailing on Rona but was based in long-term commitment to the notion that the land was theirs by right of occupation and cultivation. The Shoemaker suggested to Donald *Mhòr* that they raid 'a decent bit of ground more convenient to Rona.' This they rejected in favour of the area 'where they came from.' As articulated by Callum Mackay:

> Traditionally the people came from; they were removed from these areas of Fearns and Eyre. And they were desirous of getting back to what their ancestors had had ... Some of the Mackays were in Eyre and Fearns ... the MacLeods ... also ... They thought that they weren't taking anything out of the hands of the Laird [unclear] or anything else but what was their property. What they took out of their hands by removing their ancestors. They weren't a people who were careless ... who didn't care whether they were ... breaking the law or not that's not the kind of people they were at all. They were very desirous in keeping the law ... although they had for the benefit of their families they had to break it in this sense just to take it at that time ... it's just from their own personal experience that made them take that move ... getting the land what their ancestors possessed and what they needed because of their families ... there was nine in our own family.

33 British Parliamentary Papers, XXXII, 1884–1885, Commission of Inquiry into the Condition of Crofters and Cottars in the Highlands and Islands of Scotland. The Commission took evidence on Raasay on 22 May 1883.

Although forced to break the law, they did not recognise the legitimacy of that law as it was made for and by 'the laird only.'[34]

Despite the power of this testimony questions can be raised over the accuracy of the claim that the Rona people were raiding 'the land what their ancestors possessed'. For Sharpe the depopulation of the southern half of the island was accomplished more by emigration than by migration. Emigration began in 1803, before the reorganisation of the agricultural system. Runrig was abandoned in the second decade of the nineteenth century and crofting established. Large-scale sheep farming began in 1824, although clearance was not evident until the late 1830s, and by 1855 twelve townships, the vast majority in the south and east of the island, 'were more or less depopulated'. Much of this depopulation was achieved through assisted large-scale emigrations taking place in 1852 and 1854 but one hundred 'or a little more, left the island without record, probably during 1851 and 1854, but before the 1861 census' possibly to Skye and other parts of Scotland although the records fail as this juncture. Sharpe is certain, however, that the few families which remained after this major movement were forcibly cleared shortly afterwards. This inevitably raises questions over the validity of the belief that the Raasay raiders were re-taking 'what their ancestors had had', what was 'their property' as they may well have been unrelated to the original inhabitants. It is of course perfectly possible that, both at the time and within the contemporary community, the belief in rights to land was developed and held so as to anchor the legitimacy of the "return to a homeland". Perhaps of greatest interest is the fact that the belief does not come through in the written archive. What emerges from popular memory is a much greater depth of connection to land and landscape which may find some support from within the historiography. Key here is the few families from Screapadal, Hallaig, Leac, Fearns, Castle and Manish who were forcibly evicted after the 1854 emigration. For Sharpe a combination of clearance, the more benign but large-scale emigrations and the emotional impact of this significant socio-cultural upheaval gave rise to 'a powerful folk memory' of the creation of the Raasay sheep farm: the belief that all the established small-tenantry had been evicted from 'their property'.[35] Finally, there remains the possibility offered by those who were cleared but who did not emigrate. Whilst their destination remains uncertain it was very likely to have been Rona or Skye. People living on the island today trace their ancestry to these locations. It may very well be then that this smaller part of a wider movement provided a tangible and kin-based foundation for the belief (and justifying narrative) in rights to land based on past occupation.

A further potential issue with the memory of raiding on Raasay as here captured is that at first glance it may well have a tendency towards the anecdotal. For instance, the naming of the hillock associated with the resistance to arrest appears at first glance to be of little consequence. Engaged with at greater depth,

34 Interview Callum Mackay, *Raasay*.

35 Richard Sharpe, *Raasay: a study in island history* (London, 1977), pp. 59–67; Richard Sharpe, *Raasay: documents and sources* (London, 1978), pp. 192–299.

however, what it reveals is, critically, the close links between people and places; nature and culture (see Chapter 7). Furthermore, when viewed in the context of disturbances on Raasay as a whole this naming reveals the depth of feeling for land and the motivational power deriving from a particular landscape, questions our understanding of the symbolic and ritualised qualities of the land raid and places land seizure after 1914 more firmly in the tradition of the earlier Land Wars.

Within land seizure on Raasay is evident combinations of long and short-term motives; a pattern which matches that for many other sets of disturbances. There is also a combination of motives common to Highland disturbance as a whole and something much more locally specific. Once again this is a pattern repeated elsewhere but it also demonstrates the utility of the fine-grained approach adopted here. Interweaving between the oral tradition and the written archive has permitted a much more nuanced interpretation to emerge and one that is significantly closer to that currently held by the local population. This is a positive shift not least because the impact and consequences of these actions remain active and constitutive on Raasay to the present day. The same can be said for land disturbances in the Park district on the island of Lewis, but here the contemporary impact has perhaps been even more dynamic.

The Park District of Lewis

Undoubtedly the most celebrated disturbance in Park was the Deer Raid of 1887 in which many hundreds of (mainly) cottars and squatters from the Lochs district of the island set out to "drive" the forest. Their aim was to slaughter as many deer as possible, in part as symbolic gesture but also to obtain food. There was land hunger too and a desire to generate publicity and attract public sympathy for their cause. Whilst land was not forthcoming for some considerable period (and, significantly for their relative importance, as a result of post-war raiding) the Deer Raid did at least induce a government enquiry into the social and economic conditions on Lewis.[36]

This significant event has also generated a movement to memorialise land disturbances on Lewis more generally, with a total of six monuments erected by the end of 2013. The disturbances of the 1920s are recognised in a memorial to the Coll and Gress land seizures, whilst the Park Deer Raid has its own monument (see Figures 6.5 and 6.6). Whilst these monuments can be attributed to the work of a committee – *Cuimhneanchain nan Gaisgeach* – the driving force behind this was Angus 'Ease' Macleod.

Ease was also my main interviewee for Park and his source material was partly archival (verified by consulting the original) and partly generated through his own interaction with and understanding of the Park community. Ease was born in the district and whilst less than ten years old at the time of the post-World War One

36 N. A. S. AF 67/68, Treasury to Lothian, 20 December 1887.

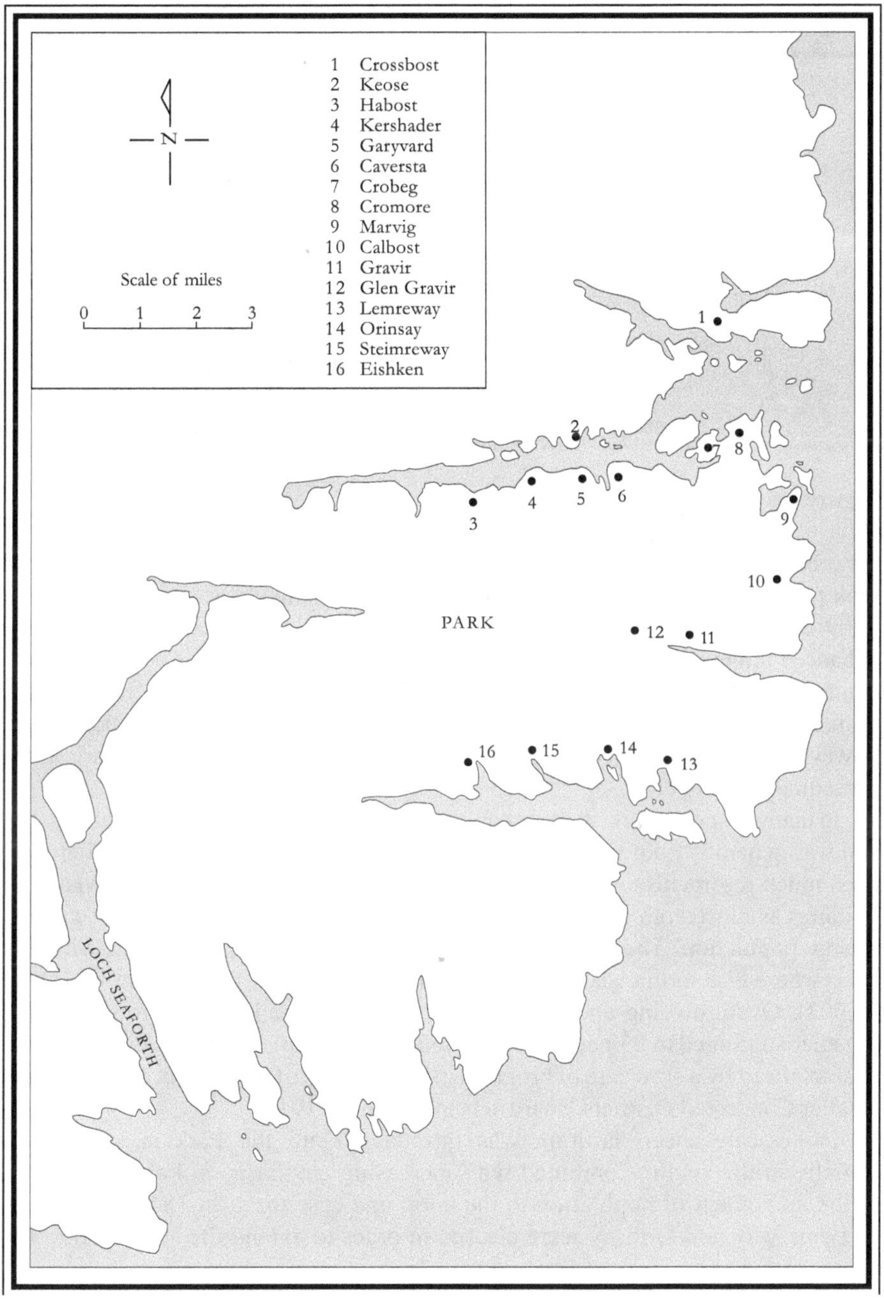

Figure 6.4 Park

Figure 6.5 Coll and Gress memorial

disturbances, was intensely interested in land issues and sought out those who took part in the incidents in the district. In short, Macleod became an intentional tradition bearer himself. In what follows, his testimony offers a different and enhanced understanding of events after 1914 (filtered through his own passionate commitment to the crofter cause and to land issues more specifically), of which the raids at Orinsay and Stimervay constitute the most significant. These disturbances, however, can only be fully understood in the context of the history of Park in the preceding crofting era.

In many respects Park shared characteristics common to Lewis as a whole. The soil was generally poor with isolated pockets of good levels of fertility. There had been much re-organisation of the population with accompanying sub-division of holdings as nineteenth century landlords attempted improvement whilst retaining a large population. The result was a demographic pattern at odds with virtually everywhere else in the islands, with population levels not peaking until 1911 (at 29,603). Overcrowding and squatting were at endemic levels, therefore, which together amounted to 23 per cent of the total population in 1921.[37] Lewis was also characterised by a slow rate of progress in the creation of new crofts with just three smaller Congested Districts Board schemes prior to 1918.

Large-scale sheep farming was introduced into the Park area in 1802, initially in the south. Combined with increasing emphasis on kelping, this led to the movement of population to the north and east coast. In 1843 the crofters of Lemreway and Orinsay were cleared in order to extend the sheep farm. The

37 Bob Chambers, 'For Want of Land: A Study of Land Settlement in the Outer Hebrides, Skye and Raasay between the Two World Wars', unpublished PhD. in progress, University of Edinburgh. I am very grateful to Bob for allowing me sight of this important work.

Figure 6.6 Park Deer Raid memorial

Table 6.1 Population figures for the crofting townships of Park

Township (number of crofts)	Date										
	1830	**1841**	**1851**	**1861**	**1871**	**1881**	**1891**	**1901**	**1911**	**1921**	**1931**
Habost (13)	49	53	68	89	96	98	113	121	111	105	87
Kershader (12)	66	70	81	84	104	114	103	111	101	93	94
Garyvard (11)	38	46	63	77	94	103	101	74	100	117	99
Caverstay (6)	?	29	?	38	42	78	45	54	64	47	45
Cromore (28)	124	127	170	182	221	259	271	294	284	240	209
Crobeg (1)	41	9	50	30	10	11	6	3	3	8	2
Marvig (23)	115	98	146	189	206	206	205	225	206	181	160
Calbost (14)	55	67	105	122	158	183	197	200	187	189	151
Gravir (69)	197	233	270	326	353	368	389	416	468	385	341
Lemreway (33)	144	179	?	209	236	245	261	316	339	289	228
Orinsay (14)	119	148	D	D	D	D	4	2	5	35	91
Stimervay (0)	46	62	89	D	D	D	D	D	D	?	?
Eishken (17)	104	D	D	11	17	29	11	14	14	10	12
Totals (224 crofts)	1098	1121	1042	1357	1357	1694	1706	1830	1882	1699	1519

Note: D=Township depopulated.

Source: Personal information Mr A. MacLeod, Stornoway; but based on independently verified census figures.

majority of the population of Orinsay went to Crossbost. Stimervay survived as a crofting township until 1857, when the crofters agreed to give up their lease in exchange for permission to re-occupy Lemreway. The three townships are within five miles of each other, and over time the populations intermixed.[38]

38 N. A. S. AF67/151, Sir Robert Greig to Scottish Office, 27 October 1922; AF67/292, Board memo, December 1929.

Where Park had previously supported 28 townships, the population in the second half of the Nineteenth Century was concentrated into fewer than half that number, with approximately two thirds of the land area closed to crofting. The result of this was overcrowding in the townships, with practically every croft supporting more than one family.[39] Moreover, and as evidenced in Table 6.1, except for those townships experiencing further reorganisation, Park townships reflect the more general Lewis pattern of continued growth of population into the twentieth century.

The pattern revealed here and elsewhere is of a narrowing of residential possibilities combined with population growth. This was a major motivation to protest and must raise the question, when combined with attempts to identify more ideologically-driven motives, why so few of the original 28 townships were subject to land agitation. In part, at least, this was the product of the geography of the area. Orinsay and Stimervay were the last unpopulated locations in the northern part of Park with access to a safe anchorage. Other suitable locations were far to the south and inaccessible. The cottars of the district decided to concentrate on Orinsay and Stimervay, and if settlement had been accomplished with ease, which it was not, then they would have attempted other locations.[40]

Agitation for these lands began as early as 1880. Shortly after the conversion of the farm to deer forest the Park Deer Raid took place to be followed by the aforementioned government enquiry and the posting of troops on the island. There was, however, a general failure to gain land and so agitation continued and a smaller and less well documented raid took place in 1891. To Hunter, only Orinsay was raided, but Ease had been told that Stimervay was seized also at this time. Orinsay was occupied by Crossbost people returning 'to their own village' whilst Stimervay was raided by ten people from Gravir, ten from Crowmore and ten from Calbost. Some cultivation and house building took place, but the raid was again unsuccessful. Hunter notes that 35 raiders were jailed. It is likely, therefore, that he amalgamated the two locations and identified only Orinsay.[41]

These two key ex-townships, by then a single farm of approximately 4,000 acres, were first considered for a scheme in 1913, although proposals for four new holdings at Stimervay were dropped before it got to the Scottish Land Court. Unfortunately, the combination of the general unsuitability of the ground ('On Steimreway the old arable with the exception of about an acre is decidedly poor quality, shallow, steep and rocky'), war-time financial constraints, and the intransigence of Major Matheson (the proprietor) forced suspension of the scheme.[42] After the war a new proprietor was in place, Lord Leverhulme, whose

39 Neil MacRitchie, for example, one of the Orinsay raiders, shared No. 38 Gravir with three other families plus two maiden aunts. Source: personal correspondence Angus Macleod, 4 December 1992.

40 Personal correspondence Angus Macleod, 4 December 1992.

41 Hunter, *The Making*, pp. 171–4, and p. 181; Interview Angus Macleod, 5 November 1992.

42 N. A. S. AF83/352, report by Neil MacLean, BoAS, 27 January 1913.

Table 6.2 The raiders of Orinsay and Stimervay and their residence

	Raider	Residence	No. of families on croft
Orinsay	Donald Montgomery	17 Lemreway	3
	Angus Macmillan	8 Lemreway	4 (?)
	John Carmichael	16 Lemreway	7
	Kenneth Macmillan	4 Lemreway	3
	Kenneth Kennedy	8 Lemreway(1)	4 (?)
	Murdo MacInnes	2 Lemreway	2
	Donald Nicolson	16 Lemreway	7
	Neil MacRitchie	38 Gravir	4
	Angus Nicolson	16 Lemreway	7
	Kenneth Kennedy	33 Lemreway	2
	Murdo Macmillan	4 Lemreway	3
	Donald Nicolson	20 Lemreway	3
	Louis Macmillan	5 Lemreway	2 (?)
Stimervay	Donald Morrison	9 Calbost	5
	Peter Chisholm	8 Lemreway(1)	4 (?)
	Donald Nicolson	16 Lemreway	7
	John Nicolson	16 Lemreway	7
	Donald Carmichael	26 Lemreway	2 (?)
	'Dallan' Nicolson	16 Lemreway	7

Note: Average size Park croft 5 acres plus 26,000 acres outrun. Deer Forest 42,000 acres.
Source: Conversation with and letters from Angus MacLeod.

views and negotiations have been extensively documented both elsewhere and earlier in the present work. The Board was persuaded not to reactivate the scheme for Orinsay until Leverhulme's development plans were given a chance of success. As elsewhere on the island this both provoked much resentment amongst the landless ex-servicemen and revealed tensions within the crofting tenantry. The first direct threat to Orinsay came in 1919 when Kenneth Nicolson and others from Lemreway stated their intention to seize land there in the Spring of 1920. They were driven to this as 'The Committee and Crofters of Lemreway compel us to leave as there is enough room for us there ... we are preparing huts for the spring'. Earlier, Neil McRitchie from 38 Gravir had written to the Board of Agriculture stating that he was married with eight children under 13 years old and lived on the croft with a number of other close relatives. He, along with two other squatters was in danger of being put off the land by the croft-holder, his brother.[43] Actual raiding in the area, however, was delayed until 1921, by which time an additional layer of motivation had been added. They wrote

43 AF67/147, 19 October 1919 and 16 December 1919; AF83/354, Neil McRitchie to Board of Agriculture, 26 February 1918.

> to let you know that we do not intend to stop our raiding ... for Lord Leverhulme's schemes, as his schemes will not profit no one, possibly may be his schemes will profit those that is near him in Stornoway ... but we are about 30 miles from Stornoway and do not intend to derive any profit from it ... Meetings were held in some places throughout the island in favour of Lord Leverhulme, but none in our district and neither would any in our district support same.[44]

This combination of the friction of distance, the proprietor's development plans, and differing aspirations was also proving divisive. As already discussed, crofters had greater sympathy towards experimenting with Leverhulme's ideas, particularly if they lived closer to Stornoway, whilst those without land and living on a kinsman's croft were more widely in favour of raiding. From Gravir too came further affirmation of inter-tenantry conflict. 'I think that I am more entitled to a Croft than people that didn't serve their King and Country. I then beg to inform you that I and a few more is [*sic*] going to make a croft and a home in Steamrava [Stimervay] near Orinsay. Steamrava was once under the Crofters Act ... If we don't get there we are determined to make a home in some of the populated villages of Park.'[45] These sentiments serve additionally to expose the close connection between disturbance, vernacular and traditional environmental beliefs, and the crofting landscape.

The 1921 raid on Orinsay proved decisive. Leverhulme was provoked into agreeing to the reinstatement of the smallholdings scheme, and all but one of the crofts created went to raiders. The proprietor was determined to go no further, however, and the Board refused to proceed other than on the basis of an agreed scheme. The reaction from within was inevitable and predictable. In October 1922 correspondents from Crowmore wrote that 'We are aware that Oronsay has been allotted and Steemradth [*sic*] has been taken possession of. We therefore hereby inform the Board that it is our intention to take possession of Arnish in the near future.'[46] Land at Stimervay had been cultivated in 1921 at the height of the agitation for Orinsay, and in spring 1922 it was subject to a more prolonged seizure. Whilst the Board of Agriculture felt able to set up a settlement scheme at Orinsay, the same was not the case for its near neighbour Stimervay. This was due in part to the unsuitability of the ground but mainly because of the 'exceptional sporting value' of the land and the associated high compensation costs. In this instance, therefore, they took no action to regularise the situation and simply left the raiders where they were. The proprietor did the same as he believed that the Board would intervene to establish raiders on the land (very likely, as we have seen) even if he took legal action to achieve the opposite. The outcome of this mutual inertia was

44 N. A. S. AF83/354, Kenneth Macmillan and Murdo McInnes for Orinsay raiders 2 February 1921.

45 N. A. S. AF83/763, letter Alexander Campbell to Board of Agriculture, 7 December 1921.

46 N. A. S. AF67/151, letter Angus Macleod to Scottish office, 18 October 1922

one of the very few land seizures in which virtually nothing official happened after the seizure; there was no overt response, with raiders simply being left in place. Despite a lack of footpath, fencing, schooling or church, families survived here for some considerable period and one or two into the 1940s.[47]

Orinsay and Stimervay, along with their close neighbour, Lemreway, were therefore closely intertwined, both at the time and subsequently. The depth of this interweaving is revealed in part through an engagement with some of the detail of the raiding families (see Table 6.2).

Two observations may be made. Firstly, there were only two raiding families who did not come from Lemreway. Local tradition suggests that this should not be interpreted as raiding drawing upon a narrow support base, but as reflecting the belief that Lemreway, Gravir and Calbost people were entitled to first refusal for Orinsay and Stimervay.[48] Second, raiding in Park reflects the close kin-links evident in many raids if studied in detail. A good example of this is Number 8 Lemreway. This croft supported a number of families plus Peter Chisholm, who raided Stimervay. His cousin Angus Macmillan also lived there, was one of the first to go to Orinsay, and is reputed to have taken a principal role in the agitation (but was not the letter writer). Other Macmillan relatives resided at Number 4 Lemreway. Of the seven male members of that croft, four went to Orinsay, one became a lay preacher, one settled in Glasgow and the remaining male inherited the croft. The two daughters married in Lemreway and Crowmore. At Stimervay, the Nicolsons from Number 16 Lemreway provided two of the raiders. Three other families from the same croft went to Orinsay.[49] Interestingly, when compared to the 1891 Orinsay/Stimervay raid, numbers taking part were fewer and fewer townships were represented. The written evidence can only partly explain this. Threats to raid Stimervay from Gravir were never carried through, as the Gravir people turned their attention to Glen Gravir, part of the township common. In October 1922, shortly after Stimervay was occupied, the Land Court received notification that seven Gravir cottars had begun house building here.[50]

This notwithstanding, Ease clearly felt that he had been told that there were people from wider locations who had been planning to take part in the Stimervay raid but that they ultimately took no part. He suggested that approximately ten

47 N. A. S. AF67/292, Notes on raiding in Lewis, December 1929; N. A. S. AF67/151, letter from Sir Robert Greig to Scottish Office, 27 October 1922. Earlier the same month Thomas Wilson, the Board's sub-commissioner on the island had reported that 'I am afraid that the proprietor will not take legal proceedings (Lord Leverhulme being opposed on principle to the adoption of such) … It is the main source of weakness in the Lewis administration that the public at large quite understand …. hence much of the illegal taking possession of recent years.' See also Chambers, *Life On The Edge*.

48 Interview Angus Macleod, *Lewis*.

49 Angus Macleod, Lewis, interview 5th November 1992; Angus Macleod, personal correspondence 4 December 1992, 26 July and 17 August 1993.

50 D.A.F.S. 118777/G/S Gravir, 13 October 1922.

other families, mainly from Calbost, were actively preparing to go there. However, during the transportation of building materials an accident resulted in the drowning of representatives of two of these families with the result that most of the Calbost contingent abandoned their plans. This was compounded by a shooting accident which resulted in the death of Donald Carmichael, one of the Stimervay raiders. His family decided to remain on the land, but Allan Finlayson (the local blacksmith), who had been amongst the first to go to Stimervay, was with Carmichael when he was killed and out of grief he returned to squat at Marvig.[51]

As with every case study here utilised what is held in the memory of land agitation at Park suggests greater depth of interpretation possibilities. Certain aspects of this: more detail; a greater range and depth of motivation, for instance; serve to complement and deepen what is held in the formal archive. In so far as answers to questions of leadership in protest have always proved elusive, regardless of the geography and chronology of events scrutinised, there is no doubt that the popular memory of events in the Highlands after 1914 can offer some help.

A Leading Role?

Staying with Lewis for the moment, it has already been noted that local tradition identifies Angus MacMillan as taking a leading role in the agitation. Crucially, however, if he was the catalyst for what followed, and this is by no means certain, he neither emerges from the archive in this way nor was he an influence from without as with Donald Macrae and the Park Deer Raid, for instance. It is this ambiguity and lack of clarity from the archive which makes this particular topic an intractable one.

This question of leadership in the agitation is consequently an under-explored one, and yet it bears directly on the question of outside influence and control of the raiding. If a leader can be identified, and links between that leader and external groups established, this may alter our understanding of the nature of Highland protest. Alternatively, land raiding may be seen to fit into the pattern of historical and contemporary decision making within the crofting tenantry, and as such would stress the close communal links between incident and population.

In her study of a Lewis township Parman argues that there are both formal and informal leaders in a crofting township. However, the 'effective decision making occurs through casual discussion, rumour and the quiet role of a few invisible leaders, who mobilize opinion and in some cases carry out direct action.' Decisions are, in effect, made communally, as a discursive process which is both slow and consensual. The most important discourse is that which occurs before the decision. If the decision has to be made at a formal meeting it is known beforehand. The pre-decision discourse takes the form of the initiation of the subject followed

51 Angus Macleod personal letter 26 July 1993. The Carmichaels were, along with the Morrisons the last two families in occupation.

by a hypothetical discussion. Positive responses to such initiations are rarely achieved; instead, a level of agreement comes about 'by the default of negation.' Hypothetical objections are raised, and if not resolved by informative comments, the decision is postponed.[52]

Parman describes those who initiate such discourse as 'ripple-starters.'

> Discussion and decision come about as if a pebble had been dropped into a pool. The ripple-starters are those who involve themselves extensively in township affairs ... with humour, readiness to have "a quick drink with the boys" and skilfulness [sic] in conveying significant information without being seen as gossips, such individuals serve as informal leaders. They do not put themselves forward, but they exert irrepressible force towards decision making.[53]

It is hard to imagine popular memory retaining ripple-starters and so it is unsurprising that Angus Macleod did not believe that 'there was any outstanding leader either in Lochs or elsewhere in Lewis.' He suggested that the Land League was of assistance in the success of the agitation, but did not take a prompting role in the onset of raiding. In his view this arose 'spontaneously' from within the townships as a result of cumulating frustrations. The men were in daily contact with each other, either working the sheep, at the fishing, or Ceilidh House.[54] As part of her ethnographic study of an Isle of Skye township Sharon Macdonald discusses such places. These were often residences of local significance. In Carnan for instance (the name is fictional) one such was the Church of Scotland Manse, whilst the house that was Macdonald's base for her fieldwork was another and was where all the local post and newspapers were delivered up until the 1950s. The Ceilidh House was where local history was 'witnessed' by the younger generation and, according to Ease, 'was the debating society of the village where all snippets of information was [sic] exchanged.'[55] So there was no formally labelled "house" as such, it would just arise organically and out of everyday interactions. In this way there would be no need to formalise a meeting. Once the subject of land raiding arose, and with a majority in favour, 'very quickly a count would be made of the heads of families' there assembled to determine whether this constituted the majority of the opinion within the township. If this was the case, the decision had been taken, informally, by consensus and from within the community.[56]

52 Susan Parman, *Scottish Crofters: A Historical Ethnography of a Celtic Village* (Belmont, CA, 2004), pp. 89 and 94–6.

53 Parman, *Scottish Crofters*, p. 95.

54 Angus Macleod, personal correspondence 26 July and 17 August 1993.

55 Angus Macleod, personal correspondence 26 July and 17 August 1993; Sharon Macdonald, *Imaging Culture. Histories, Identities and the Gaelic Renaissance* (Oxford, 1997), p. 112.

56 Angus Macleod, personal correspondence 26 July and 17 August 1993.

Similarly, both Lachlan Mackintosh and Roderick Nicolson (in a joint conversation) agreed that those who raided Camusunary and Robaston on the Strathaird Estate, Skye, took group decisions and the majority prevailed. This produced the initial raid and the determination to hold the land which led to some of the raiders being gaoled. On their release, however, the majority were against further action, and so all returned to the family crofts.[57]

The question of leadership and outside influence is less clear cut on Raasay. Here, as has already been noted, The Shoemaker acted as advisor to the raiders and was seen by the Board as influential in the agitation as they did with virtually every correspondent. This does not axiomatically follow, however. At times there would be substance to this and as corroborated by local officials, the organiser of the local agitation was the letter writer as well. Thus, Thomas Wilson, the sub-commissioner with responsibility for Raasay, asserted that

> The writer of the letters ... is Mr John M. Macleod ... whom I know well. Upon his statements no reliance can be placed. He is very hostile to Mr David J. Munro, the Factor and Manager for Messrs Wm Bairds and Co., and I have no doubt he is the author of the raid.[58]

Recollections over how protest actions were structured and organised (admittedly never easy to retain a clear memory/tradition of) suggest that such automatic connections were not always the case, however. Rather than being the instigator and driving force behind protest actions the letter writer, as at Coll and Gress, may have been chosen by those who were driving events along for their eloquence (as the most educated person in the district) and ability. At Coll and Gress it was suggested that those who wrote the letters 'might not have been the leaders' although they were undoubtedly 'very supportive of the leaders'.[59]

Nevertheless, on Raasay, and to Callum Mackay, The Shoemaker 'was the main leader.' Others, however, disagreed. Roderick MacLeod believed that the raiders were without a leader, although The Shoemaker was in the forefront of the agitation and 'very keen on them sticking to the raid.' Further, The Shoemaker's connections to the Highland Land League (confirmed by his son) raises the question as to the degree of influence the League had over the decision to raid the land. In this all Raasay interviewees were in agreement: the raiders did not act in support of the wider political aims of the League, and outside influences were slight. The decision to raid was made for and by themselves. The Shoemaker did

57 Lachlan Mackintosh and Roderick Nicolson, *Elgol*.

58 N. A. S. AF67/149, T. Wilson to Board of Agriculture, 11 May 1920.

59 In this case the source of this opinion – George Stewart – was, once again, both a tradition bearer and deeply interested in the history of his particular district on Lewis. Whilst this does not unquestionably validate this memory it does at least situate this recollection in something a little more substantial that pure opinion. Interview George Stewart, Lewis, 7 November 1992.

not go to the raiders to persuade them to raid. They went to him as a respected and self-educated person who was also a relative. This later fact would have been important to the raiders. The close, kinship-based connections between the Park raiders have already been noted and this is equally the case for Raasay. For Callum Mackay, the composition of the group was determined by their kin links, the decision to raid being discussed and made 'quite privately' despite majority support on Rona.[60]

Beyond this important fact of kin links the popular memory of land seizure on Raasay fails to unequivocally identify a definite leader. It is possible, however, to draw two important inferences from this. Firstly, this equivocation gives further weight to the presence of "ripple starters" as the driving force behind land disturbances. Such people, moreover, are much more likely to be present within the local community thereby strengthening the assertion that outside influence on the decision to seize land was indirect at best. As Callum Mackay has stated, the decision to raid came 'from their own personal experience...getting the land what their ancestors possessed and what they needed because of their families.'[61] More broadly, in terms of motive to land seizure, "family" can be understood in three senses: as extended family typified by kinship links; as nuclear family, often under threat of expulsion from the croft, (i.e. from their own kin); as part of the basis and means of transmission of the ideology of land-as-past-claim. Whichever sense is utilised, the notion of raiding undertaken "for the family" is openly articulated most clearly in the oral tradition. As such it also reveals the ongoing centrality of the relationship between family, croft and land still visible and informing identities in the Highlands today.[62]

Conclusion: Memory, Place and Protest

Place is at one and the same time spatial, temporal and psychological. To recognise this – that it represents the grounding of a melange of human and non-human traffic – is to recognise also that memory is fundamental to that grounding. From this recognition the events of the Highland Clearances, for instance, emerge as a form of 'topocide' – where the memory of place is at once challenged by but also (and here we see it generating protest) set against that which has changed.[63] In this

60 Interview Callum Mackay, *Raasay*; Interview Murdo James Macleod, *Raasay*; Roderick Macleod 5 October 1991, Ose, Skye.

61 Interview Callum Mackay, *Raasay*.

62 One of the projects the author is currently undertaking seeks to investigate exactly this relationship in the contemporary Highlands. Preliminary findings indicate precisely this.

63 John Douglas Porteous, 'Topocide: The Annihilation of Place', in John Eyles and David M. Smith (eds), *Qualitative Methods in Human Geography* (Cambridge, 1988), pp. 75–93.

way, memory of the social, cultural and non-human associations and configuration of spaces makes place but is thus unquestionably of the present. Active and constitutive of spaces, places and identities, memory thus has both agency and works through specific sites (not always a physical location). There is, in short, a geography to memory.

Recent research on *Geography and Memory* has powerfully reminded us that this underpins that other critical relationship: between identity and place.[64] Memory too, in its fluid and mutable nature, serves to remind us that both relationship(s) and identity/place individually are equally inconstant, unfixable and always in a state of "becoming". Here too is a call to prioritise "private" or "personal" memory over that of collective memory, as it is with the individual that collective memory rests and is fundamentally made. Although there is something of an artificial divide about this claim, as suggested by Rothberg's view that memory simultaneously carries both sides of our relationship with the past, it does usefully point to the position of individual personal testimonies within collective memory, as the repository where these reside.[65]

As with every oral history there are inevitably questions of factual reliability and objective validity raised over the material gathered here. However, such has been the extent of the engagement with and response to these questions amongst oral historical practice more generally, that, in terms of this book and chapter, it is more useful to draw attention to the powerfully creative work that memory (especially 'collective' memory) is able to do.[66] A particularly potent discussion of this creative capacity is to be found in Andy Wood's *The 1549 Rebellions and the Making of Early Modern England* in which he convincingly reveals the many different ways in which the narrative of Kett's rebellion was re-worked in popular memory and the different uses it was put to. Wood believes that in this instance memory's fallibility is an asset; its porous boundaries permitting borrowings and adaptations from other histories. More importantly and precisely, as Wood puts it: 'just as the memory of the commotion time remained a field of conflict, so it was possible for plebeian dissidents to take this negative characterisation of Kett's rebellion and to turn it on its head.'[67] That is, to use it as a resource.

Here, then, is found the power and possibilities of collective memory amongst the land-working tenantry in the Highlands of Scotland. Claims to past land and landscape have rightly been seen (by earlier scholars and commentators) to have

---

64 Owain Jones and Joanne Garde-Hansen (eds), *Geography and Memory: Explorations in Identity, Place and Becoming* (Basingstoke, 2012).

65 Michael Rothberg, *Multidirectional Memory: Remembering the Holocaust in the Age of Decolonization* (Stanford CA, 2009).

66 Perhaps one of the first responses to such issues is of course to be found in Paul Thompson's *The Voice of the Past* (Oxford, 2000). One of the best collections of discussions around these questions is to be found in Robert Perks and Alistair Thomson (eds), *The Oral History Reader* (London, 2006).

67 Wood, *The 1549 Rebellions*, p. 247.

been a powerful ideologically-based motivating factor in disturbances. Such motives and claims, both now and in the immediate post-Clearance Highlands, have been maintained (and re-worked) within the collective memory which inheres to specific places and events, and more widely across the region. In part from this creatively forged collective memory – with individual memory its necessary locus – a distinct identity emerged to form one of the key bases of struggles around that self-same understanding of land and landscape. From memory's multi-directional and anachronistic qualities – 'its bringing together of now and then, here and there'[68] – powerful ideologically-based motives to protest emerge and are carried forward into the late twentieth century at the very least.

It is thus reasonable to assert that collective memory can constitute a powerful resource for the political culture of subordinate groups. Protesters of the post-World War One generation frequently explicitly referred to the events of the earlier Land Wars (if not the Clearances) in their threats – saying they would do the same. We may legitimately speculate that their late twentieth century contemporaries were perhaps similarly drawing on a creatively forged collective memory of post-1914 events to make sense of their position in the world and the very early attempts at estate buyout that were just beginning to become apparent.

Beyond question, remembered histories neither represent nor emerge from a hermetically sealed culture and knowledge base. At the same time they remain firmly attached to specific places, spaces and landscapes. Such histories are therefore best utilised in the context employed here: in the spirit, if not the actuality, of microhistory, and with a much greater depth of engagement with a limited number of events of protest. The events that form the subject of this chapter were selected on the basis that each was driven by a different primary motive. Deeper investigation has largely corroborated this opinion, but it has also revealed the full range of motivation underpinning these actions. Similarly, whilst placing these events into the wider context of economic, socio-cultural and landscape change does not significantly alter the understanding of post-1914 disturbance which emerged in earlier chapters, it does nevertheless add more layers of understanding and a more rounded appreciation of the connections between space, the crofting landscape, and the vernacular environmental sensitivities which underlay acts of protest. Finally, a focus on these individual events has allowed us to gain a deeper perspective on the aftermath of such affective actions. For instance, in Park the agitation for land continued well into the 1930s, with the last action occurring in July 1934, when cottars from Harris wrote attempting to gain the land which still showed 'signs of our Forefathers' labour.'[69]

Protest is never clear-cut, hygienic or straightforward. It emerges from affective encounters between bodies (and other 'dividual' things, as Thrift has it) in places.[70]

68 Rothberg, *Multidirectional Memory*, p. 5.

69 R. I. P. D. 5543, Park, 13 July 1934.

70 Thrift, *Space*, p. 86.

It is messy, mutable, and leaves 'distinct and identifiable traces on bodies, things and places. To put it simply: there is always an aftermath.

In viewing protest in this way – as constituted by and interacting with an embodied sense of being in the world, we are pointing a way towards a more convincing grounding of these events in the landscape in which (and from which) they were performed and played out. In turning to a consideration of the place of space and everyday expressions of environmental ethics the following (and penultimate) chapter will argue that the crofting landscape is and was a dwelling place of contextualised lived practices which gave rise to a potent protest culture.

Chapter 7
Spacing and Dwelling: Performing Protest's Tasks in the Crofting Landscape

I am only asking what I have a claim on as the dwelling place of my forefathers.... I would not be Justified in applying for land elsewhere.

This book was born out of the realisation that there were two interlinked significant issues within Highland protest after 1914 which demanded further attention. The first was that post-1914 disturbance was of considerably greater significance and complexity than has been allowed hitherto. From this and from the range of issues and questions exposed by this close questioning, came the twinned realisation that it no longer seemed tenable to pursue grand narratives of class and hegemony by way of protest interpretation. This is by no means an isolated epiphany as it mirrors the trajectory of protest studies more generally. As recently articulated by Katrina Navickas, in our new histories of protest class is by no means abandoned; it is simply made more nuanced, recognised as complexly manifest in protest, and accepted as but one possible register of identity amongst many others.[1]

In the preceding chapters, the focus of discussion has been primarily that of Highland events. In what follows, whilst this focus is never abandoned it is used as a foundation and a testing ground for new ways of looking at and interpreting protest. In many respects, Navickas's 2011 paper in *Social History* is a close relation of Charlesworth's "agenda", published in *Rural History* some 20 years earlier, although the journals in which they were published betray something of the differences between them. Both are "state of the nation" pieces and both identify methodological and conceptual ways forward. One of the significant differences between the two is that the more recent paper can be seen as far more optimistic than the earlier one. Alongside a number of other important new perspectives Navickas identifies environmental history as 'offering great potential for these new histories'.[2] It is this potential, particularly when enhanced by efforts to make the nature/culture binary more problematic – the "stuff" of the best environmental history – which this chapter seeks to bring to fruition. In so doing, the concern here will be to address questions of the formative role of space and local environments in protest performances, viewed in particular through the lens of new thinking in landscape studies.

1 Navickas, *What happened.*
2 Navickas, *What happened*, p. 201.

Spacing Protest's Performances

Space matters. This statement is something of a truism to historical geographers with their concerns to identify "movements" and to focus on the local, regional and national. And, in their micro-historical methodologies, the same can be said for protest historians. As Carl Griffin has recently argued, a protesting crowd both turns the social world upside down and also transforms the space it occupies. (His focus is the Captain Swing riots but this can be equally applied to land invasions.) Taking the vestry room, 'the space in the church which as well as fulfilling an ecclesiastical role … was also where poor relief was often dispensed' as an example, Griffin asserts that 'when invaded by a group of irate labourers demanding more generous doles [it] is immediately changed into an arena of conflict'.[3] Protest, then, is a form of spatial transgression and inversion. In refusing to leave land when they were required to leave it, in entering into or perhaps even just threatening to enter into deer forests and large farms, crofters and cottars were inverting otherwise fixed and placid spaces into fluid arenas of conflict.

More generally, historians have turned to space with varying degrees of reluctance. There has been, nevertheless, a concerted effort, amongst social and cultural historians in particular, to take a spatial turn. This approach leans very heavily on philosophers of space such as Bourdieu, de Certeau and Lefebvre and proceeds from the perspective that the spatial setting reflects human cultural traditions and values, and that past activity leaves traces which can be discerned in present landscapes. Thus far, this "turn" can hardly be said to be new; it is something that landscape historians have pursued since W.G. Hoskins invented the approach in the 1950s. Fiona Williamson, however, claims that social historians have subsequently sought to extend this spatial perspective much further. Working from this enhanced perspective, and mirroring debates over landscape within historical and cultural geography, space has come to be conceptualised neither solely as inert setting nor wholly as symbolic representation of past human activity but also as constitutive of that agency; albeit with still some hesitancy over fully embracing this powerful perspective. Thus we are left with the view that 'surroundings played *some part* [my italics] in the ordering and creating of identities, and thus the subsequent performance of social relations'.[4]

This greater emphasis on space as a building block of human agency has been more often in its origins the focus of historians of early modern protest. Instrumental in this has been the work of David Rollinson and Andy Wood. Both proceed from the belief that 'popular and official cultures conceive of space in different ways' and that 'space is not neutral in its shaping effects on the way the populations

3 Griffin, *Affecting Violence*, p. 142

4 Fiona Williamson, 'Introduction' in Fiona Williamson (ed.) *Locating Agency: Space, Power and Popular Politics* (2010), p. 5.

inhabiting it grew up'.[5] Significantly both seek to ground their case studies in the dynamics of local spaces. For Rollinson it is Gloucestershire, whilst for Wood it is the Peak District, the locale from which he was first concerned to enter the debate over the utility of the class motif in the historiography of early modern England. Subsequently Wood expanded his thinking to critique the then dominant interpretation of food and anti-enclosure riots and looked instead to a model of popular politics as providing a more nuanced perspective on these disturbances. This model has stimulated much important research, particularly when it has been allied with the spatial turn. In his study of the relationships between popular politics and agency in the later Stuart alehouse, for instance, Mark Hailwood refused to align his view with any single dominant narrative arguing that all are equally flawed, all fail to capture the complex and ever-changing dynamics of alehouse culture and yet all can be equally evidently in play at any given point in time. His suggestion was that only a much closer attention to the relationship between agency, space and time, on a very small scale – perhaps on a day-to-day basis – can reveal a full understanding of the multifarious performances in play in this alehouse space.[6]

There is much merit in this turn to space, but what it generally lacks is an attempt to fully explore the instrumental role of local environments in underpinning and shaping the beliefs that generated protest. Moreover, attention to the issue of protest can also address Williamson's concern over the turn to space, namely that 'it privileges rich over poor and public over private space'.[7] An exploration of popular protest does permit us access to the spatial constructs of the dominated and is equally bound up with a multiplicity of performances.

This would certainly appear to be the view of Katrina Navickas who, in a series of compelling papers, has engaged with a number of spatially-orientated concerns. She has, for instance, discussed the dynamic and symbolic qualities of the moors and fields used for radical political meetings. She further highlights the power enmeshed in walking and asserts that 'by climbing the peaks, protestors gained control over the environment over their authorities in a symbolic as well as physical way.'[8] What Navickas is pointing towards in this work is the existence of senses of space that are differentiated both politically and culturally. Nevertheless, there is less of a sense of the shaping and formative role of such

---

5 David Rollinson, 'Exploding England: the dialectics of mobility and settlement in early modern England', *Social History*, Vol. 24, No. 1 (1999): 3–7.

6 Andy Wood, *The Politics of Social Conflict: the Peak Country, 1520–1770* (Cambridge, 1999); Andy Wood, 'Social conflict and change in the mining communities of north-west Derbyshire, c.1600–1700', *International Review of Social History*, Vol. 38, (1993): 31–58; Wood, *Riot, Rebellion*; Williamson, *Locating Agency*, p. 8; Mark Hailwood, 'Alehouses, popular politics and plebeian agency in early modern England, in Williamson, *Locating Agency*, pp. 51–76.

7 Williamson, *Locating Agency*, 5.

8 Navickas, *Moors and Fields*, p. 105.

spaces here and, whilst landscape is not viewed as wholly inert, neither is it portrayed as being as dynamic and constitutive as other commentators would allow. In a subsequent paper, however, Navickas does move towards this view through a return to a focus on Luddism and its spatial context. Taking her cue from Charlesworth's "agenda", Navickas asserts that it is wrong to categorise Luddism as an urban phenomenon. Her focus here is on those semi-rural, semi-urban 'edgelands' which convey a powerful sense of liminality and transgression.[9] Overt Luddist incidents were only the most visible and therefore most easily captured parts of a repertoire of activities which underscored this movement and which, by and large, took part in the countryside. For Navickas, it is very important to pay close attention to the micro-spaces of protest events because they reveal the shaping role of the dynamics of local topographies in protest performances. Local environments carry an affective charge which can, in certain circumstances, generate resistance.

The power and utility of the spatial perspective notwithstanding, most recently Navickas has turned to a focus on place in the belief that this admits a temporal dimension to the pure physicality of space. And, once we add in a consideration of custom, Navickas asserts that what emerges are the important linkages of people to places in particular localities.[10] In her discussion there are strong elements of some aspects, but perhaps not all, of the direction in which many geographers have travelled most recently. For some, space and place are now more convincingly seen as inextricably and co-constitutively intertwined; with place, as Nigel Thrift puts it, made up of 'particular rhythms of being that confirm and naturalise the existence of certain spaces'. Most significant for an understanding of protest performances is the assertion that places are an embodied (the sheer physicality, physical presence and affective charge of being in place), part of a complex and much larger 'spatial dance' with other human and non-human performers. In other words, this most recent (re)turn to questions of space and place has been paralleled by a turn to performance and performativity amongst human geographers with an interest in the construction of social identity and power relations. In this view, first articulated by Gregson and Rose amongst others, space is understood as being brought into being 'through performance and as a performative articulation of power'. The former connects to the act whilst the latter speaks of the interaction of power with the performance. In this way, Gregson and Rose assert, performers are (re)connected to 'power's social script'. What this also implies is that space – the stage upon which the performance is played out – is called into being by performances and it too is performative of power relations. But, because the distinction between actor and audience can, at times, become fuzzy and because

9 Paul Farley and Michael Symmons Roberts, *Edgelands: Journeys Into England's True Wilderness* (London: Jonathan Cape, 2011).

10 Katrina Navickas, *'Why I am tired of turning': a theoretical interlude* [History Working Papers Project, 2011]. Available at: http://www.historyworkingpapers.org/?page_id=225 [Accessed 20 October 2012].

slippage can occur, these can also be spaces in and out of which power relations can come into question. In these performances, moreover, gaps are left open through which new spaces are called into existence by 'reworking the spatial technologies we hold dear'.[11] Highland land invasions did exactly that. They reworked the spatial technology of sheep run and deer forest back into that of the crofting taskscape.

Acknowledgement of the agency of the non-human is a central consequence of the recent recognition of the hybridity of nature/culture relations. Biehler, for instance, sees flies as active agents in attempts to reorder urban and domestic space in Chicago in response to a severe typhoid outbreak in 1902. As she asserts, flies are 'beings ... engaged with the changing flows of urban life, and with shifting, competing human practises'. Through its irreducible omnipresence, the fly took an active role in the US state's attempts to 'manage peoples' interactions with nature'.[12] Explorations of the interaction between the human and non-human have found their way into the study of rural resistance. One aim of such studies has been to explore the cultural role of trees (and other flora) in rural life and relationships and the damage that both human and non-human actors can do to them. Griffin has shown that the failure of the English State's sylviculture schemes in the New Forest had less to do with local human-led resistance than it had to do with the forest mangers' inability to consider the non-human actors (mice and rabbits) that were co-constitutively producing affects which allow for resistances. More broadly, Griffin has argued for trees as the 'living capital' of those instigating major socio-economic change in the nineteenth century English countryside. In this view attacks on trees became forms of everyday resistance to these changes by those who had been denied access to these resources. David Kent observed similar resistances to state-led attempts to manage fauna on the River Tweed in mid nineteenth century England.[13]

11 Nigel Thrift, 'Space: the fundamental stuff of Geography', in Nicholas J. Clifford, Sarah Holloway, Stephen Rice and Gill Valentine (eds), *Key Concepts in Geography* (London: Sage, 2009), pp. 85–96; Nigel Thrift, *Non-representational Theory: Space, Politics, Affect* (London, 2007); Nicky Gregson and Gillian Rose, 'Taking Butler elsewhere: performativities, spatialities and subjectivities', *Environment and Planning D: Society and Space*, Vol. 18 (2000): 434 and 441.

12 D. Biehler, Flies, manure and window screens: medical entomology and environmental reform in early-twentieth-century US cities *Journal of Historical Geography* 36 (2010): 68–78.

13 David Kent, 'Power, Protest, Poaching, and the Tweed Fisheries Acts of 1857 and 1859: "Send a Gunboat!"', *Northern History*, Volume 42, No. 2, September 2005, pp. 293–315; Carl Griffin, 'More-than-human histories and the failure of grand state schemes: sylviculture in the New Forest, England', *Cultural Geographies*, Vol. 17, No. 4 (2010): 451–72; Carl Griffin, 'Protest practice and (tree) cultures of conflict: understanding the spaces of 'tree maiming' in eighteenth- and early nineteenth-century England', *Transactions of the Institute of British Geographers*, Vol. 40, No. 1 (2008): 91–108.

Interventions such as these, which appear to draw together the perspectives of environmental history and historical geography, are regrettably few. Even fewer are those which view rural resistance through this lens.[14] To do so, however, to investigate expressions of local and vernacular ecological beliefs and how, over time, these can come increasingly into conflict with official, central government agency led constructions of conservation, must inevitably draw inspiration from Karl Jacoby's 'moral ecology'. This is a fascinating and insightful way of conceptualising particular acts of rural resistance which encapsulate and draw upon vernacular constructions of ecological ethics. In his key monograph Jacoby utilises a number of case studies to reveal a clash between two distinct ways of life, both underpinned, he asserts, by two widely contrasting sets of 'laws'. One based in local and quotidian senses of place and formed of traditional and vernacular nature/culture relations; the other that of professional and national conservation.[15]

The development of the concept of moral ecology is one of the best examples of the profound influence and extension of Edward Thompson's essay on the moral imperatives underpinning and legitimising the actions of eighteenth century English food rioters and it is easy to identify a number of parallel perspectives here. Jacoby, for instance, is able to write of 'local resistance', of the 'transformation of previously acceptable practices into illegal acts' and of the criminalisation of customary activities. Moving beyond Thompson, however, Jacoby asserts that local working peoples had their own laws and regulations, community prescriptions of what was and what was not allowed, which were rooted in shared and localised understandings of the interactions of ecology, economy and society. These, however, came increasingly into conflict with new state conservation policies which 'redefined the rules governing the use of the environment'. Vernacular activities and prescriptions became re-inscribed as 'environmental banditry'. Nevertheless, what was now law-breaking was frequently still legitimised by support from within, providing the law breakers did not transgress locally accepted codes.[16]

Furthermore, in exactly the same way that an earlier generation of historians either ignored events of protest or were ideologically opposed to the study of it, early historians of these struggles between conservation and indigenous populations were characteristically sympathetic to the aims of conservation. Thus 'rural folk' were seen 'as operating with a flawed understanding of the natural world' and the history of conservation was viewed as the triumph of 'the unfolding of an ever-more enlightened attitude towards the environment.' This is a dualism that Jacoby finds no favour with, preferring instead to view these tensions as

14 Perhaps the most important set of interventions comes from Brian Short. See, in particular his 'Conservation, Class and Custom: Lifespace and Conflict in a Nineteenth-century Forest Environment', *Rural History*, Vol. 10, Issue 2 (1999): 127–54.

15 Karl Jacoby, *Crimes Against Nature* (Berkeley 2001).

16 Jacoby, *Crimes*, p. 2.

underlain by wider and deeper layers of complexity that, from the indigenous populations' perspective, is underpinned by a distinct moral universe: a "bottom up" understanding of nature.[17]

Thus, in the nineteenth century Adirondacks, a robust and long-lived ideology of common rights and a relatively sophisticated ecological code was maintained within the local population. When this came into conflict with increasing state control and new conservation laws and with the forest police who enforced them, resistance took the form of timber stealing, poaching and fire raising. Here fire setting could be about revenge; but it could also be an attempt to cover evidence of other forms of resistance – timber stealing, for instance. It could also be a way to preserve income – as a member of a fire-fighting crew – or to encourage new growth for foodstuffs. But, at the same time, this could also be an explicit rejection of attempts by the Forest Commission to recast definitions of what it is to be a good citizen – to be a member of a fire-fighting team. Finally, since new conservation laws made it illegal to burn fields at the time of year when it had been traditional to do so, some fire raising – taking place in those proscribed months and spaces – was undoubtedly a reassertion of a perceived and continuing validity of past spaces and cultures.[18]

Such fluidity makes it impossible to fall back on established interpretations. Poaching, arson and timber stealing have often been seen as activities that were covert – usually undertaken at night and often the work of individuals. The poaching, arson and timber stealing we encounter in Jacoby's case studies goes well beyond such lazy categorisation. These could just as easily be activities carried on in the open and by large groups and, as such, they also reflect the ever-present problems associated with categorising and compartmentalising something as dynamic and fluid as disorder. In that it is the base for the very fluidity which challenges these interpretative dualisms, moral ecology offers the possibility of a more holistic understanding and of the articulation of a more convincing link between social relations, protest in the round and the active and constitutive role of place and space.

Highland protest has similarly been interpreted as a clash between competing ideologies, albeit in the service of the view which holds that class and hegemonic conflict is the narrative which can capture all variations of such events. The whole philosophy of this book and the weight of the evidence here revealed, suggest that this monocausal view can no longer be sustained. Importantly, there is no desire here to replace one grand narrative with another. Rather, by turning to moral ecology and to related concepts, what is revealed are the more powerful and embracing associations – to vernacular environmental beliefs; to work tasks – which much more firmly ground protest performances in an embodied "world" and which recognise and encompass conflict within the tenantry rather than blanding it out into classical class conflict. This is not to deny class as generator of conflict

17 Jacoby, *Crimes*, p. 3.

18 Jacoby, *Crimes*, pp. 48–80.

but to suggest that it is but one register of competing identities amongst many. One such, and perhaps of greater significance than class in Highland protest, was the array of beliefs, practices and traditions which governed how crofters and cottars interacted with their environment; how they worked "their" land. As with Jacoby's environmental bandits, these quotidian expressions of resource utilisation were swept away almost entirely by top-down views on appropriate landscape utilisation, but became the means to resistance and reassertion of a particular way of performing work practices in place. In this reading, then, protest performances of every type, but perhaps the refusal to hand back land in deer forests gained under the Defense of the Realm Regulations most particularly, became the re-creation of the crofting landscape and the reassertion of customary attitudes to resource utilisation. Indeed, in many respects incursions into and the breaking of ground in deer forests was the more transgressive work-based act. To borrow from Mackenzie, the action of spade, plough and seed disrupts the land's connections to class-based interests and to top-down authorised land-working practices. To break land and to plant in a supposedly pristine "wilderness" (it is, of course, no such thing) is to challenge and subvert elite sporting discourses.[19] To work the land, moreover, reconnects it to past practices which exposes the myth of an unchanging 'scape and places work tasks and the intersection of the human and non-human at the centre of a counter-discourse of land and landscape.

A further engagement with the intersection between the non-human and Thompson's moral economy can be found in David Featherstone's re-thinking of the Eighteenth Century Irish peasant movement, the Whiteboys.[20] As Featherstone shows, and in common with the crofting tenantry, the Whiteboys held particular views over what were valid relations between human and non-humans. Enclosure walls and ditches and the cattle and sheep they housed were understood as 'enemies'; attacks upon them could be undertaken not so much because 'they were symbolic of hated masters or middlemen' but because walls, ditches, cattle and sheep constituted, for the Whiteboys, an unacceptable set of associations between the non-human and human.[21] The superficially obvious comparison to be made here is with the Whiteboys' near-contemporaneous Clearance resistors as they sought to physically counteract the re-organisation of their relationships to land, sea, flora and fauna. It was from this re-organisation that the crofting landscape emerged, thereby raising the possibility of a disjuncture in vernacular resource utilisation. Nevertheless, there can be no doubt that those who worked the land took with them (materially and mentally) sufficient of their customary practices and associations to ensure continuity. Re-assertion of the crofting landscape, as

19 A. Fiona, D. Mackenzie, 'A working land: crofting, communities, place and the politics of the possible in post-Land Reform Scotland', *Transactions of the Institute of British Geographers* 31.3 (2006): 383–98.

20 Featherstone, *Skills*.

21 Featherstone, *Skills*, p. 293.

articulated by the protest performances of any period up to and beyond the 1920s, was a re-assertion of those self-same practices and associations.

Subaltern interventions and assertions of particular associations of the human and non-human, such as land invasions and attacks on enclosure walls and ditches, must be understood spatially and 'as part of the ongoing constitution of the world'.[22] Protest historians simply must pay attention to spatial configurations, therefore. There is an active and dynamic relationship at play here in which space is something far more than the backdrop and setting for acts of resistance. People derive emotional and bodily attachments to and from their space; from moving through and encountering their everyday world. Attempts to alter and arrest those movements and encounters (as with the Clearances) are generative of acts of resistance, even if that resistance comes some considerable time (as with the Land Wars) after that which is being resisted. People engage with and are engaged by landscape on an emotional, material and bodily level which involves the imagination in meaning making, permits the process of imagining the self and drives a sense of belonging that is rooted in the very fabric of lifespace. Dispossession from, or an enforced re-working of such 'scapes[23] means the loss not just of a living and a home, but it is also to lose at least part of one's self. From birth, people's lives are spaced and timed through their interactions with the material: the soil; the sea; the walls; the trees; the animals; the tools; even the climate. Attempts by local inhabitants to resist dispossession and rejection of the(ir) landscapes must be understood as attempts to recapture these powerful spatial formations.[24]

In essence, this is a plea for the recognition of landscape as something far more than either an analytical device or a locale of empirical research; beyond the approach of the landscape historian and the perspective which understands all landscapes as cultural products: a symbolic register of cultural and historical processes. What both of these "gazes" on landscape deny is landscape's active and instrumental role; what they permit is the perpetuation of the unhelpful nature/culture Cartesian dualism in which humanity is always at one remove from nature. More helpful is the view of landscape as space-shaping; bound up with narratives of order and meaning, both now and in the past, which are based in and shaped by landscape itself. It thus becomes 'a milieu of engagement and involvement' in

22 Featherstone, *Skills*, p. 298.

23 This is a deliberate contraction to reflect the "more than land" nature of the entity with which we are dealing here. Landscape arrives with us via the common morphological process of compounding. In this instance this is a noun + noun compound. For some time now commentators have, through morphological analogy, been coining new compounds in order to better reflect the aspects and affects of the 'scape they wish to draw attention to; thus "memoryscape" and "ethnoscape". I will go on to argue that the most persuasive analogous compound is that of "taskscape".

24 It is at this point entirely appropriate that I thank Carl Griffin for his encouragement to fully develop this line of thinking.

which 'the self is not simply "in" the world – it is *of* it.'[25] Acting in conjunction with bodily experience, landscape is most convincingly understood as the very basis of experience and the world in which and from which we (human and non-human) live; and not merely as a scene for us to view or (artistically) reproduce. In this reading, the body is neither separate from nor subordinate to the mind with body and 'scape both, and at the same time, expressive of being in the world.

This sense of being in, of, and from the world lies at the heart of the view taken here that a holistic and more satisfying interpretation of Highland protest is one that it is understood to be informed by and expressed through landscape encounters and the dwelling perspective. In this view, which is derived from the phenomenology of Martin Heidegger, any act of building, living or even thinking, essentially the taking up physical space and existing in relation to other physical objects (including other people), is formed in the context of already being in the world. This, in turn, inevitably affects that forming, with the act of being underscoring the act of dwelling.[26] This position has been related more formally to landscape by Tim Ingold. His aim was to move away from what he saw as the crude dualisms of much of landscape thinking and to replace these with a sense of landscape as gathering meanings from the world – as a critical register of being/dwelling – emphasising practical human engagement with the world, bodily agency and the interactions between them. In placing the emphasis here, on the interactions between people and environments, Ingold suggests that the unhelpful and unrealistic binary divisions between self and landscape, culture and nature, consequently 'dissolve altogether' and emerge as 'agents of change and that which is changed'. Culture and, therefore, history, are continuously made through this interaction 'with the land and with the beings – human and non-human – that dwell therein'.[27] In this symbiotic connection between people and landscape, nature and environment are recognised as active agents with space emerging from and acting on dynamic and contextualised lived practices. As articulated by John Wylie in his contemplation of the place of dwelling in Tim Robinson's work on Arran and Connemara, this interweaving of life and landscape may well be understood as 'concordant life forms percolating through each other … a weaving to which all elements equally contribute'. It is important to acknowledge that this clarity of vision is deployed by Wylie in the service of what he sees as considerable hesitancy in Robinson's work with this dynamic and interwoven view of landscape. The stronger claim made by Robinson, Wylie argues, is the 'non-coincidence of culture and land'.[28]

25 John Wylie, *Landscape* (Abingdon, 2007), pp. 149–51.

26 George Steiner, *Heidegger* (London, 1992); Martin Heidegger, *Poetry, Language, Thought* (New York, 1971).

27 Tim Ingold, *The Perception of the Environment* (London, 2000), pp. 56 and 133; Wylie, *Landscape*, p. 159.

28 John Wylie, 'Dwelling and displacement: Tim Robinson and the questions of landscape', *Cultural Geographies*, Vol. 19, No. 3 (2012): 373.

From the perspective of the actions of cottars and crofters in protest, the interweaving of people, landscape and lived practices remains persuasive. Moreover, such practices, Ingold argues, are principally, but not exclusively, work tasks, thereby leading him to reformulate landscape as 'taskscape'.[29] In this construction, the taskscape is made up of a network of interactions, most importantly those between material space and the senses, but also those between identities, senses of place and landscapes of practice. Arising out of this composite, time-rich and formative presence, taskscapes holds the only partially-erasable, records of the lives and work of past generations who have dwelt within it and who have left and gained there something of themselves. In ways similar to the carrying of memory across generations and the consequent creation of a material and collective narrative of the popular memory of rights to land, what was written into the bodies of those displaced by the Clearances would have been the performed tasks of the pre-clearance taskscape. Moreover, they would have carried with them important, task-based continuities into the crofting 'scape. Finally, with the addition of the material remains and ghostly hauntings of the pre-clearance world, the record of past lives and past associations would have endured within mind and across body, space and landscape. In short, and partly because the Clearances failed to create a *tabula rasa*, for those who had been cleared and for their descendants, the pre-clearance taskscape remained comprehensible. A consequence – and it was carried away from the Highlands – for those who worked, or whose family had worked the land, was that tasks and forms of association between the human and non-human and between the pre- and post-clearance taskscapes became a resource, model and a motivation for actions in protest. This also suggests why protestors' idealisation and materialisation of their desires was the croft – a product of the very self-same processes that they were seeking to overturn. Conceptualised as the crofting taskscape, this became a resource for protest and a metonym for that which has been lost and which should be regained. It was also the material manifestation of the Highland Gael's genealogical imperative. In sum, the argument here is that dwelling, taskscape and moral ecology may well be more effective prisms through which to refract our understanding of popular land based protests precisely because they place the emphasis on vernacular environmental expressions and tasks undertaken in a dynamic and formative 'scape. Evident in the now-substantial range of books recalling "lost" times, and in the names and stories attaching to seemingly insignificant places and pieces of rock, this relationship between vernacular environmental sensibilities, tasks and landscape is rarely more clearly expressed than when the following discussion turned to the question of identity.

> I think in a community like this your sense of identity, your sense of culture is the only thing that keeps you here

---

29 Tim Ingold, The temporality of the landscape', *World Archaeology*, Vol. 25, No. 2 (1993): 155–8.

> Q – And what gives you that sense of identity and culture?
>
> The ground does, absolutely nothing else. I walk down the croft which has been in our family since the sixteenth-century and even as a young girl I used to walk down the croft and think if only everybody, I mean it was home, it was always home to me it's still home to me, um, if every single person who ever called this home could come back and stand shoulder to shoulder on this croft how far would they span? – A long way aye – It's the same ground I'm tilling today to plant potatoes and it's the same ground they tilled, same footsteps, same places. [pause] It gives you a very strong sense of yourself and who you are and where you come from; there's nothing worse than having that vacuum in your life ... [Land] is the only thing that keeps us clinging on by our fingernails to these rocks, these windy rocks.[30]

What can be drawn from these musings are strong elements of what Edward Said has identified as the poetics of the land; something more-than-material and a resource for, and bound up with the negotiation of identity.[31] Further revealed here is a sense of a nexus of interconnections between identity, collective memory and sense of place made meaning *full* by landscape. This sense of place identity does and did come from access to land and from a particular view of landscape but, crucially, it is a landscape to *work*: 'It's the same ground I'm tilling today to plant potatoes and it's the same ground they tilled, same footsteps, same places.' This is, then, an engagement with and an expression of landscape as an enduring record of the lives and works of past and present generations who have dwelt within it. Landscape as made meaning *full* by the tasks performed in it. To quote the director of the Stornoway Arts Centre: 'You're seen as a bit strange round here if you don't have a few sheep on your croft'.[32] This sense of an existence defined by access to and possession of land – land to rent not to own – this very particular sense of rootedness in landscape, is, it can be further suggested, a key part of the inheritance and ordinary, everyday heritage of crofting society. This sense of rootedness in landscape, then, gives Highlanders their sense of place and, in part at least, their sense of identity as Highlanders. It is their heritage because the holding of land is seen as a valued legacy from previous generations.[33] This sense of place identity is apparent and underlies acts of land protest and, both then and now, it is legitimated in and by reference to the past and through a number of interconnecting factors. This legitimation comes partly from the continuing importance of kinship links

30 Interview, Marissa Macdonald, Lewis, 6 April 1998.

31 Edward Said, *Culture and Imperialism* (New York, 1994).

32 Interview, Roddie Murray, Lewis, 8 April 1998.

33 In identifying heritage as "a valued legacy of previous generations" I am here following John and Margaret Gold's definition of heritage. J.R. and M.M. Gold, *Imagining Scotland*, 1995, p. 140.

and genealogies for contemporary Highlanders. It comes partly also, from a belief in rights to land conferred by past occupation and inheritance.

Tasks, Protests and the Crofting Landscape

The emphasis placed on taskscape here is one that is shared with Katrina Navickas and her suggestion that the peripheral and liminal spaces of Luddism (moor, turnpike, industrial village and suburb) were set within the wider 'task-scape' [her hyphenation] of common, wood and moor. Resistance to change was both undertaken in and utilised local environments.[34] There is, however, a sense in which the heterogeneous associations between human and non-human, which Featherstone saw in the Whiteboy movement and Jacoby saw in struggles in America's national parks, remain mute in Navickas's task-scapes. The boundaries between self and landscape, culture and nature, are breached but not broken down.

As Brian Short has demonstrated in a memorable passage, conflict over litter-taking in Ashdown Forest was grounded in the everyday lives of individuals which, in turn, were enmeshed in the fabric of the landscape thereby ensuring interaction between material space and the senses.

> The Forest provided raw materials, fuel and a space within which to work, to court and socialise. Family members worked together here and social relations among local families, and access to its raw materials would have made the vital difference between poverty, the lot of many, and pauperism … It was also a space within which landowners, tenant farmers, cottagers and landless labourers were bound in a mutuality of exchange and network of employment contracts which were dependent upon a local discourse concerning exactly what could and could not be undertaken on the Forest …. activities which were socially recognised, which were part of the landscape, and which … gave a sense of belonging to a community.[35]

In the Scottish Highlands also, activity, embodied experience and complex associations all came together to structure resistance which was centred on contested representations of landscape and the right to dwell in a particular taskscape. In March 1915, for instance, an applicant for land in Sconser deer forest on the island of Skye wrote, 'I am only asking what I have a claim on as the dwelling place of my forefathers…. I would not be Justified [*sic.*] in applying for land elsewhere'.[36]

---

34 Katrina Navickas, 'Luddism, Incendiarism and the Defence of Rural 'Task-Scapes' in 1812', *Northern History*, Vol. 48, No. 1 (2011): 63.

35 Short, *Conservation, Class and Custom*, p. 142.

36 R. I. P. D. 1611, Sconser, Skye, 8 April 1915.

The close connection between disturbance and work tasks was embedded in every act of land seizure. These events were far from passive, reactive or conservative in nature but were instead, proactive, affective assertions of a particular landscape, which always centred on work tasks. Land was ploughed, seeded and manured. Cattle, horses and sheep were placed on the land, which was allotted to individuals who often built homes and byres on it and from which work tasks were performed. In every instance of land seizure, such tasks were at the centre of the performative space of the protest event. Protest motives were rooted in past livelihoods and lifeworlds and in deep formative and interactive relationships with local spaces. Within these, protestors were legitimising, through work practices, their claims to rights to land. Thus, to return to Harris and to Scaristaveg in 1926 once again, those who seized land there told the local police that they had chosen that particular ground as it had been worked by their forefathers. They immediately marked out lots for each other and commenced ploughing. This sequence of events was repeated in 1927. In March of that year, five of the raiders, all of whom were cottars, were found guilty both of a breach of an interdict preventing them going onto the land, and contempt of court. They were all sentenced to two months imprisonment. On release, they returned to the raided land and recommenced work. A further prison term followed but in the face of this the raiders retained possession and continued to work the land throughout 1928. This sequence of events was repeated in 1927 and the raiders continued to work the land throughout 1928. By the spring of 1929, byres and stackyards had been illegally erected on the seized land and the raiders were continuing to actively prevent estate employees from performing their own work tasks on the contested land. Finally, even the weapons of resistance chosen by the Scaristaveg raiders relate to work tasks. Police officers were deployed in an effort to ensure estate work could be carried out. This was resisted by the raiders by the (by now) infamous soaking of the officers with the contents of the piss bucket – which had been retained for use in the tweed-making process.[37]

Protest here and elsewhere seems to have been driven by a distinct understanding of what constituted acceptable work practices in the landscape. Thus, as part of the long running agitation and associated disturbances surrounding the farm of Elgol on Skye in 1923 and as at Scaristaveg the local police reported that raiders there had prevented farm workers from ploughing the disputed land. The raiders 'went straight to where the ploughman was at work … and ranged themselves in a line in front of the horses … The ploughman Anderson endeavoured to get the horses forward but they refused to pass the men', who then proceeded to unyoke the horses from the plough. Both plough and horses were removed from the field, and the proprietor's cattle driven off the ground. Only when these

37 This summary is drawn from the extensive material to be found in a number of different Scaristaveg files, but principally N.A.S. AF67/66 and AF83/795. Correspondence here dates from March 1926 and continues through to June 1929. See also AF83/797, AF83/798, AF83, 800 and R. I. P. D. 61109/1 Scaristavore;

unacceptable task actions had been halted did the raiders move to work the land in a way that was acceptable to them – by laying seaweed. In a further example, what was unacceptable to those agitating for land at Forsinain in Sutherland (all cottars) was that the land in question was being run by six crofters as a club farm.[38] Together these examples further remind us, if any more were necessary, of the moral certainties which underlie much protest activity and which were discussed in full in Chapter 5.

Even when the protestors' actions were little more than gestural these were still centred on work tasks and on the gaining of land, and were placed at the heart of the symbolic and performative space of the land seizure. One example of this comes from Kirkton Farm in Caithness. The farm was raided on 28 May 1920. At eleven in the morning fourteen men marched to the farm, proclaimed formal possession, and then marched home again. On 14 June, as forewarned, a significantly bigger group of over thirty 'left Portskerra in procession headed by a piper'. They took with them both sheep and cattle which they proceeded to drive onto the disputed land as formal and symbolic gesture of occupation. In celebration of this action they held a dance both on the land and back in Portskerra that evening.[39]

Further affirmation of the power and centrality of the crofting taskscape to the protest performance emerges from actions at Meavig (part of North Harris Deer Forest) in 1914 and 1919. The earlier set of events were little more than gestural, with the local police reporting the action as lacking both support and serious intent, yet they still involved the assertion of work practices, with six men from the neighbouring townships of Ardhasaig and Bunavoneader marking out lots for themselves as a prequel to their seizure. Three of these men, once the war had ended, took part in a significantly bigger and formally-declared seizure in the same location in May 1919. Here the act of declaration was the physical breaking of soil and the planting of potatoes, followed by house-building some two months later.[40]

Events at Meavig took a further turn, however, and, in so doing, they revealed the heterogeneous antagonistic associations that were set in motion as the landscape of sport came into conflict most directly with that of crofting. As soon as the raiders' house building activities became obvious they were opposed by the Estate Factor. This opposition was made less on the grounds that such actions were illegal but because of where the houses were being built. Norman Robertson argued that they had been deliberately positioned close to, and within clear sight of, the gamekeeper's cottage. This was, it was claimed, in order to give them a better understanding of the keeper's movements and thereby enable them to poach game more effectively and thus to materially affect the sporting value of

38 N.A.S. AF 67/158, Police report copied to Scottish Office, 21 April 1923; N.A.S. AF67/65, Alexander Finlayson to Board of Agriculture; 3 March 1920.

39 N.A.S. AF67/65, Police reports copied to Scottish Office 28 May 1920 and 14 June 1920.

40 N.A.S. AF67/45, Police reports to Scottish Office, 4 February 1915 and 1 May 1919.

the estate. Interestingly, this antagonistic view was not shared by the Board of Agriculture's local official, Thomas Wilson, a man often thought to be showing signs of undue sympathy towards the crofter and cottar cause by both the landlords and his superiors in Edinburgh. According to sub-commissioner Wilson, 'save that the potato crop is growing they [the raiders] do no harm to the ground.' What is revealed here, therefore, is not only conflict over appropriate landscape utilisation but also the multi-dimensional tensions between tenantry, the estate and the agencies of government.[41]

A further indication of the gestural and symbolic nature of the 1915 seizure at Meavig lies in the fact that it took place in February. This was outside the principal raiding months of March through to June, when over half the total seizures took place and which constitute the raiding season as established in Chapter 3. On one level, these instances can be simply understood as a purely pragmatic set of actions that reflect the practicality of the protestors' needs but, on another level, a connection to taskscape can be clearly discerned. It would seem very likely that the reason why the period between July and October was relatively lacking in protest activity was because this was when everyday work tasks were at their most intense. From March through to June was the period when the vital spring preparation took place. It would also be the period when the need to obtain land was at its most intense; any later and crops could not be taken from it for another year. This link between disturbance, work tasks and the agricultural/tenurial cycle can be pushed even further. The traditional time for the breaking and renewing of a lease was either Whitsun (the seventh Sunday after Easter) or Martinmas (11 November). Perhaps in an attempt to legitimise protest by linking it to a time of tenancy changes, prospective raiders would often threaten to seize land on one of these dates. Thus, on Boreray Island and in one instance of many, notice was given of the intent to seize land at Martinmas term.[42]

The putative raiders at Boreray stand also as exemplars of another important strand in post-1914 protest: that of making a formal and often formalised pre-visit which was widely understood as not going as far as to constitute a formal seizure. At Boreray and at many other places, the land was formally marked out well before prospective raiders notified those they needed to that they were going to 'take steps to enter into possession' of the marked out land.[43]

Marking out and walking over were two of the most frequent and important performances of protest. The strong temptation is to see these actions as nothing more than purely symbolic social constructivism: an attempt to write counter-hegemonic ideology into the landscape. However, these actions, and they occurred

41 N.A.S. AF67/299, T. Wilson to Board 18 July 1919; Norman Robertson, estate factor to Board, 29 July 1919.

42 N.A.S. AF67/62 D. Morrison on behalf of Boreray cottars to Board of Agriculture; AF67/151, P. MacDonald to Scottish Office, 15 October 1922.

43 N.A.S. AF67/62, D. Morrison on behalf of Boreray cottars to Board of Agriculture; AF67/151.

whenever (and wherever) protest performances took place, were far more than solely representational. These were unquestionably a set of embodied and transgressive practices grounded (literally and metaphorically) in everyday life. As such – as performances enacted in very practical contexts – these are also 'ideas in action' which speak directly to some of the most recent and important theory writing in human geography. One aspect of this is the view that understands humans as in constant interaction 'with their environs', with the (more than physical) world 'the context from, with and within which what we call subjects and objects emerge'.[44]

With marking out and walking over, the key to any enhanced understanding of these aspects of the protest performance is surely the physicality of these actions. To dwell and then to construct and to cultivate arises out of people's relational and practical engagement with their surroundings because, as Crouch asserts, 'space is grasped through the doing'. Involving, in part at least, a legacy from previous generations, people 'come literally to carry the forms of their dwelling in their bodies'.[45] When people are denied the performance of that dwelling, transgressive acts seem inevitable. The protestors were imprinting their beliefs in their rights to land and reasserting a socially-shaping taskscape through the placing of their bodies in a socially-defined, exclusionary, and hence contested, space. When, in December 1919, 21 ex-servicemen from the Lochboisdale area of North Uist walked over Askernish Farm, led by two pipers, they were declaring their rights over that land by perambulation. These acts of organised trespass appear almost as precursors to the English Mass Access movement of a decade later.[46] Combined with the physical act of marking out ground, they are also, and much more significantly, about using the body to make a local political and affective statement. This also serves to remind of the potency of the topographical nature of landscape. To walk to and through the Highland landscape is no easy task. It requires considerable commitment; as did the making and re-making of the cultivation plots (anachronistically known as "lazy beds") which were one important aspect of the taskscape protestors were seeking to re-assert. In Wylie's words, 'gazing upon landscape ... [is] ... an eventful actualisation and distribution of selves and landscape ... through attending ... to the depths and folds of an

44 Ben Anderson and Paul Harrison (eds), *Taking-Place: Non-representational Theories and Geography* (London, 2010), pp. 6–8

45 David Crouch, 'Spacing, performing and becoming: tangles in the mundane', *Environment and Planning A*, Vol. 35 (2003): 1945–1960; Tim Ingold, *The Perception of the Environment: Essays on Livelihood, Dwelling and Skill* (London, 2000), p. 186.

46 N.A.S. AF67/147, Police report, 11 December 1919; Benny Rothman, *1932 Kinder Trespass: Personal View of the Kinder Scout Mass Trespass* (Timperley, 1982); Tom Stephenson, *Forbidden Land* (Manchester, 1989).

immanent plane from which distinctive selves and landscapes arise and with which they are always entwined'.[47]

The fact that the raiders would often march to and around the land is a potent gesture too. One aspect of the power of processing was the fact that all individuals became subsumed, literally, into a collective body, combined with the evoking of a military discipline. To borrow Griffin's words, 'the practice of disciplined marching did not simply serve the practical purpose of getting efficiently to' the targeted land 'but also acted to tell the communities through which they traversed that they were coming'. Perhaps observed by police, the factor and other estate workers and reported to the absentee landlord, 'the fear engendered was psychosomatic, a fear manifested in the body of bodies unseen', articulating and exemplifying the spectral geography of the protest performance.[48] The march and walking over speaks, too, of beating the bounds and of other ritualised, customary actions related to territory marking. But it also reminded authority that here were a disciplined people, used to military service, and it reminded them too of the all too recent recruiting promises of "a land fit for heroes". Beyond the potent political gesture, however, walking over, and indeed the wayfaring and seafaring nature of everyday crofting life, speaks also of and returns us to the notion of dwelling. For Ingold both '*becoming knowledgeable*' [his italics] of and to live in the world is to move. To trespass and, thus, to transgress boundaries imposed from without is to reaffirm knowledge of and from a place. It is a meaningful act in which worlds are narrated into existence.[49]

As already suggested, there is also a strong element of the spectral to these transgressive hauntings and imagined landscapes of resistance – elements of both presence/absence in the landscapes which the protestors sought to write. In their actions and correspondence there are clear statements of what Wylie would call 'love', in this instance for particular spatial arrangements.[50] As was stated in a petition from representatives of 77 crofts in the township of North Tolsta

> We are convinced that all the available farms in this Island should, without any further delay, be allotted into Small Holdings for the landless men who have fought, or have given their sons to fight, on land and sea, in defence of their King, Country and liberty … No one but a Lewisman can understand the Lewisman's love for, and pride in, being in possession of a holding in his own island … we

---

47 John Wylie, 'Depths and folds: on landscape and the gazing subject', *Environment and Planning D: Society and Space*, Vol. 24 (2006): p. 322.

48 Griffin, *Affecting violence*, pp. 145–6.

49 Bob Bushaway, *By Rite: Custom, Ceremony and Community in England 1700–1880* (London, 1982); Tim Ingold, 'Footprints through the weather-world: walking, breathing, knowing', *Journal of the Royal Anthropological Institute*, Vol. 16, No. s1 (2010): p. S121.

50 John Wylie, 'Landscape, absence and the geographies of love', *Transactions of the Institute of British Geographers*, Vol. 34, No. 3 (2009): 275–89.

> have a repugnance to congregating in towns, in spite of all urban facilities that may be provided for us .... Our ideal life is that of a crofter fisherman[51]

It was this 'love for ... being in possession of a holding' which drew (it was frequently claimed) otherwise law-abiding citizens into breaking the law. What is further evident here is not so much Tuan's "Topophilia" (the fusion of self and landscape) but, following Wylie, that love generated by 'loss, withdrawal and absence'.[52] Members of the land-working tenantry believed that prior generations of their families had been victims of clearance ('thence some of our forebears have been evicted and driven like slaves to make a living in alien shores'[53]) and had land to which they were entitled withdrawn from and denied them. For Robert Macfarlane, appropriately writing in a Hebridean context, those 'landscapes we bear with us in absentia' are amongst the most important we possess. Here Macfarlane speaks of the affective power of recalled-but-absent landscapes and suggests that these are 'the landscapes in which we live the longest, warped though they are by time and abraded though they are by distance ... but [such landscapes] exist as powerful presences too, with which we maintain deep and abiding attachments.'[54]

The imagined geography of absence and of expropriated crofting land was undoubtedly central to the decision of the protestors to act but its presence was as much, if not more, important. The Cleared crofting landscape was not a wholly eviscerated one – people and things remained. The consequence of this was that claims to land could be maintained materially as well as mentally. Not only did the remains of a past way of life litter the landscape in the form of abandoned houses, redundant field boundaries and the stories that were told about them, but people were able to both gaze on and poach on land that had been formally emptied of their (and their ancestors') presence.

Apart from some fragmented and isolated commentary, the role of poaching in Highland social and spatial relations has been grievously under-explored.[55] The same can be said, perhaps even more so, for the covert and everyday forms of resistance which have come to occupy a central place in new protest studies. Regretfully, this work does not address that lacuna. Nevertheless, the fact of poaching serves to remind that the associations at play in the Highland taskscape and in Highland protest were hybrid geographies of the human and non-human. Protestors did not enter into a *tabla rasa*, but, crucially, the associations of flora and fauna there present – sheep, deer, salmon and large single-tenanted farms were

---

51 N. A. S. AF83/363, Petition from North Tolsta, 8 February 1919.

52 Wylie, *Landscape*, p. 284.

53 N. A. S. AF83/358, copy letter John Mackay, Crowlista, Lewis 25 March 1919, threatening raid on the farm.

54 Robert Macfarlane, *The Old Ways* (London, 2012), p. 198.

55 One of the most open and frank accounts of what at times can amount to a "poaching war" can be found in: Michael Wigan, *Grimersta* (private publication, 2000).

rejected by the crofting tenantry in ways deeply reminiscent of the clash between elite and everyday discourses of environmental beliefs.

Moral ecology, taskscape and dwelling appear to be powerful lenses through which to view Highland protest. It might be said, moreover, that the protests were themselves tasks and this further appears as a motive and motif in these events. It generated conflicts within the tenantry in protest forms other than the land raid and in the point of formal recognition of the occurrence of an act of land seizure by agencies of government. Returning briefly to the Raasay raiding, and to the events of 1921 in particular, in April of that year the local police inspector stated that the raiders had actually first arrived over a month earlier but he had not reported this at the time as they had done no work and he did not view it as a seizure. But now, as they had returned, marked off plots, and commenced planting potatoes, this was officially reported as a land seizure.[56]

The refusal to hand back land temporarily leased to crofters under Defence of the Realm agreements has already been identified as a form of protest. Most significantly, every aspect of this protest-type directly relates to formative work tasks. At their most basic, these agreements were ostensibly about maximising food production, and landlords could consequently be hesitant over being seen to prioritise sport over subsistence needs if they denied tenants access to cultivable land. More significant, however, was the act of refusal itself. In these agreements, those without access to the means to the assertion of their landscape had been handed the means. As with other land settlement legislation, but perhaps more directly than in any other case, the Defence of the Realm agreements were mechanisms by which the crofting landscape could be re-imagined. Such was the power of this mental and material taskscape that it is surprising that more sets of tenants did not emulate those at Western Bunloit, who refused to withdraw from the land that they had gained in Balmacaan deer forest, or those at Inverkirkaig who had gained land in that eponymous deer forest. According to an internal Board of Agriculture memo, the first applications from local crofters for enlargements into Inverkirkaig Deer Forest came in 1910. These were refused by the then proprietor (and were very hard to achieve under the existing legislation) but, in 1914, a new proprietor was more favourable and, eventually, a Defence of the Realm agreement was obtained. At the same time, the proprietor allowed local crofters to (illegally) graze their stock in the forest. In 1921, it was reported that 'there were approximately 1000 head of sheep and 15 cattle in the forest' with numbers increasing. This situation continued for some considerable time. In 1936, ownership of the estate changed and the new proprietor moved to regularise the situation. He offered 'approximately 2,000 acres subject to the crofters agreeing to give up part of their existing common grazings which surround Glencanisp Lodge. This offer was refused'. The proprietor then attempted to get the stock removed. Anxious to avoid an upsurge in land agitation, the Board of Agriculture opened negotiations to establish a scheme of land settlement. Discussion continued into

56 N.A.S. AF67/149, Police report, 9 April 1921.

1937 when three to four miles of fence between the original common grazing and the deer forest was destroyed. Fires were set in the Forest again the following year.[57] In this instance, therefore, actions easily recognised as protest elide into something more everyday, with the fact of protest centring on work tasks ensuring a smooth transition between the two.

Such certainties could be as much divisive as they were cohesive. Indeed, divisions within the tenantry have already been shown to have led to protest which, in turn, raises serious questions over established interpretations which see only unity. But, even here, and in further reinforcement of the view which sees protest as driven by and expressive of work tasks, conflict within the tenantry was made manifest in and sought to assert work tasks and particular taskscapes. In 1917, Eoligarry was the last remaining large farm on the island of Barra. Here, and at this time, land seizures were undertaken by two distinct groups, each of which had very different desires. Cottar/fishermen from the east side of the island aspired to small plots for crofts and to continue their dual occupation, whilst crofter families from the west side (approximately 100) wanted the land to extend their crofts. They responded to the initial land seizures by threatening seizures of their own. A near-anarchic situation rapidly developed, with cattle from both groups freely grazing the farm, illegal cultivation taking place, and cottars making their occupation permanent by (illegal) house building. This conflict continued for a number of years and, at times, came close to violence.[58] What this conflict on Barra and, indeed, all conflict within the tenantry which led to acts of protest, points up is that taskscape can encapsulate and be made up of antagonisms as well as notions of authentic dwelling. We must further recognise, to borrow from Owain Jones, that what ultimately was to generate protest were the rhythmspaces of the crofting taskscape.[59]

Conclusion: Spacing Protest Cultures

The intent behind this chapter was to refract all that which preceded it through the lens of recent thinking, in cultural and historical geography in particular, but also in environmental and social history. The intention has been to explore the ways in which the reactions to earlier socio-economic and cultural changes are implicated in and imbricated with the interlocking cycles that build themselves into the form of the landscape. In keeping with this multi-disciplinary focus, what has emerged

---

57 N.A.S. AF 67/156, R. McLeod to Scottish Office, 12 June 1923; D.A.F.S. 38609 and 38609/2 Glencanisp, Board internal memorandum, July 1937.

58 N.A.S., AF67/143, Report by (sub-commissioner) T. Wilson to Board of Agriculture, 7 November 1917; R. I. P. D. 1164/C; Police report of near violent confrontation, 25 February 1920; N.A.S. AF67/148.

59 Owain Jones, 'Geography, memory and non-representational geographies', *Geography Compass*, Vol. 5, No. 12 (2011), pp. 875–85.

is a hybrid interpretation of social protest. Here attention has been paid to nature/culture interactions, to vernacular environmental beliefs and to the dynamic and formative role of landscape in the lifeworlds of the Highland tenantry. Much benefit has been derived from the utilisation of Ingold's dwelling perspective which, in turn, has opened up the possibility of the important recognition and exploration of the active and dynamic relations between protest and space. Together, space/place, landscape and work tasks formulated a belief system and a moral ecology from below out of which protest performances must now be seen have emerged. What such acts embody, through a particular set of emotional relations, is a desire to dwell, a deep sense of rootedness in a particular 'scape and the performance of a set of tasks and associations with the non-human which speak of a vernacular and quotidian environmental ethics. Further encapsulated and materialised as the taskscape, Highland conflict can now be seen to draw on and to manifest a right to dwell in a socialised space which runs counter to that of the prevailing hegemonic spatial arrangements. The crofting townships which emerged after 1914 were re-established as a direct consequence of the assertion of this counter-hegemonic taskscape, and the monuments to land disturbances erected in the 1990s and earlier, are testimony to the power of transgressive space.

Finally, an inclusive Taskscape, interweaving as it does the crofting, farming, and sporting landscapes, admits the ghillie and the stalker, the beater and blacksmith on equal terms to the crofter. After all, they might also actually be or have been crofters, cottars or squatters themselves. This also admits into the protest performance – as it must be understood as much from above as it is from below – the landowners, their solicitors and factors, and the representatives of central government. Dwelling, therefore, does not privilege one group above another but recognises instead the heterogeneous associations through which *all* come together in the performance of the taskscape. The crofting landscape, then, was and is a dwelling place of contextualised lived practices from which protest emerged and within which protest was about land and land was about work.

Conclusions

> The blueprint for land reform published this week by the Secretary of State for Scotland has matched our hopes and exceeded our expectations. Let there be no mistake. If these proposals are translated into legislation, the pattern of landownership, and the balance of social relationships which accompany it will be transformed for ever.'[1]

The story of the study of social protest has something of the bell curve about it. Initial indifference is superseded by a passionate politically, ideologically and philosophically-inspired deep commitment, out of which emerged a body of work of major significance, both within the study of social protest and social and cultural history and historical geography more generally. Very rapidly, however, the work became the new orthodoxy to which all had to refer and which ultimately was to lead to a slowing down, if not complete tailing off (certainly of the more innovative work) of engagement with questions of rural resistance. Undoubtedly this allowed attention to shift away to broader questions of domination and subordination, of hidden transcripts and of local political negotiation.

For protest studies more generally, so too the study of Highland events more specifically. The study of Highland land disturbances – before, during and after the 1880s – follows closely the paradigmatic trajectory just described. Not until the 1960s and 1970s and the rise of the history from below movement are these fundamentally important events given due attention. If they had received any consideration prior to this then they were understood as little more than knee-jerk reactions to economic downturn and summarily dismissed. The incoming generation of protest historians did not wholly reject the catalytic effect of short-term economic woes (as is entirely correct) or abandon economically driven perspectives but turned instead to cultural and historical materialism. From an initial concern with the moral economy of the clan, questions of class consciousness and conflict rapidly arose which further lead Charles Withers, for instance, to draw heavily on Gramsci's hegemony in order to explain the means to the transformation of the Highland culture region and the resistances to that process.

In common with its broader counterpart, the legacy of the Highland literature has been to encourage studies which either turns to protest as a minor part of a wider set of concerns or turn away from it altogether. Of central but far from malign influence in the evolution of the engagement with Highland land disturbances has been James Hunter's magisterial *The Making of the Crofting*

1 Editorial, *West Highland Free Press*, 8 January 1999.

Community. An articulation of the full chronological breadth of the protests of crofters and cottars was inevitably central to this work, although it is likely that the fact that this was not sole focus lead to the passing over of detail and significant elements of the range of forms therein deployed. Such has been the impact of Hunter's work, moreover, that if it became not quite the last word on the topic, it most certainly became the Highland equivalent of Rudé and Hobsbawm's *Captain Swing*: impossible to ignore but of such impact that it has led subsequent commentators to believe little more can be said. This is certainly not the case, not least for the fact that Hunter's work was first published almost 40 years ago. Our perspectives are long overdue for revision, therefore, and there is much fertile new thinking on space, place, protest and landscape which these can draw on. This has been one of the motivating factors behind the present volume.

A further factor has been much more recent Highland history. In 1976 Hunter was able to close *The Making* on a guardedly optimistic note. His was a future whose success was more or less determined by what he felt could be captured in a quotation from the equally magisterial *The Cheviot, the Stag and the Black Black Oil*: 'the people do not own the land. The people do not control the land'. Over 30 years later Hunter had grounds for even greater optimism, writing that

> today you can stand on any one of more than 500,000 acres in widely separated parts of the Highlands and islands and, on asking some local person who owns that acre, get the reply … "Us" … This represents a magnificent achievement on the part of many people … They have established that depopulation can be reversed, businesses created and homes built in localities where these things formerly seemed impossible[2]

Part of the warp and weft of this volume which draws both these views and earlier events together is that of the land and the crofting landscape. Land and landscape are what the Land Wars were fought over and it is here contended that the achievements of community ownership that Hunter was able to celebrate in 2012 would have been significantly more limited had not the protestor forbears of today's community owners not taken the actions they did some ninety years earlier. Community land ownership has arrived as a consequence of the hugely significant 2003 Land Reform (Scotland) Act which amounts to a significant challenge and ultimate re-working of established property rights. This was made possible by the Scottish devolution settlement of 1999 and by the fact that land issues have, for some time, been a central part of 'the Scottish psyche'.[3] A newly

2 James Hunter, *From the low Tide of the Sea to the Highest Mountain Tops* (Kershader, Isle of Lewis, 2012): p. 193.

3 Chenevix-Trench and Philip quoted in Charles, R. Warren, and Annie, Mckee, 'The Scottish Revolution? Evaluating the impacts of post-devolution land reform', *Scottish Geographical Journal*, Vol. 127, No. 1 (2011): 17–39.

empowered Scottish Parliament had both the energy and means to address these issues which has resulted in somewhere between one-third and a half of the total land acreage of the Outer Hebrides now in community hands. For Fiona Mackenzie, in the broadest terms the consequence of this is that once what were places of impossibility are now places of possibility, where 'for the first time the people of North Harris can look at their land and know it belongs to them. We now have so many opportunities that can benefit not just us but all the generations to come'.[4] These initial community buyouts and the various Trusts set up to manage them attempt to re-work local human and non-human associations and, particularly in the case of the North Harris Trust, create differential geographies of place which, in many respects, are reminiscent of Jacoby's moral ecologies.

This contemporary manifestation of a historically deep way of seeing land and land ownership had led on each estate to a re-negotiation of the meaning of "community" as it relates to land – the central register of identity in the Highlands – and the concomitant destabilising of the supposedly fixed boundaries framing ownership and belonging. As Mackenzie suggests, 'historically-resonant collective rights, *duthchas*, are re-cast through the rules of membership and the legal structure of the land owning body'.[5] Here is the counter hegemony of the land working tenantry – in the form of the croft land and taskscape to work – coming to a form of full fruition.

Indeed the link between community ownership and actions in protest is apparent on more levels than this general point around the struggles and successes of land agitation. Take, for instance, one of the most celebrated early buy-outs, that of North Lochinver Estate in Assynt. This Estate was carved out of one of the Deer Forests to which local crofters had been given rights of access in 1917 and which they refused to give up when their Defence of the Realm tenancy expired. Alternatively, the Galson trust on Lewis is one of the most dynamic but they owe their ability to buy the land as much to the raiding of the 1920s, which persuaded Lord Leverhulme to agree the re-establishment of crofting tenure across it, as they do to the provisions of the Land Reform (Scotland) Act of 2003. Protest matters, therefore, and in the Scottish Highlands after 1914 it mattered more than has hitherto been accepted.

A parallel and no less important binding thread holding this work together has been the desire to test and move beyond dominant paradigms. The trajectory in the historiography of Highland protest closely matches certain key aspects of that of protest studies more generally, not least in the fact that it has drawn directly upon it. So an initial burst of intense activity was followed by a period of stasis in which the Whiggish paradigm gets re-worked with the study *of* great men replaced by studies *by* great men. Indeed, such has been the field of force that has built up around these works that it has facilitated a shift in Highland

---

4 David Cameron quoted in Hunter *From the low tide*, p. 146.

5 A. Fiona, D. Mackenzie, *Places of Possibility: property, nature and community land ownership* (Oxford: 2013): p. 14.

historiography and contexts away from this important perspective. It is thus time for a return to a focus on land disturbance and timely too, as there is a recent and ongoing reappraisal of some of the key tenets of protest studies more generally. This book, then, has been driven by the interwoven aims of an in-depth explication of events of land disturbance after 1914, a re-appraisal of these events drawing upon some of the most recent thinking in human geography and landscape studies and from this, a belief that this re-worked understanding makes a contribution to protest studies more generally.

If nothing else has been achieved, however, it must now be clear that the land agitation after 1914 carries a greater weight than previously imagined, in the now-obvious evidential base alone. More than that, such is the depth and breadth of the available evidence that is has forced re-appraisal not just of the chronology and geography of these events but also of the forms taken in what amounts to a significant (and largely successful) challenge to authority. To take a singular view then, to focus virtually exclusively on the detail and dissection of Highland land disturbances, permits a much more convincing understanding of the importance of the post-1914 events in relation to those of the earlier Land Wars. In addition where other less focussed works are compelled to generalise and therefore to ignore forms and occurrences of protest, attention to such level of detail reveals a significantly less homogenous set of events. Flowing from all of this we are now able to advance a much more nuanced analysis of these events which suggests that the more rewarding perspective to take is a spatial one, as a strictly chronological approach does a disservice to the nature of the enduring opposition in some places. In challenging the dominant explanation and perspective in this way and hinting at new ways of looking at events of rural resistance more generally, there is nonetheless no attempt to deny the existence of strong elements of continuity between these events and those of the earlier Land Wars and their interpretation. Continuity comes particularly from the evident economic, political and ideological motives underlying the decision to protest, with the latter in particular to be found at the heart of the protest movement. Kinship links between and across the generations often determined the composition of the raiding party and sustained the attachment to the family croft and when disassociated from that croft impelled and maintained the desire to reclaim it. The collective expression of this desire became the legitimating notion for land seizure.

Notwithstanding the rewards of a greater attention to the evidential base, the forced seizure of land previously expropriated under the drive to agricultural improvement and sporting estates remains the more significant form of protest after 1914, particularly in relation to the effect of such protest and perhaps only because a significant number of threats of seizure progressed into the full occupation of land. Similarly to the threat, land raids were a complex mixture of single event and repeated actions, the latter not always undertaken by the same groups. By 1914, in many instances the land raid had taken on ritualistic aspects – each party to the event recognised and performed a particular pattern of behaviour. Only when landowners, as in the case of Lewis or much of South Uist, reacted in ways more akin to those of an earlier period did protestors respond accordingly and only when participants went beyond these bounds did authority consider reacting in a way more associated with the violent response to the disturbances of the 1880s. Nevertheless recourse to the popular memory of these events serves to remind us of the continuing depth of commitment required to undertake land seizures. Disturbance was far from clear-cut and neither wholly ritualistic or gestural. Protest performances were in actuality affectively powerful, drawing on a desire for land which went beyond the purely economic and the need to subsist. It is critically important, therefore, that we recognise the depth of emotional commitment required to plan and carry through a protest performance of whatever form.

This was certainly something felt and recognised by authority. Notwithstanding a revival in 1926, individual incidents of protest certainly declined after 1924 to virtual non-existence by 1939. Nevertheless the fear of the affecting violence of the protest performance was such that authority – central government; landlords; their agents – continued to act as they had when protest was at its peak well into the 1930s.

A major part of this was the sheer intensity of the incidence of threats to seize land; often from multiple locations but made on the same day. In total over 400 written threats to seize land survive in the archive, far in excess of the number of seizures. This surplus cannot be accounted for wholly by multiple threats relating to a single incident or place and so the threat must have existed as separate protest device, utilised to put pressure on the authorities to demonstrate the correspondents' serious intentions and as means of accelerating the land allocation process. As protest device it was highly successful as there is no instance in which written threat failed to provoke the Board of Agriculture into at least considering the break-up of the threatened land. The threat also on occasion accelerated the process of the break-up and re-allocation of land. Finally threat could force the Board of Agriculture to allocate holdings to those they deemed unsuitable to gain one. Unequivocally this was a powerful protest tool which demands attention in its own right.

Alongside the threat and actual seizure, three further forms of protest performance are recognisable in this period and together they amount to a protest repertoire somewhat wider, in form and actual numbers, than has hitherto been identified. Where others generalise, what emerges from the monocular attention to disturbance essayed here is the conviction that the geography of events after 1914 may be better understood less as manifestation and representation of a single, region-wide class consciousness, but more convincingly as a number of different, albeit interleaving geographies.

This is not to deny that the tenantry's perception of the Highland region was based on beliefs distinct from those of their landlords. Given, however, that the tenantry were no longer acting solely as a class for itself this undoubtedly led to a further re-articulation of regional identity along class lines. The emergence and creation of a fluid and distinct region – always in process – is clearly here a social act which contains the potential for and actuality of contestation and conflict. Further, within the tenantry and between the tenantry and authority, relations of domination and subordination emerge in which the subordinate configuration (however constituted) will enter into struggle with the dominant culture in a process of resistance or usurpation. Based on conflicting conceptions of landownership and use rights within the tenantry, the making and re-making of the region involved a cultural conflict surrounding contested notions of the Highlands and drawing upon conflicting ideological bases to land and landscape, and the proper performance of tasks within it. It was these work tasks and the landscape in which to perform them which gave rise to Highland land disturbances.

This regional and intra-regional geography is further complicated by the fact that actors saw protest performances as linked and interchangeable. If we accept that this represents a broadening of the repertoire when compared to events before 1914 (by no means certain) then this challenges both the notion of continuity to and categorisation of protest based on type. In addition, consideration of events of protest in the context of intra-regional divisions, principally between the various islands and between the islands and the mainland clearly demonstrates that a full understanding of the chronology of protest rests with a full understanding of the local geographies of protest. This is apparent in a number of distinct ways. In the Outer Hebrides, for instance, whilst greater levels of intensity of disturbance have long been recognised, what is only now clear is that these endured far longer than has been hitherto suggested. Additionally, an intra-regional perspective makes clear the variations in typology evident across the region and over time. On the mainland whilst the recognition of new protest forms means that disturbance was longer lasting than looking only at land seizures would suggest, it is also clear that motives to protest lacked the depth of ideological commitment recognised for other areas of the Highlands. This motivational variation is most clearly suggested by the (relative) prevalence of protest types other than the raid and threat on the mainland. Explanation of these variations lies in part with the continued overcrowding on islands such as Harris/Lewis and Barra. Given, however, that other islands, such as North Uist, demonstrate similar population characteristics, then explanation must also lie with the impact on the nature of protest of landlord development policies, both contemporaneous and historical. Further, on the mainland whether it was a function of landlords' lack of concern or whether a function of the considerable area of these inland estates, protest more easily and more often (comparatively speaking) metamorphosed into its informal form. The commitment to protest was clearly there; it simply took the most appropriate form. Once again, the need to investigate protest in its local context is clearly demonstrated. Finally, what the geography of overt acts of protest clearly delineates is what we might recognise as the heartland of the protest movement. A clear function of the efficiency of the Clearances and hence a small population, protest occurred predominantly on the islands and on the outer Hebrides in particular, where the popular memory of earlier events – clearance and the response to them – was at its strongest and most easily retained.

This fracturing of any regional-wide pattern must also raise doubts over the extent to which we can recognise in disturbance after 1914 a new and decisively different protest movement or a variation on that which had pertained before. Key here in any debate around questions of continuity is the role and impact of World War One. Whilst this gave strong impetus to agitation and provided different means to effect change, we can at first suggest that it did not substantively alter the nature of protest. In the land raid and underlying legitimation (of all types), protest remained recognisably the same as events of the 1880s and earlier. On the other hand there is strong countervailing evidence to support the assertion that World War One does in fact mark a significant disjuncture in Highland protest, particularly when it came to the context in which it was performed. Important here was firstly the impact of the war on public opinion and the attitudes of local and national authorities towards the crofting tenantry's cause, and secondly, the belief that a promise of land in return for war service had been made and not kept. Together this altered context brought a reinvigorated determination amongst the tenantry to have the land and enhanced sympathies towards the facilitating of that aim from governmental and public opinion, both of which suggests discontinuity with earlier events.

Against these suggestions of discontinuity, however, must be weighed the fact of the intense but relatively short-lived nature of the eruption of land agitation after November 1918. This looks very different from the levels of protest experienced in the first 13 years of the twentieth century. In this earlier period whilst there were some signs of an incipient revival in protest events they had not come close to reaching the intensity of that of the 1880s. Between 1919 and 1923, however, and again after 1925, that intensity was matched and perhaps even surpassed. Here, truly, we might argue are direct links with the earlier Land Wars. And yet discontinuities continue to emerge. By the end of the war governmental response to disturbance had been significantly re-shaped. Driven by public opinion and a greater level of sympathy from within, authority (principally the Board of Agriculture) moved proactively to both introduce legislation which proved reasonably effective in attempting to address the land issue and to act on that legislation. We can, however, go further than that. The public declarations of opposition by successive governments to the fact that land seizure often resulted in the law breakers being allocated land eventually lead to a formal ban on this occurring. Nevertheless evidence presented here has revealed that Ministers' private fears of the political capital to be made from their inability to halt or even control seizures, by the Labour party within Parliament and the Highland Land League without, often over-rode their desire to maintain their public stance and frequently resulted in the bar being ignored.

Whether this somewhat labyrinthine discussion over questions of continuity with an earlier phase of disturbance actually provides a definitive answer must be open to some doubt. What it does do, however, is further reinforce the assertion that disturbance, wherever and whenever it is found, is complex and ever-shifting. Indeed the fluid and mutable nature of Highland land agitation is further demonstrated by the fact that a first glance at the decision to protest reveals a strong sense of continuity with the traditions written into earlier protest. In other words, actors in the post-1914 disturbances based their actions on the belief that land was both past claim and, as the means of existence, present right. Given less emphasis elsewhere but seen here as a vital signpost to a more rounded understanding, this was land to work in the form of the crofting landscape. In and through kin, land and landscape were intimately connected but at the same time they could also be expressive of fracture and disjuncture. To recognise this is perhaps to depart most radically from established narratives of the events of the Highland Land Wars, a claim only exacerbated by the anatomisation of individual events which unequivocally demonstrate that not all participants participated for the same reasons or mix of reasons. What this leads to is a set of serious questions over whether it is possible and desirable to maintain the view of Highland disturbance as class war (or wars) driven by a growing consciousness of class. The view taken here, and substantiated by the evidence, is that at best we should now view class conflict as one register of disturbance amongst many. Greater emphasis needs to be placed on an understanding of these events as fluid, uneven and ever-changing skirmishes which may have class as a referent but are equally revelatory of internal divisions within the tenantry and which were also motive to protest. In moving to protest performances crofters, cottars and squatters at various times took action independent of other groups and often in opposition to those groups.

At the same time it is equally important to recognise that conflict within protest was multi-faceted. Indeed it was not solely within the tenantry or even between the tenantry and landowners. We can also see in actions in disturbance conflict between landowners, their agents, and agencies of government and their representatives in the locality. Furthermore, relations between central government departments and their sub-commissioners in the Highlands were far from straightforward and, to return to the tenantry, we can also see conflict between those who undertook protest and those who did not and between those who went to war and those who did not. In short, protest was expressive of and drew on complex alliances and antagonistic associations which suggest that the more rewarding perspective to take on the post-1914 disturbances is one based on much greater sensitivity to the microspaces of oppression, resistance and proactive protest. In the context of events of Highland protest this greater sensitivity to these microspaces is best achieved through close and culturally-informed attention to individual event and through the utilisation of a range of evidences; not least the collective memory of these events.

We must acknowledge that remembered histories neither represent nor emerge from a hermetically sealed culture and knowledge base. At the same time they remain firmly attached to specific places, spaces and landscapes. Such histories are therefore best utilised in the context employed here: in the spirit, if not the actuality, of microhistory. Interwoven with a close reading of the documentary evidence, factual validity can emerge from what has been recalled but perhaps the more significant assertion is that memory's fallibility and porous boundaries need to be recognised as both asset and resource. Memory services the relationship between place and identity and in its plasticity is able to turn negative experiences and connotations of that relationship into a resource for change and resistance. In the Highlands of Scotland claims to past land and landscape have been maintained (and re-worked) within the collective memory which inheres to specific places and events, and more widely across the region. In part from this creatively forged collective memory a distinct identity emerged to form one of the key motives to struggles around that self-same understanding of land and landscape. In this way that which is recalled adds more layers of understanding and a more rounded appreciation of the connections between space, the crofting landscape, and the vernacular environmental sensitivities which underlay acts of protest. In addition, a focus on these individual events has allowed us to gain a deeper perspective on the aftermath of the affective encounters between the human and non-human which make up all forms of land disturbance.

It is hard to over-estimate the positive legacy of the land disturbances of this period but it is equally important to recognise that events of protest have serious repercussions and post-existences. The impact of these largely successful actions on landowner, farmer-tenant, shepherds and sportsmen and their implications for wider governmental and social policy is obvious. Less obvious are the consequences for the tenantry of the land settlement scheme that almost inevitably followed from any land seizure of remotely serious intent. There was often clear dissatisfaction with the way in which the land had been broken up and to whom it had been allocated. After acquiring an estate or farm, the Board of Agriculture had on occasion to evict squatters and raiders already on the ground and deal with further threats to seize land (and the occasional re-occupation) by those frustrated that they (or family members) had failed to gain a holding. When discussed elsewhere these schemes have generally been portrayed as beneficial and clearly there were significant long-term benefits for those who achieved a new holding or extension of an existing holding. But in the short-term, as indicated by the post-scheme threats, actual land seizures and by grazing and other disputes noted here, the legacy for the local community was often one of conflict and ongoing tensions. What, then, seems to have been left behind once land disturbance reached some sort of conclusion is a little-studied endgame. These were clearly not new counter-hegemonic expressions and neither were they proto-movements, although elements of both are clearly present. They serve once more to remind us of the affective underpinnings of the act of protest and reveal the ongoing breadth of conflicts and tensions around land which must have fed into the stresses of unresolved and wider issues that were played out in the Highlands in the period after World War Two.

From this and from the direct statements of protestors themselves, it must now be clear that the depth of commitment to land apparent in these disturbances goes beyond the purely economic and towards the ideological and cultural, even if it is equally clear that protest was also more than ideological. The material form of that ideology, and what it was attempting to materialise, was the landscape of crofting agriculture. Indeed, this fundamental aspiration – to re-imagine the crofting landscape back into being – was perhaps the one constant linking the diverse nature of protest after 1914 with that which preceded it. Critically, however, this was not a mythologised landscape of a "lost Golden Age" but an embodied, peopled 'scape in which lifespaces and livelihoods were played out. Beyond doubt there are important symbolic and cultural meanings written into the crofting landscape and it can be read and understood as a deeply ideological cultural construct. But this is a more-than-representational 'scape. Reconceptualising it as taskscape draws attention to the embodied, dynamic and constitutive processes written into it and which it in turn writes. From this the suggestion can be made that rather than the landscape's symbolic qualities it is far more likely to be the right to dwell in a socialised space which runs counter to that of the hegemonic that will have driven people to acts of resistance and reassertion. Protest drew on the dynamic and formative role of landscape in the lifeworlds of the Highland tenantry and involved the effectual and affectual embodying of transgressive space. Highland land disturbances involved also the coming together of loose and fluid associations of individuals often bound by kin and deep attachments to particular places. Transgressive acts involved assembling, marching, walking over and the formal taking of possession. They were assertions of appropriate associations of the human and non-human in the form of the placing (or the refusal to remove) cattle and sheep from the contested ground. To take possession frequently involved the driving of pegs into the ground as plot markers, the breaking of the earth, the sowing of seeds and potatoes and the prevention of tasks being performed on the land by those deemed inappropriate to be there. If not formally seizing land people could refuse to leave it when their lease expired or wholly ignore the need for formal tenurial arrangements which led them once again to place cattle and sheep on the ground under assault. Protestors were also – in this embodying of transgressive space – placing bodies where they had no right to be. And very often all it took to be equally effectual was the affecting violence and transgressive force of the threat to bodily re-work hegemonic spatial arrangements.

More often than not it would seem, in undertaking these actions protestors believed that they had a right to occupy these spaces based on a firmly-held belief in rights to land maintained by custom and inheritance. Space and landscape were the props upon which the crofting tenantry based their resistance. Drawing on Noel Castree's work on indigenous rights, we can see the place-project the crofting tenantry were undertaking as a struggle for a differential geography; an assertion of the right to make their own spatial configuration and landscape. In this, of course, they were drawing on previous and ongoing spatial formations in the shape of the crofting taskscape. Spaces and places are drawn together and materialised in the form of acts of resistance and reassertion, but perhaps less as a reflection of their mutually constitutive properties and more as the mutually beneficial entwining of their meanings.[6]

Land is never static, is always actively doing and bound up with social identities. As place its meanings and the cultural and memory work it does are contingent. As space/landscape it is also and at the same time, constitutive of lifespaces. In their protest performances cottars and crofters were aiming to recapture land and landscape and reanimate it with particular lifespaces primarily constituted (and constitutive) of work tasks. Such tasks, moreover, may be said to encapsulate strong elements of everyday expressions of environmental ethics expressed as customary land-working practices – Jacoby's moral ecology in other words – which brought them directly into conflict with "top down" views on appropriate landscape utilisation. Taken together space/place, landscape and work tasks formulated a belief system and moral ecology from below out of which protest performances emerged.

This book was born out of the realisation that we have not paid sufficient attention to land disturbances in the Highlands of Scotland after 1914 when compared to that given to earlier events. Unlike the various groups who have memorialised these acts of resistance and reassertion, history has given less weight to the later Land Wars than it has to those of the 1880s. And yet disturbance after 1914 and after 1918 in particular, was of lasting significance and successfully re-worked the crofting landscape of the Outer Hebrides in particular. This significance is to be found in the response of (local and national) authority and public opinion to these actions and their depth, diversity and sheer volume. For an understanding of Highland protest and perhaps for protest studies more generally, significance also emerges from the fact that the old shibboleths of an inert "space-as-backdrop", class consciousness and class conflict are insufficiently flexible to embrace the fluid, complex and dynamic view of protest this diversity and depth demands.

Land agitation in the Highlands, whether expressive of a crofting taskscape or not, unquestionably emerged from a deep cultural tradition which spoke of customary rights to land and customary inheritance of land. The perceived denial of that custom and those rights underlay and impelled protest performances. There is a multiplicity to protests' performances, then, in its actants (from below *and* above), the stage upon which this is played out and in the materiality of its embodied form. Equally undeniably the performances and associations drawn into and of the land agitation were deeply conservative demonstrations of adherence to the orthodoxy of 1886 – the crofting taskscape writ into law. Nevertheless, it would seem that the self-same deep cultural tradition – apparent in and often maintained through Gaelic poetry – had, by 2013, transformed these limited ambitions into something akin to James Hunter's optimistic hopes for the Highlands with which this Chapter opened. It is therefore entirely appropriate that we close this book with an extract from an optimistic poetic response to Norman MacCaig's *A Man in Assynt*.

6 Noel, Castree, 'Differential geographies: place, indigenous rights and "local" resources', *Political Geography*, Vol. 23 (2004): 133–67.

A passion for Assynt
By Mandy Haggith

This ice-sculpted loch-and-cnocan space is still
the most beautiful corner of the land.
The air prevaricates on,
the ups still lift,
the hollows still astound
with sphagnum art and puddle-craft.
The tide glides out
and slides back in again.
Tourists (though he wouldn't use the word
not seeing himself as one) continue to come,
maybe even wearier now of our much newer civilisation:
the clock's tyranny out there is strong as ever.
Here, natural rhythms perpetuate,
day and night, moon and season.

His questions pointed at true north,
a compass bearing that has driven
men in boats and folk inland
on a journey he'd be proud of.

Who owns this land?
Loch Roe, Clachtoll, the pools in Stoer,
the fanks, Clashnessie Bay,
our litany of mountains -
Cul Beg, Cul Mor, Suilven, Canisp –
they're ours, the local people's,
crofters, women even, all who live here
who fought and won,
raised the funds to share the rights
to this rock-bog-wood-loch land.

We possess and it belongs to us
but what he knew was that
we owned it all already
and though we have the title now
its text does not express the two-way deal:
it is also us who belong to it.
It remains masterless.

Suilven's snow-clad, sun-drenched,
an iced pudding in a bowl of cream,
as delicious as it's always been
and always will be.
Nothing we do changes the mountains,
though I swear they gleamed
the day we bought them.

He asked if owning has anything to do with love.
I answer him, everything and nothing.
It's a marriage made in a solicitor's office,
the deeds are silent about what matters.
Yet it was passion for this place
that drove the people to rewrite its history,
to wrest the land from rich and absent men.

The mountains are unaffected.
Lochans do not care.

…

The land lives, despite what we do,
or fail to do. Schemes start,
abort. Traditions
grow and cease.
The land lives on.

A tide of people ebbed
and turned: new generations
replenish the land, coming into our own,
coming in, coming in,
to renew the unrequitable passion.[7]

7 I am very grateful to the poet for her permission to use this extract. The full poem can be found here – http://www.northwordsnow.co.uk/issues/NNow_16_for_web.pdf

Bibliography

Manuscript Sources

National Archives of Scotland; Allotments and smallholdings, AF 66.
National Archives of Scotland; Congested Districts, AF 42.
National Archives of Scotland; Highland Development, DD 15.
National Archives of Scotland; Highland Development, SEP 12.
National Archives of Scotland; Home Office Papers (Highland disturbances), HH 1.
National Archives of Scotland; Minute Books, AF 76
National Archives of Scotland; *Scottish* Office Crofting Files, AF 67
National Archives of Scotland; *Scottish* Office Estate Management Files: *AF83*.
Scottish Government, Rural Payments & Inspections Directorate (Saughton House, Edinburgh); Estate Management Files (uncatelogued).

Printed Primary Sources

Annual Board of Agriculture Reports (Edinburgh: 1918–1938).
Agrarian Offences Scotland (Edinburgh: 1888).
Annual Reports of the Congested Districts Board (Edinburgh: 1897–1913).
Annual Reports of the Land Court (Edinburgh: 1912–1939).
Crofters Commission Reports 1888– (Edinburgh: 1899).
Crofting Parishes (Edinburgh: 1888).
Deer Forests Commissioners Report London: 1895).
Dundee Advertiser 1918–1939).
Employment of Military in Case of Disturbance (London: 1908, 1914).
Enlargement of Holdings (Edinburgh: 1888).
Glasgow Herald 1918–1939).
Lews Cottars (Edinburgh: 1888).
Oban Times 1918–1939).
Royal Commission on the Interests of the Population of the Highlands and Islands (London: 1890, 1890–1891).
Report of the Committee on Land Settlement (Edinburgh: 1928).
Report of the Inter-Departmental Committee on Riots (Edinburgh: 1895).
Report on Land Settlement (Edinburgh: 1944–1945).
Riot Compensation (Edinburgh: 1912–1913).
The Scotsman 1918–1939.
The Stornoway Gazette 1918–1939.

Secondary Sources

Archer, John, *By a Flash and a Scare: Arson, Animal Maiming and Poaching in East Anglia 1815–1870* (Oxford: Clarendon Press, 1990).

Archer, John, *Social Unrest and Popular Protest in England, 1780–1840* (Cambridge: Cambridge University Press, 2000).

Arnold, Rollo, 'The "Revolt of the Field" in Kent 1872–1879', *Past and Present*, Vol. 64 (August 1974): 71–95.

Bak Janos, M. and Beneke, Gerhard (eds), *Religion and Rural Revolt* (Manchester: Manchester University Press, 1984).

Baines, Dudley, *Migration in a Mature Economy: Emigration and internal migration in England and Wales, 1861–1900* (Cambridge: Cambridge University Press, 1985).

Baker, Alan, 'On ideology and historical geography,' in Baker, Alan, R. and Billinge, Mark (eds), *Period and Place* (Cambridge: Cambridge University Press, 1982).

Baker, Alan, 'Reflections on the relations of historical geography and the Annales school of history', in Alan Baker and Derek Gregory (eds), *Explorations in Historical Geography* (Cambridge: Cambridge University Press, 1984).

Bartlett, Thomas, 'An End to Moral Economy: The Irish Militia Disturbances of 1793', *Past and Present*, Vol. 99 (May, 1983): 41–64.

Beames, Michael, 'Peasant Movements: Ireland 1785–95', *Journal of Peasant Studies*, Vol. 2, No. 4 (1975): 502–6.

Beames, Michael, 'Rural Conflict in Pre-Famine Ireland', *Past and Present*, Vol. 81 (1978): 75–91.

Beckett Ian F. V. and Simpson, Keith (eds), *A Nation in Arms: A Social Study of the British Army in the First World War* (Manchester: Tom Donovan Publishing 1985).

Belloff, Max, *Wars and Welfare: Britain 1914–1945* (London: Edward Arnold, 1984).

Biehler, Dawn, 'Flies, manure and window screens: medical entomology and environmental reform in early-twentieth-century US cities', *Journal of Historical Geography*, Vol. 36 (2010): 68–78.

Billinge, Mark 'Hegemony, Class and Power in late Georgian and early Victorian England: towards a cultural geography,' in Baker, Alan, R. and Billinge, Mark (eds), *Explorations in Historical Geography* (Cambridge: Cambridge University Press, 1984).

Binfield, Kevin *Writings of the Luddites* (Baltimore: The Johns Hopkins University Press, 2004).

Blomley, Nicholas, 'Making Private Property: Enclosure, Common Right and the Work of Hedges' *Rural History*, Vol. 18 (2007): 1–21.

Blum, Jerome, *The End of the Old Order in Rural Europe* (Princeton: Princeton University Press, 1978).

Bohstedt, John, *Riots and Community Politics in England and Wales, 1790–1810* (Harvard: Harvard University Press, 1983).

Bohstedt, John, *The Politics of Provisions* (Farnham: Ashgate, 2010).

Bohstedt John, and Williams. Dale E. 'The Diffusion of Riots', *The Journal of Interdisciplinary History*, Vol. XIX, No. 1 (1988): 3–22.

Booth, Alan, 'Popular loyalties and public violence in the north-west of England 1790–1800', *Social History*, Vol. 8, No. 3 (1983): 295–313.

Braddick, Michael, and Walter, John, 'Introduction', in Michael Braddick and John Walter (eds), *Negotiating Power in Early Modern England* (Cambridge: Cambridge University Press, 2001).

Braddick, Michael, and Walter, John (eds), *Negotiating Power in Early Modern Society: Order, Hierarchy and Subordination in Britain and Ireland* (Cambridge: Cambridge University Press, 2001).

Bruce, Steve, 'Social change and collective behaviour: the revival in Eighteenth Century Ross-shire', *British Journal of Sociology*, Vol. XXIV (1983): 554–72.

Buchanan Sharp, *In Contempt of All Authority: Rural Artisans and Riot in the West of England, 1586–1660* (Berkeley: University of California Press, 1992).

Buchanan, Joni, 'Clearance, Conflict and Crofting', *Scottish Trades Union Review*, No. 32, 1986, 4–6.

Buchanan, Joni, *The Lewis Land Struggle* (Stornoway: Acair, 1996).

Burnett, Ray, 'Land Raids and the Scottish Left,' *Cencrastus*, No. 18 (1984): 7–12.

Burnett, John A. *The Making of the Modern Scottish Highlands*, 1939–1965 (Dublin: Four Courts Press Ltd, 2011).

Bushaway, Bob, *By Rite: Custom, Ceremony and Community in England 1700–1880* (London: Humanities Press, 1982).

Caird, James, B. 'The Creation of Crofts and New Settlement Patterns in the Highlands and Islands of Scotland', *Scottish Geographical Magazine*, Vol. 103, No. 2 (1987): 67–75.

Caird, James, B. et al., 'Park: A Geographical Study of a Lewis Crofting District', *Geographical Field Group* (Nottingham, 1958).

Caird, James, B. and Moisley, Harold, 'Leadership and innovation in the crofting community of the Outer Hebrides', *Sociological Review*, Vol. IX (1961): 85–102.

Calhoun, Craig, *The Question of Class Struggle: The Social Foundations of Popular Radicalism during the Industrial Revolution* (Chicago: University of Chicago Press, 1982).

Cameron, Ewen A. 'The Political Influence of Highland Landowners: a reassessment', *Northern Scotland*, Vol. XIV (1991): 27–45.

Cameron, Ewen A. 'Congested District to Objective One: The Scottish Highlands in the twentieth century', in T.M. Devine and R.J. Finlay (eds), *Scotland in the Twentieth Century* (Edinburgh, 1996).

Cameron, Ewen A. *"Land for the People" The British Government and the Scottish Highlands, c.1880–1930* (East Linton: Tuckwell, 1996).

Cameron, Ewen A. '"Unfinished Business": The Land Question and the Scottish Parliament', *Contemporary British History*, Vol. 15, Issue 1 (2001): 83–114.
Cameron, Ewen, A. 'Land agitation and reform in the Highlands and Islands', in Michael Lynch (ed.) *The Oxford Companion to Scottish History* (Oxford: Oxford University Press, 2001).
Cameron, Ewen A. 'Communication or Separation? Reactions to Irish Land Agitation and Legislation in the Highlands of Scotland, c.1870–1910' *English Historical Review*, Vol. 120, No. 487 (2005): 633–66.
Cameron Ewen A. 'Setting the heather on fire: the land question in Scotland', in Matthew Cragoe and Paul Redman (eds), *The Land Question in Britain, 1750–1950* (London: Palgrave Macmillan, 2010).
Cameron, Ewen A. and Robertson, Iain J.M. 'Fighting and bleeding for the land: the Scottish highlands and the Great War', in Elaine Macfarlane and Catriona Macdonald (eds), *Scotland and the Great War* (East Linton: Tuckwell Press, 1998).
Carter, Ian, 'The Peasantry of Northeast Scotland' *Journal of Peasant Studies*, Vol. 3, No. 2 (1976): 151–91.
Carter, Ian, 'The Scottish Peasantry,' in Raphael Samuel (ed.), *People's History and Socialist Theory* (London: Routledge and Kegan Paul, 1981).
Castree, Noel, 'Differential geographies: place, indigenous rights and "local" resources', *Political* Geography, Vol. 23 (2004): 133–67.
Charlesworth, Andrew, 'Social Protest in a Rural Society: The Spatial Diffusion of the Captain Swing Disturbances of 1830–1831', *Historical Geography Research Series*, Issue 1 (London: Geo Abstracts Ltd, 1979).
Charlesworth, Andrew, 'An Agenda for Historical Studies of Rural Protest in Britain, 1750–1850', *Rural History*, Vol. 2, Issue 2 (1991): 231–40.
Charlesworth, Andrew, 'From the Moral Economy of Devon to the Political Economy of Manchester, 1790–1812', *Social History*, 18 (1993): 205–17.
Chambers, Bob, *Life On The Edge: Growing up in Steimreway* (Stornoway: The Islands Book Trust, 2011).
Chase, Malcolm, *The Peoples' Farm: English Radical Agrarianism 1775–1840* (Oxford: Clarendon Press, 1988).
Chase, Malcolm, *Chartism: A New History* (Manchester: Manchester University Press, 2007).
Cloke, Paul, and Owain, Jones, 'Dwelling, place, and landscape: an orchard in Somerset', *Environment and Planning A*, Vol. 33, No. 4 (2001): 649–66.
Coats, Anthony, 'Contrary Moralities: Plebes, Paternalists and Political Economists', *Past and Present*, No. 54 (1972): 130–33.
Collier, Adam, *The Crofting Problem* (Cambridge: Cambridge University Press, 1953).
Connolly, Samuel, 'Violence and Order in the Eighteenth Century,' in P. O'Flanagan, P. Ferguson and K. Whelan (eds), *Rural Ireland 1600–1900*. (Cork: Cork University Press, 1987.

Connolly, Samuel, 'The Houghers: Agrarian Protest in Early Eighteenth-Century Connacht', in Charles Philpin (ed.), *Nationalism and Popular Protest in Ireland* (Cambridge: Cambridge University Press, 1987).
Coull, James, 'Crofters' Common Grazings in Scotland', *Agricultural History Review*, Vol. XVI (1968): 142–54.
Clark, Samuel, *The Social Origins of the Irish Land Wars* (Princeton, NJ: Princeton University Press, 1979).
Comann Eachdraidh Uibhist a Tuath (collective authorship), *Croft Histories: Balranald and Paiblesgarry* (Stornoway: Comann Eachdraidh Uibhist a Tuath, 1988).
Cragoe, Matthew, and Redman, Paul (eds), *The Land Question in Britain, 1750–1950* (London: Palgrave Macmillan, 2010).
Craig, David *On the Crofters Trail* (London: Jonathan Cape, 1990).
Crawford, Ian, 'Kelp burning', *Scottish Studies*, Vol. 1 (1962).
Crawford, Ian, 'Feannagan Tomaidh (Lazy Beds)', *Scottish Studies*, Vol. VI (1966).
Crouch, David, 'Spacing, performing and becoming: tangles in the mundane', *Environment and Planning A*, Vol. 35 (2003): 1945–1960.
Curtis, Louis, *Coercion and Conciliation in Ireland 1880–1892* (Princeton: Princeton University Press, 1963).
Devine, Tom, *The Great Highland Famine* (Edinburgh: John Donald, 1988).
Devine, Tom, 'Social Responses to Agrarian 'Improvement': The Highland and Lowland Clearances in Scotland', in Rab Houston and Ian D. Whyte (eds), *Scottish Society, 1500–1800* (Edinburgh: Edinburgh University Press, 1989).
Devine, Tom, *Clanship to Crofters War* (Manchester: Manchester University Press, 1994).
Devine, Tom, *The Great Highland Famine: Hunger, Emigration and the Scottish Highlands in the Nineteenth-century* (Edinburgh: John Donald, 1997).
Dewey, Clive, 'Celtic agrarian legislation and the Celtic revival: historicist implications of Gladstone's Irish and Scottish Land Acts, 1870–1886', *Past and Present*, Vol. 64 (1974): 30–70.
Dodgshon, Robert, *Land and Society in Early Scotland* (Oxford: Oxford University Press, 1981).
Dunbabin, John, 'The revolt of the field: The agricultural labourers movement in the 1870s,' *Past and Present*, No. 26 (1963): 68–97.
Dunbabin, John, *Rural Discontent in Nineteenth Century Britain* (London: Faber and Faber, 1974).
Eastwood, David, 'Communities, protest and police in early nineteenth-century Oxfordshire: the enclosure of Otmoor reconsidered', *Agricultural History Review*, Vol. 44, No. 1 (1996): 35–46.
Emsley, Clive and Walvin, James (eds), *Artisans, Peasants and Proletarians 1760–1860* (London: Croom Helm, 1985).
Farley, Paul, and Symmons Roberts, Michael, *Edgelands: Journeys into England's True Wilderness* (London: Jonathan Cape, 2011).

Featherstone, David, 'Skills for heterogeneous associations: The Whiteboys, collective experimentation, and subaltern political ecologies', *Environment and Planning D: Society and Space*, Vol. 25 (2007): 284–306.

Fenton, Alexander, *Scottish Country Life* (Edinburgh: John Donald, 1989).

Ferguson, Calum, *Children Of The Black House* (Edinburgh: Birlinn, 2003).

Fraser Darling, Frank, *West Highland Survey: An Essay in Human Ecology* (Oxford: Oxford University Press, 1955).

Fraser Grigor, Iain, *Mightier than a Lord* (Stornoway: Acair, 1979).

Fraser Grigor, Iain, *Highland Resistance: The Radical Tradition in the Scottish North* (Edinburgh: Mainstream, 2000).

Fisher, Chris, *Custom, Work and Market Capitalism* (London: Croom Helm, 1981).

Geary, Dick, *European Labour Protest* (London: Methuen, 1984).

Geddes, Arthur, 'Lewis,' *Scottish Geographical Magazine*, Vol. 52, No. 5 (1936): 217–31.

Geddes, Arthur, *The Isle of Lewis and Harris* (Edinburgh: Edinburgh University Press, 1954).

Geddes, Michael, 'Uneven Development and the Scottish Highlands,' Working Paper 17, *Urban Regional Studies Group* (University of Sussex, 1979).

Giddens, Anthony, *Central Problems in Social Theory* (London: Palgrave Macmillan, 1979).

Gilbert, Anne 'The new regional geography in English and French-speaking countries', *Progress in Human Geography*, Vol. 12, No. 2 (1988): 208–28.

Goodwin, Jeff, Jasper, James, M. and Poletta, Frank (eds), *Passionate Politics* (Chicago: Chicago University Press, 2001).

Gold, John, R., and Margaret M. Gold. 'Land reform in north-west Scotland: a study of the social and economic impact of the land settlement programme', *Patterns of Regional Geography: An International Perspective*, Vol. 3 (1990): 35.

Goodman, David, and Redclift, Michael, *From Peasant to Proletarian* (London: Basil Blackwell, 1981).

Gordon, Seton, 'Isles of the Outer Hebrides', *Scottish Geographical Magazine*, Vol. 57, No. 3 (1941): 115–19.

Gregory, Derek, 'Contours of crisis: sketches for a geography of class struggle on the early Industrial revolution in England' in Alan Baker and Derek Gregory (eds), *Explorations in Historical Geography* (Cambridge, 1984).

Gregson, Nicky, and Rose. Gillian, 'Taking Butler elsewhere: performativities, spatialities and subjectivities', *Environment and Planning D*, Vol. 18, No. 4 (2000): 433–52.

Griffin, Carl, 'Affecting violence: language, gesture and performance in early nineteenth-century English popular protest', *Historical Geography*, Vol. 36 (2008): 139–62.

Griffin, Carl, 'Protest practice and (tree) cultures of conflict: understanding the spaces of "tree maiming" in eighteenth- and early nineteenth-century England',

Transactions of the Institute of British Geographers, Vol. 40, No. 1 (2008): 91–108.

Griffin, Carl, J. 'Swing, Swing redivivus or something after Swing? On the death throes of a movement, December 1830–December 1833', *International Review of Social History*, Vol. 54, No. 3 (2009): 459–97.

Griffin, Carl, J. 'More-than-human histories and the failure of grand states schemes', *Cultural Geographies*, Vol. 17, No. 4 (2010): 451–72.

Griffin, Carl, J. 'The violent Captain Swing?' *Past and Present*, Vol. 209 (2010): 149–80.

Griffin, Carl, J. 'Becoming private property: custom, law, and the geographies of "ownership" in 18th- and 19th-century England', *Environment and Planning A*, Vol. 42, No. 3 (2010): 747–62.

Griffin, Carl, J. *Rural War* (Manchester, Manchester University Press, 2012).

Griffin, Carl, J. and Evans, Adrian, 'On historical geographies of embodied practice and performance', *Historical Geography*, Vol. 36 (2008): 5–16.

Hailwood, Mark, 'Alehouses, popular politics and plebeian agency in early modern England, in Fiona Williamson (ed.) *Locating Agency: Space, Power and Popular Politics* (Cambridge: Cambridge Scholars Publishing, 2010).

Halbwachs, Maurice, *On Collective Memory* (Chicago: University of Chicago Press, 1992).

Hamish Fraser, W. 'Patterns of protest', in Tom Devine and Rosalind Mitchinson, (eds) *People and Society in Scotland, Vol. 1, 1760–1830* (Edinburgh: John Donald, 1998).

Hanham, Hubert, 'The problem of Highland Discontent 1880–1885', *Transactions Royal History Society*, Vol. 19 (1969): 21–65.

Harrison, Mark, '"To Raise and Dare Resentment": The Bristol Bridge Riot of 1793 re-examined', *The Historical Journal*, Vol. 26, No. 3 (1983): 557–85.

Harper Marjory, *Scotland No More?: The Scots Who Left Scotland In The Twentieth Century* (Edinburgh: Luath Press, 2012).

Harper, Marjory, and Evans, Nicholas, J. 'Socio-economic Dislocation and Inter-war Emigration to Canada and the United States: A Scottish Snapshot', *The Journal of Imperial and Commonwealth History* Vol. 34, No. 4 (2006): 529–52.

Harvie, Christopher, *No Gods and Precious Few Heroes* (London: Edward Arnold, 1980).

Hechter, Michael, *Internal Colonialism: The Celtic Fringe in British National Development 1536–1966* (London: Routledge and Kegan Paul, 1978).

Heidegger, Martin, *Poetry, Language, Thought* (London: Harper and Row, 1972).

Hindle, Steve, *On the Parish? The Micro-Politics of Poor Relief in Rural England c.1550–1750* (Oxford: Oxford University Press, 2004).

Hipkin, Stephen, 'Sitting on his penny rent: conflict and right of common in Faversham Blean, 1596–1610', *Rural History*, Vol. 11, No. 1 (2000): 163–77.

Hobsbawm, Eric, J. 'The machine breakers', *Past and Present*, Vol. 1, No. 1 (1952): 57–70.

Hobsbawm, Eric, J. *Primitive Rebels: Studies in Archaic Forms of Social Movement in the 19th Century* (Manchester: Manchester University Press, 1959).
Hobsbawm, Eric, J. *Bandits* (Worthing: Littlehampton Book Services, 1969).
Hobsbawm, Eric, J. 'Peasant Land Occupations', *Past and Present*, No. 62 (1974): 120–52.
Hobsbawm, Eric, J. and Rudé, *Captain Swing* (London: Readers Union, 1970).
Holton, Robert J. 'The Crowd in History: some problems of theory and method', *Social History*, Vol. 3, No. 2 (1978): 219–31.
Horn, Pamela, *The Rural World: Social Change in the English Countryside 1780–1850* (London: Hutchinson, 1980).
Howell, David, *Land and People in Nineteenth-Century Wales* (London: Routledge and Kegan Paul, 1977).
Howell, David W. 'The Rebecca riots', in Trevor Herbert and Gareth E. Jones (eds), *People and Protest in Wales 1815–1880* (Cardiff: University of Wales Press, 1990).
Howkins, Alun, *Poor Labouring Men: Rural Radicalism in Norfolk 1870–1923* (London: Routledge and Kegan Paul, 1985).
Howkins, Alun, 'From Diggers to Dongas: the Land in English Radicalism, 1649–2000', *History Workshop Journal*, Vol. 54, No. 1 (2002): 1–23.
Howkins, Alun, *The Death of Rural England: A Social History of the Countryside Since 1900* (London: Routledge, 2003).
Huggett, Frank E. *The Land Question and European Society* (London: Thames and Hudson, 1975).
Hunter, James, 'The Emergence of the Crofting Community: The Religious Contribution 1798–1843', *Scottish Studies*, Vol. 18 (1974): 95–116.
Hunter, James, 'The politics of highland land reform, 1873–1895', *The Scottish Historical Review*, Vol. 53, No. 155, Part 1 (1974): 45–68.
Hunter, James, 'The Gaelic Connection: Highlands, Ireland and Nationalism 1873–1922', *Scottish Historical Review*, 59 (1975): 178–204.
Hunter, James, *The Making of the Crofting Community* (Edinburgh: John Donald, 1976).
Hunter, James, *The Claim of Crofting: The Scottish Highlands and Islands 1930–1990* (Edinburgh: Mainstream, 1991).
Hunter, James, *On the Other Side of Sorrow: Nature and People in the Scottish Highlands* (Edinburgh: Mainstream, 1995).
Hunter, James, *Last of the Free* (Edinburgh: Mainstream, 1999).
Hunter, James, *From the Low Tide of the Sea to the Highest Mountain Tops* (Kershader, Isle of Lewis: Islands Book Trust, 2012).
Ingold, Tim, 'The temporality of the landscape', *World Archaeology*, 25:2 (1993): 24–174.
Ingold, Tim, 'Earth, sky, wind and weather', *Journal of the Royal Anthropological Institute* (N.S.), 13: s1, (2007) pp. S19–38.
Ingold, Tim, 'Footprints through the weather-world: Walking, breathing, knowing', *Journal of the Royal Anthropological Institute* (N.S.), 16: s1 (2010a): S121–39.

Ingold, Tim, 'Ways of mind-walking: Reading, writing, painting', *Visual Studies*, Vol. 25, No. 1 (2010b): 15–23.

Ingold, Tim, *Being Alive: Essays on Movement, Knowledge and Description* (Routledge: London, 2011).

Ingold, Tim, and Vergunst, Jo, L. (eds), *Ways of Walking* (Aldershot: Ashgate, 2008).

Ingram, Martin, 'Ridings, Rough Music and the "Reform of Popular Culture" in Early Modern England', *Past and Present*, No. 105 (1984): 79–103.

Jacoby, Karl, *Crimes Against Nature: Squatters, Poachers, Thieves and the Hidden History of American Conservation* (Berkeley, CA: University of California Press, 2001.

Jackson, Peter, *Maps of Meaning* (London: Routledge, 1989).

Jones, David, J.V. *Before Rebecca: Popular Protests in Wales 1793–1835* (London: Allen Lane, 1973).

Jones, David, J.V. 'Crime, Protest and Community in Nineteenth-Century Wales,' *Llafeir*, Vol. 1, No. 3 (1974): 5–15.

Jones, Owain, '"The Breath of the Moon": The Rhythmic and Affective time-spaces of UK Tides', in Tim Edensor (ed.), *Geographies of Rhythm* (Aldershot: Ashgate 2008).

Jones, Owain, 'Geography, memory and non-representational theory', *Geography Compass*, Social Geography Section, Vol. 5, No. 12 (2011a): 875–85.

Jones, Owain, 'Lunar-solar rhythm patterns: Towards the material cultures of tides', *Environment and Planning A*, Vol. 43 (2011b): 2285–303.

Jones, Owain, and Garde-Hansen, Joanne (eds), *Geography and Memory: Explorations in Identity, Place and Becoming* (Basingstoke: Palgrave Macmillan, 2012).

Jones, Peter, 'Swing, Speenhamland and rural social relations: the "moral economy" of the English crowd in the nineteenth century', *Social History*, Vol. 32, 3 (2007): 271–83.

Jones, Peter, 'Finding Captain Swing: protest parish relations and the state of the public mind in 1830', *International Review of Social History*, Vol. 54, No. 3 (2009): 429–58.

Jones, R. Merfyn, *The North Wales Quarrymen 1874–1922* (Cardiff: University of Wales Press, 1981).

Kent, David, 'Power, Protest, Poaching, and the Tweed Fisheries Acts of 1857 and 1859: "Send a Gunboat!"', *Northern History*, Vol. 42, No. 2 (2005): 293–315.

Knott, J.W. 'Land, kinship and Identity: The Cultural Roots of Agrarian Agitation in 18th and 19th Century Ireland', *Journal of Peasant Studies*, Vol. 12, No. 1 (1984): 93–108.

Knox, Susan, *The Making of the Shetland Landscape* (Edinburgh: John Donald, 1985).

Knott, John, 'Land, kinship and identity', *Journal of Peasant Studies*, Vol. 12, No. 1 (1984): 93–108.

Leneman, Leah, 'Land settlement in Scotland after World War 1', *The Agricultural History Review*, Vol. 37, Part 1 (1989): 52–64.

Leneman, Leah, *Fit For Heroes* (Aberdeen: Aberdeen University Press, 1989).

Kynaston, David, *King Labour: The British Working Class 1850–1914* (London: George Allen and Unwin, 1976).

Lewis. Gavin, 'The Peasantry, Rural Change and Conservative Agrarianism', *Past and Present*, Vol. 81, No. 1 (1978): 119–43.

Fisher, Chris, *Custom, Work and Market Capitalism* (London: Croom Helm, 1981).

Lindley, Keith, *Fenland Riots and the English Revolution* (London: Ashgate, 1982).

Logue, Kenneth, *Popular Disturbances in Scotland 1780–1815* (Edinburgh: John Donald, 1989).

Lorimer, Hayden, 'Cultural geography: the busyness of being "more-than-representational"', *Progress in Human Geography*, Vol. 29, No. 1 (2005): 83–94.

MacAskill, John, '"The most arbitrary, scandalous act of tyranny": The Crown, Private Proprietors and the Ownership of the Scottish Foreshore in the Nineteenth Century', *The Scottish Historical Review*, Vol. 85, No. 2 (2006): 277–304.

MacCuish, Donald, J. 'Crofting legislation since 1886', *Scottish Geographical Magazine*, Vol. 103, No. 2 (1987): 90–94.

Macdonald, Sharon, *Imaging Culture. Histories, Identities and the Gaelic Renaissance* (Oxford: Berg, 1997).

Macleod, John, *When I Heard the Bell: The Loss of the Iolaire* (Edinburgh, Birlinn Ltd, 2010).

MacLeod, Finlay, *Crowdie and Cream* (London, 1994).

Macfarlane, Robert, *The Old Ways* (London: Hamish Hamilton, 2012).

MacInnes, Allan, 'Crown, Clans and Fine: The civilizing of Scottish Gaeldom', *Northern Scotland*, Vol. 13 (1993): 31–55.

MacInnes, Allan, *Clanship, Commerce and the House of Stuart, 1603–1788* (Edinburgh: Tuckwell Press, 1996).

MacInnes, John J. 'Religion in Gaelic Society', *Transactions of the Gaelic Society of Inverness*, No. 52 (1980–2): 222–40.

Mackenzie, A., Fiona, D. 'A working land: crofting communities, place and the politics of the possible in post-Land Reform Scotland', *Transactions of the Institute of British Geographers*, Vol. 31, No. 3 (2006): 383–98.

Mackenzie, A., Fiona, D. 'Re-stor(y)ing North West Sutherland, Scotland', *Scottish Geographical Journal*, Vol. 126, No. 3 (2010): 162–84.

Mackenzie, A., Fiona, D. 'A common claim: Community land ownership in the Outer Hebrides, Scotland'. *International Journal of the Commons*, North America, February 2010. Available at: <http://www.thecommonsjournal.org/index.php/ijc/article/view/151/141>. Date accessed: 30 April 2013.

Mackenzie, A., Fiona, D. *Places of Possibility: property, nature and community land ownership* (Oxford: Wiley-Blackwell, 2013).

Mackenzie, A., Fiona, D., MacAskill, J., Muro, G. and Seki, E., 'Contesting land, creating community, in the Highlands and Islands, Scotland', *Scottish Geographical Journal*, Vol. 120, No. 3 (2005): 159–80.

Maclean, M. and Carrell, C. (eds), *As an Fhearann. From the Land* (Edinburgh: Mainstream Publishing, 1986).

MacLean, Sorley, 'The Poetry of the Clearances,' *Transactions of the Gaelic Society of Inverness*, Vol. 38 (1937–1941).

MacPhail, Ian M.M. *The Crofters' War* (Stornoway: Acair, 1989).

Manning, Roger, *Village Revolts: Social Protest and Popular Disturbances in England 1509–1640* (Oxford: Oxford University Press, 1988).

Mansfield, Nick, 'The National Federation of Discharged and Demobilized Soldiers, 1917–1921: A View from the Marches', *Family and Community History*, 7 (2004): 19–32.

Mason, John, 'The Duke of Argyll and the Land Question in Late Nineteenth-Century Britain', *Victorian Studies*, Vol. 21, No. 2 (1978): 149–70.

Massey, Doreen, 'Spatial history: rethinking the idea of place', *History Workshop Journal*, Vol. 39, No. 1 (1995): 182–92.

Mather, Alexander, *State-aided Land Settlement in Scotland* (Aberdeen: University of Aberdeen, 1978).

Meek, Donald, E. 'Gaelic Poets of the Land Agitation,' *Transactions of the Gaelic Society of Inverness*, Vol. 49 (1977): 309–76.

Meek, Donald, E. '"The Land Question Answered from the Bible": The Land Issue and the Development of a Highland Theology of Liberation,' *Scottish Geographical Magazine*, Vol. 103, No. 2 (1987): 84–9.

Meek, Donald, E. 'The Role of Song in the Highland Land Agitation,' *Scottish Gaelic Studies*, Vol. XVI (1990) n.p.

Mills, Denis, 'Peasants and Conflict in Nineteenth-Century Rural England: A comment on two recent articles,' *Journal of Peasant Studies*, Vol. 15, No. 3 (1988): 395–400.

Mintz, Sidney, 'The Rural Proletariat and the Problem of Rural Proletarian Consciousness,' *Journal of Peasant Studies*, Vol. 1, No. 3 (1974): 291–325.

Mitchinson, Rosalind, 'The Highland clearances', *Scottish Economic and Social History*, Vol. 1, No. 1 (1981): 4–24.

Mowat, Ian R.M. *Easter Ross 1750–1850: The Double Frontier* (Edinburgh: John Donald, 1981).

Navickas, Katrina, 'The Search for General Ludd: the Mythology of Luddism', *Social History*, Vol. 30, No. 3 (2005), 281–95.

Navickas, Katrina, 'Moors, Fields, and Popular Protest in South Lancashire and the West Riding of Yorkshire, 1800–1848' *Northern History*, 46 (2009): 93–111.

Navickas, Katrina, 'What happened to class? New histories of labour and collective action in Britain', *Social History*, Vol. 36, No. 2 (2011): 192–204.

Navickas, Katrina, 'Luddism, Incendiarism and the Defence of Rural 'Task-scapes' in 1812', *Northern History*, Vol. 48, No. 1 (2011): 59–73.

Navickas, Katrina, 'Why I am tired of turning': a theoretical interlude, [*History Working Papers Project*, 2011]. Available at: http://www.historyworkingpapers.org/?page_id=225 [Accessed 20 October 2012].

Neeson, Jeanette, *Commoners, Common Right, Enclosure and Social Change in England 1700–1820* (Cambridge: Cambridge University Press, 1993).

Newby, Andrew, 'Edward McHugh, the National Land League of Great Britain and the 'Crofters' War', 1879–1882', *The Scottish Historical Review*, Vol. 82, No. 213, Part 1 (2003): 74–91.

Newby, Andrew, *Ireland, Radicalism, and the Scottish Highlands* (Edinburgh: Edinburgh University Press, 2006).

Newby, Andrew, 'Land and the "Crofter Question" in Nineteenth-Century Scotland', *International Review of Scottish Studies*, Vol. 35 (2010): 7–36.

Newby, Howard, *The Deferential Worker* (London: Penguin, 1979).

Newby, Howard, *Green and Pleasant Land? Social Change in Rural England* (London: Harmondsworth/Hutchinson, 1979).

Nicolson, Nigel, *Lord of the Isles: Lord Leverhulme in the Hebrides* (London: Weidenfeld & Nicolson, 1960).

Nield, Keith, and Seed, John, 'Waiting for Gramsci', *Social History*, Vol. 6, No. 2 (1981): 209–27.

Offer, Avner, *Property and Politics 1870–1914: Landownership, Law, Ideology and Urban Development in England* (Cambridge: Cambridge University Press, 1981).

Orr, Willie, *Deer Forests, Landlords and Crofters* (Edinburgh: John Donald, 1982).

Parman, Susan, *Scottish Crofters: A Historical Ethnography of a Celtic Village* (Belmont, CA: Wadsworth Publishing 2004).

Pawson, Eric, and Cant, Garth, 'Land rights in historical and contemporary context', *Applied Geography*, Vol. 12, No. 2 (1992): 95–108.

Perks, Robert, and Thomson, Alistair (eds), *The Oral History Reader* (London: Routledge, 2006).

Poole, Steve, "A lasting and salutary warning": incendiarism, rural order and England's last scene of crime execution', *Rural History*, Vol. 19, No. 2 (2008): 163–77.

Porteous, John Douglas, 'Topocide: The Annihilation of Place', in John Eyles and David M. Smith (eds), *Qualitative Methods in Human Geography* (Cambridge: Polity Press, 1988).

Pretty, David, *The Rural Revolt that Failed* (Cardiff: University of Wales Press, 1989).

Pringle, Trevor R. 'The privation of history: Landseer, Victoria and the Highland myth', in Denis Cosgrove and Stephen Daniels (eds), *The Iconography of Landscape: Essays on the Symbolic Representation, Design and Use of Past Environments* (Cambridge: Cambridge University Press, 1988).

Randall, Adrian, 'The Shearmen and the Wiltshire outrages of 1802: trade unionism and industrial violence,' *Social History*, Vol. 7, No. 3 (1982): 283–304.

Randall, Adrian, *Before the Luddites* (Cambridge: Cambridge University Press, 1991).

Randall, Adrian, '*Captain Swing*: a retrospect', *International Review of Social History*, Vol. 54 (2009): 419–27.

Randall, Adrian, *Riotous Assemblies: popular protest in Hanoverian England* (Oxford: Oxford University Press, 2006).

Randall, Adrian, and Charlesworth, Andrew (eds), *Markets, Market Culture and Popular Protest in Eighteenth Century Britain* (Liverpool, 1996).

Reay, Barry, 'The Last Rising of the Agricultural Labourers. The Battle in Bossenden Wood, 1838', *History Workshop Journal*, Vol. 26, No. 1 (1988): 79–101.

Reay, Barry, *The Last Rising of the Agricultural Labourers* (Oxford: Clarendon Press, 1990).

Reay, Barry, *Microhistories: Demography, Society and Culture in Rural England 1800–1930* (Cambridge: Cambridge University Press, 1996).

Reed, Mick, 'Social change and social conflict in Nineteenth Century England: a comment', *The Journal of Peasant Studies*, Vol. 12, No. 1 (1984): 109–23.

Reed, Mick, 'Class and Conflict in Rural England: Some Reflections on a Debate', in Reed, Mick, and Wells, Roger (eds), *Class, Conflict and Protest in the English Countryside 1700–1880* (London: Frank Cass, 1990).

Reed, Mick 'Nineteenth-Century Rural England: A Case for "Peasant Studies"?,' *Journal of Peasant Studies*, Vol. 14, No. 1 (1986): 78–99.

Richards, Eric, 'Structural change in a regional economy', *Economic History Review*, Vol. 26, No. 1 (1973): 63–76.

Richards, Eric, 'How tame were the Highlands during the Clearances?', *Scottish Studies* (1973): 35–50.

Richards, Eric, *A History of the Highland Clearances, Vol. 1* (London: Croom Helm, 1985).

Richards, Eric, *A History of the Highland Clearances, Vol. 2* (London: Croom Helm, 1985).

Richards, Eric, 'Agricultural Change, Modernization and the Clearances', in Donald Ormand (ed.), *The Ross and Cromarty Book* (Golspie: The Northern Times, 1984).

Robertson, Iain J.M. '"Two steps forward; six steps back": the dissipated legacy of Captain Swing', *Southern History*, Vol. 32 (2010): 85–100.

Robertson, Iain J.M. 'The role of women in social protest in the Highlands of Scotland, c.1880–1939', *Journal of Historical Geography*, Vol. 23, No. 2 (1997): 187–200.

Rollinson, David, 'Exploding England: the dialectics of mobility and settlement in early modern England', *Social History*, Vol. 24, No. 1 (1999): 1–16.

Rose, Mitch, 'The seductions of resistance; power, politics, and a performative style of systems', *Environment and Planning D: Society and Space*, Vol. 20 (2002): 383–400.

Rothman, Benny, *1932 Kinder Trespass: Personal View of the Kinder Scout Mass Trespass* (Timperley: Willow Publishing, 1982).

Rothberg, Michael, *Multidirectional Memory: Remembering the Holocaust in the Age of Decolonization* (Stanford CA: Stanford University Press, 2009).

Rudé, George, *The Crowd in History* (London: Lawrence and Wishart, 1964).

Rudé, George, *Protest and Punishment* (Oxford: Oxford University Press, 1978).

Rule, John, and Wells, Roger (eds), *Crime, Protest and Popular Politics in Southern England 1740–1850* (London: Hambledon Continuum, 1997).

Said, Edward, *Culture and Imperialism* (New York: Alfred A. Knopf, 1994).

Salman, Redcliffe, *The History and Social Influence of the Potato* (Cambridge: Cambridge University Press, 1949).

Samuel, Raphael, and Driver, Felix, 'Rethinking the idea of Place', *History Workshop Journal*, Vol. 39, No. 1 (1995): 1-t-1.

Scott, James, C. *The Moral Economy of the Peasantry* (New Haven, CT: Yale University Press, 1976).

Scott, James, C. 'Hegemony and the Peasantry', *Politics and Society*, Vol. 7, No. 3 (1977): 267–96.

Scott, James, C. *Weapons of the Weak: Everyday Forms of Peasant Resistance* (New Haven, CT: Yale University Press, 1987).

Scott, James, C. *Domination and the Arts of Resistance: Hidden Transcripts* (New Haven, CT: Yale University Press, 1992).

Scotland, Nigel, *Methodism and the Revolt of the Field* (London: Humanities Press, 1981).

Sebold, Guy, L. 'The Essence of Military Group Cohesion', *Armed Forces & Society*, Vol. 33, No. 2 (2007): 286–95.

Shanin, Theodore, *Peasant Societies* (London: Penguin, 1971).

Sharpe, Richard, *Raasay: A Study In Island History* (London: Grant and Cutler, 1978).

Sharpe, Richard, *Raasay: A Study In Island History, Vol. 2: Documents And Sources* (London: Grant and Cutler, 1978).

Shaw, Frances, J. *The Northern and Western Isles of Scotland. Their Economy and Society in the Seventeenth Century* (Edinburgh: John Donald, 1980).

Short, Brian, 'Conservation, class and custom: lifespace and conflict in a nineteenth-century forest environment', *Rural History*, Vol. 10, No. 2 (1999): 127–54.

Sider, Gerald, M. 'The ties that bind: culture and agriculture, property and propriety in the Newfoundland village fishery', *Social History*, Vol. 5, No. 1 (1980): 1–39.

Sider, Gerald, M. *Culture and Class in Anthropology and History: A Newfoundland Illustration* (Cambridge: Cambridge University Press, 1986).

Smout, Tom, C. *A Century of the Scottish People 1830–1950* (London: Fontana Press, 1987).
Snell, Keith, *Annals of the Labouring Poor* (Cambridge: Cambridge University Press, 1985).
Snowden, Frank, *Violence and Great Estates in the South of Italy* (Cambridge: Cambridge University Press, 1986).
Steiner, George, *Heidegger* (London: Branch Line, 1992).
Stevenson, John, *Popular Disturbances in England 1700–1870* (London: Longman, 1979).
Stephenson, Tom, *Forbidden Land* (Manchester: Manchester University Press, 1989).
Thomis, Malcom, *The Luddites* (London: David and Charles, 1970).
Thomis, Malcom and Grimmett, Jo, *Women in Protest 1800–1850* (London: Croom Helm, 1982).
Thompson, Paul, *The Voice of the Past* (Oxford: Oxford University Press, 2000).
Thompson, Edward, P. *The Making of the English Working Class* (London: Penguin, 1968).
Thompson, Edward, P. 'The Crime of Anonymity' in Douglas Hay et al., *Albion's Fatal Tree* (London: Penguin, 1975).
Thompson, Edward, P. *Whigs and Hunters*. (London: Penguin, 1977).
Thompson, Edward, P. 'Eighteenth Century English Society: Class Struggle without Class', *Social History*, Vol. 3 (1978): 133–65.
Thompson, Edward, P. *Customs in Common* (London: The Merlin Press, 1991).
Thomson, William, P.L. *The Little General and the Rousay Crofters* (London: John Donald, 1981).
The Islands Book Trust (collective), *Aimhreit am Fhearainn: The Land Struggle in Skye and Lewis* (Stornoway: The Islands Book Trust, 2012).
Thrift, Nigel, *Non-representational Theory: Space, Politics, Affect* (London: Routledge, 2007).
Thrift, Nigel, 'Space: the fundamental stuff of Geography', in Nicholas J. Clifford, Sarah Holloway, Stephen Rice and Gill Valentine (eds), *Key Concepts in Geography* (London: Sage, 2009).
Thuente, Mary Helen, 'Violence in Pre-Famine Ireland: The Testimony of Irish Folklore and Fiction,' *Irish Historical Review*, Vol. 15, No. 2 (1985): 129–47.
Tilly, Charles, *Popular Contention in Great Britain, 1758–1834* (Harvard: Harvard University Press, 1995).
Tilly, Charles, Tilly, Louise, and Tilly, Richard, *The Rebellious Century* (Cambridge MA: Harvard University Press, 1975).
Tilly, Charles, and Wood, Lesley J. *Social Movements, 1768–2008* (London: Paradigm, 2004).
Tindley, Annie, *The Sutherland Estate, 1850–1920: Aristocratic Decline, Estate Management and Land Reform* (Edinburgh: Edinburgh University Press, 2010).

Tindley, Annie, 'They sow the wind, they reap the whirlwind:' estate management in the post-clearance Highlands, c.1815–c.1900', *Northern Scotland*, Vol. 3 (2012): 66–85.

Tindley, Annie, and Richards, Eric, 'Turmoil among the crofters: Evander McIver and the "Highland Question", 1873–1903', *Agricultural History Review*, Vol. 60, No. 2 (2012): 191–213.

Turnock, David, *Patterns of Highland Development* (London: Macmillan, 1970).

Turnock, David, *The Historical Geography of Scotland since 1707* (Cambridge: Cambridge University Press, 1982).

Underdown, David, *Revel, Riot and Rebellion: Popular Politics and Culture in England 1603–1660* (Oxford: Clarendon Press, 1985).

Urry, John, 'Social Relations Space and Time,' in Derek Gregory and John Urry (eds), *Social Relations and Spatial Structures* (London: Macmillan, 1985).

Vogel, Ursula, 'The Land Question: A Liberal Theory of Communal Property,' *History Workshop*, Issue 27, No. 1 (1989): 107–35.

Walter, John, 'Grain, riots and popular attitudes to the law,' in John Brewer and John Styles (eds) *An Ungovernable People* (London: Hutchinson, 1980).

Walter, John, 'Public Transcripts, Popular Agency and the Politics of Subsistence in Early Modern England' in Braddick Michael, and Walter John (eds), *Negotiating Power in Early Modern England* (Cambridge: Cambridge University Press, 2001).

Warren, Charles, R. and McKee, Annie, 'The Scottish revolution? Evaluating the impacts of post-devolution land reform', *Scottish Geographical Journal*, Vol. 127, No. 1 (2011): 17–39.

Wells, Roger, 'The Revolt of the South West 1800–1801. A Study in English Popular Protest', *Social History*, Vol. 2, No. 6 (1977): 713–44.

Wells, Roger, 'Crime and Protest in a Country Parish: Burwash, 1790–1850', in Rule, John, and Wells, Roger (eds), *Crime, Protest and Popular Politics in Southern Britain* (London: Hambledon Continuum 1997).

Wells, Roger, 'The Moral Economy of the English Countryside', in Randall, Adrian and Charlesworth, Andrew (eds), *Moral Economy and Popular Protest: Crowds, Conflict and Authority* (London: Macmillan, 1999).

Wigan, Michael, *Grimersta* (Private Publication, 2000).

Williams, David, *The Rebecca Riots* (Cardiff: University of Wales Press, 1986).

Williams, Dale, E. 'Morals, Markets and the English Crowd in 1766,' *Past and Present*, No. 104 (1984): 56–73.

Williams, Raymond, *Marxism and Literature* (Oxford: Oxford University Press, 1977).

Williams, Raymond, 'Base and superstructure in Marxist cultural theory', in Raymond Williams (ed.), *Problems in Materialism and Culture* (London: Verso, 1980).

Williamson, Fiona, 'Introduction', in Fiona Williamson (ed.), *Locating Agency: Space, Power and Popular Politics* (Cambridge: Cambridge Scholars Publishing, 2010).

Williamson, Fiona (ed.) *Locating Agency: Space, Power and Popular Politics* (Cambridge: Cambridge Scholars Publishing, 2010).
Winstanley, Michael, J. *Ireland and the Land Question* (London: Methuen, 1984).
Withers, Charles, W.J. 'The Scottish Highlands outlined: an assessment of the cartographical evidence for the Highland-Lowland boundary', *Scottish Geographical Magazine*, Vol. 98, No. 3 (1982): 143–57.
Withers, Charles, W.J. *Gaelic in Scotland 1698–1981* (Edinburgh: John Donald, 1984).
Withers, Charles, W.J. 'Highland-Lowland Migration and the Making of the Crofting Community, 1755–1891,' *Scottish Geographical Magazine*, Vol. 103, No. 2 (1987): 76–83.
Withers, Charles, W.J. *Gaelic Scotland: The Transformation of a Culture Region* (London: Routledge, 1988).
Withers, Charles, W.J. '"Give us land and plenty of it": the ideological basis to land and landscape in the Scottish Highlands,' *Landscape History*, Vol. 12, No. 1 (1990): 45–54.
Wolf, Eric, R. *Peasant Wars of the Twentieth Century* (London: Harper & Row, 1969).
Wood, Andy, 'Social conflict and change in the mining communities of north-west Derbyshire, c.1600–1700', *International Review of Social History*, Vol. 38, No. 01 (1993): 31–58.
Wood, Andy, *The Politics of Social Conflict: the Peak Country, 1520–1770* (Cambridge: Cambridge University Press, 1999).
Wood, Andy, *Riot, Rebellion and Popular Politics in Early Modern England* (London: Palgrave, 2002).
Wood, Andy, *The 1549 Rebellions and the Making of Early Modern England: The 1549 Rebellions and the Ideology of Popular Protest* (Cambridge: Cambridge University Press, 2010).
Wood, John, D. 'Transatlantic Land Reform: America and the Crofters' Revolt 1878–1888, *Scottish Historical Review*, Vol. LXIII, No. 175 (1984): 79–104.
Wylie, John, 'Depths and folds: on landscape and the gazing subject', *Environment and Planning D: Society and Space*, Vol. 24 (2006): 519–35.
Wylie, John, *Landscape* (Abingdon: Routledge, 2007).
Wylie, John, 'Landscape, absence and the geographies of love', *Transactions of the Institute of British Geographers*, Vol. 34, No. 3 (2009): 275–89.
Wylie, John, 'Dwelling and displacement: Tim Robinson and the questions of landscape', *Cultural Geographies*, Vol. 19, No. 3) (2012): 365–83.
Yeo, Eileen, and Yeo, Stephen, *Popular Culture and Class Conflict 1590–1914* (London: Harvester Press, 1981).

Index

FSC
www.fsc.org
MIX
Papier | Fördert gute Waldnutzung
FSC® C083411

Kolibri 360 GmbH
Ferdinand-Jühlke-Straße 7
99095 Erfurt, Deutschland
produktsicherheit@kolibri360.de